Five hundred copies of the first edition
of this book have been numbered
and signed by the author.

This is copy number __411__

An International Rule of Law

VIRGINIA LEGAL STUDIES *are sponsored by the School of Law of the University of Virginia for the publication of meritorious original works, symposia, and reprints in law and related fields. Titles previously published are listed below.*

Studies Editors: Carl McFarland, 1967–73
Richard B. Lillich, 1973–

Central Power in the Australian Commonwealth, by the Rt. Hon. Sir Robert Menzies, former Prime Minister of Australia. 1967.

Administrative Procedure in Government Agencies—Report by Committee Appointed by Attorney General at Request of President to Investigate Need for Procedural Reforms in Administrative Tribunals (1941), reprinted with preface and index 1968.

The Road from Runnymede: Magna Carta and Constitutionalism in America, by A. E. Dick Howard. 1968.

Non-Proliferation Treaty: Framework for Nuclear Arms Control, by Mason Willrich. 1969.

Mass Production Justice and the Constitutional Ideal—Papers and proceedings of a conference on problems associated with the misdemeanor, held in April 1969, under the sponsorship of the School of Law, edited by Charles H. Whitebread, II. 1970.

Education in the Professional Responsibilities of the Lawyer—Proceedings of the 1968 National Conference on Education in the Professional Responsibilities of the Lawyer, edited by Donald T. Weckstein. 1970.

The Valuation of Nationalized Property in International Law—Essays by experts on contemporary practice and suggested approaches, edited by Richard B. Lillich. v. I, 1972; v. II, 1973; v. III, 1975.

Legislative History: Research for the Interpretation of Laws, by Gwendolyn B. Folsom. 1972.

Criminal Appeals: English Practices and American Reforms, by Daniel J. Meador. 1973. Out of print.

Humanitarian Intervention and the United Nations—Proceedings of a conference held in March 1972, with appended papers, edited by Richard B. Lillich. 1973.

The United Nations, a Reassessment: Sanctions, Peacekeeping, and Humanitarian Assistance—Papers and proceedings of a symposium held in March 1972, edited by John M. Paxman and George T. Boggs. 1973.

Mr. Justice Black and His Books—Catalogue of the Justice's personal library, by Daniel J. Meador. 1974.

Legal Transplants, by Alan Watson. 1974.

Limits to National Jurisdiction over the Sea, edited by George T. Yates III and John Hardin Young. 1974.

Commentaries on the Constitution of Virginia (in two volumes), by A. E. Dick Howard. 1974.

The Future of the United States Multinational Corporation—Proceedings of a conference held in 1974, edited for the J. B. Moore Society of International Law by Lee D. Unterman and Christine W. Swent. 1975.

Dictionary of Sigla and Abbreviations to and in Law Books before 1607, edited by William Hamilton Bryson. 1975.

An International Rule of Law

By
Eberhard P. Deutsch

University Press of Virginia

Charlottesville

THE UNIVERSITY PRESS OF VIRGINIA
Copyright © 1977 by the Rector and Visitors
of the University of Virginia

First published 1977

Library of Congress Cataloging in Publication Data

Deutsch, Eberhard Paul, 1897–
　An international rule of law.

　(Virginia legal studies)
　Includes bibliographical references and index.
　1. Hague. International Court of Justice. I. Ti-
tle. II. Series.
JX1971.6.D48　　341.5′5　　77–22311
ISBN 0–8139–0614–8

Printed in the United States of America

To the Memory of
R L D
Who, while Living,
Inspired the Inception,
And whose Spirit, When She had Passed,
Encouraged the Completion,
of this Book

Contents

Preface

In the physical sciences, man has made such giant strides in so many directions as to penetrate a number of areas of hitherto occult mysticism, which lie literally beyond the bounds of his own highly developed comprehension. But in the political sciences, man seems to remain lost in the same prehistoric morass in which his tribal ancestors wandered about, and out of which he has apparently never been able to find his way onto the highway of ratiocination. Throughout the ages, the desire to wield and retain political power has motivated strong tribes, as it has great nations, in using force or the threat of force, as a dominant weapon over the rule of reason, in shaping the broad political destinies of the human race. Perhaps the very threat of human extinction, posed by man's progress in the physical sciences beyond limits within his own ultimate control, has itself prepared him to make concessions to a rule of reason over one of self-destructive force, in an effort to bring order out of chaos in his long-retarded political evolution.

At the end of the First World War, an effort was made to break through this stasis of political science, by seeking to beat a well-marked path toward reasoned solutions of international problems through the Covenant of the League of Nations and the Statute of the Permanent Court of International Justice. But the physical sciences had not yet yielded to mankind the secrets of a completely self-destructive force; and significant sectors of the human family did not yet feel impelled to abandon the struggle for dominance of the power of might among nations in favor of a reasoned rule of political science in a world of sovereign States. The holocaust of Hiroshima brought the Second World War to a close, with a foreboding of such far greater destructive forces as to constrain even the major powers, in a position to magnify and unleash them, to pause and consider the inevitable effects of retaliatory measures *inter se,* and to pledge renewed and wider scope to the rule of reason as a guide for the conduct of all nations, large and small, toward each other.

On June 26, 1945, the San Francisco Conference on International Organization adopted the Charter of the United Nations, "based on the principle of the sovereign equality of all its Members," [1] in order "to bring about by peaceful means, and in conformity with the principles of justice and international law, adjustment or settlement of international disputes or situations which might lead to a breach of the peace." [2]

At the same time, for the purpose of providing a means of moving toward this objective and accomplishing these aims, the Conference adopted, as "an integral part of the present Charter," the Statute of the "International Court of Justice [which] shall be the principal judicial organ of the United Nations." [3]

But the jurisdiction of the Court was not compulsory. It was based on voluntary declarations of adherence which, even when filed at all, ordinarily were conditioned on such emasculating reservations as individual nations saw fit to attach to them—and the menace of ever-increasing force has continued to darken the world's horizons.

This constantly advancing threat to the very existence of the world, continues to render its great powers receptive to proposals within the sphere of political science, toward maintenance of peace and security through the rule of reason, at least insofar as attainment of that goal is promised with a minimal surrender of national sovereignties.

The plan for a reconstitution of the International Court of Justice, described in this book, contemplates no real surrender of sovereignty, while vesting in that tribunal unreserved, universal, and uniform compulsory jurisdiction over the justiciable controversies of all nations with each other, on what is sincerely believed to be a universally acceptable basis.

Such a reconstitution will by no means serve as a panacea for all the world's political ills. But its plan takes full cognizance of the Aristotelian doctrine of the supremacy of distributive over

---

[1] U. N. CHARTER art. 2, para. 1.　　　[2] *Id.* art. 1, para. 1.　　　[3] *Id.* art. 92.

corrective justice, through its assumption that the mere avail-
ability of a tribunal with compulsory jurisdiction to adjudicate
all international disputes in strict accord with legal principles,
will itself tend to impel diplomatic adjustment of most controversies among nations.

The world has no greater need than for an effective instrumentality to compel adjudication under an international rule
of law, and to induce the peaceful settlement, of disputes among
nations. The following pages detail and illustrate a workable
plan for bringing the rule of law into being.

EPD

New Orleans
January 1977

Acknowledgments

So many people necessarily contribute, in one way or another, to the formulation of even a single thought, and so countless many more inevitably participate in formulating and weaving together the myriad of thoughts which bring so far-reaching a book as this into being, that I do not even know who most of them may be; and I could not name them within more than twice the reach of this volume, if I knew every one. So I refer expressly to only two, whose assistance in my work was most tangible, ever-present, and immediate, without disparaging in the slightest the innumerable others with whom I have had the privilege of contact throughout my life, and whose aggregate contributions made through me as their mere conduit really created the conceptual judicial structure presented and described in the pages of this book.

From the beginning, I had the inestimable privilege of consulting, whenever I wished to do so, with the Honorable Russell B. Long, formerly a ranking member of the Foreign Relations Committee of the Senate of the United States, enthusiastically devoted to the cause of peace through law in the world, in the history of which he is destined to become a significant figure. In addition to making available to me a wealth of invaluable source material, he gave me and obtained for me practical suggestions and advice as to work-a-day international relationships, without which this work could never have attained its present scope.

And I shall never be able to express adequate appreciation to my distinguished author-brother Hermann who, one evening, when he had reviewed the skeletal plan of my opus, said quite simply, "you are projecting a monumental masterpiece"; and when I had put together the book somewhat roughly in accordance with that plan, he brought his infinitely skillful master-craftsmanship to bear on the manuscript and suggested revisions which made it far more readable.

Among the many secondary works which were of use in researching this book, I would like to make special mention of Judge Manley O. Hudson's seminal work, *The Permanent Court of International Justice 1920–1942* (1943), which provides a magnificent insight into the early, formative period of the Permanent Court, and especially the debates of the 1920 Committee of Jurists.

My special thanks to Mrs. Elaine Kern, whose stenographic work put this volume into readable form.

I also would like to extend my deepest appreciation to Professors Richard B. Lillich and Kenneth R. Redden and to Charles Bayar.

To all of these, named and unnamed, for whatever of merit there may be in this presentation of a plan for attainment of a Rule of Law among nations, to the concept, evolution, design, creation, and depiction of which I have devoted the greater part of more than ten years of my life, I tender my deepest and sincerest gratitude.

EPD

New Orleans
January 1977

Foreword

In December 1967, the American Bar Association Journal published an article by Mr. Deutsch on *A Judicial Path to World Peace*.[1] It was a condensed version of this book.

Judge Orie L. Phillips, Senior Judge of the United States Court of Appeal for the Tenth Circuit, said of that article, "I am convinced . . . that Mr. Deutsch deserves the thanks of the International bar and the appreciation of the nations of the world for his brilliant proposal in . . . 'A Judicial Path to World Peace.'"[2]

While I was a member of the Foreign Relations Committee of the Senate, I introduced a joint resolution in the Congress to request the President of the United States to take up Mr. Deutsch's plan and present it to the United Nations. At that time, I discussed the plan with the Honorable Harland Cleveland, Assistant Secretary of State, and he was quite sympathetic to it, although he had little hope for its ultimate adoption by the nations of the world, primarily because of Russian opposition to compulsory jurisdiction of the Court over the Soviet Union under any circumstances.

Mr. Deutsch's plan is really a brilliant one. It provides for appointment of judges for life (with voluntary retirement at seventy and compulsory retirement at seventy-five) and for a two-thirds majority of the entire Court to overrule a plea to the jurisdiction of the Court. This latter provision, it seems to me, is a fair settlement of the Connally Amendment question, under which the United States may determine for itself whether a case involves a domestic or an international issue.

Having been familiar with Mr. Deutsch's work in the international field for many years (he introduced and managed to get

---

[1] Deutsch, *A Judicial Path to World Peace*, 53 A.B.A.J. 1115 (1967).
[2] 54 A.B.A.J. 338 (1968).

through the negative veto in Austria, which saved that government for the West, while he was on the staff of General Mark Clark, High Commissioner of the U.S. in the Military Administration of Austria following World War II) , I am convinced that some such plan as Mr. Deutsch has presented can be worked out, even against Russian intransigence.

Either man will learn to live by a rule of law or he will destroy himself. To live by man-made law requires a court in which men of all nations can have confidence. The court must earn that confidence, which is not likely to happen so long as judges are bound by national loyalties and even face the possibility of reprisals if they place the cause of justice above their national ties. Without reforms of the nature suggested by Mr. Deutsch, the world court can never achieve its objective. The hope men can resolve their international differences in a court, rather than on a battlefield, will continue to be thwarted.

Mr. Deutsch's proposal would move us much closer to the day when all men "shall beat their swords into plowshares. . . ." This may not remove all the impediments to a universal rule of law, but it would bring us much closer to that day.

Experience with a reconstituted world court would demonstrate to us what, if any, further reforms might be necessary to achieve the noble ideals that dictated the establishment of such an institution.

The idea of compulsory jurisdiction of the World Court, under such conditions as Mr. Deutsch proposes, is an excellent one. Scholars and students of international law, in reading *An International Rule of Law* objectively, must agree with me on this. I commend the book in the highest terms.

Russell B. Long
United States Senator

January 1977

Abbreviations

Hague Convention of 1899 – Convention with Certain Powers for the Pacific Settlement of International Disputes, July 29, 1899, 32 Stat. 1779, T.S. No. 392 (effective Sept. 4, 1900).

Hague Convention of 1907 – Convention with Other Powers for the Pacific Settlement of International Disputes, Oct. 18, 1907, 36 Stat. 2199, T.S. No. 536 (effective Jan. 6, 1910).

HAGUE CONVENTIONS – THE HAGUE CONVENTIONS AND DECLARATIONS OF 1899 AND 1907 (J. Scott ed. 1918).

M. HUDSON, TRIBUNALS – M. HUDSON, INTERNATIONAL TRIBUNALS (1944).

M. HUDSON, P.C.I.J. – M. HUDSON, THE PERMANENT COURT OF INTERNATIONAL JUSTICE 1920–1942 (1943).

H. LAUTERPACHT, DEVELOPMENT – H. LAUTERPACHT, THE DEVELOPMENT OF INTERNATIONAL LAW BY THE INTERNATIONAL COURT (1958).

H. LAUTERPACHT, FUNCTION – H. LAUTERPACHT, THE FUNCTION OF LAW IN THE INTERNATIONAL COMMUNITY (1933).

COMM. III – 1 LEAGUE OF NATIONS, RECORDS OF THE FIRST ASSEMBLY, COMMITTEES, at 273–617 (1920).

LEAGUE DOCUMENTS – LEAGUE OF NATIONS, DOCUMENTS CONCERNING THE ACTION TAKEN BY THE COUNCIL OF THE LEAGUE OF NATIONS UNDER ARTICLE 14 OF THE COVENANT AND THE ADOPTION BY THE ASSEMBLY OF THE STATUTE OF THE PERMANENT COURT (no date).

1926 PROCEEDINGS (SIGNATORIES) – LEAGUE OF NATIONS, MINUTES OF THE CONFERENCE OF STATES SIGNATORIES OF THE PROTOCOL OF SIGNATURE OF THE STATUTE OF THE PERMANENT COURT OF INTERNATIONAL JUSTICE, HELD AT GENEVA FROM SEPTEMBER 1ST TO 23RD, 1926 (no date).

1929 PROCEEDINGS (SIGNATORIES) —LEAGUE OF NATIONS, MINUTES OF THE CONFERENCE REGARDING THE REVISION OF THE STATUTE OF THE PERMANENT COURT OF INTERNATIONAL JUSTICE AND THE ACCESSION OF THE UNITED STATES OF AMERICA TO THE PROTO-COL OF SIGNATURE OF THAT STATUTE, HELD AT GENEVA FROM SEPTEMBER 4TH TO 12TH, 1929 (1929).

1920 PROCEEDINGS—P.C.I.J., ADVISORY COMM. OF JURISTS, PROCES-VERBAUX OF THE PROCEEDINGS OF THE COMMITTEE, JUNE 16TH–JULY 24TH, 1920 (1920).

1920 DOCUMENTS—P.C.I.J., ADVISORY COMM. OF JURISTS, DOCU-MENTS PRESENTED TO THE COMMITTEE RELATING TO EXISTING PLANS FOR THE ESTABLISHMENT OF A PERMANENT COURT OF IN-TERNATIONAL JUSTICE (no date).

1929 PROCEEDINGS—P.C.I.J., COMM. OF JURISTS ON THE STATUTE OF THE PERMANENT COURT OF INTERNATIONAL JUSTICE, MIN-UTES OF THE SESSION HELD AT GENEVA, MARCH 11TH TO 19TH, 1929 (1929).

Prize Court Convention of 1907—Hague Convention (XII) of 1907 Relating to the Creation of an International Prize Court, HAGUE CONVENTIONS, at 188.

S. ROSENNE, I.C.J.—S. ROSENNE, THE INTERNATIONAL COURT OF JUSTICE (1957).

1–2 S. ROSENNE, LAW AND PRACTICE—1–2 S. ROSENNE, THE LAW AND PRACTICE OF THE INTERNATIONAL COURT (1965).

R. RUSSELL, CHARTER—R. RUSSELL, A HISTORY OF THE UNITED NATIONS CHARTER (1958).

Vienna Convention—Vienna Convention on the Law of Treaties, *opened for signature* May 23, 1969, U.N. Doc. A/CONF. 39/27 (1969), *reprinted in* U.N. CONF. ON THE LAW OF TREATIES, OFFICIAL RECORDS (DOCUMENTS), U.N. Doc. A/CONF. 39/1/ Add.2 (1971); 8 INT'L LEGAL MATERIALS 679 (1969).

Introduction

Nearly 2,500 years ago an "Athenian stranger" is reported to have declared that "the state in which the law is above the rulers, and the rulers are the inferiors of the law, has salvation, and every blessing which the gods can confer." [1] In the thirteenth century, Bracton wrote that "the king must not be under man but under God and under the law, because law makes the king. . . . [T]here is no *rex* where will rules rather than *lex*." [2] Some four hundred years later, Sir Edward Coke, the father of the common law, exalted it as "the perfection of reason." [3] Finally, in 1885, Professor A. V. Dicey tied the concept of the rule of law to the judicial standard by which alone it can have force and meaning. The threefold meaning of the rule of law, said Dicey, is that the law is administered "in the ordinary legal manner before the ordinary courts of the land," that "every man, whatever be his rank or condition, is subject to the ordinary law of the realm," and that the general principles of individual liberty are "the result of judicial decisions." [4] In a colloquium held at the University of Chicago in 1957,[5] participants from a dozen countries, including Poland and the Soviet Union, concluded that the rule of law as understood in the West includes the concept of "the

[1] PLATO, LAWS bk. IV, in 4 THE DIALOGUES OF PLATO 243 (B. Jowett transl. 1871).

[2] BRACTON, ON THE LAWS AND CUSTOMS OF ENGLAND f. 5, at 33 (G. Woodbine ed., S. Thorne transl. 1968); *see also* 2 W. HOLDSWORTH, A HISTORY OF ENGLISH LAW 253–55 (3rd ed. 1923).

[3] E. COKE, THE FIRST PART OF THE INSTITUTES OF THE LAWS OF ENGLAND, OR A COMMENTARY UPON LITTLETON § 138, at f. 97b (14th ed. 1789).

[4] A. DICEY, INTRODUCTION TO THE STUDY OF THE LAW OF THE CONSTITUTION 188, 193, 195 (10th ed. 1959). *See generally id.* at 181–205.

[5] The transcript of the Chicago Colloquium has not been published. *See* Wade, *Introduction to id.* at cviii–ix.

supremacy of law over government," and "must be secured principally, but not exclusively, by the ordinary courts." [6]

The immediate problem is to translate some such definition
into international terms. This is, of course, extremely difficult,
since by its very nature international law is coordinate, based on
voluntary accord, as opposed to the obligatory or subordinate
nature of law imposed within a State. But even a tentatively
acceptable rule of international law must be based on some acceptable concept of international law itself. Thomas Hobbes envisioned this concept in the nature of a transition from national
law governing men to international law governing nations. He
wrote:

Concerning the Offices of one Soveraign to another, which are comprehended in that Law, which is commonly called the *Law of Nations*, I need not say anything in this place; because the Law of
Nations, and the Law of Nature, is the same thing. . . . And the
same Law, that dictateth to men that have no Civil Government,
what they ought to do, and what to avoyd in regard to one another,
dictateth the same to Common-wealths, that is, to consciences of
Soveraign Princes, and Soveraign Assemblies.[7]

Professor Lauterpacht (later Judge Sir Hersch Lauterpacht of
the International Court of Justice) wrote:

There is no reason why the original hypothesis in international law
should not be that the will of the international community must be
obeyed. . . . [A]lthough in many cases the will of the international
community must be deduced from the mere fact of its existence . . .
the organs of the formation of [that] will . . . are . . . States them-

---

[6] *Id.* at cix. The rule of law "is a characteristic doctrine of the common law that
the judiciary, in ordinary legal proceedings, may pronounce upon the legal validity
of the acts of the king's ministers and servants and hence, in the United States,
upon the validity of administrative, executive and legislative action. . . ." Pound,
Rule of Law, in 13 Encyclopedia of the Social Sciences 463 (1934).

[7] T. Hobbes, Leviathan pt. 2, ch. 30, at 185 (1651). Professor Hold-Ferneck of
the University of Vienna conceived the relation between sovereign States to be one
of comity, international law being merely the expression of a *modus vivendi.*
A. Hold-Ferneck, Lehrbuch des Voelkerrechts 12, 86, 88 (1930). Professor Brierly
of Oxford, later Chairman of the International Law Commission, considered that
international society, "in the matter of its law, [is still] at the primitive stage."
J. Brierly, The Law of Nations 52 (1928).

selves, their consent being given by custom or treaty, and being capable of impartial ascertainment and interpretation by international tribunals.[8]

Thus the rule of international law, like its domestic counterpart, would be brought under the protective aegis of the judiciary.

In a given social environment, tribunals for the adjudication of legal disputes have quite often arisen before the advent of any codified system of law. Sir Henry Maine said that "it is certain that, in the infancy of mankind, no sort of legislature, nor even a distinct author of law, is contemplated or conceived of." In that era, "the only authoritative statement of right and wrong is a judicial sentence . . . which is breathed for the first time by a higher power into the judge's mind at the time of adjudication."[9] Holdsworth states that "from the medieval period onwards, the appeal of those who were discontented with the policy pursued by the state has been either an appeal to the courts for the proper enforcement or for the proper interpretation of the law, or an appeal to Parliament for a change in the law."[10] Dicey defined state law as "any rule which will be enforced by the courts"; and he concluded that any rule not subject to ordinary judicial process was not a rule of law at all.[11] Professor Lauterpacht was convinced that "there is substance in the view that the existence of a body of clear rules of conduct is not at all essential to the existence of

[8] H. LAUTERPACHT, FUNCTION at 421.

[9] H. MAINE, ANCIENT LAW 8 (2d ed. 1863). Professor Nicolas Politis of the University of Paris, Delegate of Greece to the League of Nations, wrote that "le développement juridique ne commence pas tant par la fixation du droit que par l'institution d'un juge." N. POLITIS, LA JUSTICE INTERNATIONALE 252–53 (1924), citing J. DUBS, LE DROIT PUBLIC DE LA CONFÉDÉRATION SUISSE, pt. 2e, at 105–06 (1879). Thomas Walker, Professor of International Law at Cambridge and London, declared: "Observance precedes Command, and the Administrator the Law-Giver." T. WALKER, THE SCIENCE OF INTERNATIONAL LAW 17 (1893).

[10] 10 W. HOLDSWORTH, *supra* note 2, at 646.

[11] A. DICEY, *supra* note 4, at 40. This definition was accepted in the United States by Professor John Chipman Gray of Harvard. J. GRAY, THE NATURE AND SOURCES OF THE LAW 255 (1909). Professor Goodhart of Oxford states that "this Anglo-American interpretation places the main emphasis on recognition by the courts because they have always played such a dominant role in the system of government in those countries." Goodhart, *The Rule of Law and Absolute Sovereignty*, 106 U. PA. L. REV. 943, 953 (1958).

law, and that the decisive test is whether there exists a judge competent to decide upon disputed rights and to command peace."[12]

"The idea of resolving international disputes," declares Shabtai Rosenne of the International Law Commission, "through international third parties . . . on the basis of law and justice, as an alternative to direct settlement . . . by means of violence after diplomacy has failed, is a deep-rooted human aspiration."[13] That yearning found some expression in the Nuremburg War Crimes Tribunal, whose underlying purpose was described by Mr. Justice Jackson, in his closing address of July 26, 1946, in terms of a judicial rule of international law:

In drawing the Charter of this Tribunal, we thought we were recording an accomplished advance in international law. . . . The Agreement of London, whether it originates or merely records, at all events marks a transition in International Law which roughly corresponds to that in the evolution of local law when man ceased to punish local crime by 'hue and cry' and began to let reason and inquiry govern punishment.[14]

The entire function of a law of nations is, in the last analysis, the preservation of peace through exclusion of self-help and the application to international disputes of principles of justice, ordinarily by some sort of judicial process; "for that which prevents a civil war in a nation is that which may prevent it abroad, viz., justice; and we see where that is notably obstructed, war is kindled between the magistrates and people in particular kingdoms and states. . . . Thus peace is maintained by justice. . . ."[15]

As shown, law, to be given effect as the embodiment of justice,

[12] H. LAUTERPACHT, FUNCTION at 424.

[13] S. ROSENNE, THE WORLD COURT 11 (1962).

[14] 19 TRIAL OF THE MAJOR WAR CRIMINALS BEFORE THE INTERNATIONAL MILITARY TRIBUNAL 398 (1948). Nevertheless, as recently as 1964, the late Professor C. Wilfred Jenks of London expressed the following view: "Since the Second World War remarkable advances have been made in virtually every sector of international organisation except the judicial sector. There has been no comparable advance in international adjudication. . . ." C. JENKS, THE PROSPECTS OF INTERNATIONAL ADJUDICATION 1 (1964).

[15] Penn, *An Essay Towards the Present and Future Peace of Europe, reprinted in* 394 INT'L CONCIL. 571 (1943).

needs judicial application. The history of Western democracies demonstrates that, with some notable exceptions, the ultimate authority of courts, even within the State, is not really dependent on forcible execution of judgments, but arises rather from inherent respect for, and generally recognized acceptance of, judicial decrees. This is no less true in controversies among nations: "Frequently the only guarantee of the effectiveness of the legal decision" in international adjudication, said Professor Lauterpacht, "is the impersonal authority of the law. This factor reduces, but does not substantially impair, its function as an instrument of peace." [16]

Just as in the case of domestic jurisprudence, so the history of international law has its beginnings in the organization of early tribunals for the arbitration of disputes among political entities. As far back as the seventh century B.C., tribunals of sorts, such as the Delphic amphictyony, were established in ancient Greece to provide for third-party adjudication of asserted violations by the city-states of a rudimentary system of customary law, and so to bring to the inter-State community the constructive values of legal discipline in place of the destructive effects of warfare.[17]

In early medieval times, the judicial function was a prerogative of royalty—an integral part of the machinery of absolutism within the State. Law did not reach supremacy in the concept of government until courts were given independent status. The first significant breach in the wall of judicial prerogative came when, in 1215, the barons demanded and obtained its surrender by King John. In 1305, a wealthy Norman lawyer and pamphleteer, Pierre Dubois, suggested the formation of a World Court to which nations might bring their disputes for settlement according to law.[18] And in 1623, another Frenchman, a somewhat obscure lawyer named Émeric Crucé, published a book which elaborated on the

---

[16] H. LAUTERPACHT, FUNCTION at 398.

[17] 1 C. PHILLIPSON, THE INTERNATIONAL LAW AND CUSTOM OF ANCIENT GREECE AND ROME 36 (1911); 2 *id.* at 5–11. With the growth of the Macedonian, Roman, and Byzantine empires, this method of third-party settlement of inter-State controversies fell into disuse, apparently because the larger imperialist states were unwilling to submit disputes to such impartial adjudication. *Id.*

[18] P. DUBOIS, DE RECUPERATIONE TERRE SANCTE (1305).

details of Dubois's proposed Court.[19] In 1625, Hugo Grotius, the father of modern international law, wrote:

Christian kings and states are bound to pursue this method [arbitration] of avoiding wars. . . . [I]t would be advantageous, indeed in a degree necessary, to hold certain conferences of Christian powers, where those who have no interest at stake may settle the disputes of others, and where, in fact, steps may be taken to compel parties to accept peace on fair terms.[20]

Perhaps the most remarkably succinct and practical proposal for such a tribunal was suggested in 1693 by William Penn in his *Essay Towards the Present and Future Peace of Europe:*

Now if the sovereign princes of Europe, who represent that society or independent state of men that was previous to the obligations of society, would, for the same reason that engaged men first into society, viz., love of peace and order, agree to meet by their stated deputies in a general diet . . . and there establish rules of justice for sovereign princes to observe one to another . . . before which sovereign assembly should be brought all differences depending between one sovereign and another that cannot be made up by private embassies before the sessions begin; and that if any of the sovereignties that constitute these imperial states shall refuse to submit their claims or pretensions to them, or to abide and perform the judgment thereof, and seek their remedy by arms . . . all the other sovereignties, united as one strength, shall compel the submission and performance of the sentence, with damages to the suffering party, and charges to the sovereignties that obliged their submission.[21]

Unquestionably, the greatest obstacle over the years to establishment of, adherence to, and confidence in a permanent international court has arisen out of strong and near universal aversion to surrender of sovereignty in advance to such a tribunal. In his *Essay Towards the Present and Future Peace of Europe,* William Penn said, with regard to the suggestion "that sovereign princes and states will" by the establishment of such a court "be-

[19] É. CRUCÉ, LE NOUVEAU CYNÉE (1673). *See also* É. CRUCÉ, THE NEW CYNEAS (T. Balch transl. 1909).

[20] H. GROTIUS, 2 DE JURE BELLI AC PACIS ch. 23, § 8 (The Classics of International Law No. 3, J. Scott ed., F. Kelsey transl. 1925).

[21] Penn, *supra* note 15, at 573.

come not sovereign," that "if this be called a lessening of their power, it must be only because the great fish can no longer eat up the little ones, and that each sovereignty is equally defended from injuries, and disabled from committing them. . . ." [22] Nearly five hundred years earlier, King John had perforce set an example on the domestic level by surrendering his sovereignty to the barons, by allowing them to "distress and harass" him to compel his compliance with their decrees. [23] Surely, every obligation into which a nation enters represents, *pro tanto*, an abrogation of that nation's sovereignty, for it thus binds itself to do, or to refrain from doing, some act which it would otherwise be free to do or not to do. Every Member of the United Nations has surrendered some portion of its sovereignty, *quoad hoc* the binding obligations which it has assumed under the Charter; and, except for the veto power reserved to the five permanent members of the Security Council, each Member actually has gone much further by agreeing, in advance, in Article 108 of the Charter itself, to be bound by any amendment thereto adopted. Equally, of course, an agreement by a nation to submit a dispute with another nation to arbitration is an abdication of sovereignty in that respect — and this may also be carried even further by an agreement (not uncommon) to arbitrate any and all disputes that may arise under a treaty or a series of treaties. [24] From that point it is only a short step to an agreement by a nation to submit any and all

---

[22] *Id.* at 579. In the fifth century B.C., an Athenian envoy is reported to have told the Lacedaemonian Assembly:

We are not the first who have aspired to rule; the world has ever held that the weaker must be kept down by the stronger. And we think that we are worthy of power; and there was a time when you thought so too; but now, when you mean expediency you talk about justice. Did justice ever deter anyone from taking by force whatever he could? Men who indulge the natural ambition of empire deserve credit if they are in any degree more careful of justice than they need be.

THUCYDIDES, HISTORY OF THE PELOPONNESIAN WAR bk. I, para. 76, at 49 (American ed. B. Jowett transl. 1883).

[23] MAGNA CHARTA ch. 61, in 2 G. SMITH, HISTORY OF THE ENGLISH PARLIAMENT 556 (1892).

[24] Professor Lauterpacht has suggested that the doctrine *rebus sic stantibus* cannot logically be applied to an arbitration agreement, "for it is difficult to see how any change of circumstances can justify the refusal to have a dispute settled by law." H. LAUTERPACHT, FUNCTION at 431 n.1.

justiciable disputes which it may have with other nations to an established permanent international tribunal.

One of the very real problems in that regard, however, arises from the desire of nations to assure, as nearly as possible, an absence of bias from any tribunal which is to adjudicate their rights and liabilities. Even courts, it must be conceded, are subject at times to political partisanships, and international disputes are peculiarly fraught with political overtones. Another primary fear of nations, one closely related to the sovereignty issue discussed above, turns on the prospect of international organs intruding into matters solely within their "domestic jurisdiction." [25]

Of course, an international tribunal serves no really useful purpose unless a nation may be required to appear before it in respect to the demand of another nation for adjudication of a dispute between them. As stated by Professor Lauterpacht: "The absence in international society of compulsory jurisdiction of courts is tantamount to a general recognition of the right of self-help." [26]

Ultimately, the most important — the absolutely indispensable — factor to bring about acceptance of compulsory jurisdiction of an

[25] *See, e.g.,* the Connally Amendment to reservation (b) of the Declaration of the United States of America Recognizing the Jurisdiction of the International Court of Justice, [1971–72] I.C.J.Y.B. 84. This Declaration, when reported to the floor of the U.S. Senate as S. RES 196, contained a reservation regarding domestic jurisdiction. Senator Connally of Texas proposed the addition of the words "as determined by the United States" to Reservation (b), 92 CONG. REC. 10763 (1946). He later stated: "We do not propose to have a Court of 15, 14 of whom will be alien judges—I do not reflect upon them—decide that a domestic question is an international question. . . ." *Id.* at 10840. The Connally Amendment was added to S. RES 196, *id.* at 10841, which was then passed by a vote of sixty to two. *Id.* at 10850.

At present, nineteen States have domestic jurisdiction reservation clauses in their declarations of adherence to the jurisdiction of the International Court of Justice: Australia ([1971–72] I.C.J.Y.B. 57), Botswana (59), Canada (60), France (63), Gambia (64), India (65), Israel (66), Kenya (68), Khmer Republic [Cambodia] (68), Liberia (69), Malawi (71), Malta (72), Mauritius (73), Mexico (74), New Zealand (75), Pakistan (77), the Philippines (78), the Sudan (81), Swaziland (81), and the United States of America (84). Of these, six States reserve the determination of what lies within their domestic jurisdiction to themselves: Liberia, Malawi, Mexico, the Philippines, the Sudan, and the United States. *See generally* Wright, *Domestic Jurisdiction as a Limit on National and Supra-National Action,* 56 Nw. U.L. REV. 11 (1961).

[26] H. LAUTERPACHT, FUNCTION at 395.

international tribunal over disputes among sovereign nations is assured independence of the international judiciary. "The real difficulty lies not in the inability of international law to protect important interests of States, but in the apprehension that it would be dangerous to expose such interests to the risks of a decision by judges whose impartiality is regarded as problematical." [27] Since the time of Aristotle, political philosophers have agreed that the persons who exercise judicial authority should be independent of all those who wield political—that is, legislative or executive—power. Montesquieu submitted that "there is no liberty if the judiciary power be not separated from the legislative and executive." [28] According to Blackstone, "in this distinct and separate existence of the judicial power . . . consists one main preservative of the public liberty; which cannot subsist long in any state, unless the administration of common justice be in some degree separated both from the legislative and also from the executive power." [29] And unquestionably "it was the attainment of independence by the [British] judges . . . which gave emphasis to Dicey's conception of the rule of law. . . ." [30] This British principle was not extended to the American colonies, and one of the principal complaints of the colonists against

[27] *Id.* at 202.

[28] 1 MONTESQUIEU, THE SPIRIT OF THE LAWS 152 (The World's Great Classics, T. Nugent transl. 1899).

[29] 1 W. BLACKSTONE, COMMENTARIES *259. "I know not whether a greater improvement has been made in government than to separate the judiciary from the executive and legislative branches, and to provide for the decision of private rights in a manner wholly uninfluenced by reasons of state, or considerations of party or of policy." Remarks by Daniel Webster in the Convention To Amend the Constitution of the State of Massachusetts, Dec. 30, 1820, in 3 THE WORKS OF DANIEL WEBSTER 27 (1851). "The separation of the judiciary from the administrative power of the state, no doubt affects the security of every citizen, and the liberty of all." 1 A. DE TOCQUEVILLE, DEMOCRACY IN AMERICA 206 (H. Reeves transl. 1835).

[30] Wade, *supra* note 5, at ciii. The English Act of Settlement of 1700, 12 & 13 Will. 3, c. 2, § 3 provided that "Judges [*sic*] Commissions be made *Quandiu* [*sic*] *se bene gesserint.*" "Of all officers of government, those in whose appointment any participation of popular suffrage is the most objectionable, are judicial officers. While there are no functionaries whose special and professional qualifications the popular judgment is less fitted to estimate, there are none in whose case absolute impartiality, and freedom from connexion with politicians or sections of politicians, are of anything like equal importance." J. MILL, CONSIDERATIONS ON REPRESENTATIVE GOVERNMENT 106 (People's ed. 1867).

George III, as set forth in the Declaration of Independence, was that "he has made Judges dependent on his Will alone for the tenure of their Offices." Alexander Hamilton wrote:

the general liberty can never be endangered . . . so long as the judiciary remains truly distinct from both the legislative and executive. . . . [Since] nothing can contribute so much to its firmness and independence as permanency in office, this quality may therefore be justly regarded as an indispensable ingredient in its constitution; and, in a great measure, as the citadel of the public justice and the public security.[31]

In Canada, judges appointed by the Governor in Council are prohibited from taking seats in Parliament by the Canada Elections Act of 1960.[32] In England, by way of contrast, the same rule is supported by immemorial custom.[33]

Nevertheless, the exercise of a judicial function, however disinterestedly it may be performed, is by no means a short, straight path to an Utopian international rule of law. Existence, and even universal acceptance, of a permanent international tribunal to adjudicate disputes among nations can no more assure a universal rule of law than an efficient fire department can guarantee an absence of incendiarism. It is submitted, however, that creation of a deservedly trusted adjudicative process, with universal jurisdiction over international disputes, would be a significant achievement in the development of world peace through law.

Just as it can within a State, so law can play only a limited role among States. But inevitably law must be a constituent element of permanent peace, and if administered ethically, it will ultimately bring about the acceptance of common standards of morality. "The reign of law, represented by the incorporation of obligatory arbitration as a rule of positive international law, is not the only means for securing and preserving peace among nations. Nevertheless it is an essential condition of peace." [34]

Unquestionably, States remain reluctant to submit disputes of

[31] THE FEDERALIST No. 78, at 211 (G. Hopkins ed. 1802) (A. Hamilton).

[32] CAN. REV. STAT. Supp. 1, c. 14, § 21 (1) (h).

[33] *See* 2 A. TODD, ON PARLIAMENTARY GOVERNMENT IN ENGLAND 324–25 (2d ed. 1889).

[34] H. LAUTERPACHT, FUNCTION at 437.

great substantive importance for judicial determination because of their very importance, coupled with the fear of adverse adjudication as opposed to the hope of favorable diplomatic negotiation. Political factors must and will continue to play an important role in international relations, but this by no means diminishes the importance of legal issues which may remain subject to adjudication.

One need not naïvely expect that a judicial clarification of questions of competence or similar legal issues will set all conflicts at rest as legal issues rarely comprise the whole controversy. But it may be expected that [nations] . . . will be able to move ahead on the political level where interests can be composed and conciliated. What seems to be required in the years to come is that [nations] . . . free themselves from a certain antijudicial bias . . . and that resort to legal arguments be not confined merely to the debates.[35]

The whole function of compulsory international adjudication is to apply "the rule of law" in an endeavor to maintain peace in the world, however uncertain and unsteady it may be. "The point is not whether international law can prevent a war, but whether it can make a contribution to preventing a war, and whether a well-founded appeal to international law can strengthen the case of whoever appeals to it. And *that* it can."[36]

A fundamental reconstitution of the International Court of Justice may well achieve ultimate acceptance of compulsory jurisdiction of that tribunal over all nations, by assuring the Court's completely nonpolitical character through independent judges and effective prohibition of invasion of domestic jurisdiction. It is to the outline and explanation of such a proposal that this book is devoted.

[35] Gross, *The United Nations and the Role of Law*, 19 INT'L ORG. 537, 560 (1965). This, in a sense, is what Rosenne refers to as "the political contexture of international adjudication." S. ROSENNE, I.C.J. at 8.

[36] Address by Dr. Ealco van Kleffens, President of the General Assembly of the United Nations, at Princeton University, Nov. 29, 1954.

An International Rule of Law

Greater than the force of
mighty armies is the impact
of an idea whose hour has come.

Victor Hugo

CHAPTER I

Universal Compulsory Jurisdiction

Ever since the beginning of the twentieth century, and to some extent even earlier, there have been strong currents—engendered by a deep-seated human yearning for world peace—moving toward establishment of a permanent international tribunal with compulsory jurisdiction over all nations of the world and dedicated to the peaceful adjudication of their disputes. Each of the great statesmen who labored assiduously in the vineyards of international organization at the Hague Peace Conferences of 1899 and 1907, at Versailles in 1919, and at San Francisco in 1945, was striving to lay a firm foundation for the support of a sturdy structure to embody the idealistic concept of an international tribunal as an instrument to achieve the ultimate ideal of permanent peace. The most farsighted idealist would not presume to assert that their goal has yet been closely approached, much less achieved; nor, on the other hand, would the starkest realist deny that there has been progress in that direction. Both would agree, however, that the permanent international tribunals established in the twentieth century as agencies for peaceful adjudication—but with the extent and very existence of their jurisdiction dependent solely upon the will of the litigants—never could have achieved the destiny which their creators envisioned for them.

The Permanent Court of International Justice, organized in 1922 under a Statute adopted by the League of Nations pursuant to Article 14 of its Covenant, unquestionably rendered some noteworthy decisions and scholarly opinions, which have become significant milestones along the tortuous paths of international law. But Article 14 merely provided that "[t]he Court shall be competent to hear and determine any dispute of an international character which the parties thereto submit to it." It is widely recognized that the Permanent Court's inability to consider such disputes on its own initiative was a major factor in its failure to make an effective contribution to the preservation of world peace.

Article 92 of the Charter of the United Nations declares that "[t]he International Court of Justice shall be . . . [its] principal judicial organ, . . . " and it provides that the Court is to "function in accordance with the annexed Statute, which is based upon the Statute of the Permanent Court of International Justice. . . ." Under Article 36 of the present Statute, only States which file declarations of adherence are subject to the jurisdiction of the Court—and then only under the conditions which they may stipulate. At the present time (1974), less than 50 of the over 130 Member States of the United Nations have of record any declarations of adherence to the International Court of Justice, and only 2 States may be said to have truly submitted themselves unconditionally to the compulsory jurisdiction of the Court.[1] Under these conditions, it must be conceded that the International Court of Justice has fallen into the pattern of its late lamented predecessor: while sometimes handing down learned and significant opinions, it has proved impotent as an instrument to further the "purposes and principles" of the United Nations (as set forth in Article 1 of the Charter) ; specifically, "the prevention and removal of threats to the peace" through "adjustment or settlement of international disputes" in "conformity with the principles of justice and international law."

Rightly or wrongly, most nations have withheld their declarations of adherence altogether or have made their adherence conditional, for three principal reasons. First, there has been an understandable reluctance on the part of the so-called great powers to surrender their "sovereignty" to the extent apparently necessary for unconditional submission to compulsory jurisdiction of an international court. Second, most countries have hesitated to submit their important international problems to judges whose supposedly strong national allegiances might change their perspective from one of disinterest to one of expedient partisanship. Finally, there has been an especially marked unwillingness on the part of all nations to entrust a mere majority of a quorum of an international tribunal with the power to determine which

---

[1] These States are Haiti and Nicaragua. *See* [1971–72] I.C.J.Y.B. 64, 76.

matters lie within a State's domestic jurisdiction and which fall within the permissible scope of international adjudication.

The plan for reconstitution of the International Court of Justice set forth in this book contemplates that it be composed of disinterested judges, and that it have compulsory jurisdiction over all justiciable international disputes among nations, and yet be trusted confidently to deny its own right to adjudicate domestic issues. All this, moreover, can be accomplished without undue surrender of sovereignty on the part of any State, certainly none beyond that already surrendered by adherence to the Charter of the United Nations itself.

With the waging of war in a nuclear age becoming more and more destructive, and with universal disarmament emerging as a definite subject of international negotiation, "adjustment or settlement of international disputes" in "conformity with the principles of justice and international law" can all the more likely be achieved by establishment of a universally acceptable international tribunal, having compulsory jurisdiction over all nations. The major practical difficulty lies in fixing the conditions under which disarmament is to be accomplished, the Court established, and both maintained with a minimal surrender of national sovereignty. In his Annual Report for 1955 to the General Assembly of the United Nations, then Secretary-General Dag Hammarskjöld submitted that "it is surely in the interest of all Member States to restrict as much as possible the sphere where sheer strength is an argument and to extend as widely as possible the area ruled by considerations of law and justice. In an interdependent world, a greater degree of authority and effectiveness in international law will be a safeguard, not a threat, to the freedom and independence of national States."[2] A decade earlier, the First Committee (on the International Court of Justice) of the Fourth Commission (on Judicial Organization), in its report at the San Francisco Conference of June 12, 1945, ventured "to foresee a significant role for the new Court in the international relations of the future. . . . It is confidently anticipated that the jurisdiction of this tribunal will be extended as time goes on, and

---

[2] Sec'y-Gen., Report, 10 U.N. GAOR, Supp. 1, at xiii, U.N. Doc. A/2911 (1955).

past experience warrants the expectation that its exercise of this jurisdiction will command a general support." [3]

The proposed reconstitution of the International Court can be accomplished only by amendment by the Statute of the Court, which requires "a vote of two thirds of the members of the General Assembly," and ratification "in accordance with their constitutional processes by two thirds of the Members of the United Nations, including all the permanent members of the Security Council." [4] It is suggested, however, that the reconstitution be put into effect, not through revision of the present Statute, but by adoption of a complete new text embodying the principles outlined briefly above. A draft proposal of such a new Statute forms Appendix C of this volume.

Perhaps the single most important factor in purging an international tribunal of bias, or in quelling suspicions of bias, is internationalization of its judges for life. The late Judge Hersch Lauterpacht of the International Court of Justice, one of the world's greatest modern scholars in the field of international law, stated in *The Development of International Law by the International Court* (a revised edition of his 1934 work on the Permanent Court of International Justice, published only two years before his death) : "If government by men, and not by laws, is resented within the State by individuals, any appearance of it is likely to be viewed with even greater suspicion on the part of sovereign States in relation to judges of foreign nationality. The problem of judicial impartiality, however exaggerated it may be on occasions, is an ever-present problem in relation to international tribunals. . . ." [5]

The proposed Statute of the International Court of Justice provides that the Court "shall be composed of a body of independent judges." [6] Those are the identical words used in Article 2 of the original Statute of that Court and in the same article of the original and revised Statutes of the Permanent Court of International Justice, into which they were incorporated from similar language in Article 2 of the 1907 Hague Draft Convention

[3] Doc. 913, IV/1/74 (1) , 13 U.N.C.I.O. Docs. 381, at 393 (1945) .

[4] I.C.J. STAT. art. 69; U.N. CHARTER art. 108.

[5] H. LAUTERPACHT, DEVELOPMENT at 40.   [6] I.C.J. STAT. (P) art. II, para. 1.

Relative to the Creation of a Judicial Arbitration Court.[7] By use of the term "a body of independent judges," the 1920 Committee of Jurists, which drafted the original Statute of the Permanent Court, intended that the judges of that Court were (insofar as humanly possible) to be absolutely independent of the governments of which they were nationals.[8] In September 1927, a committee of judges of the Permanent Court (in a report rendered with reference to the advisability of permitting appointment of judges *ad hoc* by litigants in cases submitted for advisory opinions), themselves conceded that "[o]f all influences to which men are subject, none is more powerful, more pervasive, or more subtle, than the tie of allegiance that binds them to the land of their homes and kindred and to the great sources of the honors and preferments for which they are so ready to spend their fortunes and to risk their lives."[9] As early as 1920, Mineitciro Adatci, a distinguished international scholar and diplomat, a member of the Committee of Jurists which drafted the Statute of the Permanent Court of International Justice, and destined to become that Court's President, expressed the view that the judges of that Court should be required, on appointment, to "deify themselves," a status which he suggested might be achieved by means of their internationalization.[10] In 1923 Judge Edwin B. Parker of the United States was appointed Umpire of the Mixed Claims Commission to adjudicate claims between the United States and Germany. Shortly after Judge Parker's death in 1929, Professor Edwin M. Borchard of the School of Law of Yale University wrote of him that he "early made it clear that as a judge [on the Commission] he regarded himself as denationalized. . . ."[11]

Some interesting statistics on inherent prejudices of national judges of the Permanent Court of International Justice were gathered by Professor Lauterpacht and published in 1933 in his *Function of Law in the International Community,* but only after he had given due "consideration of the expediency and appropri-

[7] The text of this Draft Convention is found in HAGUE CONVENTIONS at 31.

[8] R. RUSSELL, CHARTER at 380 (1958).

[9] 4 P.C.I.J. ANN. R. (ser. E) 75 (1928).

[10] 1920 PROCEEDINGS at 187.

[11] Borchard, *Judge Edwin B. Parker,* 24 AM. J. INT'L L. 139, 140 (1930).

ateness of this line of investigation." He found "that in no case have national (*ad hoc*) judges voted against their state," a circumstance which "cannot be regarded as a mere coincidence." He considered the result "profoundly disturbing," particularly in light of the fact that in several cases, the dissenting opinions of national judges were "delivered against the unanimous or practically unanimous view of the Court." [12] The experience of the International Court of Justice since 1947 has confirmed the conclusions reached by Professor Lauterpacht regarding a marked tendency for judges to reach conclusions favorable to their own States.[13]

Professor Lauterpacht had concluded in 1933 that the indispensable impartiality of the judges of any permanent international tribunal, "presupposes on their part the consciousness of being citizens of the world." [14] To this end, the proposed Statute of the International Court of Justice provides that each judge is required to renounce his nationality upon his accession, and is deemed a citizen of the world.[15] The spouse of each judge will also be presumed to have renounced her (or his) nationality upon the judge's accession and will likewise become a citizen of the United Nations, with correlative worldwide immunities, for the life of the judge. The spouse would retain United Nations citizenship for two years after the death of the judge, thereupon being eligible for, and obligated to take, citizenship in any country of her choice.[16]

The United Nations, however, is not itself a State. It accordingly has no domestic laws for the government of matters of personal status, rights, and liabilities of members of the Court and their spouses—such as marital community, devolution and inheritance, capacity to contract, and innumerable other issues. To

[12] H. LAUTERPACHT, FUNCTION at 230–32.

[13] *See* S. ROSENNE, I.C.J. at 152. Rosenne notes, however, that this tendency is stronger among judges *ad hoc* than among titular judges. For example, judges *ad hoc* have formed minorities of one in favor of their own countries on several occasions, but never a titular judge. Also, Rosenne sees the partiality of judges towards their homelands as a possible consequence of their legal training and outlook, and not necessarily as a manifestation of bias.

[14] H. LAUTERPACHT, FUNCTION at 238–39.

[15] I.C.J. STAT. (P) art. IV, para. 1.   [16] *Id.*, para. 2.

fill this gap, it is proposed that each judge and his spouse be deemed to have their national domicile at the seat of the Court and each retired judge and his spouse (as long as they are deemed to be citizens of the United Nations as provided in the Statute) be considered to have theirs at the judge's permanent residence. The law of their natural domicile is to apply only insofar as their personal status, rights, and liabilities may not be defined by their United Nations citizenship.[17]

As a concomitant of the suggested internationalization of judges, it is proposed that their election be for life [18] (with certain retirement privileges and requirements [19]), instead of for nine years as under the present Statute.[20] As further assurance of the independence of the judges, the proposed Statute retains the provision of the original Statute that the salaries and allowances of judges may not be decreased during their tenure and remain free of any and all taxation.[21]

Under the proposed Statute, the court would remain at fifteen members, there being no apparent reason for any change in their number.[22]

Much has been said and written about the possibility of retrograding the caliber of the Court through the provisions for election of its members in groups for fixed terms, as under the present Statute, but it has never been suggested that any of the present members of the Court leave anything to be desired in individual scholarly attainments in international law, and in absolute personal and judicial integrity. With the possible exception of a suggestion of a moderate predominance by Latin America over other world areas, there has been no strong criticism of regional distribution of membership on the Court. It is proposed accordingly that the judges in office at the time of adoption of the proposed Statute be automatically retained in office for life and continue to sit under the terms of the proposed Statute.[23] Life tenure of the judges under the proposed Statute will minimize the necessity for revision of the present substantive method of filling vacancies on

---

[17] *Id.*, para. 4.   [18] *Id.* art. III, para. 1.
[19] *Id.* art. VI, paras. 2–3; *Id.* art. VII, para. 7.   [20] I.C.J. Stat. art. 13, para. 1.
[21] I.C.J. Stat. (P) art. VII, paras. 3, 10.   [22] *Id.* art. II, para. 2.
[23] *Id.* art. III, para. 2.

the Court. Instead of election of five judges *en bloc* every three years as at present) , elections will take place only to fill vacancies and will rarely involve more than a single judgeship.[24]

Election of judges under the proposed Statute may nevertheless give rise to national or regional alignments and difficulties in securing majorities, especially in light of the recent increased membership of the United Nations. Under these circumstances, it is advisable to modify the present election machinery to establish a simplified procedure, somewhat along the lines of election by pluralities, to avoid any possible impasse in achieving bloc majorities. Vacancies would be filled simply by election by the General Assembly and the Security Council (without right of veto) from nominations which each nation would be privileged to make directly.[25] But election would be by plurality among nominees receiving a majority of votes cast in both bodies, without the necessity of "absolute majorities" of entire memberships.[26]

If judges are to have life tenure, it is advisable to fix age limits for nominees for judgeships. Absolutism or relative statistical certainty of result in setting age limits for judges is impossible of attainment; but it is suggested, as a fair basis for assuring adequate maturity with full physical and mental vigor, that judges be between the ages of fifty and sixty-five when elected.[27]

Article 18 of the present Statute of the Court provides that "[n]o member of the Court can be dismissed unless, in the unanimous opinion of the other members, he has ceased to fulfil the required conditions." It has not been necessary to put this provision to a practical test, since the present limited nine-year term for judges gives some assurance of ultimate control by the General Assembly and the Security Council. But in view of the life-tenure provision of the proposed Statute, it is preferable that a judge be subject to dismissal, on impeachment by a majority of the General Assembly and by a vote of two-thirds of the members of the Security Council, without right of veto.[28] Dismissal of a judge will carry with it loss of United Nations citizenship for himself and his spouse, automatic reversion to their citizenship

---

[24] *Id.*, para. 3.   [25] *Id.*, paras. 1, 3–4, 6, 11.   [26] *Id.*, para. 6.
[27] *Id.* art. II, para. 2.   [28] *Id.* art. VI, para. 4.

at the time of his election, and loss of emoluments of office and pension rights.[29]

The proposed Statute provides, as does the present, that a judge may resign at any time, except that it is now proposed that a judge may not resign while under impeachment. On resignation, the judge forfeits United Nations citizenship of both himself and his spouse: they will be eligible for, and must within six months take, citizenship in a State of their choice.[30]

It is proposed that judges shall have the right to retire at any time after reaching seventy, and that they shall be retired automatically at seventy-five.[31] On retirement, the judge is to receive, for life, his full salary if he has served ten years or more, and a ratable portion if he has served less than ten years.[32]

As an added safeguard to the guaranty of fair hearings – in view of the new paramount requirement for compulsory, unreserved submission to the jurisdiction of the Court – the provisions for required recusation of judges are broadened considerably under the proposed Statute. Any member of the Court may request, at any time and for any reason, that he be permitted to recuse himself from participating in a cause. Any member may suggest, for any reason, that any other member of the Court should not sit in a particular case, and any party may suggest to the Court that, for a stated reason, any member should not sit.[33] In the event of a dispute as to whether a judge should be allowed or required to recuse himself from participation in hearing and determination of a cause, the matter is to be decided by the Court, but the judge whose recusation is under consideration is not to participate in this decision.[34]

The requirement of the present Statute for a quorum of nine judges to constitute the Court is raised to eleven by the proposed Statute,[35] subject to the provision – to which further reference will be made hereunder – that a full Court of fifteen judges must sit, at the request of any party to the cause, for hearing and determination of any question as to the jurisdiction of the Court.

The present Statute of the International Court of Justice pro-

[29] *Id.*, para. 5.   [30] *Id.*, para. 1; *see also* I.C.J. STAT. art. 13, para. 4.
[31] I.C.J. STAT. (P) art. VI, paras. 2–3.   [32] *Id.* art. VII, para. 7.
[33] *Id.* art. XIII, para. 7.   [34] *Id.*   [35] *Id.* art. XIII, para. 2.

vides,[36] as did the Statute of the Permanent Court,[37] that if the panel of the Court does not include a national of a party to a case before it, the party (or both parties, if there is no national of either on the bench) may designate a judge (or judges) *ad hoc,* to sit with the Court and to take part in the decision on terms of complete equality with the titular judges. There is no present provision for appointment of judges *ad hoc* to meet other contingencies, such as the absence of a quorum. It is provided in the Rules of Court that judges *ad hoc* "shall not be taken into account for the calculation of the quorum," and that, in the absence of a quorum, a session is simply to be adjourned "until a quorum has been obtained."[38] While the present Statute contains no requirement that a judge *ad hoc* be of the nationality of the appointing party, judges *ad hoc* have been nationals of the States by which they were appointed, except on rare occasions. This has been the inevitable consequence of the premise that the very purpose of the provisions for designation of judges *ad hoc* is to place representatives of the parties themselves on the bench for determination of a particular case.[39] On the other hand, the whole idea of national judges is completely foreign to the basic concept of the proposed Statute; so no need is recognized for national judges *ad hoc*. Only when additional judges are required to complete a quorum or to break a tie will there be any need for judges *ad hoc,* and they should not be designated by the parties nor should they be nationals of the countries-litigant.[40] Therefore it is provided in the proposed Statute that whenever there is an insufficient number of judges to constitute the bench, or if the judges are equally divided in their votes as to decision of a case, the Court itself is simply to designate a judge or judges *ad hoc* from the ranks of retired judges willing and able to serve, or from persons, not of the nationality of any party to the cause, previously nominated but not elected to the Court.[41]

Like the present Statute, the proposed Statute requires that all questions before the Court or any chamber thereof be decided by

36 I.C.J. STAT. art. 31, paras. 2–4, 6.   37 P.C.I.J. STAT. art. 31.
38 I.C.J.R. 29.   39 Report of M. de Lapradelle, 1920 PROCEEDINGS 693, at 721–22.
40 I.C.J. STAT. (P) art. XIV.   41 *Id.,* para. 1.

a majority of the judges who participate in the hearing.[42] As discussed previously, in the event of a tie vote, the Court is to designate an additional judge or judges to sit with the Court or chamber for rehearing and determination of the question or cause, instead of following the current practice of allowing a second, or casting, vote to the President of the Court.[43] The proposed statute, like the present one, provides for the rendition of written opinions—majority, dissenting, and concurring—and naming of the judges subscribing to each.[44]

There is one exception to this rule: the determination of controversies involving jurisdiction. In that case, if a party to a cause submits that an issue lies within its own domestic jurisdiction, at least ten judges must agree that the issue lies within the subject-matter jurisdiction of the Court before it can be taken up.[45] A question of this sort could conceivably be heard by a quorum of eleven judges, yet a party to a cause may also request that it be heard by a full Court of fifteen judges.[46]

Some changes are proposed with reference to the constitution and functioning of chambers of the Court. The provision for a standing chamber for summary disposition of causes referred to it is retained. While the Court has never had occasion to form a chamber to hear a particular case or categories of cases, its right to do so is retained in the proposed Statute.[47] The proposed Statute provides, however, that a case is to be heard before a chamber of the Court only at the request or by the consent of the parties, or by direction of the Court,[48] provided that any party which shall have objected to a hearing before a chamber is to have a right of appeal to the full Court from the judgment of the chamber.[49] In the event of an appeal, the members of the chamber which determined the cause are to be eligible to sit as members of the full Court on the appeal, which will be presented on the record as

---

[42] *Id.* art. XVI, para. 1; I.C.J. STAT. art. 55, para. 1.

[43] *See* I.C.J. STAT., art. 55, para. 2.

[44] I.C.J. STAT. (P) art. XVI, para. 2; I.C.J. STAT. arts. 56–57.

[45] I.C.J. STAT. (P) art. VIII, para. 4.

[46] *Id.* art. XIII, para. 6.   [47] I.C.J. STAT. (P) art. XIII, para. 3.

[48] *Id.*, para. 4.   [49] *Id.* art. XVI, para. 4.

made up before the chamber, except as otherwise ordered by the Court.[50]

No change is proposed in the nature of parties having access to the Court except that, in addition to States (both Members and non-Members of the United Nations), the jurisdiction of the Court over public international bodies is spelled out expressly. The Court will continue to be without jurisdiction over private parties as complainants, respondents, or otherwise.[51]

Jurisdiction of the Court, *ratione materiae,* remains unchanged under the proposed Statute, except for clarification of and emphasis on the absence of any jurisdiction over essentially domestic issues as such.[52] The jurisdiction of the Court as to subject matter will extend to (*a*) the interpretation of treaties; (*b*) questions of international law; (*c*) the determination of any fact which, if established, would constitute a breach of an international obligation; (*d*) the nature and extent of any reparation to be made for the breach of an international obligation; and (*e*) any matter which, under any international agreement, is to be referred, in event of dispute, to the Court or to any predecessor international tribunal.[53] The jurisdiction of the Court will also continue to extend to (*a*) any justiciable matter referred by the parties to the Court for determination; (*b*) all matters specially provided for adjudication by the Court under the Charter of the United Nations; and (*c*) matters referred to the Court for advisory opinions by the General Assembly, the Security Council, or other organs or agencies of the United Nations which may be authorized by the General Assembly to request such opinions.[54]

The proposed Statute provides explicitly that "the Court shall have no jurisdiction over, and nothing contained in the present Statute shall be construed as requiring any Member of the United Nations to submit to the Court for adjudication, any matter essentially within the domestic jurisdiction of any State."[55] The principal criticism of the Court has been that its jurisdiction over States exists in effect, at their own option—subject, first, to the filing by each State of a declaration of its acceptance of the Court's jurisdiction, and, second, to any conditions which a State might

[50] *Id.*   [51] *See generally id.* art. IX.   [52] *Id.* art. VIII, para. 3.
[53] *Id.,* para. 1.   [54] *Id.,* para. 2.   [55] *Id.,* para. 3.

see fit to attach to its declaration.[56] Thus, for instance, a number of States have from time to time conditioned their acceptance of the jurisdiction of the Court, by excepting therefrom matters which they themselves may deem to fall within their own domestic jurisdictions. The Connally Amendment to reservation (b) of the United States declaration of adherence falls within this category and is typical of conditions attached by several other nations to their acceptances of the Court's jurisdiction.[57] In addition, each State which conditions its adherence on the principle of "reciprocity" is permitted to limit that adherence by any condition which another State, *vis-à-vis* which it is called to appear before the Court, may have attached to its own acceptance of the Court's jurisdiction.[58] Unquestionably, much of the virility contemplated for the Court has been lost through these emasculating reservations. It is not suggested that the reservations are unjustified, although it has frequently been submitted that they are. But whether warranted or not, there can be no question that they have rendered the Court impotent in many situations in which it should have been in a position to function effectively.

Much less can be said in support of optional or conditional jurisdiction of the International Court of Justice, however, when firm assurances are given to all nations that the Court is to be so constituted as to guarantee an objective attitude toward the cause of every nation, although the Court is to be the sole arbiter of whether a matter placed before it is one of domestic or of international concern. On the assumption, therefore, that proponents of optional or conditional jurisdiction of the Court would concede the absence of any need for its safeguards in the face of assurances of the tribunal's impartiality, the proposed Statute provides that any "dispute as to the jurisdiction of the Court shall be determined by the Court."[59] But it goes further. It provides

[56] I.C.J. Stat. art. 36, para. 1–3.

[57] While nineteen States have domestic jurisdiction clauses in their declarations of adherence, six of them have provisions, similar to the Connally Amendment, which predicate the determination of what lies within domestic jurisdiction on the opinion of the State concerned rather than on principles of international law. *See* Introduction, *supra* at note 25.

[58] *See* Norwegian Loans case, [1957] I.C.J. 9, at 22–28.

[59] I.C.J. Stat. (P) art. VIII, para. 4.

that the Court is not to exercise jurisdiction over a cause in the event that a State which is party to the cause objects on the grounds that the proceeding is one essentially within its own domestic jurisdiction, unless at least ten judges (two-thirds of the Court's entire membership) concur in holding that the matter under consideration is within the Court's jurisdiction. The proposed Statute also contains the mandatory directive that "any doubt as to whether a matter is essentially within the domestic jurisdiction of a State shall be resolved by the Court in favor of such domestic jurisdiction." [60]

Much has been said about the asserted impossibility of the dispensation of truly impartial justice among nations compelled to appear before an international tribunal, if it is to be composed of judges, whatever their *bona fides,* trained under different judicial systems and adhering to different—even completely incompatible—jurisprudential philosophies. Again, with all that has been said and remains to be said on both sides of this question, it must be remembered that the world is growing ever smaller. Civilized concepts of the inalienable rights of free men and of free nations are finding their way into what were once the far corners of the earth. Public international law is falling more and more into universally recognized patterns. In his Annual Report for 1955, Mr. Hammarskjöld conceded that "[o]ne may recognize that the reluctance of Governments to submit their controversies to judicial settlement stems in part from the fragmentary and uncertain character of much of international law as it now exists. . . . [However,] [t]he beginnings of a 'common law' of the United Nations, based on the Charter, are now apparent; its steady growth will contribute to stability and orderliness." [61]

With an international tribunal whose members are almost certain to display objective points of view toward international disputes laid before them, it would seem safe to set forth guides for determination of these disputes. These guides are found in the original Statute,[62] and are carried forward with some modification into the proposed Statute.[63] For instance, Article 38 the Statute of the Permanent Court of International Justice did not expressly

---

[60] *Id.*   [61] *See* note 2 *supra.*
[62] I.C.J. STAT. art. 38.   [63] I.C.J. STAT. (P) art. VIII, para. 5.

direct that tribunal to be guided by general principles of international law in reaching its decisions. On the other hand, its framers definitely "considered that it would be one of the Court's important tasks to contribute [by its judgments] to the development of international law."[64] When the present Statute of the International Court of Justice was drafted, its framers supplied this legislative omission by providing, at least parenthetically, that the Court, "whose function is to decide in accordance with international law such disputes as are submitted to it," is to apply to the adjudication of such disputes substantially the same legal criteria as were enumerated in the former Statute.[65] The proposed Statute provides affirmatively that "[t]he Court shall adjudicate disputes before it in accordance with generally accepted, applicable principles of international law, giving due consideration, in its deliberations, to" somewhat modified criteria.[66] For example, among the criteria to be applied by the Court under its present Statute are "the general principles of law recognized by civilized nations."[67] On the assumptions that the term "principles of law" should now be broadened and that all nations must be presumed to be more or less civilized in this latter half of the twentieth century, the comparable provision of the proposed Statute speaks instead of "general principles of law, equity and justice recognized among nations."[68] These principles, which the Court would be directed to apply in reaching its conclusions, are: (*a*) provisions of international conventions establishing rules of international

[64] Subcomm. of the Third Comm., Report, COMM. III, Annex 7, at 534. The Third Committee considered this question in the context of a proposal by Argentina that the Court should apply "the rules drawn up by the Assembly of the League of Nations in the performance of its duty of codifying international law." *Id.*, Annex 3, at 519. The Subcommittee rejected this proposal on the grounds that codification of international law was premature and, as put by Sir Cecil Hurst, the proposal "excludes every possibility of considering the judgments [of the Court] as precedents building up law." Subcomm. of the Third Comm., Minutes of the 7th Meeting, *Id.* at 386. *See also* Summary Report of Fifth Meeting of Committee IV/1, Doc. 240, IV/1/15, 13 U.N.C.I.O. Docs. 163, at 164 (1945).

[65] I.C.J. STAT. art. 38; *see* Observations by the Chilean Delegation on Article 38 of the Statute of the Proposed International Court of Justice, Doc. 263, IV/1/16, 13 U.N. C. I. O. Docs. 493 (1945).

[66] I.C.J. STAT. (P) art. VIII, para. 5.

[67] I.C.J. STAT. art. 38, para. 1 (c).

[68] I.C.J. STAT. (P) art. VIII, para. 5 (d).

conduct expressly recognized among nations; (*b*) international custom, as evidence of generally accepted practice; (*c*) judicial precedents recognizing principles of international law; (*d*) general principles of law, equity, and justice recognized among nations; and (*e*) legal writings of recognized authorities in international law.[69] The proposed Statute omits the old provision that the Court is to have the power "to decide a case *ex aequo et bono, if the parties agree thereto.*"[70] This power, essentially one of judicial legislation, is not considered to constitute a proper judicial function in any case.

As the Court is authorized to do, and has done under its present Statute, it will be empowered to make rules of procedure to implement the proposed Statute.[71]

Finally, under the proposed Statute, jurisdiction of the Court over international disputes would be compulsory as to all Member states of the United Nations.[72] All declarations of acceptance of the jurisdiction of the Court under its present Statute would serve no further purpose. Of the previously discussed reasons underlying optional or conditional jurisdiction of the International Court of Justice, most, if not all, of them dissipate when the Statute of the Court assures completely objective judges, of unquestionable integrity, appointed for life, declining to adjudicate any but genuinely international questions, and determining real international issues as fairly as human frailties will permit. That the proposed Statute of the International Court of Justice involves, in the last analysis, no undue surrender by any nation of its national sovereignty must also be evident from the Court's mere decretal authority, with no power to enforce its decrees.[73]

It is not suggested, of course, that the proposed Statute is equivalent to a handbook of scientific formulae, coupled with an infallible electronic computer, by which complex international problems can be solved with mathematical precision to the entire satisfaction of all concerned; nor is it submitted that under the influence of the proposed Statute, differences of opinion

---

[69] *Id.,* para. 5.   [70] I.C.J. STAT. art. 38, para. 2.

[71] I.C.J. STAT. (P) art. XIX, para. 1.

[72] I.C.J. STAT. (P) art. VIII, para. 1.

[73] *See* chapter 18 *infra.*

among members of the Court in the determination of issues before the tribunal will become infrequent or even less likely to occur. It is argued simply that, under its provisions, any nation of the world may safely agree in advance to lay its disputes with any other nation before the Court for adjudication, without reservations and with full confidence in the integrity of that body to give fair answers to the questions at issue, under universally recognized equitable principles.

CHAPTER II

Ratification without Reservations

Paragraph I of Article XX of the proposed Statute provides that [r]eservations shall not be admissible in ratifications of the present Statute, which shall come into force unconditionally, as written, for all Members of the United Nations, after it shall have been adopted by a vote of two-thirds of the members of the General Assembly, upon deposit with the Secretary-General of instruments of ratification thereof, without reservations, in accordance with their respective constitutional processes, by two-thirds of the Members of the United Nations, including all of the permanent members of the Security Council.

A reservation is simply a provision inserted in the ratification of a treaty, by which the ratifying nation stipulates that it does not accept some clause of the treaty, or ratifies the treaty only subject to a stated condition. Sometimes a treaty is ratified subject to an "understanding," which partakes of the nature of a reservation, and expresses the understanding of the ratifying body as to the meaning or intent of a clause in the treaty, and stipulates that the ratification is based on that understanding.[1] In the past, when most treaties were negotiated and executed between only two so-called "high contracting parties," reservations were less frequent than they are today, when so many treaties are multilateral.

There is, moreover, a pronounced relationship between the form of government of a State and the frequency with which it incorporates reservations into its ratification of treaties, as well as the origin of these reservations. The governments of most nations are parliamentary in form, and the executive authority is

[1] An understanding, strictly speaking, is the statement of a country ratifying or acceding to a treaty, as to its construction of a clause in the treaty. This would not ordinarily be binding on a tribunal, which might hold simply that the country's understanding was not correct. If, however, the country's ratification or accession is stated clearly to be contingent on its understanding, the latter becomes, in effect, a binding reservation.

ordinarily appointed from among the members of the parliament, by that body itself or subject to its approval. Such executive authority is accordingly representative of and directly responsible to the parliament of which it really forms a mere extension. When, therefore, a treaty is negotiated by the executive authority of such a nation, the legislative body will frequently approve it without reservations. Any reservations to the treaty will have been those originally negotiated by the executive. Under Article 2, Section 2, of the Constitution of the United States, the Senate must advise and consent to the ratification of a treaty by a vote of not less than two-thirds of its members present and voting. Under the same Article however, the President is accorded the power to "make Treaties," to undertake direct negotiations with foreign powers. Accordingly, when the executive authority of the United States concludes a treaty, it must submit the instrument for advice and consent to ratification to a Senate which, as a legislative body, has often had no part whatever, direct or indirect, in its formation.

As a consequence, while the original treaty may well contain executive-negotiated reservations, the United States Senate has shown a marked tendency to insert its own reservations, or to withhold advice and consent altogether.[2] In order to minimize the chances of this occurring, the executive authority frequently consults with influential members of the Senate during negotiation of a treaty or invites them to participate in the negotiations. But even such participation is not really tantamount to assurance of ultimate ratification of the treaty. The most outstanding example of this lesson involved the failure of the Senate, in 1935, to advise and consent to the 1929 Protocol for accession of the United States to the Statute of the Permanent Court of International Justice.[3]

[2] Two very recent examples of this which spring to mind are (*a*) the failure of Congress thus far to grant the Soviet Union most-favored-nation treatment, as called for in the Agreement with the Union of Soviet Socialist Republics Regarding Trade, Oct. 18, 1972, in 11 INT'L LEGAL MATERIALS 1321 (1972); and (*b*) the assertion by the Senate of a veto power over any assistance in nuclear technology negotiated by President Nixon with Egypt and Israel during his recent Middle East trip. Wash. Post, July 11, 1974, at A2, col. 2.

[3] The circumstances of this case were as follows. On February 24, 1923, President Harding asked the Senate to advise and consent to the adherence by the United States to the 1920 protocol of signature to the Statute of the Permanent Court of

When treaties are made simply between two nations, the legal effect of a reservation would seem to be clear. A treaty, after all, is nothing more than a contract—a contract between nations. Under the law of contracts, the binding effect of an agreement is conditioned, in the first instance, on "a meeting of the minds." There is, in other words, no contract unless the parties thereto have reached complete agreement as to all of its terms. This principle of the law of contracts applies equally to treaties, a formal condition of which is ratification under the constitutional processes of the contracting parties. Therefore, when one of the parties to a treaty ratifies it subject to one or more reservations, there has been no ultimate meeting of the minds—no agreement as to all of the terms of the compact, and the convention has really never come into being.

International Justice. S. Doc. No. 309, 67th Cong., 4th Sess. (1923). Almost three years later, the Senate gave its advice and consent, but incorporated therein five reservations:

a) that adherence not entail any legal relation with the League of Nations or obligation under the Treaty of Versailles;

b) that the United States nonetheless participate in the election of judges;

c) that the United States pay a fair share of the Court's expenses as determined by Congress;

d) that the United States retain the right to withdraw its adherence and that the Court's Statute not be amended without the consent of the United States; and

e) that the Court not render any advisory opinion, except publicly, after due notice to all States and after public hearing or opportunity for hearing given to any State concerned; furthermore, the Court may not, without the consent of the United States, "entertain any request for an advisory opinion touching any dispute or question in which the United States has or claims an interest." S. Res. 5, 69th Cong., 1st Sess., 67 CONG. REC. 2824-25 (1926).

Negotiations with other governments, the 1926 Conference of Signatories, and the 1929 Committee of Jurists finally produced a draft protocol incorporating the Senate's reservations. *See* 1st Comm., Report, LEAGUE OF NATIONS OFF. J., Spec. Supp. 75, Annex 5, at 441 (1929). There was, however, a question whether the protocol sufficiently incorporated the Senate's reservation related to advisory opinions. Several additional reservations were approved by the Senate. Despite two favorable reports on the protocol from the Senate Foreign Relations Committee (S. REP. No. 758, 72nd Cong., 1st Sess. [1932]; S. EXEC. REP. No. 1, 74th Cong., 1st Sess. [1935], the resolution of adherence to the protocol received a majority vote on January 29, 1935, but failed to achieve consent by the necessary two-thirds vote. 79 CONG. REC. 1146-47 (1935).

But the situation is different as to multipartite treaties. It obviously is difficult to hammer out the terms of such a treaty on a basis satisfactory, in all of its details, to all of the parties. The consequence is that ratifications, when they are given at all to such treaties, are frequently accompanied by reservations of varying degrees of substantive importance. It may be assumed that, among many parties to a multilateral treaty, some nations will ratify without any reservations; some, with what may be termed minor reservations; and a number of others, with reservations relating to important provisions. Such a situation gives rise to a number of interesting legal questions. For instance, does the treaty come into effect as to *any* of the participating countries, when there has been no unequivocal agreement as to all of its terms among all of the nations which are parties to the instrument? If the treaty does come into effect at all, which nations are bound to which others, and under what terms?

The International Court of Justice has had occasion to pass on these questions, although the opinion of the Court is somewhat nebulous, and its answers are still subject to considerable doubt. On November 16, 1950, the General Assembly of the United Nations requested the Court to render an advisory opinion as to the nature, validity and effect of reservations in ratifications of, or accessions to, the Convention on the Prevention and Punishment of the Crime of Genocide, as well as the effect of objections to such reservations.[4] The Court split seven to five in its decision. The majority found, in the first place, that "it could certainly not be inferred from the absence of an article providing for reservations in a multilateral convention that the contracting States are prohibited from making certain reservations. . . . The character of a multilateral convention, its purpose, provisions, mode of preparation and adoption, are factors which must be considered in determining, in the absence of any express provision on the subject, the possibility of making reservations, as well as their

---

[4] G.A. Res. 478, 5 U.N. GAOR, Supp. 20, at 74–75, U.N. Doc. A/1775 (1951), *reprinted in* Advisory Opinion on Reservations to the Convention on the Prevention and Punishment of the Crime of Genocide, [1951] I.C.J. 15, at 16–17. The Genocide Convention was adopted as G.A. Res. 260 (III) A, U.N. Doc. A/810 at 174 (1949); the text is at 78 U.N.T.S. 277.

validity and effect."[5] The majority judges next went on to hold that "it is the compatibility of a reservation with the object and purpose of the Convention that must furnish the criterion for the attitude of a State in making the reservation on accession as well as for the appraisal by a State in objecting to the reservation."[6] This led to the opinion of this group of judges that, "[a]s no State can be bound by a reservation to which it has not consented, it necessarily follows that each State objecting to it will or will not, on the basis of its individual appraisal within the limits of the criterion of its object and purpose stated above, consider the reserving State to be a party to the Convention. In the ordinary course of events, such a decision will only affect the relationship between the State making the reservation and the objecting State. . . ."[7] Accordingly, the Court held:

that a State which has made and maintained a reservation which has been objected to by one or more parties to the Convention but not by others, can be regarded as being a party to the Convention if the reservation is compatible with the object and purpose of the Convention; otherwise, that State cannot be regarded as being a party to the Convention.

. . . that if a party to the Convention objects to a reservation which it considers to be incompatible with the object and purpose of the Convention, it can in fact consider that the reserving State is not a party to the Convention;

that if, on the other hand, a party accepts the reservation as being compatible with the object and purpose of the Convention, it can in fact consider that the reserving State is a party to the Convention. . . .[8]

Four of the five dissenting judges,[9] convinced that the holding of the majority would inevitably create "[s]uch a state of things [as] can only cause the utmost confusion among the interested States,"[10] recommended that, "[i]n the interests of the international community, it would be better to lose as a party to the Convention a State which insists in face of objections on a modifi-

---

[5] Advisory Opinion, *supra* note 4, at 22.   [6] *Id.* at 24.
[7] *Id.* at 26.   [8] *Id.* at 29–30.
[9] Vice-President Guerrero, Judges Sir Arnold McNair, Read, and Hsu Mo.
[10] *Id.* at 44.

cation of the terms of the Convention, than to permit it to become a party against the wish of a State or States which have irrevocably and unconditionally accepted all the obligations of the Convention." [11] The fifth dissenter, Judge Alvarez of Chile, agreed generally with the other dissenting judges but concluded that the replies to the request of the General Assembly for an advisory opinion should be phrased as follows:

If the reservations proposed by a State are not accepted by one or several others of the States parties to the convention, the reserving State is not to be considered as a party to the convention.

If the reservations are accepted by the majority of other States, then the convention is transformed, and another convention takes its place; the States which have not accepted the reservations are not parties to the new convention.

Finally, if the reservations are accepted by certain States but objected to by others, then there is no convention at all. [12]

One must, of course, accept the majority opinion of the Court as representing the present state of international law with reference to the nature, validity, and effect of reservations to treaties and objections thereto. The strong minority views, however, may fairly be said to accentuate the considerable and persistent doubt surrounding the subject.

The situation with regard to the Genocide Convention is especially interesting and particularly illustrative of the involved morass into which reservations to a multipartite treaty may lead. At the time of the 1951 Advisory Opinion discussed above, only twenty-eight States had deposited instruments of ratification of, or accession to, the Genocide Convention with the Secretary General of the United Nations, and five of these States had ratified or acceded with reservations. By August of 1973, some seventy-six nations had deposited their instruments of ratification or accession; of these, fifty-six had ratified or acceded without reservations, and the remaining twenty had filed reservations—some relatively minor, but many of considerable substantive importance. [13]

---

[11] *Id.* at 47.   [12] *Id.* at 55.

[13] Multilateral Treaties in Respect of Which the Secretary-General Performs Depositary Functions, List of Signatures, Ratifications, Accessions, etc. as at 31 December 1972, at 67–68, U.N. Doc. ST/LEG/SER.D/6 (1973), lists seventy-five

As of the same time, twelve nations had entered and deposited objections to all or some of the reservations,[14] giving doubtful or no effect to the Convention, at least as far as the reserving and objecting nations are concerned. Two of these countries based their objections expressly on the 1951 Advisory Opinion. Thus, the Government of Brazil stated, in its objection, that it "considers the said reservations as incompatible with the object and purpose of the Convention," and that its position "is founded on the Advisory Opinion of the International Court of Justice of 28 May 1951 and on the resolution adopted by the sixth session of the General Assembly on 12 January 1952, on reservations to multilateral conventions." Brazil added that it "reserves the right to draw any such legal consequences as it may deem fit from its formal objection to the above-mentioned reservations."[15] Similarly, the Government of (Nationalist) China objected to the reservations of some ten States, because it "consider[ed] the above-mentioned reservations as incompatible with the object and purpose of the Convention and, therefore, by virtue of the Advisory Opinion of the International Court of Justice of 28 May 1951, would not regard the above-mentioned States as being Parties to the Convention."[16]

"The Government of the Kingdom of the Netherlands," for its part, "declare[d] that it considers the reservations . . . in respect of Article IX of the Convention . . . to be incompatible

---

instruments of ratification and accession. The German Democratic Republic filed an instrument of accession in March 1973. Statement of Treaties and International Agreements Registered or Filed and Recorded with the Secretariat During the Month of March 1973, at 32, U.N. Doc. ST/LEG/SER.A/313 (1974).

The twenty States which have filed reservations to the Genocide Convention along with their instruments of ratification or accession are the following (those marked with an asterisk [*] had reservations on file at the time of the 1951 Advisory Opinion): Albania, Algeria, Argentina, Bulgaria,* Burma, Byelorussian SSR, Czechoslovakia,* Finland, Hungary, India, Mongolia, Morocco, the Philippines,* Poland,* Romania,* Spain, Ukrainian SSR, the Union of Soviet Socialist Republics, and Venezuela. The text of these reservations may be found in Multilateral Treaties in Respect of Which the Secretary-General Performs Depositary Functions, *supra* at 68–71. The instrument of accession filed by the German Democratic Republic in March 1973 also contained a reservation, the text of which is not yet available.

[14] Multilateral Treaties in Respect of Which the Secretary-General Performs Depositary Functions, *supra* note 13, at 71–72.

[15] *Id.* at 71.　　[16] *Id.* at 72.

with the object and purpose of the Convention. . . . [T]herefore [it] does not deem any State which has made or which will make such reservation a party to the Convention." [17] The Government of the United Kingdom stated simply that it "do [*sic*] not accept the reservations to articles IV, VII, VIII, IX or XII of the Convention made by" eighteen named states; [18] while Greece declared unequivocally "that we have not accepted and do not accept any reservation which has already been made or which may hereafter be made by the countries signatory to this instrument or by countries which have acceded or may hereafter accede thereto." [19] The foregoing are fairly illustrative of the others. It may reasonably be said that the Genocide Convention has, to all practical intents and purposes, been largely emasculated by the reservations of the parties thereto.

In the same resolution which brought about the 1951 Advisory Opinion of the International Court of Justice, the General Assembly also

[i]nvite[d] the International Law Commission:
   (*a*) [i]n the course of its work on the codification of the law of treaties, to study the question of reservations to multilateral conventions both from the point of view of codification and from that of the progressive development of international law. . . .[20]

This study was made; draft articles which contained a group of articles on reservations and objections thereto were prepared by the Commission for a contemplated convention on the law of treaties.[21] These draft articles became the nucleus of a convention ultimately submitted to international conferences of plenipotentiaries of more than a hundred nations held in Vienna in 1968 and 1969. On May 22, 1969, the Vienna Convention on the Law of Treaties was finally adopted.[22] While the Convention, by its express terms, "applies only to treaties which are concluded by States after [its] entry into force," this provision is stated to be "[w]ithout prejudice to the application of any rules set forth in

[17] *Id.*   [18] *Id.*   [19] *Id.*   [20] *See* G.A. Res. 478, note 4 *supra.*
[21] Int'l L. Comm'n, Report, 21 U.N. GAOR, Supp. 9, at 20, U.N. Doc. A/6309/Rev. 1 (1966) (draft articles with commentary).
[22] U.N. CONF. ON THE LAW OF TREATIES, OFFICIAL RECORDS (DOCUMENTS) 281, U.N. Doc. A/CONF.39/11/Add.2 (1971).

the present Convention to which treaties would be subject under
international law independently of the Convention"; [23] and, of
course, many of the rules in the Vienna Convention are simply
restatements of long-established rules of international law.

In any event, Articles 19 through 23 of the Vienna Convention
deal with reservations to treaties and objections thereto, and a
brief outline of their relevant provisions is given hereunder.
Reservations are permitted under the Vienna Convention, unless
(*a*) the terms of the treaty in question prohibit the reservations
expressly, (*b*) the treaty provides that only specified reservations
may be made, and the reservation in question is not enumerated,
or (*c*) in the absence of *a* or *b*, "the reservation is incompatible
with the object and purpose of the treaty." [24] Furthermore, reservations expressly authorized by a treaty do not require acceptance;
but if it is evident from the limited number of parties involved,
and from the general object and purpose of the treaty, that application thereof "in its entirety between all the parties is an essential condition of the consent of each one to be bound by the
treaty, a reservation requires acceptance by all the parties." [25]
Acceptance of a reservation by another contracting State "constitutes the reserving State a party to the treaty in relation to that
other State; . . . and objection by another contracting State to
a reservation does not preclude the entry into force of the treaty
as between the objecting and reserving States unless a contrary
intention is definitely expressed. . . ." Reservations are considered to have been accepted by a State if it has raised no objection thereto within twelve months.[26] Finally, an accepted
reservation "modifies for the reserving" and accepting States, in
their relations to each other, "the provisions of the treaty to which
the reservation relates to the extent of the reservation," but "the
reservation does not modify the provisions of the treaty for the
other parties thereto *inter se"*; and "[w]hen a State objecting to a
reservation has not opposed the entry into force of the treaty between itself and the reserving State, the provisions to which the

---

[23] Vienna Convention art. 4.   [24] *Id*. art. 19.   [25] *Id*. art 20 (2) .

[26] *Id*. arts. 20 (4) (a) – (b) , (5) . Note, however, that a ratification or accession
which contains a reservation is not effective until at least one other contracting
State has accepted it. *Id*. art. 20 (4) (c) .

reservation relates do not apply as between the two States to the extent of the reservation." [27]

Despite the foregoing effort at codification of the applicable rules, and the precedent of the 1951 Advisory Opinion of the International Court of Justice, as already indicated, the problem is still by no means free from doubt. As pointed out, for instance, in the joint opinion of four of the five dissenting judges in that case,

a reserving State may or may not be a party to the [Genocide] Convention according to the different viewpoints of States which have already become parties. Under such a system, it is obvious that there will be no finality or certainty as to the status of the reserving State as a party as long as the admissibility of any reservation that has been objected to is left to *subjective* determination by *individual* States [emphasis added]. It will only be objectively determined when the question of the compatibility of the reservation is referred to judicial decision; but this procedure, for various reasons, may never be resorted to by the parties. If and when the question is judicially determined, the result will be, according as the reservation as judicially found to be compatible or incompatible, either that the objecting State or States must, for the first time, recognize the reserving State as being also a party to the Convention, or that the reserving State ceases to be a party in relation to those other parties which have accepted the reservation. Such a state of things can only cause the utmost confusion. . . .[28]

In its majority opinion, on the other hand, the Court stated that the underlying characteristics of a multilateral convention are relevant to the determination of the admissibility of reservations, but only "in the absence of any express provision on the subject." [29] In response to this implied suggestion by the Court, the General Assembly of the United Nations, at the January 1952 plenary session in Paris, adopted a Resolution recommending "that organs of the United Nations, specialized agencies and States should, in the course of preparing multilateral conventions, consider the insertion therein of provisions relating to the admis-

[27] *Id*. art. 21.   [28] Advisory Opinion, *supra* note 4, at 44.   [29] *Id*. at 22.

sibility or non-admissibility of reservations and the effect to be attributed to them." [30]

Returning to consideration of the proposed Statute of the International Court of Justice, the advice of this Resolution has been taken. As stated at the outset of this chapter, the proposed Statute has been drafted in contemplation of ratification with no reservations thereto being permitted; the Statute, if ratified, will take effect automatically as to all Members of the United Nations, and precisely as written.[31] The great weakness of both the Permanent Court of International Justice and the International Court of Justice has been the absence of compulsory jurisdiction, the root of which lay in the privilege of States to refrain totally from adhering to the Court's jurisdiction, or to adhere subject to any number of reservations. As has been pointed out in detail in chapter 1, all the provisions of the proposed Statute, whatever their apparent goal, have been framed with the overriding purpose of establishing a Court to whose compulsory jurisdiction in international matters no nation could submit and still harbor the fear of intrusion into its domestic affairs or an unacceptable loss of sovereignty. To permit ratification of the proposed Statute with reservations would, especially in light of Article 21 of the Vienna Convention discussed above,[32] create precisely the sort of jurisdictional patchwork currently in existence, negate the very terms of the Statute itself,[33] and frustrate its purpose. Ratification of the proposed Statute without reservations is thus a necessary condition for realistic compulsory jurisdiction of the Court, and a clause to that effect is therefore included in the terms of ratification.[34]

---

[30] G.A. Res. 598, 6 U.N. GAOR, Supp. 20, at 84, U.N. Doc. A/2119 (1952).

[31] I.C.J. STAT. (P) art. XX, para. 1. The proposed Statute, once adopted by a vote of two-thirds of the members of the General Assembly, comes into force after ratification by two-thirds of the Members of the United Nations, including all permanent members of the Security Council. Thus it may be said that the proposed Statute is, in effect, a treaty.

[32] *See* text at note 27 *supra.*   [33] *See* I.C.J. STAT (P) art. VIII, para. 1.

[34] *See* note 31 *supra.*

CHAPTER III

Internationalization of Judges

It must be conceded generally, today as it was in 1945, that permanent peace can be achieved in the world—as it must ultimately be—only when there is available to the nations of the world an international tribunal in whose judges' complete independence and integrity they could have implicit confidence, with compulsory jurisdiction over all of them, and with plenary power to adjudicate all disputes among them. It will be recalled that, as early as 1920, M. Mineitciro Adatci of Japan, a member of the Committee of Jurists who drafted the Statute of the Permanent Court of International Justice, of which he was later to become President, suggested that the judges of the proposed new Court should give unqualified assurance of their impartiality by "deifying themselves" through internationalization.[1] In 1923, Judge Edwin B. Parker of the United States was appointed umpire of the Mixed Claims Commission between the United States and Germany. Shortly after Judge Parker's death in 1929, Professor Edwin M. Borchard of the Yale Law School wrote of him that he "early made it clear that" in his official capacity, "he regarded himself as denationalized."[2] In 1927, a committee of judges of the Permanent Court of International Justice, considering adoption of a rule permitting litigants at interest to appoint judges *ad hoc,* in cases submitted for advisory opinions as well as in contentious cases, reported that "of all influences to which men are subject, none is more powerful, more persuasive or more subtle, than the tie of allegiance that binds" judges "to the land of their homes and kindred."[3] Moreover, Professor (later Judge Sir Hersch) Lauterpacht, that renowned authority on public international law, stated that impartiality of international judges

[1] 1920 PROCEEDINGS at 187.

[2] Borchard, *Judge Edwin B. Parker,* 24 AM. J. INT'L L. 139–40 (1930).

[3] [1927] P.C.I.J., ser. E, No. 4, at 187.

"presupposes on their part the consciousness of being citizens of the world."[4]

The most important single way, therefore, by which the independence and integrity of the International Court of Justice could be assured, is to provide for the "internationalization" of its judges; and so the revised Statute of the Court requires that each member of the Court upon his accession should renounce his allegiance to the country of which he was a national when elected and is to be deemed to have become, for his natural lifetime, a citizen of the United Nations. The question nevertheless inevitably arises as to whether it is really possible, as a practical matter, to eliminate partisan considerations altogether from the makeup of an international tribunal. It must be conceded of course that the system of nomination and election of judges necessarily involves political processes, and even political considerations, while at the same time tending toward selection of candidates of the highest possible caliber.

The provision of the present Statute of the International Court of Justice, like that of its predecessor, requiring that it "be composed of a body of independent judges," unquestionably still recognizes that political considerations must inevitably enter into their selection, but also unquestionably contemplates that, once elected, the judges are to be completely independent of control by their own countries, or even by the United Nations as an organization. This contemplated assurance of independence of the judges could, it is submitted, be strengthened immeasurably by the provision for their "internationalization" under the proposed new Statute of the Court, coupled with the companion provision for their life tenures.

It has been suggested that judges would be unwilling to give up their right to vote in national elections, and that they will

---

[4] H. LAUTERPACHT, FUNCTION at 238–39. The British Commissioner in the London Commission of 1853, in submitting his suggestion as to the choice of an umpire, referred to the person concerned as entitled "to take rank among that class of citizens of the world in whom every nation takes a pride, whose fame is the common property of all, and whose feelings, sympathies and interests may be fairly considered as not confined to one place or people, but equally and indifferently spread over the whole world." J. MOORE, HISTORY AND DIGEST OF INTERNATIONAL ARBITRATIONS TO WHICH THE UNITED STATES HAS BEEN A PARTY 395 (1898).

accordingly decline to serve on condition of giving up their nationality. In Canada, however, "every judge appointed by the Governor in Council" is "disqualified from voting at an election and incapable of being registered as elector, and shall not vote nor be so registered. . . ." Yet Canadian judges are among the world's best.

It has been stated from time to time that it is helpful to the Court to have one or more of its judges familiar, at first hand, with local factors at issue in an international controversy under consideration; but this has frequently been said in circumstances indicating an evident desire to find a basis on which to retain the principle of national judgeships, thought to be necessary to gain support for acceptance of the tribunal itself, as an institution. Thus, during the course of the discussions in the 1920 Committee of Jurists, Elihu Root of the United States did say that "nations should be able to go before the Court with the certainty that their case would be fully understood"; [5] but, as stated later of Mr. Root by Judge Hudson, "he urged the participation of national judges chiefly, however, as a practical way for getting States to consent." [6] Nevertheless, it must be conceded that Judge Hudson did himself find "that national judges have served a useful purpose in familiarizing other judges with special features of their national laws, and at times with their national psychology as affected by the particular case." [7] Further, too, the record does show that, in 1944, an Informal Inter-Allied Committee on the Future of the Permanent Court of International Justice, which had begun to meet in London during the previous year, recommended that the contemplated new Court should continue to sanction the use of national and *ad hoc* judges because they "fulfill a useful function in supplying local knowledge and a national point of view." [8] No logical reason appears, however, why such special features of national laws, national psychology, local knowledge, and national points of view should not be supplied by evidence, by legal or other literature, or by presentation of counsel. It is far safer for a judge to be informed as to the background of a controversy in

[5] 1920 PROCEEDINGS at 532, 538.   [6] M. HUDSON, P.C.I.J. at 132.
[7] *Id.* at 359.   [8] 1920 PROCEEDINGS at 169–70, 531.

contentious proceedings than to rely on his own preconceptions thereof.

This principle leads to an understanding as to why memberships of national judges, even openly partisan, on arbitral tribunals is accepted practice in the settlement of international controversies. Such an *ad hoc* commission is established to bring about an amicable adjustment of a particular dispute, ordinarily by reformation of an agreement on a compromise basis, as between representatives of the parties with the assistance of an umpire. A permanent judicial tribunal, however, exists to adjudicate controversies by construing the rights and liabilities of the parties judicially—without fear or favor—on the basis of law and justice rather than to seek a common meeting ground on which the parties ought to reach agreement. Efforts to justify the right of judges who are nationals of parties to a dispute, to sit in judgment on their controversy before a permanent international court of justice, on the ground that such a practice is sanctioned by arbitral precedents are therefore clearly fallacious.

In the discussions on this point in the 1920 Committee of Jurists, M. Loder of the Netherlands, destined to become the first President of the Permanent Court of International Justice, opposed the suggestion that a judge of the Court should be permitted to participate in the decision of a case to which the country of which he is a national is a party, because this would be "a characteristic essentially belonging to arbitration." [9] That Committee itself, in recommending adoption of the system of national and *ad hoc* judges on the stated ground that "States attach much importance to having one of their subjects on the bench, when they appear before a court of justice," conceded that under this system the proposed Court "more nearly resembles a Court of Arbitration than a national Court of Justice." [10] Rosenne's submission that "the institution of national and *ad hoc* judges" is sanctioned because "deeply rooted in the history of international arbitration and judicial settlement" is accordingly not supportable.[11]

As stated by Sir Hersch Lauterpacht, then a judge of the Court: "The problem of judicial impartiality, however exaggerated it

[9] *Id.*   [10] *Id.* at 721–22.   [11] S. Rosenne, I.C.J. at 147.

may be on occasions, is an ever-present problem in relation to international tribunals—in particular those of an institutional character as distinguished from *ad hoc* tribunals."[12] It should of course be borne in mind in this connection that Professor Lauterpacht had much earlier stated unequivocally that the "borderline between explaining the legal views and defending the interests of the State concerned is in such cases so shadowy as to become utterly unreal."[13]

When proposals concerning incompatibilities and challenges were being made and discussed in connection with preliminary plans to be submitted to the 1920 Committee of Jurists, Baron Descamps of Belgium took the position that the Statute should contain no provision for challenges, but should set out a statement of incompatibilities instead.[14] Judge Hudson suggested that although there had never been an express provision for challenges and the situation had never arisen in practice, "it must be open to a party . . . to raise [such] a question for the Court's decision," and that a party "might inform the President of facts which would lead to his initiative in the premises."[15] The proposed Statute of the Court provides expressly, in paragraph 7 of Article XIII, that "any party to a cause before the Court may suggest to the Court that, for a particular reason given, a member of the Court should not take part in the decision of the case."

During the extensive discussions which were had in the 1920 Committee of Jurists on the problem as to whether judges of the nationality of one of the parties to a cause before the proposed Court should be permitted to participate in the determination thereof, Lord Phillimore of Great Britain cited the famous *Alaska Boundary Arbitration* of 1903, in which Lord Alverstone, the British arbitrator, voted to sustain the position of the United States as against that of Great Britain, and so to refute the contention of M. de Lapradelle of France that "a national judge would always record his disapproval of a sentence unfavorable to his country."[16]

Some interesting statistics were gathered on this direct point

[12] H. LAUTERPACHT, DEVELOPMENT at 40. [13] H. LAUTERPACHT, FUNCTION at 232.
[14] 1920 PROCEEDINGS at 170, 173. [15] M. HUDSON, P.C.I.J. at 370.
[16] 1920 PROCEEDINGS at 172, 198, 531, 533, 535.

by Professor Lauterpacht and were published in 1933 in his *Function of Law in the International Community,* after due "consideration of the expediency and appropriateness of this line of investigation." Of fifteen cases in which "national judges"— judges *ad hoc*—had been involved up to that time, they had voted with the majority in favor of their own countries in three, and in the remainder they had dissented from opinions against their governments.[17] Professor Lauterpacht found "that the result of the analysis here undertaken cannot be regarded as a mere co-incidence," but that, on the contrary, the fact "that in no case have national judges voted against their State," was "profoundly disturbing," and in "several cases . . . aggravated by the circum-stance that the dissenting opinion was delivered against the unanimous or practically unanimous view of the Court."[18] There are later statistics which demonstrate that, as a general rule, and in most cases, national judges—especially judges *ad hoc*—have voted in favor of their own countries, although there have been some exceptions to this rule, which tend rather to prove than to disprove it; but there has never been an instance in which a national judge has dissented from a majority opinion in favor of his own country.[19]

Judge Hudson suggested that mere statistics may tend to be misleading and a conclusion either way "should not be based on a mere tabulation of the votes which led to the adoption of the Court's judgments."[20] This view is undoubtedly fortified to some extent by a dictum in the opinion of Judge Levi Carneiro of the International Court of Justice, in the *Anglo-Iranian Oil Co.* case in 1952, that "it is inevitable that everyone of us in this Court should retain some trace of his legal education and his former legal activities in his country of origin. This is inevitable, and even justified. . . ."[21] For whatever the statistics are worth, it is at least interesting to note that, on some fourteen occasions from 1922 until 1970, a judge *ad hoc* has formed a minority of one on the side of his own country.

It is, of course, impossible to tell to what extent judges *ad hoc*

---

[17] H. LAUTERPACHT, FUNCTION at 230, 232.   [18] *Id.*
[19] S. ROSENNE, I.C.J. at 240–45.   [20] M. HUDSON, P.C.I.J. at 355.
[21] [1952] I.C.J. 161.

may have influenced the decision of cases, but in the case of *The "S.S. Lotus"*, the Court consisted of eleven regular judges and the Turkish judge *ad hoc*, and the twelve were evenly divided. A judgment in favor of Turkey was reached by the President's casting vote, so that the result was actually attributable directly to the participation of the Turkish judge *ad hoc*.[22] In the judgment of July 18, 1966, in the *South West Africa* case, on the question of the right of Ethiopia and Liberia to stand in judgment, the Court stood seven to seven, with Judge *ad hoc* van Wyk voting against the right of the plaintiffs so to stand and Judge *ad hoc* Manefo in favor. The casting vote by the President, Sir Percy Spender, threw the decision against that right.[23] Of course, had neither judge *ad hoc* been in the case, the result would have been the same.

All of these statistics, as suggested by Judge Sir Hersch Lauterpacht, cannot be coincidental, and while they do not furnish mathematical evidence of any rule, they do at least tend to show that a Court composed of judges who have no nationalities will certainly function with a greater degree of judicial independence than one which includes judges of the nationalities of one or more of the parties before the Court. So the proposed Statute of the Court provides for internationalization of judges, with compulsory jurisdiction over all nations, to insure equality of treatment for all with complete judicial independence of the members of the Court.

[22] [1927] P.C.I.J., ser. A. No. 10, at 4, 32.

[23] [1966] I.C.J. 6. In the *Free Zones* case, [1932] P.C.I.J. ser. A/B, No. 46, at 202, Judge *ad hoc* Dreyfus, dissenting, stated that in the Court's earlier opinion in that case, [1930] P.C.I.J., ser. A, No. 24, at 18–19, "the casting vote of the President" had "rendered impotent" the opinion of the dissenting judges

CHAPTER IV

Nomination and Election of Judges

Generally speaking, Article III of the proposed Statute of the International Court of Justice retains the system of election of judges by the joint vote of the United Nations General Assembly and the Security Council. It provides for their election for life, for voluntary retirement at age seventy and compulsory retirement at seventy-five, and for retention of the members of the Court serving as such upon the ratification thereof.[1] It does change, however, the method of nomination. Accordingly, it may be helpful to outline not only the procedure established by the proposed Statute for the election or selection of judges but also the background in which that procedure is to be established.

In the first place, then, it must be remembered that the members of the Court are, under its new Statute, to be elected for life.[2] For over fifty years, ever since adoption of the original Statute of the Permanent Court of International Justice in 1920, the members of that Court, as well as those of the International Court of Justice, have been elected for terms of nine years.[3] In the case of the Permanent Court of International Justice, all of the judges were elected at the same time, the first group in the general election of 1921 and the second, nine years later, in the general election of 1930. (The election which was to have taken place in 1939 was postponed because of the outbreak of the Second World War.) [4] Vacancies were filled by election, but only for the unexpired term of the judge whose death or resignation created the vacancy, so that the terms of all of the judges always expired at

---

[1] Note that, under I.C.J. STAT. (P) art. VI, para. 3, the retirement at age seventy-five of judges of that age serving at the time of ratification does not take effect until six months afterwards. This provision is designed to allow ample time to nominate and elect new judges to replace them.

[2] I.C.J. STAT. (P) art. III, para. 1.

[3] P.C.I.J. STAT. art. 13; I.C.J. STAT. art. 13, para. 1.

[4] LEAGUE OF NATIONS, RECORDS OF THE TWENTIETH ASSEMBLY 6 (1940).

the same time. There had been criticism of this system on the grounds that it contained no assurance of continuity of membership on the Court, and that it was conducive to perfunctory selection of judges.[5] To correct this situation, the Statute of the International Court of Justice provided that the terms of the fifteen judges should be staggered—that is, five of the first members of the Court should be elected for three, five for six, and five for nine years, with the terms of all judges thereafter to be nine years.[6]

In 1929, when the Statute of the Permanent Court of International Justice was being revised by a Committee of Jurists, M. Nicolas Politis of Greece proposed that the terms of the members of that Court "should be increased from nine to twelve years, with the hope that, in future, it would be found possible to go even further and to appoint the international judges for life."[7] When the proposed Statute of the International Court of Justice was drawn, it was felt that the time had come to elect the members of the Court for life; experience having shown that all the judges of the two Courts, during the fifty years of the tribunals' existence, have been men of outstanding ability and unquestioned integrity. Further, election of members of the Court for life would ensure automatic continuity of membership of the Court and would give the judges the greatest possible degree of judicial independence. Finally, since the members of the Court in office at the time of adoption of the proposed Statute would be presumed to have been elected for life thereunder, there would be no need for any elections except to fill vacancies occurring by resignation, retirement, or death.

The proposed Statute provides, as did the former one, for fif-

---

[5] H. LAUTERPACHT, FUNCTION at 240–41; M. HUDSON, TRIBUNALS at 153. To the 1920 Committee of Jurists who framed the Statute of the Permanent Court, on the other hand, it was important that "[t]he possibility of new elections every nine years . . . be assured." 1920 PROCEEDINGS at 575 (statements of Baron Descamps and Lord Phillimore). It is also worth noting that the continuity of the Permanent Court did not suffer from this system as much as imagined. In the election of 1930, six of the eleven incumbent judges were reelected, and two of the four deputy judges were elevated to judgeships on the enlarged, fifteen-member Court. *See* Records of the Eleventh Assembly, Text of the Debates, LEAGUE OF NATIONS OFF. J., Spec. Supp. 84, at 134–40 (1930).

[6] I.C.J. STAT. art. 13, para. 1.   [7] 1929 PROCEEDINGS at 44.

teen judges of the Court. There has been a great deal of discussion about the size of the Court. It was suggested, at one time, that a court of nine judges would be better,[8] but this suggestion was opposed on the ground that, as "the great Powers would always be represented on the Court," the smaller countries would have a difficult time agreeing on candidates for the lesser number of posts available to them.[9] In very general terms, it was felt that the Court should be large enough to represent various systems of legal thought, yet small enough to include only persons of eminence; sufficiently large to offset inevitable absences, yet sufficiently small to permit effective conferences.[10] Originally, the bench of the Permanent Court of International Justice was composed of eleven judges and four deputy judges, with a right vested in the Assembly, upon the proposal of the Council of the League of Nations, to increase its membership to fifteen judges and six deputy judges.[11] By the Revision Protocol of 1929, which became effective in 1936, the number of judges was fixed at fifteen.[12]

Under the proposed Statute, the jurisdiction of the Court is compulsory as to all Members of the United Nations.[13] This will, of course, while tending to induce diplomatic settlement of many cases, nevertheless increase the work load of the Court to some extent, and might ultimately require more judges; but such an increase can be effected only by a revision of the Statute.

The proposed Statute of the Court provides, as does the present, that the Court may sit in sections or chambers under certain circumstances. While this has never been done, it may ultimately be necessary in order to effect reasonable dispatch of the increased

[8] Minutes of the Second Meeting of the Subcomm. of the Third Comm., COMM. III at 340 (proposal by Sir Cecil Hurst of the British Empire).

[9] *Id.* M. Raul Fernandes of Brazil pointed out that the more than thirty secondary powers would have to agree on the distribution of only four seats on a nine-man Court.

[10] 1920 PROCEEDINGS at 168–82 *passim. See also* M. HUDSON, P.C.I.J. at 147–48.

[11] P.C.I.J. STAT. art. 3.

[12] *See generally* M. HUDSON, P.C.I.J. at 135–40. Because of a question as to the status of the deputy judges after ratification of the Revision Protocol, the Assembly and Council of the League of Nations, pursuant to a resolution of the First Committee, elected fifteen judges and four deputy judges in 1930. *See* Minutes of the First Comm., LEAGUE OF NATIONS OFF. J., Spec. Supp. 85, at 8–28 (1930); *see also* note 5 *supra.*

[13] *See* chapter 1 *supra.*

case load anticipated in connection with the proposed compulsory jurisdiction of the Court.

The most important points to be borne in mind in the election of judges of the International Court of Justice, under the current Statute, are that "[t]he Court shall be composed of a body of independent judges," and that they are to be elected from among persons "who possess the qualifications required in their respective countries for appointment to the highest judicial offices, or are jurisconsults of recognized competence in international law." [14]

While neither the present Statute of the International Court of Justice, nor the Statute of the Permanent Court of International Justice, contain any age limits among the qualifications for judges of those courts, the proposed Statute provides that, at the time of his election, a judge may not be less than fifty nor more than sixty-five years of age.[15] Retirement is permitted at age seventy and required at age seventy-five.[16]

One of the earliest problems faced by those who wished to establish a permanent international tribunal was that of the method of selecting judges. The Permanent Court of Arbitration's procedure for constituting a body to decide international issues submitted to it was quite adequate, given the nature of the Court as an arbitration panel rather than a true "court." [17] Basically, the signatory or contracting Powers to the Hague Conventions each selected four persons at the most, "of known competency in questions of international law," to serve as arbitrators. When recourse was had to the Court to settle a dispute, the arbitrators who form the tribunal had to be chosen by agreements from among the list of submitted names, all of whom were considered "members of the Court." [18] Several nations, however, including

---

[14] I.C.J. STAT. art. 2.   [15] I.C.J. STAT (P) art. II, para. 2.

[16] *Id.* I.C.J. STAT. (P) art. VI, paras. 2–3.

[17] The Permanent Court of Arbitration was organized pursuant to the Hague Convention of 1899, ch. II, arts. 20–29, and strengthened by the Hague Convention of 1907, arts. 41–50. *See* HAGUE CONVENTIONS at 57–64. For general discussion of the Permanent Court of Arbitration, see N. POLITIS, THE WORK OF THE HAGUE COURT (Judicial Settlement of International Disputes No. 6, 1911). *See also* M. HUDSON, TRIBUNALS at 6–8, 157–64 (1944); M. HUDSON, P.C.I.J. at 3–36.

[18] Hague Convention of 1899 art. 23; Hague Convention of 1907 art. 44. While neither of the Hague Conventions uses the term, the members of the Permanent Court of Arbitration selected by each country have come to be known as "national

the United States, were dissatisfied with a "Court" which resolved disputes on the basis of tradition, usage, and other diplomatic influences, rather than on the determination of questions of fact and law, upon a record, and with a sense of judicial responsibility.[19] Under their influence, the Second Hague Conference of 1907 did succeed in working out a general plan for a new Permanent Court of Arbitral Justice, one "capable of insuring continuity in arbitral jurisprudence." [20] The Conference, however, was unable to evolve an agreed method for selecting the judges of the Court, because of an irreconcilable conflict between the smaller nations' concept of the equality of States, on the one hand, and the insistence on political dominance by the larger nations, on the other.[21]

---

groups," and are referred to as such in the Statutes of the Permanent Court of International Justice and the International Court of Justice. P.C.I.J. STAT. art. 4; I.C.J. STAT. art. 4, paras. 1–2.

[19] Thus, the American delegates to the Second Hague Conference of 1907 were instructed to press for "a development of the Hague tribunal into a permanent tribunal composed of judges who are judicial officers and nothing else, . . . and who will devote their entire time to the trial and decision of international causes by judicial methods and under a sense of judicial responsibility." Instructions of May 31, 1907, from Elihu Root, the Secretary of State, to the American Delegates to the Hague Conference of 1907, [1907] 2 FOREIGN REL. U.S. 1128, at 1135 (1910).

[20] See Chapter 1, *supra*, text at note 7. See also M. HUDSON, P.C.I.J. at 80–84.

[21] The provisions of the draft Convention for the Court of Arbitral Justice were hammered out in Committee of Examination B, First Subcommission of the First Commission, chaired by M. Leon Bourgeois of France. The proposal around which debate and counterproposals swirled (an arrangement similar to that of the Root-Phillimore Plan of the 1920 Committee of Jurists), submitted jointly by the United States, Great Britain, and Germany, called for a court of seventeen members, eight permanent representatives of the Great Powers (Germany, the United States, Austria-Hungary, France, Great Britain, Italy, Japan, and Russia) and nine representatives of the other signatory Powers, to be seated on the court on a rotating basis according to an appended schedule. Draft Convention Presented by the Delegations of Germany, the United States of America, and Great Britain (1st ed.), 2 [1907] HAGUE PROCEEDINGS 1019, at 1020, 1024–25; (2d ed.), *id.* at 1031–32; (3d ed.), *id.* at 1036–37, 1043–44. Between August 13 and September 5, 1907, the Committee approved all provisions of the proposal except those related to the composition of the court. *Id.* at 683. After an impassioned plea by Mr. Joseph H. Choate of the United States, a preparatory subcommittee was formed to deal with this specific problem. *Id.* at 683–89. On September 18, 1907, Mr. Alexander Nelidow of Montenegro reported to the Committee that the subcommittee had rejected the U.S.-British-German rotating system yet had failed to agree on any other one. *Id.* at 690–93. At this point Sir Edward Fry of Great Britain submitted the following

A number of projects for constituting a permanent international tribunal, submitted between the Second Hague Conference of 1907 and the 1919 Paris Peace Conference, could not meet this problem.[22] It was the organizational connection between the League of Nations and the proposed Permanent Court of International Justice, and the organization of the League itself, which suggested a solution to the imaginative mind of Elihu Root, former Secretary of State of the United States, and then a member of the 1920 Committee of Jurists, hammering out a plan for the Permanent Court at the behest of the Council of the League. He pointed out that the United States, faced with a similar problem in 1787, had responded with a bicameral Congress; one house based on equal representation, the other on proportional representation. Could not the Permanent Court be constituted in two chambers along similar lines? To go one step further; an analogous arrangement already existed between the Council and the Assembly of the League of Nations. "It was possible that the solution of the problem would be found by articulating the new organization [the Court] with the political organization of the League. . . . Would it be possible to vest the power of election of judges [of a single-chamber Court] both in the Assembly and in the Council?"[23] This proposal was incorporated in Article 2 of the

---

resolution: "The Conference believes it desirable for the signatory Powers to adopt the project for the establishment of a court of arbitral justice by omitting the provisions bearing upon the appointment of the judges and upon the rotation to be established among them." *Id.* at 694. After a last-ditch effort by Mr. Choate to have the Committee agree to *some* system of election, *id.* at 694–99, the resolution was adopted in modified form by a vote of eight for, five against, and two abstentions. *Id.* at 705. Thus, no provision was made in the final text of the resolution for the nomination or election of judges of the court, or their number.

See generally M. Hudson, P.C.I.J. at 82; D. Hill, The Problem of a World Court 25–26 (1927); *cf.* Report of the American Delegation to the Hague Conference of 1907, [1907] Foreign Rel. U.S. 1144, 1176–78 (1910).

[22] *See* J. Scott, The Project of a Permanent Court of International Justice and Resolutions of the Advisory Committee of Jurists, Report and Commentary 195–98 (Carnegie Endowment for International Peace, Division of International Law Pamphlet No. 35, 1920), for the texts of various proposals for permanent international tribunals, put forth between the Hague Conference of 1907 and the 1919 Paris Peace Conference.

[23] 1920 Proceedings at 108–09.

Root-Phillimore plan [24] and adopted by the Committee on July 6, 1920.[25]

This method of election worked easily, and eminently well, in the League of Nations as to the Permanent Court of International Justice. It was carried over into the present Statute of the International Court of Justice,[26] in the selection of whose judges it has also functioned smoothly, and apparently to the complete satisfaction of all concerned. No better or more satisfactory system for the election of judges of the Court having evolved in more than fifty years of practice, the same system is transplanted into the proposed Statute of the International Court of Justice.[27]

Almost as difficult, and actually more complex, has been the system by which candidates for election to membership on the Court have been nominated. The system of making nominations, still in effect today, was inaugurated by the 1920 Committee of Jurists. This system was simply that the nominations were to be made by the "national groups" on the Permanent Court of Arbitration rather than by the governments which had appointed the members of those national groups.[28] It was provided further that nations not represented on the Permanent Court of Arbitration might participate in the nominating process through *ad hoc* national groups, appointed by them for that purpose under the same conditions prescribed in Article 44 of the 1907 Hague Convention for appointment of members of the Permanent Court of Arbitration.[29]

The original proposals in this regard were made on June 22, 1920, by Mr. Elihu Root of the United States, and M. Bernard C. J. Loder of the Netherlands,[30] (the latter destined to become, in 1922, the first President of the Permanent Court of International Justice). M. Loder made his proposal as a suggested means

---

[24] The Root-Phillimore plan dealt with the organization and jurisdiction of the Permanent Court and was used by the 1920 Committee of Jurists as a framework within which to vote on specific proposals. It was submitted to the Committee on June 30–July 1, 1920. For the text of the plan, see 1920 PROCEEDINGS at 298–301, 326–28. *See also* H. LAUTERPACHT, FUNCTION at 239–40.

[25] 1920 PROCEEDINGS at 395. *See* P.C.I.J. STAT. arts. 4–12.

[26] I.C.J. STAT. arts. 4–12.   [27] I.C.J. STAT. (P) art. III, paras. 4–6.

[28] *See generally* M. HUDSON, P.C.I.J. at 265–66. *See also* note 21 *supra*.

[29] P.C.I.J. STAT. art. 4.   [30] 1920 PROCEEDINGS at 160, 166.

of preventing political intrigues in the elections, in light of "the moral weakness of all political bodies;"[31] but the more forceful reason for the suggestion was unquestionably its linking of the new Court to the Permanent Court of Arbitration, with the objective of mollifying a particular vocal group which was insisting that the latter body alone should conduct the elections, in order to make the judges entirely independent of the League of Nations as such.[32] As Judge Manley O. Hudson of the United States, who was elected to the Permanent Court of International Justice in 1936, later wrote: "[T]he system has worked well. It has the advantage of taking the nomination of candidates out of the hands of Governments, and of entrusting it to individuals likely to be in a position to investigate and to know the merits of possible candidates in other countries as well as in their own."[33] While the system did not preclude government activity in behalf of candidates for nomination, it was believed presumably to place a premium on competence as against nationalistic political influence.

This system of nominations by the national groups in the Permanent Court of Arbitration by no means went unopposed. It was suggested that political dealings might result from the possibility that the candidates of various countries might themselves be members of the Permanent Court of Arbitration, and that the national groups of the Court of Arbitration had been appointed for a different purpose. It was accordingly proposed that nominations be made directly by the governments.[34] These fears of prearrangement of nominations were borne out to some extent. While consultation among national groups making nominations was not expressly contemplated, it unquestionably took

[31] *Id.* at 163.

[32] The major advocate of this position on the 1920 Committee of Jurists was M. Arturo Ricci-Busatti of Italy. See 1920 PROCEEDINGS at 183, for the text of his first proposal linking the organization of the Permanent Court of International Justice to the Permanent Court of Arbitration, a proposal based on the premise that "[t]he Court of Justice should be connected as intimately as possible with the Court of Arbitration, the functions of which it merely develops." *Id.*

[33] M. HUDSON, TRIBUNALS at 147.

[34] Norwegian Amendments to the Draft Proposal Submitted by the 1920 Committee of Jurists, COMM. III at 500–501.

place extensively. In some elections, the same candidates were nominated by as many as thirty different national groups.[35] It seems likely, in fact, that national and international politics played their part rather in the nominating process than in the elections, since, in some of the elections, the voting quite obviously was a mere formal confirmation of selections prearranged among the nominating groups and their governments.[36]

Just as the 1920 Committee of Jurists was anxious to preserve a close link to the Permanent Court of Arbitration when drafting the original Statute of the Permanent Court of International Justice, so the United Nations Committee of Jurists, assembled at Washington in 1945 to draft provisions for the International Court of Justice, wanted to track, as closely as possible, the Statute of the Permanent Court of International Justice. This desire was carried so far that Article 92 of the Charter of the United Nations itself provides that the International Court of Justice, as "the principal judicial organ of the United Nations . . . shall function in accordance with the annexed Statute, which is based upon the Statute of the Permanent Court of International Justice and forms an integral part of the present Charter."

One of the first problems to confront the Washington Committee of Jurists—one on which there was quite a sharp divergence of opinion—was as to whether the system of nominating candidates for the Permanent Court of International Justice, by the national groups in the Permanent Court of Arbitration, should be made applicable to the members of the new International Court of Justice. On the one hand, this system had worked well in practice, and for that reason alone, many members of the Committee favored retaining it without change.[37] On the other hand, despite the near-universal desire of all concerned to keep

[35] *See* M. Hudson, P.C.I.J. at 267 & ns. 2–3.

[36] Mr. Elihu Root, in fact, expressed the hope that "so many concordant expressions of opinion [regarding suitable choices for membership on the Permanent Court] would be obtained from the various countries, that the election would be thereby virtually decided; the Assembly and the Council would not venture to go against this opinion." 1920 Proceedings at 409. In the election of 1930, fourteen of the fifteen judges were agreed upon "independently" by the Assembly and the Council on the first ballot. Records of the Eleventh Assembly, *supra* note 5, at 136.

[37] *See, e.g.,* the statement of Mr. John E. Read of Canada, in U.N. Comm. of Jurists, Subcomm. on Arts. 3–13, Summary of the First Meeting, Doc. Jurist 32, G/24, 14 U.N.C.I.O. Docs. 255, at 258 (1945).

the structure and organizational processes of the new Court as close as possible to those of the old, there were many influential elements which favored a change in the system of nomination of candidates for judgeships and urged adoption of a system of direct nominations by governments.[38] Great Britain proposed an entirely new method, coupled with a change in size and organization of the Court.[39] A Subcommittee, considering the two basic methods of nominations which had been proposed, decided in favor of direct nominations of single candidates by governments, as simpler and more suitable for the future than perpetuation of the old system.[40] The Subcommittee even suggested that "the simpler method of direct nomination by governments will reduce the possibility of making 'political' nominations," and that nominating only one candidate, a national, "will minimize the political intervention of the Chanceries which precede the designations made according to the present method" – the identical argument then and previously made in favor of retaining the old system.[41]

In the full Committee, it was urged again, by a group led by France and the United States, that the old system afforded "a broader base of consideration" of candidates than would a single nomination by each government and reduced the influence of political considerations, which were more likely to motivate governments.[42] When the vote was taken in the Committee on

[38] Among the nations represented on the Subcommittee on Articles 3–13 who expressed approval of direct nomination were Mexico (id. 257), Egypt (257-58), Great Britain (258), the Soviet Union, China, and the Netherlands (259).

[39] United Kingdom Proposals Regarding the Statute of the Permanent Court of International Justice, Doc. Jurist 14, DP/4, 14 U.N.C.I.O. Docs. 314 (1945).

[40] The Subcommittee approved direct nomination by governments of a single candidate by a narrow 5–4 vote, with Mexico, Great Britain, the Soviet Union, and the Netherlands in favor of a single candidate; Egypt, Canada, and Norway favoring two government-nominated candidates (one a nonnational); and China and France taking no public position. U.N. Comm. of Jurists, Subcomm. on Arts. 3–13, Summary of the First Meeting, *supra* note 37, at 259–60. The vote on the question of "direct nomination by governments" itself, however, was more decisive; six of the Subcommittee's nine members favored the proposal (*see* note 38 *supra*), only Canada and Norway favored the old system (*id.* 258–59), and France expressed no opinion in the discussion. The actual figures of the vote were not recorded.

[41] Report of Subcomm. on Arts. 3–13, Doc. Jurist 24, G/18, 14 U.N.C.I.O. Docs. 274, at 275 (1945). *See* R. Russell, Charter at 867 n.10 (1958).

[42] *See* Statement of Prof. Jules Basdevant of France, in U.N. Comm. of Jurists, Summary of Ninth Meeting, Doc. Jurist 57, G/45, 14 U.N.C.I.O. Docs. 189, at 191 (1945).

whether to change the old system of nominations by national groups, the motion was lost by a tie, although there were a number of absences and abstentions.[43] In the end, the Committee of Jurists recommended to the United Nations Conference at San Francisco that the traditional method of nominations by national groups be retained, but, at the same time, the Committee submitted to that Conference for consideration, as an alternative, the basic system of having each government nominate one of its nationals to a list of candidates for election.[44]

At San Francisco, the alternative texts submitted by the Committee of Jurists, came first before Technical Committee 1 (on the International Court of Justice) of Commission IV on Judicial Organization. In this Committee there was, interestingly enough, no real controversy over the matter of the system of nominations of members of the Court. The reasons favoring the existing system of nominations by national groups were reviewed by the French representative, who argued that that system had worked very well, and, above all, "guarantee[d] a choice which is not based on political considerations." [45] Great Britain's proposal for nominations by each government was opposed also on the grounds that, since only one national of any government might sit as a member of the Court, all governments whose nationals were already judges of the Court "would nominate fruitlessly since any other nominees of their own nationality could not be elected." [46] The Committee then voted overwhelmingly to retain the old system of nominations by national groups in the Permanent Court of Arbitration.[47]

43 *Id.* at 194–95. The vote was 16–16, with four countries not voting. Immediately after the vote, Dr. Arturo Garcia of Peru suggested that, since the Colombian delegate was due momentarily, the vote be retaken when he arrived. The Chairman, Mr. G. H. Hackworth of the United States (later President of the International Court of Justice) , ruled that the votes counted as of the time of voting.

44 U.N. Comm. of Jurists, Report on a Draft of Statute of an International Court of Justice Referred to in Chapter VII of the Dumbarton Oaks Proposals, Doc. Jurist 86, G/73, 14 U.N.C.I.O. Docs. 821, 824–27 (1945) .

45 Comm. IV/1, Summary Report of Eighth Meeting, Doc. 418, IV/1/32, 13 U.N.C.I.O. Docs. 179 (1945) .

46 *Id.* at 180. In the case of an election to fill a single vacancy, under the system of nomination of one national by his own government, fourteen States would perforce nominate a candidate with no chance of being elected.

47 *Id.* The vote in favor of maintaining the old system of nomination was 32–8.

This was ultimately adopted by the full Commission on Judicial Organization (and therefore by the Conference on International Organization) [48] and was embodied in appropriate Articles of the Statute of the International Court of Justice.[49]

Sentiment in favor of direct nominations by governments nevertheless persists. It has been pointed out that, while the method of nominations by national groups had functioned satisfactorily, such nominations had really been made, in most, if not all, instances, by the governments themselves, through their national groups in the Permanent Court of Arbitration. As stated by Judge Manley O. Hudson of the Permanent Court of International Justice, "some of the national groups have clearly conceived it to be their function to express their Governments' will." [50] Moreover, even though the Secretary-General of the United Nations is supposed to communicate directly with the national groups regarding nominations,[51] he does so in practice through the appropriate Foreign Ministries.[52]

When, therefore, consideration is given to revision of the Statute of the International Court of Justice, it is provided, with full recognition of the salutary purpose which the system of nominations by national groups had served in the earlier period of a Court with no compulsory jurisdiction and composed of judges with limited terms, that candidates for life membership on the new, mature Court having compulsory jurisdiction should be nominated directly and simply by the member governments of the United Nations. But the governments are not required to nominate only persons of their own nationalities, as had previously been suggested. Such a limitation had never applied to nominations by the national groups on the Permanent Court of Arbitration, many of whom had, as stated, frequently joined in nominating a single candidate.

Paragraph 3 of Article III of the proposed Statute of the

[48] The entire Statute of the International Court of Justice, submitted by Committee 1, was approved by the Commission without debate. Comm'n IV, Verbatim Minutes of Second Meeting, Doc. 1007, IV/12, 13 U.N.C.I.O. 53, at 59 (1945).

[49] I.C.J. STAT. art. 4, paras. 2–3; arts. 5–6.   [50] M. HUDSON, P.C.I.J. at 266.

[51] I.C.J. STAT. art. 5, para. 1.

[52] S. ROSENNE, I.C.J. at 124–25. Such also was the practice of the Secretary-General of the League of Nations. M. HUDSON, P.C.I.J. at 266 n. 97.

International Court of Justice provides that, whenever a vacancy shall have occurred, or is about to occur, in the membership of the Court, the Secretary-General is to "invite each of the members of the General Assembly to nominate . . . not more than two persons of any nationality . . . qualified, and in a position, to serve as members of the Court." [53]

In summary, the proposed Statute provides that the system of nomination of judges be revised to allow governments to nominate directly two persons of any nationality; that the system of electing judges remain unchanged except that judges are to be elected for life; that sitting judges are to hold their places for life; that judges may retire at seventy and must retire at seventy-five; and that sitting judges who have passed these ages continue to hold office for six months after the adoption of the proposed Statute. Elections will accordingly be held only to replace judges who have died or retired.

[53] Note, however, that this provision is still subject to the retained provision that no two members of the Court may, at the time of their elections, be of the same nationality. I.C.J. STAT. (P) art. II, para. 2.

CHAPTER V

Qualifications of Judges

Obviously, there is no such profession as that of "international judge," from whose ranks members of an international tribunal might, as a matter of course, be selected. Few individuals, indeed, are so outstanding as to qualify inherently for this unique, high judicial office. Moreover, the number of persons serving as international judges, at any one time, is very limited. For these reasons, the post is one not normally considered to be offering itself as a specific career for which men are, or could ordinarily be, trained.[1]

The actual selection of judges for the International Court of Justice, as for its predecessor, the Permanent Court of International Justice, thus has been determined across a broad spectrum of innumerable factors, many of them really fortuitous. There is, nevertheless, a clear distinction between the qualifications required of, or desirable in, a member of a temporary or *ad hoc* tribunal, appointed to dispose of a particular controversy, and those of a member of a permanent international court, available at all times to hear by juridical processes and to adjudicate by judicial standards whatever disputes may arise among any of the world's nations.[2]

A primary qualification of international, as of all, judges, is that of moral integrity. The Hague Conventions of 1899 and 1907 required that members of the Permanent Court of Arbitration should be "of the highest moral reputation." [3] The Statute of the Permanent Court of International Justice, as well as that of

[1] M. HUDSON, TRIBUNALS at 32.

[2] Specifically, the members of an *ad hoc* tribunal are selected on the basis of their competence in dealing with a particular dispute or class of disputes, while members of a permanent tribunal "may have to possess a general competence to deal with a great variety of disputes." *Id.*

[3] Hague Convention of 1899 art. 23; Hague Convention of 1907 art. 44. *See* chap. 4, *supra*, at note 18. This phrase was employed also in Article 2 of the 1907 Hague Draft Convention Relative to the Creation of a Judicial Arbitration Court. *See* chap. 1, *supra*, text at note 7.

the International Court of Justice, has provided that these tribunals "shall be composed of a body of independent judges . . .
from among persons of high moral character. . . ."[4] While this
provision seems to serve little purpose, in that it is inconceivable
that nations would nominate for such high judicial office persons
who were not "of high moral character,"[5] it has been carried over
verbatim into the proposed Statute of the International Court of
Justice—to emphasize the need for a sense of responsibility with
which international judges should be imbued, both before and
after their selection.[6] Nonetheless, nationality has been a particularly significant factor in the selection of judges. While the diverse
nationality of the judges has worked out quite well in the past in
practice, it has been a subject which has given rise to some confusion in theory. The Statutes of both the Permanent Court of
International Justice and the International Court of Justice provide, *in haec verbae,* that these Courts are to "be composed of a
body of independent judges, elected regardless of their nationality. . . ."[7] One area which illustrates both a difference between
ad hoc and permanent tribunals, and a continuing concern regarding nationality of judges, is that of the representation of
parties to a case on the bench. In the case of members of a tribunal set up to adjudicate a particular controversy, it is usual to
select a panel of persons of nationalities other than the parties to
the dispute; or to have only one person of nationality other than
the parties to the dispute; or to have one national of each party,
with a third person, a nonnational of either, to compose the
bench. But in a permanent tribunal, the situation is different.
The members of the tribunal are set, and may be called upon to
hear disputes among any particular nations as the occasion may
warrant. For such cases, it has generally been felt that the bench
should contain nationals of both parties, to "protect their interests" and to provide the tribunal with specialized knowledge
regarding the various legal systems.[8]

[4] P.C.I.J. STAT. art. 2 ("from amongst persons. . . .") ; I.C.J. STAT. art. 2.

[5] M. HUDSON, P.C.I.J. at 146.   [6] I.C.J. STAT. (P) art. II, para. 1.

[7] P.C.I.J. STAT. art. 2; I.C.J. STAT. art. 2.

[8] *See* 1920 PROCEEDINGS at 528–29, 532–33 (statements of Lord Phillimore, Mr.
Root and M. Hagerup) . There was some opposition to this idea from Dr. B. C. J.
Loder, later to be elected the first President of the Permanent Court of Interna-

The Statutes of both the Permanent Court of International Justice and the International Court of Justice provide expressly that if the membership of the Court includes a national of one of the parties litigant, the other might designate one of its own nationals as a judge *ad hoc* to sit with the Court for the hearing and determination of the particular case at issue, and that if the Court's membership does not include a national of either party to the dispute, each might designate such a judge *ad hoc* of its own nationality to sit on the bench for the trial of that case.[9] Under the proposed Statute of the International Court of Justice, the judges of the Court are to give up their nationalities when elected, so that there could not be on the Court under any circumstances a national of any party before the Court. There is no need—and no provision has been made—for national judges *ad hoc* to serve in such cases.[10]

Another area in which concern regarding the nationality of judges is evident is that of nomination and election. The Statutes of both the Permanent Court of International Justice and the International Court of Justice provide that candidates for judgeships on these Courts nominated by each national group of the Permanent Court of Arbitration, might not exceed four, "not more than two of whom shall be of their own nationality."[11] The 1920 Committee of Jurists proposed that the number of nominees to be submitted by any national group in the Permanent Court of Arbitration be limited to two "of any nationality."[12] At another time, the Committee reached agreement on a maximum of six nominations by any national group, no more than two of

---

tional Justice. *Id.* at 531. At the meeting of the United Nations Committee of Jurists, which drafted the Statute of the International Court of Justice, a proposal by Dr. Abdul-Majid Abbass of Iraq that judges who are nationals of the parties to a case should always be excluded was voted down by a 23–2 count. U.N. Comm. of Jurists, Summary of Fourth Meeting (Revised), Doc. Jurist 46 (22), 35, 14 U.N.C.I.O. Docs. 117, 126–29 (1945).

[9] P.C.I.J. STAT. art. 31; I.C.J. STAT. art. 31.

[10] I.C.J. STAT. (P) art. IV, para. 1 Of course, as to litigation involving the United Nations itself, all judges will be citizens of that organization. *See* chapter 3 *supra.*

[11] P.C.I.J. STAT. art. 5; I.C.J. STAT. art. 5.

[12] Report of M. de Lapradelle, 1920 PROCEEDINGS at 693, 708–09.

whom could be nationals.[13] The final determination was to fix the number of permissible nominees at four, dividing that number between nationals and nonnationals.[14] This provision was stated to have been adopted "to give the different groups a largeɪ opportunity to propose candidates of universally known competence but of a nationality other than that of the nominating group."[15]

Now it must be remembered that, originally, there were no staggered terms of judges of the Permanent Court of International Justice. The nine-year terms of all of the judges expired at the same time, and individual vacancies could occur only by resignation or death.[16] The limitation of the number of permissible nominees to four by any one national group, therefore, contemplated that number of nominations when an entire slate of nine judges (or perhaps of two or more) was to be elected. In order to limit, even further, the number of nominees permitted when only a single vacancy was to be filled—at a so-called "by-election" —a clause was added providing that "[i]n no case must the number of candidates nominated be more than double the number of seats to be filled."[17] In this latter instance, no provision was made for division of nominees as between nationals and nonnationals, and no key to that problem has been found. The question has never arisen as a practical matter; and, interestingly enough, the provision was carried over into the Statute of the International Court of Justice, without further clarification.[18] In drafting the proposed Statute of the International Court of

[13] Dr. Loder made this proposal as an amendment to the Root-Phillimore plan. *Id.* at 379–80. It was adopted by the Committee on July 8, 1920, and incorporated into Article 6 of the plan. *Id.* at 431. The drafting Committee, however, inserted the provision for nomination of only two candidates by each national group. Drafting Committee's Text of a Scheme for the establishment of the Permanent Court of International Justice, *id.* at 561–62. This change was approved (*see* note 12 *supra*) despite the vigorous objections of M. Francis Hagerup. *Id.* at 555, 612.

[14] Minutes of the Sixth Meeting, COMM. III at 302–04 (motion of M. La Fontaine of Belgium).

[15] Report of the Third Comm., *id.*, Annex 16, at 568. The proposal for four nominations equally divided between nationals and nonnationals was made earlier by Mr. Root. Proposal of Mr. Root, 1920 PROCEEDINGS at 166. *See generally* M. HUDSON, P.C.I.J. at 154–55.

[16] *See* chapter 4, *supra*, text at notes 4–5; P.C.I.J. STAT. art. 13.

[17] P.C.I.J. STAT. art. 5.   [18] I.C.J. STAT. art. 5, para. 2.

Justice, with its elections of judges for life and with vacancies by resignation, retirement, or death to be filled as occasion might require, it is provided simply that each member of the General Assembly might nominate not more than two persons for each such vacancy, with no required division of the nominations between nationals and nonnationals.[19]

The nationality of candidates for judgeships on international tribunals has also been an issue in relation to representation of nations on the bench. The Statute of the Permanent Court of International Justice provided that, "[i]n the event of more than one national of the same Member of the League being elected . . . the eldest of these only shall be considered as elected." [20] This provision contemplated possible selection of two nationals of the same country at the same election and did not clearly prohibit election to fill a vacancy with a national of a State, one of whose other nationals was already a member of the Court. Further, in referring to "more than one national of the same Member of the League," the Statute might conceivably have been taken to refer, literally, only to members of the League, thus containing no prohibition against election of more than one national of a nonmember of the League.[21] In the drafting of these provisions, however, the 1920 Committee of Jurists stated in their report, that "[t]he Court can never include more than one judge of the same nationality," in order "to ensure the representation of the main forms of civilisation and the principal legal systems of the world; and to enable as many States as possible to have a share in the composition of the Court. . . ." [22] When the Statute of the International Court of Justice was prepared, these ambiguities were eliminated by providing in simple, direct terms, that no two members of the Court "may be nationals of the same state." [23]

The proposed Statute of the International Court of Justice, like the original, requires that, in the selection of members of the

[19] I.C.J. STAT. (P) art. III, para. 3.   [20] P.C.I.J. STAT. art. 10.
[21] M. HUDSON, P.C.I.J. at 159n.15.
[22] Report of M. de Lapradelle, *supra* note 12, at 713–14.
[23] I.C.J. STAT. art. 3, para. 1. The provision regarding election of two nationals of the same State was retained. I.C.J. STAT. art. 10, para. 3. *See* I.C.J. STAT. (P) art. III, para. 6.

Court, every effort shall be made to reflect in the Court as a whole a composite of the principal civilizations and legal systems of the world.[24] Article 9 of the Statute of the Permanent Court of International Justice contained a substantially similar provision, to which some opposition was originally expressed on the grounds that, since the Court was to apply international law, "there was no need to have national systems of law represented."[25] The 1920 Committee of Jurists, however, stated in its report:

The Committee, in expressly recommending that the principal legal systems should be represented, had in mind, not that there were distinct systems of International Law, . . . but that there were distinct systems of legal education. . . . The intention is to try and insure that, no matter what points of national law may be involved in an international suit, all shall be equally comprehended; . . . so that the Bench may really and permanently represent the legal conceptions of all nations.

[T]he various forms of civilisation must also be represented. This is an essential condition, if the Permanent Court of International Justice is to be a real World Court for the Society of all Nations.[26]

In any event, all of these provisions have a direct relevance to the nationality of candidates for judgeships on the International Courts and demonstrate quite clearly that nationality has always been an important factor in the system established under these successive Statutes for the selection of members of the Court. For this reason, it is difficult to understand why the Statutes of both the Permanent Court of International Justice and the International Court of Justice have provided that the judges of each of these Courts are to be elected "regardless of their nationality"; and extensive research has not disclosed any logical, underlying purpose of this provision. Of course, no such provision is contained in the proposed Statute of the International Court of Justice, in which the judges will give up their nationalities when elected. There are only two qualifications of judges, under the proposed Statute, in which nationality plays any part. First, no

---

24 I.C.J. STAT. art. 9; I.C.J. STAT. (P) art. II, para. 5.

25 1920 PROCEEDINGS at 363, 365 (statements of Dr. Loder and M. Hagerup).

26 Report of M. de Lapradelle, *supra* note 12, at 710.

two of the judges "shall have been of the same national origin"; [27] second, membership on the Court is expressly limited to nationals of Members of the United Nations.[28]

The proposed Statute of the International Court of Justice, like the present one, provides that judges are to be selected from among those "who possess the qualifications required in their respective countries for appointment to the highest judicial offices, or are jurisconsults of recognized competence in international law." [29] Obviously, professional background is an important consideration, and it would seem to go without saying that the legal profession—or perhaps rather, training in the law—would be, or should be, a paramount requirement for any judgeship. There have been instances, nevertheless, of members of temporary international commissions who were not drawn from the legal profession and who have rendered eminently satisfactory services. On the other hand, it hardly seems conceivable that a judge of a permanent international tribunal having general jurisdiction over disputes among nations should not have studied international law extensively.

No rule, however, can be formulated by which competence in international law can be evidenced or measured. Diplomats, some professional soldiers, lawyers who have served with foreign ministries, some professors of international law, and some national judges, may all have the requisite knowledge to be classed as learned in international law. Among these, perhaps, diplomats—especially those with legal training—are probably considered best fitted, by background and practical experience, to serve as members of a permanent international tribunal. While professional soldiers normally have only a modicum of technical legal education, they are ordinarily logical thinkers along international lines. Many military officers, for instance, have had valuable experience as military attachés at the embassies of their countries throughout

---

[27] I.C.J. STAT. (P) art. II, para. 2.   [28] *Id.* art. II, para. 1.

[29] *Id.;* I.C.J. STAT. art. 2. *See also* P.C.I.J. STAT. art. 2. Article 2 of the 1907 Hague Draft Convention Relative to the Creation of a Judicial Arbitration Court provides that its judges "shall [fulfil] conditions qualifying them, in their respective countries, to occupy high legal posts, or be jurists of recognized competence in matters of international law." HAGUE CONVENTIONS at 31–32.

the world. In addition, such military personnel are very often men of broad practical perspective in viewing intricate problems of international relationships, as a number of Allied officers demonstrated so abundantly in the military administrations of occupied areas following the Second World War. However, no professional soldier has ever served as a judge of either the Permanent Court of International Justice or the International Court of Justice.[30]

Lawyers who have had practical experience in public international law have generally gained it while serving in the foreign offices of their countries; but both they and academicians are inclined to overlook the broad forest of work-a-day international relationships, while examining too closely the obscure trees of abstract legal theory. As early as 1929, the Assembly of the League of Nations adopted a recommendation by the Conference of Signatories of that year that candidates for judgeships on the Permanent Court of International Justice "should possess recognised practical experience in international law. . . ." This recommendation was opposed, however, on the grounds that it placed undue emphasis on the experience of legal advisers to ministries of foreign affairs.[31]

---

[30] Judge Hardy C. Dillard of the United States, a current member of the International Court of Justice, is a 1924 graduate of West Point. He resigned his commission, however, and began his legal studies at the University of Virginia in September of the same year. *See* WEST POINT ALUMNI FOUNDATION, REGISTER OF GRADUATES AND FORMER CADETS OF THE UNITED STATES MILITARY ACADEMY 379 (1971).

[31] This recommendation, which included provisions for not only practical experience, but also minimum proficiency in the official languages of the Court (French and English), and written statements of candidates' qualifications, originally took the form of an amendment to the Statute, proposed at the meeting of the 1929 Committee of Jurists. Since "none of these three questions necessitate[d] a modification of the existing texts," and to facilitate agreement to them, they were presented in the form of a recommendation, and adopted by the Committee as such. Report of the Committee of Jurists on the Question of Amendment of the Statute of the Court, in First Comm., Minutes, Annex 5, LEAGUE OF NATIONS OFF. J., Spec. Supp. 76, at 71–72, (1929). At the 1929 Conference of Signatories, the question was reopened for debate, and the recommendation was again adopted. *See* First Comm., Report, in Records of the Tenth Assembly, Text of the Debates, Annex 4, LEAGUE OF NATIONS OFF. J., Spec. Supp. 75, at 433, 436. At the Tenth Session of the Assembly of the League of Nations, the First Committee (Constitutional and Legal Questions) again debated the recommendation, with strong opposition to it being put forth by Denmark, Latvia, and especially Norway, on the

The provision of the Statutes of the Courts that the persons selected as judges should "possess the qualifications required in their respective countries for appointment to the highest judicial offices" met some opposition at the time of its adoption and has also been the subject of some criticism since that time. In the 1920 Committee of Jurists, Senõr Rafael Altamira of Spain, who later became one of the first judges of the Permanent Court of International Justice, suggested that some "national judges rarely have the opportunity of dealing with international questions." [32] M. de Lapradelle of France, a professor at the University of Paris and a legal adviser to the French Foreign Office, explained that, while it was desirable "to reconcile the continental and Anglo-American points of view, the former of which preferred to have as international judges jurisconsults who were not judges by profession, whereas the latter preferred national magistrates," it was still necessary "to exclude national judges who had not specialised in International Law from appointment as international judges." [33]

Judge Manley O. Hudson, who served for eight years as a member of the Permanent Court of International Justice, erst-

---

grounds that it was not in the spirit of the Statute to give such detailed instructions to the national groups regarding the choice of candidates and that the recommendation regarding practical experience in international law was "dangerous" in the sense that "[t]hose who were familiar [with it] were diplomatists and the agents of the Ministries for Foreign Affairs" (statement of M. Duzmans of Latvia). The part of the recommendation dealing with practical experience in international law was nevertheless adopted by the First Committee by a vote of 27–13; the part regarding proficiency in the official languages, unanimously; and the part regarding written statements of qualifications, with only Cuba in opposition. First Comm., Minutes, *supra*, at 9–11. Norway persisted in its opposition, however, by offering an amendment to the report of the First Committee deleting the recommendation. M. Politis of Greece, who had drafted the report, defended the recommendation, stating that "competence" should include "both a theoretical and practical knowledge of international law." The First Committee report was thereupon adopted by the Assembly of the League by a vote of 32–15. Records of the Tenth Assembly, Text of the Debates, *supra*, at 119–21. *See also* M. HUDSON, TRIBUNALS at 39.

[32] 1920 PROCEEDINGS at 612.

[33] *Id.* at 553. The Committee of Jurists had adopted Article 2 of the Descamps plan (*see id.* at 373) with wording from the 1907 Draft Convention on the Judicial Arbitration Court added. *Id.* at 450. The drafting Committee eliminated this wording for the reasons set forth by M. de Lapradelle. *See* Drafting Committee's Text, *id.* at 561. Wording to the effect that those qualified for high judicial office in their own countries could serve as judges on the Court was later reinstated in the Article. *Id.* at 611–12.

while world-renowned professor of international law at Harvard
University, wrote as late as 1944 that "[t]he text of the Statute is
open to criticism, for the possession of the qualifications required
for national judges would in many cases give no indication of
fitness for service as an international judge; the formal national
requirements may be very slight—as in the United States of
America. . . ."[34] Judge Hudson went on:

In general, the questions dealt with by international courts differ very
materially from those which come before national courts, and the
approach to their solution should be very different. Even where national courts deal with international questions, they must apply
national law and they are usually concerned with international law
only as it may have been incorporated into the national law. Moreover, a person who has long served as a judge of a national court is
likely to be so engrossed in the particular system of his own national
law that he may lack the freedom of mind necessary for dealing with
disputes governed by a different system of law, and possibly between
States each of which has a national law of other character. . . . For
these reasons, service in national courts ought not to be regarded as a
necessary qualification for international judges.[35]

Nevertheless, the provision as to qualification of candidates for
national judgeships as a prerequisite for international judgeship
is retained in the proposed Statute of the International Court of
Justice, with full recognition of the fact that such qualification
alone is an insufficient criterion; but it is felt that it embraces,
at least in theory, an understanding of the philosophy of the law
and that most important of all traits in judges, national or international—a judicial temperament.

In this connection, it may be of interest to review the background qualifications and prior professional experience of the
seventy-eight judges of both the Permanent Court of International
Justice and the International Court of Justice who have served as
members of those Courts during the half century since the establishment of the former tribunal. Fifteen of the judges had been
ministers of foreign affairs of their countries, and thirty-three had
been advisers to such ministries. Twenty-eight had held other
high government posts. Fourteen had been members of national

[34] M. HUDSON, TRIBUNALS at 39.   [35] *Id.* at 40–41.

parliaments, and twenty-four had been national judges, while an aggregate of fifty-one had taught at universities, specializing in international law. Many had had some practical experience in the field of international law. Seven, for instance, had previously served as judges *ad hoc* of the Court itself. Seventeen had been members of other international tribunals or commissions, and the same number had appeared as counsel before such bodies. In addition, nineteen of the judges had held high diplomatic posts, and as many as fifty-four had taken significant parts in international conferences, or had been active in various international organizations. Finally, thirty-nine of the judges had previously been appointed by their own governments as members of the Permanent Court of Arbitration. It must be understood, in considering these statistics, that many of the judges had had experience in two or more of the fields cited. For instance, of the thirty-three who had been legal advisers to foreign ministries, ten were among the fifty-four who had played important roles in international conferences and about half of all of these had also served as professors at universities.

Some situations have arisen out of these very statistics, showing the inevitable disadvantages to which they may lead, requiring recusation of judges in various circumstances. In the *Société Commerciale de Belgique* case in 1939, M. C. Georges Ténékidès was permitted to sit on the Permanent Court as Judge *ad hoc* for Greece, despite the fact that he had theretofore been Legal Director of the Greek Ministry of Foreign Affairs, while negotiations concerning the controversy were in progress between the Greek and Belgian governments.[36] In the *Advisory Opinion on the Effect of Awards made by the United Nations Administrative Tribunal,* Judge Basdevant stated that he felt that he should not

---

[36] *See* 15 P.C.I.J. ANN. R. (ser. E) 24–25 (1939) for a brief biography of M. Ténékidès. He took the solemn declaration that he would "exercise his powers impartially and conscientiously," as called for by P.C.I.J. STAT. art. 20 and P.C.I.J.R. 5. *See* Twelfth Public Sitting, Société Commerciale de Belgique, [1939] P.C.I.J., ser. C, No. 87, at 162. The Belgian Government did not file an objection under Article 17 of the Permanent Court's Statute to the selection of M. Ténékidès. Letter of Sept. 26, 1938, from F. Muûls, Agent of the Royal Belgian Government, to J. Herry, Registrar of the Permanent Court of International Justice, *id.* at 296 (in French).

take part in the rendition of the Advisory Opinion "for considerations of a personal nature," since he "was closely related to the
President of the Administrative Tribunal of the United Nations."
The President of the Court agreed with this view, and Judge
Basdevant did not sit in the case.[37] Judge Sir Hersch Lauterpacht
had advised one of the parties in the *Nottebohm Case (Second
Phase)*, prior to his election to the Court. On this basis, he told
the President that, "subject to the decision of the Court he
felt . . . that he ought not to participate in the adjudication of
the case." The Court agreed, and he recused himself.[38] In 1952,
the Court had accepted the conclusion of Judge Sir Benegal Rau,
that he should recuse himself from sitting in the *Anglo-Iranian
Oil Co.* case because previously, as the representative of India
on the Security Council of the United Nations, he had participated in the discussion in that body of the complaint of the
United Kingdom against Iran for failure to comply with the preliminary measures which the Court had directed the parties to
take in that case.[39]

In light of the foregoing precedents and the general principles
which the Court has established in those cases, the proposed
Statute of the Court has provided, in paragraph 7 of Article XIII,
that any judge may recuse himself from sitting in a particular
case; that any judge or party may challenge the right of any judge
to sit in a particular case; and that the Court shall determine,
without participation of the questioned judge, his fitness to sit
in any case.

Quite obviously, the members of any international tribunal
should be conversant in the language or languages to be employed
in the proceedings before the tribunal—necessarily a factor in
selection of the members of the tribunal. In creating tribunals
ad hoc to hear particular cases, parties ordinarily specify the lan-

---

[37] Sixth Public Sitting, Advisory Opinion on the Effect of Awards made by the
United Nations Administrative Tribunal, I.C.J. Pleadings 280, at 281 (1954). *See
also* [1953–1954] I.C.J.Y.B. 97. Madame Bastid, the President of the United Nations
Administrative Tribunal at the time, is the daughter of Judge Basdevant.
S. ROSENNE, I.C.J. at 144n.3.

[38] [1954–55] I.C.J.Y.B. 88.

[39] Fourth Public Sitting, Anglo-Iranian Oil Co. case, I.C.J. Pleadings 426, at 427
(1952).

guage to be employed in the proceedings, or it is assumed that this will be one of the languages commonly in use in diplomatic intercourse—most frequently French or English; or the tribunal will itself designate the language to be employed, as an incident to this right of control over matters of procedure before it.[40] In the case of a permanent tribunal, created to hear and determine causes as they arise among any number of nations, the matter of language will inevitably be a particularly significant factor in the selection of judges.

The Statute of the Permanent Court of International Justice provided that the official languages of the Court were to be French and English. Originally, the Statute also provided that "at the request of *the parties* [emphasis added]," the Court might authorize use of a language other than French or English.[41] An amendment to the original Statute of that Court stipulated that it might authorize employment of a language other than one of the official languages in proceedings before it, "at the request of *any party* [emphasis added]," to make it clear, by direct expression, that use of a language other than French or English might be authorized by the Court even when requested by one party only. It was pointed out at the time that this was the Court's practice, in any event, under the original Statute.[42]

When the Statute of the International Court of Justice was drafted, the provision for use, in proceedings before that tribunal, of a language other than French or English was brought over from the revised Statute of the Permanent Court of International Justice, but permission for use of such other language was no longer left to the discretion of the Court. As a matter of fact, at the suggestion of the Soviet Union, the right to employ, in proceedings before the International Court of Justice, any language requested by either party was made mandatory.[43] The

[40] M. HUDSON, TRIBUNALS at 41.   [41] P.C.I.J. STAT. art. 39.

[42] *See* Draft Protocol and Amendments to the Statute of the Permanent Court of International Justice submitted by the 1929 Conference of Signatories, in First Comm., Report, Records of the Tenth Assembly, *supra* note 31, at 433, 440. *See also* M. HUDSON, P.C.I.J. at 197.

[43] U.N. Comm. of Jurists, Summary of Seventh Meeting, Doc. Jurist 40, G/30, 14 U.N.C.I.O. Docs. 162, at 171 (1945). The Soviet proposal passed unanimously. It was but one part of a concerted effort on the part of the Soviets to enhance the formal standing of the Russian language in diplomatic usage. R. RUSSELL, CHARTER at 869n.14 (1958).

Statute of that Court provides that, at the request of either party, "the Court shall . . . authorize a language other than French or English," [44] although, in practice, both Courts had always granted such requests as a matter of course.

The proposed Statute of the International Court of Justice returns the language provision to its permissive concept in providing that all pleadings are to be drawn, and all proceedings before the Court are to be conducted, in either English or French as the official languages of the Court, "unless otherwise ordered by the Court at the request of any party. . . ." [45]

The recommendation, adopted by the Assembly of the League of Nations in 1929, regarding practical experience in international law as a desirable quality in a judge of the Permanent Court also contained suggestions that the nominees for the Court be able, as a minimum, both to read the official languages of the Court and to speak one of them and that the national groups, in making their nominations, attach thereto a statement of the career of each nominee, showing that he possesses the required qualifications. [46] The Secretaries-General of the United Nations, like their predecessors in the League of Nations, when inviting the national groups of the Permanent Court of Arbitration to submit nominations for judgeships on the International Court of Justice, have continued the practice of reminding them of the foregoing language qualifications and requesting that they attach a statement of the careers of the candidates justifying their candidature. In this connection, it may be of interest to note that Judge Hudson of the United States, who served as a member of the Permanent Court of International Justice from 1936 until that Court was succeeded by the International Court of Justice, and who served also as an observer at the 1945 Conference of the Committee of Jurists convened to draft a Statute for the International Court of Justice, cautioned that "a rigorous rule" as to language qualifications of candidates for membership on the Court "might restrict the selection too narrowly, and might in effect exclude the nationals of some States from eligibility." [47]

Under Article 6 of the Statute of the International Court of

[44] I.C.J. STAT. art. 39, para. 3.   [45] I.C.J. STAT. (P) art. XV, para. 4.
[46] *See* note 30 *supra*.   [47] M. HUDSON, TRIBUNALS at 42.

Justice, carried over from the same Article of the Statute of the Permanent Court of International Justice, it is "recommended" that each national group "consult its highest court of justice, its legal facilities and schools of law, and its national academies and national sections of international academies devoted to the study of law" before making its nominations for judges of the Court. This provision also is omitted from the proposed Statute of the International Court of Justice.

Why would this provision be omitted, it might be asked, if direct nominations by governments are really to be made without political considerations, from among persons of the highest caliber and possessing so many desirable technical qualifications? Consultation with such eminent bodies and their recommendations regarding likely candidates, would obviously be so helpful. When the proposal for this provision was first made in the 1920 Committee of Jurists, as Article 8 of the Root-Phillimore plan, it was opposed by M. Ricci-Busatti of Italy, who felt that the nominating bodies "would certainly consult those persons whose advice they thought would be most useful. If this . . . [proposal] were adopted they would be under a moral obligation to consult certain bodies; if they did not take the advice offered, offence might be given, and difficulties would follow." He wanted members of the nominating bodies "to be free to consult whomsoever they might wish."[48] While adopting the provision, the Committee nevertheless stated in its report that

only a moral obligation to take this advice exists, there is no legal obligation; the nomination is not rendered void if one of these bodies is not consulted; and even if they are all consulted there is no definite obligation to choose the name of the person who has received most support from them; if any State's national group of the Court of Arbitration should decide upon another name, it is quite free to do so.[49]

In the Subcommittee of the Third Committee of the First Assembly of the League of Nations, both the Italian and British

[48] 1920 PROCEEDINGS at 436. He alone voted against adoption of this Article of the Root-Phillimore plan. *Id.* at 437. When this Article returned from the drafting Committee as Article 7 of its text, M. Ricci-Busatti abstained from voting; otherwise, approval was unanimous. *Id.* at 556.

[49] Report of M. de Lapradelle, *supra* note 12, at 707.

representatives proposed to suppress this provision as being, in effect, meaningless; but a tie vote on the proposal to omit the recommendation left it standing.[50] Somewhat similar attitudes were expressed when the same provision came up for discussion in the drafting of the original Statute of the International Court of Justice. Because the recommendation for the consultations necessarily made them optional, a proposal was made by Egypt, in the course of the deliberations of the Subcommittee on Articles 3–13 of the United Nations Committee of Jurists, that instead of merely recommending national consultations with the legal bodies before nominating candidates for international judgeships, each government should be required to enact laws compelling such consultations.[51] The members of the 1945 Committee of Jurists were in agreement that the Egyptian proposal was not feasible, since "it would be dangerous to establish a requirement, such as the obligatory consultation with a certain number of domestic bodies, noncompliance with which would afford grounds for attacking the validity of an election." [52] While, in the end, the provision for consultations was carried over without change from the Statute of the Permanent Court of International Justice into the Statute of the International Court of Justice, it appeared in the report of the Committee of Jurists in two versions, as part of the alternative proposal on nominations of judges.[53]

Omission of the provision for consultations from the proposed Statute of the Court is based on the reasoning advanced in the

[50] Subcomm. of the Third Comm., Minutes, COMM. III at 340–41. *See also* Extract from the Report of the Council for Diplomatic Litigation attached to the Italian Ministry of Foreign Affairs, *id.*, Annex 2, at 496–97; British Amendments to the Draft Scheme of the Committee of Jurists, *id.*, Annex 25, at 591.

[51] U.N. Comm. of Jurists, Subcomm. on Arts. 3–13, Summary of the First Meeting, Doc. Jurist 32, G/24, 14 U.N.C.I.O. Docs. 255, at 261 (1945). This proposal was made by Dr. Helmy Bahgat Badawi of Egypt, later elected to the International Court of Justice, on which he served nineteen years.

[52] U.N. Comm. of Jurists, Report of Subcomm. on Arts. 3–13, Doc. Jurist 24, G/18, 14 U.N.C.I.O. Docs. 274, at 278 (1945). In fact, Dr. Badawi withdrew his proposal in the face of opposition to it from the other members of the Subcommittee. The proposal thus was never put to a vote. U.N. Comm. of Jurists, Subcomm. on Arts. 3–13, Summary of the First Meeting, *supra* note 51, at 261–62.

[53] U.N. Comm. of Jurists, Report on a Draft Statute of an International Court of Justice Referred to in chapter 7 of the Dumbarton Oaks Proposals, chapter 4, *supra* note 4, at 827. *See id.* at ns. 41–53.

1920 Commission of Jurists by M. Ricci-Busatti against the original proposal in that regard. All governments are aware of the qualifications required for judges of the Court, and it must be assumed that they will consult with any and all bodies, organizations, tribunals, academies, and individuals which or who may be helpful in making a choice of outstanding candidates for judgeships. Since, for the reasons heretofore expressed during discussions and debate of such provisions, it would be highly inadvisable to make such consultations compulsory and a mere statutory recommendation that governments consult various bodies obviously would be meaningless, the provision for consultations is omitted from the proposed Statute of the International Court of Justice.

CHAPTER VI

Number and Ages of Judges

In determining the number of judges to sit on an international court, two issues have been of decisive importance. First, varying systems of nomination and election of the judges will dictate different numerical compositions of the court, depending upon whether the influence of the numerous smaller nations is to be manifested in the nomination/election process or in physical representation on the bench. The second issue is the more practical one of determining the proper number of judges to compose an effective, smooth-running tribunal.

When the proposal for a court of arbitral justice came up for discussion at the 1907 Hague Conference, the first issue had such a divisive effect that no agreement could be reached regarding the composition of the court.[1] By 1919, however, the issue had been muted by the near-unanimous opinion that an international tribunal of a permanent nature should be established.[2] The numerous official and unofficial schemes for the constitution of such a court, submitted to the Paris Peace Conference, varied as to the number of judges in the full court from as few as seven, to as many as twenty-one, with most favoring fifteen. The significance of these proposals lay in the realization that the court would be of limited membership, that its members would be selected by an

---

[1] See chapter 4, supra, note 21.

[2] Judge Antonio S. de Bustamante, in giving the establishment of the Permanent Court of International Justice "the place of honor in the list of [the 1919 treaties'] unquestionable merits," postulates a rather idealistic explanation for this development: "No one was afraid of the idea by this time, and it no longer stirred up the old storms. The flight of time is not in vain; the human conscience cannot be in contact with progress and justice without responding to their influence and assimilating itself to what they require." A. DE BUSTAMANTE, THE WORLD COURT 94 (E. Read transl. 1926). The fact that the world had just gone through the most intense period of mass destruction in its history must also be taken into account, however, in appreciating the widespread support for the Court and its parent organization, the League of Nations.

electoral college of States (either the League of Nations or a separate Congress), and that the resulting issue of the representation of the smaller nations in the electoral process could be resolved.[3] Only Italy put forth the idea of a court composed of judges from each contracting State.[4]

At the meeting of the 1920 Committee of Jurists, the size of the proposed Permanent Court of International Justice finally was faced as an independent issue. Arguments on this issue, especially in the early phase of the Committee's work, was enmeshed with other issues such as challenges, chambers, and deputy judges. Opinion, however, was divided generally into two positions. One group, led by Dr. Bernard C. J. Loder of the Netherlands and Baron Descamps of Belgium, emphasized the nature of the Court as the highest judicial authority in the world. This seemed to dictate the necessity for a very limited number of judges, since it would be difficult to find many qualified candidates. Moreover, they maintained, a smaller tribunal works together better and gives each member a greater sense of responsibility.[5] On the other hand, other representatives, led by M. Francis Hagerup of Norway, M. Albert de Lapradelle of France, and Lord Phillimore of

[3] A Memorandum summarizing and analyzing these schemes and indicating the general guidelines to be followed in drawing up a Statute for the Permanent Court was prepared by the Legal Section of the Permanent Secretariat of the League of Nations and sent to each prospective member of the 1920 Advisory Committee of Jurists on April 19, 1920. *See* Letter of May 8, 1920, from A. Hammarskjöld, Secretary-General of the United Nations, to members of the Advisory Jurists' Committee, LEAGUE OF NATIONS DOCUMENTS at 17. The Memorandum itself appears in 1920 DOCUMENTS at 1; the summary of proposals relating to the composition of the Court in *id.* at 79–87. Denmark and Norway (with one dissenting delegate) proposed a Court of twenty-one judges; the Netherlands one of seven judges; two nonofficial schemes proposed eighteen and twelve judges; and all the others settled on fifteen as the ideal number. *Id.* at 83.

[4] *See* Extract from the Project for the Establishment of the League of Nations submitted to the Preliminary Peace Conference by the Government of Italy, 1920 DOCUMENTS at 121. According to the proposal, each contracting State would appoint a judge to the Court for a six-year term. A panel would be formed from the members of the Court to hear each case. *See also id.* at 55.

[5] Dr. Loder proposed a Court of nine judges, with no right of challenge. 1920 PROCEEDINGS at 169. Baron Descamps originally proposed a Court of nine judges and six deputy judges, to be chosen from a panel of eligible judges. *Id.* at 28. While he later abandoned the idea of the panel, he continued to support nine as the ideal number of judges. *Id.* at 171. *See also id.* at 172–73.

Great Britain, pointed out that the Court must be large enough
to represent the different legal systems (as well as several nations
which would demand representation) and to allow for the inevitable illnesses and absences, and for an indispensible right of
challenge.[6]

At the same time, it was recognized that "in recommending the
number of judges for this Court, not only actual conditions prevailing at that time, but also those conditions which will prevail
in the future, should be taken into consideration. . . ."[7]

The proposal which finally emerged as Article 2 of the Root-
Phillimore plan called for eleven judges and four "supplementary" judges. Article 17 of the plan allowed for future increases
in the membership of the Court of up to fifteen judges and six
supplementary judges.[8] This proposal was adopted by the Committee by a show of hands on July 8, 1920,[9] and, after two un-

[6] M. Hagerup supported a Court of at least fifteen judges (*id.* at 170) ; M. de
Lapradelle, at least eleven (*id.* at 171–72: he later supported fifteen, *id.* at 200) ;
and Lord Phillimore, fifteen, but with more emphasis on the need for the Court
to sit *in pleno* at all times. *Id.* at 138, 169, 175. M. Mineichiro Adatci of Japan at
first supported a Court of thirteen members, with a fixed division of the judges
between the Great Powers and the other members of the League of Nations. *Id.* at
29. He later reconsidered his position and lowered this number to nine judges in
all. *Id.* at 169.

The one truly different proposal was that of M. Arturo Ricci-Busatti of Italy.
He envisioned a permanent tribunal modeled after the Permanent Court of Arbitration, with fifteen to twenty judges from which the parties would choose a
smaller tribunal of undetermined size to hear their case. *Id.* at 177. He later raised
this number to twenty-five, but this was done just before the Committee voted
down his proposal. *Id.* at 441.

[7] *Id.* at 181 (statement of Mr. Root of the United States.)

[8] In explaining the number of judges in the plan, Lord Phillimore said:

The intention . . . was that the Court should be finally composed of fifteen
judges, but the increase up to this number was to be gradual, keeping pace with
the extention of the Court's jurisdiction. As the number of 9 had been proposed
as a quorum, at least eleven judges must be appointed in order to provide for
cases of illness and other causes of absence. Eleven was the minimum number
which would ensure a genuinely representative Court.

Id. at 441. For text of the proposal, see *id.* at 298, 301.

[9] *Id.* at 442. This vote involved only Article 2 of the plan. When Article 17
came up for approval on July 12, Baron Descamps pointed out that both articles
of the Root-Phillimore plan were embodied in Article 3 of a plan he had submitted
subsequent to the Root-Phillimore plan (text at *id.* at 373) . The Committee then
adopted Article 3 of the Descamps plan, and this is what really became Article 3
of the Statute of the Permanent Court.

successful attempts to alter its terms in the League of Nations Assembly,[10] became Article 3 of the Statute of the Permanent Court of International Justice. When that Statute came up later for reconsideration, the 1929 Committee of Jurists recommended elimination of that part of Article 3 under which the Assembly of the League was authorized to increase the number of judges, "to avoid the risk of an exaggeration which might cause misconception." [11]

The concept of having deputy judges on a world court apparently originated in the Hague *project* of 1907.[12] In the discussions which took place on this subject in the 1920 Committee of Jurists, Baron Descamps suggested that, in addition to nine regular judges, there should be six *suppléants,* necessary, in his opinion, to fill such vacancies as might occur.[13] M. de Lapradelle of France agreed with Baron Descamps that there should be deputy judges available to fill vacancies. He also felt that they would help accomplish the important political purpose of satisfying countries none of whose nationals was a judge.[14] M. de Lapradelle's concurrence in Baron Descamps's recommendation was based further on his conviction that, "[i]n order to imbue future judges with the spirit which must pervade the Court there must be young judges who can from time to time do duty on the Court and keep in constant touch with it." [15] The distinction between judges and

[10] At the second meeting of the Sub-Committee of the Third Committee of the First League Assembly, held on November 25th, 1920, an informal suggestion by Sir Cecil Hurst of Great Britain that the number of judges should be reduced to nine, with seven required for a quorum, received so little support from the other delegates that he did not even bother to propose it as an amendment. LEAGUE OF NATIONS DOCUMENTS at 117. An Italian amendment which would have removed any limitation on the future number of judges, *id.* at twenty-eight, was then voted down by the Sub-Committee by an 8–2 vote. *Id.* at 118.

[11] 1929 PROCEEDINGS at 119.

[12] *See* Draft Convention Relative to the Creation of a Judicial Arbitration Court art. 2, in HAGUE CONVENTIONS at 31–32.

[13] 1920 PROCEEDINGS at 143, 195, 465.

[14] *Id.* at 200–201, 457. M. de Lapradelle supported a system of "assessors" to represent States which did not have representation on the Court. If one party had a judge and the other a deputy judge, or if both had deputy judges, the deputy judges would represent their respective nations *and* do so as full judges, rather than as assessors without a vote.

[15] *Id.* at 400–401.

deputy judges did not come up for debate again until an Italian proposal to eliminate the distinction [16] was easily defeated in the Subcommittee of the Third Committee of the First League Assembly.[17]

At the meetings of the 1929 Committee of Jurists, however, the fear was expressed quite forcefully that judges might feel justified in absenting themselves from sessions of the Court if deputy judges were available to replace them. The Committee recommended unanimously that the provision for deputy judges be abandoned, since "practical experience" had demonstrated the inadvisability of such a system.[18] Article 3 of the revised Statute of the Permanent Court of International Justice, as amended by the 1929 Committee of Jurists, accordingly provided simply that "the Court shall consist of fifteen members."

In the closing days of the Second World War, the UN Committee of Jurists met in Washington to draft a Statute for the new International Court of Justice. Again, the matter of size of the Court was tied in with the question as to method of nomination and election of judges. Great Britain, for instance, suggested that a new method of nomination of judges be combined with significant revisions in size and composition of the new Court. Briefly, each State which was a party to the Statute of the Court would designate one of its own nationals to become, *ipso facto*, a "Member of the Court." [19] "Members of the Court" were then to be elected as "Judges of the Court" by the same method of election for judges of the Permanent Court of International Justice.

[16] The Italian proposal maintains that the distinction between judges and deputy judges ". . . has no sufficient justification in a fundamental difference in mandate and duties and would thus almost certainly give rise to difficulties and embarrassments, which should be avoided as far as possible. If occasion arises, the Court itself can designate in its rules of procedure, and by rotation or otherwise, deputy-judges amongst its own members." LEAGUE OF NATIONS DOCUMENTS at 28. The British put forth a similar proposal. *Id*. at 70.

[17] *Id*. at 117. Sir Cecil Hurst of Great Britain endeavored to explain the rationale behind the concept of deputy judges to M. Ricci-Busatti of Italy, then turned about and supported the Italian proposal "under instructions from his Government."

[18] 1929 PROCEEDINGS at 28, 119.

[19] Note that nomination by governments was to replace nomination by national groups of the Permanent Court of Arbitration. *See* chapter 4, *supra*, text and notes 39–44.

The members of the Court not elected as judges were to hold themselves available, throughout their terms, as additional or supplementary judges, or as judges *ad hoc* in cases in which their countries were parties.[20] The Subcommittee on Articles 3–13 rejected this proposal because it was felt that persons of such outstanding distinction as to be worthy of membership on the Court would be unwilling to serve in a "supplementary" status, subject to call.[21]

In justification of that part of their plan under which the membership of the Court would be reduced to nine judges, the British representatives submitted that fifteen judges (seventeen, if two *ad hoc* judges had to be added for a particular case) was too large a number; that the quality of opinions of a large court tends to be low; and that a large court will produce too many separate concurring and dissenting opinions.[22] France and the Soviet Union were inclined to agree with Great Britain, but to lay greater stress on the ground that it would be easier to find nine men of outstanding eminence in the field of international law than fifteen.[23] On the other hand, many governments expressed the view that the proposed Court should be as large if not larger than the Permanent Court of International Justice. These countries felt that a larger Court, composed of nationals of a greater number of States, would have greater prestige and that its decisions would accordingly carry greater worldwide weight.[24] They also felt that only in a larger Court would it be possible to achieve the goal of representation of the principal legal systems of the world.[25] These smaller nations also called attention to the undisputed fact that

[20] United Kingdom Proposals Regarding the Statute of the Permanent Court of International Justice, Doc. Jurist 14, DP/4, 14 U.N.C.I.O. Docs. 314 (1945).

[21] Report of Subcomm. on Articles 3 to 13, Doc. Jurist 24, G/18, *id.* at 274, 276.

[22] Subcomm. on Arts. 3–13, Summary of First Meeting, Doc. Jurist 32, G/24, *id.* at 255–56 (remarks of Mr. Fitzmaurice). The Informal Inter-Allied Committee on the future of the Permanent Court of International Justice, meeting in London in 1944, also recommended a nine-man Court. *See* Official Comments Relating to the Statute of the Proposed International Court of Justice, Doc. Jurist 1, G-1, *id.* at 386, 398.

[23] *Id.* at 263–64 (remarks of Prof. Golunsky and Prof. Basdevant).

[24] U.N. Comm. of Jurists, Summary of Ninth Meeting, Doc. Jurist 57, G/45, *id.* at 189, 196 (remarks of Hafez Radaman Pacha of Egypt).

[25] *Id.* at 197 (remarks of Prof. Bilsel of Turkey).

the reason for increasing the original number of judges of the Permanent Court of International Justice from eleven to fifteen was that practical experience had proved the smaller number to be inadequate.[26] Finally, and quite frankly, these smaller countries were motivated to maintain the Court at not less than fifteen judges because the chances were much better that they would be able to effect election of one of their own nationals to such a larger tribunal.[27] In any event, following all of this discussion, the UN Committee of Jurists recommended—and their recommendation was followed in due course—that the International Court of Justice be composed, as had been its predecessor since 1936, of fifteen judges.[28]

In the eighteen years of the effective existence of the Permanent Court of International Justice, 65 new cases were filed before that Court, with 27 advisory opinions and 32 judgments being rendered.[29] The case load of the International Court of Justice has been even lighter. Up until July 31, 1974, there had been brought before the Court an aggregate of 59 cases. During the same period, the Court returned 36 judgments and 15 advisory opinions.[30] In 45 years of work, therefore, the two Courts have had for consideration 124 matters of all kinds and have entered 110 judgments and advisory opinions (an average of 2.5 per year). Frankly, it seems to be the opinion of all concerned that the

[26] *Id.* (remarks of Prof. Spiropoulos of Greece).

[27] *Id.* at 196; Subcomm. on Arts. 3–13, Summary of First Meeting, *supra* note 22, at 263 (remarks of Ambassador Roberto Cordova of Mexico).

[28] In the Subcommittee on Articles 3 to 13, the vote to keep the number of judges at fifteen, rather than reducing the number, was favorable by only a 5–4 margin. Subcomm. on Arts. 3–13, Summary of First Meeting, *supra* note 22, at 267. While no official tally was recorded, it appears from the debate that voting in favor were Canada, China, Norway, Egypt, and Mexico, with Great Britain, the Netherlands, the U.S.S.R., and France opposed. When the recommendation to retain fifteen judges for the Court came up before the full Committee of Jurists, it provoked some additional debate and remarks (*see* notes 24–27 *supra*), but was approved by a vote of 28–4. U.N. Comm. of Jurists, Summary of Ninth Meeting, *supra* note 24, at 198. The issue of the number of judges of the International Court of Justice was not reopened for debate at the May 1945 U.N. Conference on International Organizations held in San Francisco. *See* Summary Report of the Second Meeting of Committee IV/1, Doc. 146, IV/5, 13 U.N.C.I.O. Docs. 142, at 143–44 (1945).

[29] M. HUDSON, P.C.I.J. at 779.   [30] [1973–1974] I.C.J.Y.B. 5.

judges had not been overworked—and this is a considerable understatement of some of the views which have been expressed.

The Supreme Court of the United States, by comparison, is composed of only nine justices. During its 1969–70 term, for example, it considered 4112 cases, disposing of 84 of them by formal opinion and judgment, 265 by *per curiam* opinions, and the rest by summary order (albeit these were mostly discretionary denials of certiorari). It has been suggested, and is apparently the consensus, that as the case load of a tribunal increases, its method of approach is adjusted to meet its changed problems. Oral arguments are required to be shortened, briefs are obliged to live up to their name, the administrative staff is increased and strengthened, and so on. The bench of the Supreme Court has not been enlarged in over a hundred years, although the numerical work load of that Court has multiplied many times during that period: plans are just now being formulated seriously to relieve that Court of a considerable part of its work load.

Once the International Court of Justice is vested with real compulsory jurisdiction over all nations, its work load probably would not in fact increase appreciably. Most controversies among States would unquestionably be settled diplomatically to avoid the chance of unfavorable adjudication. But, in the final analysis, even if its case load should increase materially, it is felt that the Court as presently constituted should have no difficulty whatever in taking care of it.

If, however, it was found that the work of the Court should actually increase too much as a result of its new compulsory jurisdiction, the proposed Statute retains the solution of the present Statute, and improves upon it. With its new provisions as to chambers, especially that allowing an appeal to the full Court from the decision of a chamber,[31] the chambers will undoubtedly come into use—perhaps extensively—if the work load of the Court should increase materially.

The Statute of the Permanent Court of International Justice did not, nor does the Statute of the International Court of Justice, fix any age limits—either minimum or maximum—for members

[31] I.C.J. Stat. (P) art. XVI, para. 4.

of those Courts. The proposed Statute of the International Court of Justice, on the other hand, fixes the minimum age of its judges at the time of their election at fifty, and the maximum at sixty-five.[32]

In a temporary international tribunal, which is to settle a single specific controversy, the age of its members is of little significance, since they are chosen to serve only for a limited time, at the conclusion of which their services are automatically terminated. In the case of a permanent international court, on the other hand, judges must be available for the trial of any and all international disputes, whatever their time of origin, extent, or duration. In the latter case, the judges should be old enough to have the seasoning of maturity necessary to give proper perspective toward the varied, complex, and delicate problems likely to be presented to such a tribunal and, at the same time, sufficiently young to assure adequate physical and mental vigor for an extended term prior to compulsory retirement.

It is usual to fix a minimum age for judges of national tribunals. This is to give assurance that only persons of adequate maturity are elected to the judiciary, in whose character, after all, that quality must inevitably play so important a part. In the Statutes of the two Courts, it was thought that there was no need for a minimum age limit, since younger men would hardly have had either the necessary experience or reputation to warrant their selection as judges. The only provision in that regard to find its way into the Statutes of the Courts was that which brought forward the relevant provisions of national laws, in the requirement that members of the Courts must "possess the qualifications required in their respective countries for appointment to the highest judicial offices." [33]

Of the thirty-one judges who served as members of the Permanent Court of International Justice, only one was under forty-five and only four were under fifty at the time of their election.[34] The two youngest judges ever to be elected to the International Court of Justice were José María Ruda of Argentina and Charles

---

[32] *Id.* art. II, para. 2.   [33] P.C.I.J. Stat. art. 2; I.C.J. Stat. art. 2.
[34] M. Hudson, Tribunals at 43.

D. Onyeama of Nigeria, not yet fifty at the time they took office. Feodor Ivanovich Kojevnikov of the Soviet Union was just past fifty when elected. All others were older, with an average age of nearly sixty. While opinions differ widely on this point, it has seemed advisable that a minimum age limit should be provided for members of the Court, and that fifty is as close as it is possible to come to a minimum age at which the desired maturity of judgment for the consideration of diverse international problems is likely to be assured.

While maximum age limits for judges of national courts ordinarily are not established, such a qualification may have a significant place in eligibility requirements for members of a permanent international tribunal. Because of the normal desire to select men of great eminence as members of such courts, there has been a tendency to choose men well advanced in years—men whom time has crowned with worldwide renown in the field of international law. This has even occurred in the case of temporary international commissions, whose work ordinarily should be accomplished in a relatively short period. Because, for instance, judges too advanced in age even for such a task were selected as members of the American-German Mixed Claims Commission, created in 1922 under the Treaty of Versailles to settle claims arising out of the First World War, the Commission had to use four umpires over a period of ten years before it completed its task.[35]

As early as 1918, in one of the first drafts of the Covenant of the League of Nations, Col. E. M. House, a delegate of the United States to the Commission on the League of Nations, proposed that judges of the contemplated "International Court" be required to retire at age seventy-two.[36] The advisability of a maximum age limit for judges at the time of their election to the Permanent Court of International Justice was discussed at the Conference of Signatories of 1929, when revisions of the Statute of that Court

[35] *Id.*

[36] Draft Proposal of July 16, 1918, of a Covenant of a League of Nations, submitted by Col. E. M. House to Woodrow Wilson, President of the United States, in 4 C. SEYMOUR, THE INTIMATE PAPERS OF COLONEL HOUSE 28, at 31 (1928).

were being adopted.[37] During the drafting of the Statute of the International Court of Justice by the United Nations Committee of Jurists meeting in Washington, the United States proposed that judges be no older than seventy-two when elected, and compelled to retire at age seventy-five.[38] This suggestion was not adopted because it was felt that the bodies charged with electing the members of the Court could be trusted not to select persons who might become decrepit during their incumbencies.[39]

A maximum age limit of sixty-five at the time of election for judges of the International Court of Justice is fixed in the proposed Statute of the Court, primarily on the basis of the past failure of judges elected when beyond this age to survive the normal term of office. Another important consideration in the fixing of a maximum age limit for judges of the Court under the proposed Statute lies in the companion provisions for voluntary and compulsory retirement. Under the former pension system of the Permanent Court of International Justice, as transplanted into the International Court of Justice, retirement pensions are payable for life to judges who have served at least five years, and who retire after reaching age sixty-five.[40] Under the proposed Statute of the Court, judges may retire voluntarily at any time after reaching age seventy, and must retire on reaching age seventy-five.[41] Any judge who has served ten years or more at retirement is to receive full pay for life, and if he has served less than ten years, he receives for life that proportion of his full pay which his number of years of service on the tribunal bears to ten.[42] Thus, if a judge is sixty or under at the time of his election to the Court,

[37] 1929 PROCEEDINGS (SIGNATORIES) at 32–33.

[38] The Statute of the Permanent Court of International Justice With Revisions Proposed by the United States, Doc. Jurist 5, G/5, 14 U.N.C.I.O. Docs. 323, 330 (1945).

[39] U.N. Comm. of Jurists, Summary of the Third Meeting (revised), Doc. Jurist 38 (19), G/28 *id.* 92, at 95–96. The vote on the age limit proposal was ten in favor, twenty against.

[40] The size of the pension will depend upon whether he has served a full nine-year term in office. There is also a pension provision for judges who retire before the age of sixty-five. *See* [1973–1974] I.C.J.Y.B. 166.

[41] I.C.J. STAT. (P) art. VI, paras. 2–3.   [42] *Id.* art. VII, para. 7.

he may retire with full pay for life at any time after his seventieth birthday. Similarly, if he is sixty-five or younger when elected, he will receive full pay for life when required to retire at age seventy-five. If, on the other hand, a judge is sixty-five at the time of his election, he would, for example, receive a life pension of only half his pay if he retired voluntarily at age seventy, or full pay for life when subject to compulsory retirement at age seventy-five. Thus, it is felt that in order to provide a reasonable age for compulsory retirement (seventy-five) and still make it possible for each judge to qualify for a full pension (by serving ten years), sixty-five is the best maximum age for candidates for election to the International Court of Justice.

CHAPTER VII

Disabilities of Judges

The Second Hague Conference took place in 1907. The United States had continued to hold to her ideal of a truly permanent international court, and Elihu Root, then Secretary of State, instructed the delegates to the 1907 Conference, to endeavor to bring into being, "[a] permanent tribunal composed of judges who are judicial officers and nothing else, who are paid adequate salaries, who have no other occupation, and who will devote their entire time to the trial and decision of international causes by judicial methods and under a sense of judicial responsibility. . . ."[1] At that Conference, a general plan for a new Permanent Court of Arbitral Justice was worked out, but the delegates were unable to agree on a method of selecting judges, as between the small nations and the great powers. Nevertheless, the United States delegation reported that "the foundations of a permanent court have been broadly and firmly laid. . . ."[2]

When the Peace Conference was held in Paris in 1919, at the close of the First World War, there was no longer any question that some sort of an international tribunal would be established. But other problems of peace and reconstruction were transcendental, and that Conference got no further than to provide, by Article 14 of the Covenant of the League of Nations, that its "Council shall formulate and submit to the Members of the League for adoption plans for the establishment of a Permanent Court of International Justice."

In February 1920, the Council of the League requested a group of prominent jurists, which came to be known as the "1920 Committee of Jurists," among whom was Elihu Root of the United

---

[1] See chapter 4, *supra*, at note 23.

[2] Report of the American Delegation to the Hague Conference of 1907, [1907] FOREIGN REL. U.S. 1144, at 1178. See Chapter 4, *supra*, at note 25.

States, to prepare a plan for the contemplated court. This Commission of Jurists met at the Hague, and, working assiduously and availing itself of the bases for such a tribunal evolved at the Second Peace Conference in the same city in 1907, developed a concrete *projet* which it submitted to the Council on August 5, 1920. The overwhelming consideration which motivated the 1920 Committee of Jurists found expression in the text of the second Article of their draft Statute, which provided that "[t]he Permanent Court of International Justice shall be composed of a body of independent judges." [3]

In a gesture toward at least the appearance of independence of the proposed Court, after its judges should have surmounted the political barriers leading to their election, the 1920 Committee of Jurists established criteria of disqualifications, disabilities, and incompatibilities of judges *quoad* their participation in the adjudication of any particular case. The disqualification was provided by a stipulation in Article 17 that "[n]o member may participate in the decision of any case in which he has previously taken an active part, as agent, counsel or advocate for one of the contesting parties, or as a member of a national or international court, or of a Commission of Inquiry, or in any other capacity." Any doubt as to such disqualification was to be settled by the Court.[4] Article 24 of the draft Statute prepared by the 1920 Committee of Jurists contained further disqualifications in a provision to the effect that if a member of the Court should feel that, for some special reason, he should not participate in the decision of a particular case, he should so advise the President; if the President considers that one of the members of the Court should not sit on a particular case, he should give notice of this to the member concerned. In either case, if the judge and the President of the Court

[3] Text of Scheme for the Establishment of the Permanent Court of International Justice, 1920 PROCEEDINGS at 673.

[4] *Id.* at 676. This text was taken almost verbatim from the first paragraph of Article 7 of the Hague *projet*. HAGUE CONVENTIONS at 33. Baron Descamps of Belgium wanted to go even further, to disqualify a judge if he or a member of his family or any relative up to and including the third degree had any interest whatever in the case. Draft Scheme concerning the Permanent Court of International Justice, submitted by Baron Descamps, 1920 PROCEEDINGS at 373, 376.

should not agree, the disagreement should be referred to the Court for decision.[5]

The question did arise, from time to time, in the Permanent Court of International Justice as to whether a judge of that Court might properly serve on an international commission of conciliation. In 1926, it was determined, in connection with the proposed appointment of a judge of the Court as a member of a conciliation commission under one of the Locarno treaties, that such service would not be proper because the treaty conferred jurisdiction on the Court in the event of failure of the commission to reach a settlement.[6] In 1930, the Court reaffirmed this position,[7] but in 1931 and later, it seemed to find no impropriety in service by one of its judges on such a body.[8] However, in 1936, the President of the Court declined to serve as president of a commission of conciliation because of the possibility of subsequent reference to the Court of matters to come before the commission.[9]

As to disabilities, the 1920 Committee of Jurists, taking their test from a provision of the Hague Convention of 1907 for the Pacific Settlement of International Disputes, stipulated in Article 17 of the Draft Scheme that "[n]o member of the Court can act as agent, counsel or advocate in any case of an international nature."[10] This prohibition, however, did not preclude judges of the Permanent Court of International Justice from practicing law in the courts of their own countries, which some of them did quite actively; but when the Statute of the Court was revised in 1929, the last four words of this provision were deleted, so that the revised provision insured the independence, *pro tanto,* of the judges by prohibiting them from acting "as agent, counsel or advocate in any case" whatever.[11]

As stated, the 1920 Committee of Jurists established, in addition to disqualifications and disabilities, certain "incompatibilities," which they felt might impair the judicial independence of members of the Permanent Court of International Justice. Mr.

[5] 1920 PROCEEDINGS at 677.

[6] 3 P.C.I.J. ANN. R. (ser. E) 177–78 (1927) .   [7] 6 *id.* at 282 (1930) .

[8] 7 *id.* at 276–77 (1931) . *See also* 1929 PROCEEDINGS at 120.

[9] 14 P.C.I.J. ANN. R. (ser. E) 127 (1938) .   [10] 1920 PROCEEDINGS at 676.

[11] *See* First Comm., Report, *in* Records of the Tenth Assembly, Text of the Debates, Annex 4, LEAGUE OF NATIONS OFF. J., Spec. Supp. 75, at 433, 438 (1929) .

Elihu Root insisted from the start on a stipulation which would prevent a judgeship "from being considered as an incident in a political career," [12] although Lord Phillimore considered that "it was . . . an advantage for an international judge to belong at the same time to the Bench of his own country," and that the judicial functions of the House of Lords were not of a political nature.[13] After considerable discussion, the Committee proposed the following text: "The exercise of any function which belongs to the political direction, national or international, of States, by the Members of the Court, during their terms of office, is declared incompatible with their judicial duties." [14] The report of the Committee, accompanying this text, nevertheless seemed to recognize that, in order to secure the services of persons of the highest standing as judges of the Permanent Court, it might be necessary to concede that "[a] great judge or a great professor . . . must be allowed to continue" to serve as such in his own country, even after his election to the Court.[15] The Committee was by no means unanimous on what the consequences of a judge's engaging in an incompatible activity should be, but at one point it was actually suggested that such conduct ought to be considered as resignation from the Court.[16] In a Subcommittee of the Third Committee of the First Assembly of the League of Nations, M. Fromageot of France expressed himself as favoring a rule requiring "the judge" to "disengage [himself] from his previous occupations," [17] while M. Huber of Switzerland felt that this was going too far, since the Court would, in any event, have "little to do." [18] In the end, the text proposed by the 1920 Committee of Jurists was rejected, and the Statute of the Court was phrased to provide simply that the "Members of the Court may not exercise any political or administrative function." [19]

When this provision was brought up for consideration by the 1929 Committee of Jurists, M. Fromageot again suggested that the judges should "devote themselves exclusively to this high function," and should not "exercise any other functions"; [20] but a

[12] 1920 PROCEEDINGS at 462.   [13] *Id.* at 191.
[14] Draft Scheme, *supra* note 3, at 676.
[15] Report of M. de Lapradelle, 1920 PROCEEDINGS at 693, 715.   [16] *Id.* at 193, 573.
[17] COMM. III at 351.   [18] *Id.* at 350.
[19] Third Comm., Report, COMM. III at 573, 575.   [20] 1929 PROCEEDINGS at 42.

number of the members of that Committee felt that this was a matter which, in the final analysis, should be left to "the conscience of the individual judges," and the text was extended to provide simply that, in addition to the incompatibility previously specified, the judges were not to "engage in any other occupation of a professional nature, any doubt on the point to be settled by the Court." [21] The 1929 Conference of Signatories expressly stated its intention that this provision should be "interpreted in its widest sense." [22] While the Court has never defined the term "occupation of a professional nature," Judge Negulesco, on one occasion, said that it referred to "a remunerative occupation which provided the person concerned with a livelihood and in which he was continually engaged." [23]

Judge Manley O. Hudson, erstwhile professor of international law at Harvard University and a judge of the Permanent Court of International Justice from 1936 to 1942, gave a particularly apt summary, in his book on the Court, of the background and effect of this provision as to incompatibility of its judges:

> Even when a member of the Court is not strictly under a disability, it has been recognized that he should refrain from certain activities on the ground that they are incompatible with his duties as a judge of the Court. Incompatibilities are not to be so rigidly defined as disabilities and disqualifications. . . . In general, any activity which might even in remote possibility affect a judge's independence or impartiality, or might even be thought to do so, should be avoided as incompatible.[24]

The Permanent Court of International Justice had rather frequent occasion to consider questions of incompatibility. It found none in the acceptance by a judge of membership on a Mixed Arbitral Tribunal appointed under the Peace Treaties of 1919–20, nor in membership of a judge on an international commission on rules of warfare, nor even as a member of the Spanish Senate.[25] However, the Court did hold that one of its judges

21 *Id.* at 44.   22 1929 PROCEEDINGS (SIGNATORIES) at 33, 78.
23 P.C.I.J., ser. D, No. 2 (3rd add.), at 717.   24 M. HUDSON, P.C.I.J. at 372.
25 Minutes of Meetings Held during the Preliminary Session of the Court (Jan. 30–March 24, 1922), P.C.I.J., ser. D, No. 2, at 10–12 (1922) [hereinafter cited as 1922 Prelim. Sess.]; 3 P.C.I.J. ANN. R. (ser. E) 177 (1927).

should not represent his own government at a session of the International Labor Conference, and even went so far as to rule that a member of the Court should not make "an official pronouncement at a banquet regarding his government's international policy," because "any function which compelled a person to follow the instructions of his government, regardless of his personal views, was 'political.' " [26]

This latter concept, applied to the inevitable influence of a judge's nationality on his own perspective as a member of an international tribunal, gave rise to a paradox woven into the birth of the Permanent Court of International Justice and into the more than fifty years of the combined lives of that tribunal and of the International Court of Justice which succeeded it. On the one hand, as stated by M. de Lapradelle of France in the course of discussions as to whether judges who are nationals of parties to causes before the Court should be permitted to participate in the hearings thereof, "a national judge would always record his disapproval of a sentence unfavorable to his country." [27] On the other hand, the 1920 Committee of Jurists justified its recommendation for adoption of Article 28 of the proposed Statute of the Permanent Court of International Justice, providing that "[j]udges of the nationality of each contesting party shall retain their right to sit in the case before the Court," by the statement that . . . "States attach much importance to having one of their subjects on the Bench when they appear before a Court of Justice." [28] Judge Hudson suggested that "[t]his text, the substance of which was drafted by the 1920 Committee of Jurists . . . represents one of its principal achievements, for the scheme for electing the judges would probably never have been adopted without it." [29]

Despite, therefore, the constantly reiterated recognition of the principle expressed in Article 2 of the Statute of the Court, that it "shall be composed of a body of independent judges," and in order, as a practical matter, to effect consent of the States to the formation of a permanent international tribunal, the principle was sacrificed to expediency, and judges were permitted to par-

[26] 7 *id.* at 278.   [27] Report of M. de Lapradelle, *id.* at 693, 722.
[28] 1920 PROCEEDINGS at 531.   [29] M. HUDSON, P.C.I.J. at 181.

ticipate in determination of cases to which their own countries
were parties. This problem had been discussed extensively by the
1920 Committee of Jurists. The accepted rule has been that no
one should be permitted to act as a judge of his own cause,[30] but
the proponents of the principle were not successful in having it
embodied in the draft scheme of the 1920 Committee of Jurists.
Various suggestions were made during the discussions of this
question among the members of the 1920 Committee of Jurists.
M. Adatci of Japan, who had already expressed his conviction
that judges of the Court should "internationalize themselves," [31]
nevertheless now supported participation of judges in cases to
which their countries were parties, as a necessary factor to adequate consideration of such a case by the Court.[32] Mr. Elihu Root
concurred in this view, on the ground that "[n]ations should be
able to go before the Court with the certainty that their case will
be fully understood." [33] Despite recurring suggestions that national judges should be excluded from all cases in which their
countries were litigants, the Statute was drawn to permit such
participation, to avoid ruffling national susceptibilities.[34]

In point of fact, as stated by Professor (later Judge Sir Hersch)
Lauterpacht, "[t]he border-line between explaining the legal
views and defending the interests of the State concerned is in
such cases so shadowy as to become utterly unreal." [35] So then,
in order to "re-establish equality," provision was made in the
Statute for "national judges"; that is, whenever there was a national of only one of the parties on the bench, the other party
was permitted to appoint its own judge to sit with the Court, as
both parties were permitted to do when there was no national of
either on the bench.[36] This provision gave rise to something of an
anomaly, as suggested at the time by Mr. Ricci-Busatti of Italy, in
that the authority of the regular judge would stem from his pre-

[30] *See* Advisory Opinion on Article 3, Paragraph 2, of the Treaty of Lausanne,
[1925] P.C.I.J., ser. B, No. 12, at 32.

[31] *See* chapter 1, *supra*, text at note 10.   [32] 1920 PROCEEDINGS at 29, 168, 529.

[33] *Id.* at 532. *See also id.* at 538.

[34] *Id.* at 539, 565.   [35] H. LAUTERPACHT, FUNCTION at 232.

[36] P.C.I.J. STAT. art. 31. For application of this provision, see Advisory Opinion
on the Interpretation of the Greco-Turkish Agreement of Dec. 1, 1926, [1928]
P.C.I.J., ser. B, No. 16, at 8.

sumably nonpartisan international election, whereas the source of the authority of the national judge would be his partisan appointment by a party to the cause.[37] In the end, as stated, late in the course of the exhaustive deliberations of the Committee of Jurists, expediency prevailed over the principle of judicial independence, through compromise of the right of judges to sit in cases involving their own countries for the right of countries which had no national on the bench to appoint a judge *ad hoc* to the Court. On the other hand, the Committee conceded, in its report submitting its *projet,* that it would be "logical" that judges should never participate in cases in which their own countries are parties-litigant.[38]

This *projet* of 1920 was debated, and was revised in various respects, by the Council and the Assembly, and, by Resolution of the First Assembly of the League of Nations on December 13, 1920, "the Assembly unanimously declares its approval of the draft Statute of the Permanent Court of International Justice—as amended by the Assembly."[39] On December 16, 1920, a Protocol was opened for signature by the Members of the League, to declare their acceptance of the Statute and of the jurisdiction of the Court, pursuant to the terms and conditions of the Statute.[40] This Protocol provided that its ratification by the majority of the members of the League was to make the Statute effective; and such ratification (by twenty-eight nations) brought the Statute into force in September 1921.[41] Under the provisions of Article 36 of the Statute, the various nations, either when signing or when ratifying the Protocol, might declare, either unconditionally or subject to stated conditions, their recognition of the compulsory jurisdiction of the Court.

While the representatives of the United States signed the Covenant of the League of Nations, and while they also signed the Protocol for acceptance of the Statute of the Permanent Court of International Justice as well as revisions of the Statute proposed in 1929 and adopted as effective in 1936, the Senate never gave its advice and consent to ratification of any of those treaties. The United States accordingly never became a member of the

[37] 1920 PROCEEDINGS at 532.   [38] Report of M. de Lapradelle, *id.* at 721.
[39] COMM. III at 408, 617.   [40] *Id.* at 408, 627.   [41] 6 L.N.T.S. 379.

League of Nations, and, although the membership of the Permanent Court of International Justice, throughout its active life from 1922 to 1942, always included one judge from the United States, this country never became subject to the jurisdiction of that Court—conditionally or otherwise.

While the life of the Permanent Court was primarily significant in demonstrating the practical feasibility of such an international tribunal, its record of opinions during the twenty years of its functioning was not impressive. Out of sixty-five contentious cases and twenty-seven requests for advisory opinions, the court rendered a total of only thirty-two judgments in twenty years.[42] There was, however, no real fault to be found with the caliber of its judges nor with the quality, or even the result, of its opinions and decisions. But the only cases brought before the court were such as the parties in effect agreed to submit to it for adjudication. The real difficulty arose from the want of compulsory jurisdiction, under which nations might have been compelled to settle their justiciable disputes; and this want of compulsory jurisdiction, in turn, was imputable primarily to the inescapable conviction that national judges could not really be independent of their governments, which more often than not were parties to regional and ideological alignments. Instead, therefore, such disputes became the subjects of negotiation and compromise or piled up undecided, and eventually played a direct or indirect part in leading to the Second World War.

This question of compulsory jurisdiction raised by far the most important issue in 1944 and 1945 in the formulation of the new International Court of Justice as the principal judicial organ of the United Nations. In the spring of 1944, a Committee of Jurists convened at Washington to prepare a draft of a new statute for an international court. This Committee reported that "in spite of predominant sentiment" apparently opposed to any form of optional jurisdiction, it seemed unlikely that "all the nations whose participation in the proposed International Organization appears to be necessary were not in a position to accept the rule of compulsory jurisdiction."[43] The two nations whose cooperation was

---

[42] M. HUDSON, TRIBUNALS at 11.   [43] 14 U.N.C.I.O. Docs. 380 (1945).

felt by practically all concerned to be essential to the establishment of any international judicial tribunal were the United States and the Soviet Union.

The reason that the United States did not become a party to the Permanent Court of International Justice was simply that the Senate was unwilling to approve any treaty under which the sovereignty of the United States would be surrendered to an international court, with power to determine whether a dispute in which the United Nations was involved before that tribunal was in fact international, or really domestic, in character. The Soviet Union had never even signed the 1920 Protocol for establishment of the Permanent Court of International Justice. It apparently was then, and it has remained thereafter, unwilling to surrender any part of its sovereignty to any international tribunal, on any basis, for any purpose. For these reasons, it was "feared that insistence upon the realization of" the ideal of compulsory jurisdiction, "would only impair the possibility of obtaining general accord to the Statute of the Court as well as to the Charter" of the United Nations itself.[44] Similarly, it was felt that the time was inauspicious for any special effort to minimize the national allegiances of judges of the new Court, to strengthen their independence, and to encourage broader international perspectives; and it was almost universally felt that the primary interests of all concerned could best be served by departing, in the drafting of the new Statute, only to the extent absolutely necessary, from the old one.[45] And when the question again arose, in 1944 and 1945, as to the effect of nationality of judges of the proposed new International Court of Justice on their judicial independence, it was determined to avoid the danger of loss of the entire institution, by retaining the system of national and *ad hoc* judges, rather than to seek to depart, at that critical time, from what was viewed as an accepted historical precedent.[46]

In his interesting work on the International Court of Justice,

[44] 13 *id.* at 558–59.

[45] "The International Court of Justice . . . shall function in accordance with the annexed statute, which is based upon the Statute of the Permanent Court of International Justice, . . ." U.N. CHARTER art. 92.

[46] 14 U.N.C.I.O. Docs. 836 (1945) .

Shabtai Rosenne suggests that it is a mistake to "pre-suppose a strict analogy between an international court and a municipal court," since to do so "would discount the political role which the (international) Court serves"; and he asserts that, while the concept "may be extremely unpalatable from the point of view of the lawyer, it seems that the more general political factors ought to be given preference, so that recognition of the institution of national and *ad hoc* judges be accorded as a political necessity." [47] It is extremely difficult, however, to reconcile this suggestion with the author's own reiterated insistence that in the drafting of the Statute of the International Court of Justice at San Francisco in 1945, it was contemplated that "if political factors momentarily enter into play at the time of the election of the judges, once elected, the Court is granted every facility to maintain the proper degree of judicial independence." [48] In the end, in the confection of the Statute of the International Court of Justice as an adjunct to the Charter of the United Nations at San Francisco in 1945, it was agreed that, "everything being taken into account, the system of optional jurisdiction at the present time would be more likely to secure general agreement," and it was so drawn, approved, and signed.[49]

During the formulation of the final draft of the Charter and the Statute at San Francisco, President Truman expressed himself to Secretary of State Stettinius as opposed to the concept of voluntary jurisdiction of the Court. He felt, he said, "that if we were going to have a court it ought to be a court that would work, with compulsory jurisdiction." [50] The "Optional Clause" annexed to the 1920 Protocol, under which nations were permitted to file their declarations of adherence to the Permanent Court of International Justice, subject to stated conditions or reservations, had unquestionably led by 1945 to the acceptance of the concept of compulsory jurisdiction by many countries which had originally refused to subscribe to it. By carrying that optional provision forward from the old to the new Statute, it may fairly be stated that

[47] S. ROSENNE, I.C.J. at 147.

[48] *Id.* at 118. *See also* 1 S. ROSENNE, LAW AND PRACTICE at 165.

[49] 13 U.N.C.I.O. Docs. 559 (1945).

[50] H. TRUMAN, YEAR OF DECISIONS 286 (1958).

a formula was adopted, as had been suggested by President Truman, "that would make possible at least eventually, compulsory jurisdiction of the International Court of Justice." [51]

Russia, as stated above, has never declared her adherence to the International Court of Justice—with or without reservations —but she has regularly participated in the nomination and election of the judges; and one member of the Court has, in fact, always been a citizen of the Soviet Union.

In the United States, the difficulty arose, as was anticipated, in the Senate. There, a declaration of adherence to the Court was finally hammered out. Although it contained some conditions, all but one of these were of no undue significance. That one was exclusion from the jurisdiction of the Court of "disputes with regard to matters which are essentially within the domestic jurisdiction of the United States." But to this exclusion was added the Connally Amendment, which provided that the question as to whether a dispute before the Court is "essentially within the domestic jurisdiction of the United States" is to be "determined by the United States" herself. This Amendment effectively emasculated the jurisdiction of the Court in so far as the United States, and a number of other nations which followed her lead in this regard, were concerned.[52] Under the "principle of reciprocity," any nation sought to be made a defendant before the Court might decline the jurisdiction on the same grounds as were available to the plaintiff nation—so that every nation had an implied Connally Amendment *vis-à-vis* the United States and all other nations which had adopted the same condition, under the optional clause.[53]

These factors combined to provoke concerted efforts to find means to achieve uniform and universal compulsory jurisdiction of the International Court of Justice, over every nation, at the instance of any nation on terms acceptable to all nations; and, in the last analysis, to render moot most questions as to disabilities, disqualifications, and incompatibilities of judges.

[51] *Id.*   [52] *See* Introduction *supra,* text at note 25.
[53] Norwegian Loans case (Norway v. France) , [1955] I.C.J. 9, at 27.

CHAPTER VIII

Bases of Decision I

The League of Nations was established, according to its Covenant, "to promote international co-operation and to achieve international peace and security," in part "by the firm establishment of the understandings of international law as the actual rule of conduct among Governments. . . ." [1] Similarly, the Preamble to the Charter of the United Nations expresses one purpose of the formation of that organization to have been "to establish conditions under which justice and respect for the obligations arising from treaties and other sources of international law can be maintained. . . ." And the very first Article of that Charter declares that one of the purposes of the United Nations is "to maintain international peace and security" by bringing about "adjustment or settlement of international disputes" through "peaceful means . . . in conformity with the principles of justice and international law. . . ."

These quotations are a twentieth-century expression of man's age-old yearning to find ways and means to secure peaceful co-existence among the nations of the earth. It seems inconceivable that, in an age in which man has made such giant strides in the physical sciences, the apparently unlimited reach of his intellect should be inadequate to cope with international problems within the political sciences. Peace is, or must become, the masterpiece of reason, and the proposed Statute of the International Court of Justice, which will form "an integral part" of the Charter of the United Nations,[2] represents what is believed to be man's latest intellectual step forward toward the achievement of international peace, "in conformity with the principles of justice and international law. . . ." [3]

Now, despite the provisions quoted from the Covenant of the

---

[1] LEAGUE OF NATIONS COVENANT preamble. [2] See U.N. CHARTER art. 92.
[3] Id. art. 1, para. 1.

League of Nations for the establishment of international law as the rule of conduct among governments, and despite the provision in the Statute of the Permanent Court of International Justice giving that Court jurisdiction over "[a]ny question of International Law,"[4] there was no mention in the Statute of international law, strange as it may seem, among the principles according to which the Court was to adjudicate controversies brought before it. Under Article 38 of that Statute, the Court was directed to apply, in the decision of its cases: (1) treaties fixing rules recognized by the parties; (2) international custom generally accepted by law; (3) general principles of law recognized by civilized nations; and (4) judicial precedents and authoritative texts. If the parties consented, the Court also could decide its cases *ex aequo et bono.* This omission of any express mandate for application, by the Permanent Court of International Justice, of the rules of international law in the determination of disputes submitted to it seems especially remarkable in light of the history of then recent efforts to establish international tribunals for settlement of disputes by international law.

Article 48 of the Hague Convention of 1899 for the Pacific Settlement of International Disputes provided that a tribunal of the Permanent Court of Arbitration may determine its own jurisdiction in applying "the principles of international law"; but, for some reason, Article 73 of the 1907 Convention on the same subject substituted "principles of law" for "principles of international law."[5] The International Prize Court Convention of 1907, which sought creation of a permanent panel of members of a tribunal to determine appeals of nations, and even of persons, in matters relating to maritime captures in war, provided that in the absence of treaty provisions, decisions of that Court were to be rendered according to the recognized "rules of international law."[6]

While the International Prize Court never actually came into being, it did serve, in many of its attributes, as a precursor of subsequent international judicial concepts. The Prize Court would have sanctioned institution of some proceedings by indi-

[4] P.C.I.J. Stat. art. 36, para. 2 (b).   [5] *See* Hague Conventions at 72.
[6] Prize Court Convention of 1907 art. 7.

vidual parties, its jurisdiction as to subject matter was extremely limited, and it was, in a sense, an appellate tribunal from national courts; [7] but, as stated in 1912 by Elihu Root in an address before the American Society of International Law, the Prize Court was the "advance guard" of later, more extensive, international judicial organizations.[8] The members of the Prize Court were to be appointed by the States parties to the Convention. Fifteen judges were to comprise the full Court, with nine judges to constitute a quorum; and only "jurists of known proficiency in questions of international maritime law, and of the highest moral reputation" were to serve as its judges.[9] Regular sessions of the Court, aside from specific cases of capture in the course of a particular war, were not contemplated, except that provision was made for a session to adopt rules of procedure.[10] It was unquestionably understood that the judges were to be invested with complete political independence, as in the enjoyment of unqualified diplomatic privileges and immunities when serving outside their own countries.[11] The proposed International Prize Court was to be governed, in rendering decisions, in the first instance, by the provisions of any treaty between the States involved. But, in the absence of any such treaty provisions governing disposition of captures, the Court was to apply "the rules of international law"; and where there were no applicable, generally recognized, rules of international law governing the case under consideration, judgment was to be rendered "in accordance with the general principles of justice and equity." [12]

The Convention for the creation of the International Prize Court was opened for signature on October 18, 1907, but its ratification apparently was delayed by doubts raised—despite its provision on that point—as to the law to be applied in the adjudication of cases before the Court, since there had never been any codification of the rules of recognized international law of maritime warfare.[13] Great Britain, as the leading naval power of

---

[7] *See id.* arts. 3–4.

[8] Address by the Honorable Elihu Root, American Society of International Law Annual Meeting, Apr. 25, 1912, 6 AM. SOC'Y INT'L L. PROC. 4, at 13 (1912).

[9] Prize Court Convention of 1907 arts. 10, 14–15.   [10] *Id.* art. 49.

[11] *Id.* art. 13.   [12] *See* note 6 *supra.*   [13] M. HUDSON, P.C.I.J. at 76.

the world at the time, suggested that a general impression was prevalent at the Second Peace Conference at the Hague in 1907 "that the establishment of the International Prize Court would not meet with general acceptance so long as vagueness and uncertainty exist as to the principles which the court, in dealing with appeals brought before it, would apply to questions of far-reaching importance affecting naval policy and practice." [14] Accordingly, in February 1907, the British Government proposed that a conference should be held "with the object of arriving at an agreement as to what are the generally recognized principles of international law, within the meaning of . . ." the Convention (on the International Prize Court) "as to those matters wherein the practice of nations has varied and of then formulating the rules which, in the absence of special treaty provisions applicable to a particular case, the Court should observe in dealing with appeals brought before it for decision." [15]

In response to the British proposal, representatives of the world's naval powers met in London in the winter of 1908–9 and drew up the *Declaration relative au droit de guerre maritime,* which became known as the Declaration of London.[16] While it was generally conceded that the rules codified in this Declaration "correspond in substance with the generally recognized principles of international law," nevertheless a substantial number of the rules were actually new, and the Declaration was, as far as it went, of a legislative character.[17] The Declaration of London was signed in behalf of all of the countries which had been represented at the Conference at which it was evolved; but it was never ratified, and so it never came into force, and the International Prize Court never came into being.[18]

[14] Letter from Sir Edward Grey to His Majesty's Representatives, Feb. 27, 1908, BRITISH PARLIAMENTARY PAPERS, MISCELLANEOUS, No. 4, CD. No. 4554, at 1, (1909) *reprinted in* THE DECLARATION OF LONDON 13 (J. Scott ed. 1919).

[15] *Id.*

[16] For the original French text, see BRITISH PARLIAMENTARY PAPERS, MISCELLANEOUS, No. 5, CD. No. 4555, at 381 (1909). For an English translation, see THE DECLARATION OF LONDON, *supra* note 14, at 112.

[17] M. HUDSON, P.C.I.J. at 76.

[18] Perhaps this was the best result. "The Declaration of London, even if it had been ratified by the belligerent Powers in [the First World War], was admittedly incomplete; and on the matters with which it did purport to deal would have

The question as to the law to be applied by international tribunals has always been a troublesome one and has never been answered to the satisfaction of judges and statesmen. The 1907 Convention for the Estblishment of a Central American Court of Justice directed that, in the adjudication of questions of fact, the Court was to act according to "its free judgment," but that, in its determination of questions of law, the court was to be governed "by the principles of international law." [19] The draft Convention, worked out at the Second Peace Conference at the Hague in 1907, for the creation of a Court of Arbitral Justice as a tribunal "of free and easy access, composed of judges representing the various juridical systems of the world, and capable of insuring continuity in arbitral jurisprudence (Art. 1) ," contained no direction as to the principles of law which the Court was to apply in reaching its decisions.[20] It may very well be that it was contemplated that, because of the nature of this Court as an arbitral tribunal, the parties before it would agree to, or the Court itself would announce, the rules by which any particular controversy before the Court was to be settled.

There is, unquestionably, a fundamental difference in determining the law by which settlement of a particular dispute among nations is to be governed by an *ad hoc* arbitral commission created for that purpose and the establishment of rules of law to govern adjudication of all international disputes which might in future come before a permanent judicial tribunal. On the other hand, there seems to be no reason whatever why the parties to any such dispute before any type of tribunal, whether *ad hoc* or permanent, should not agree, if they wish and can, on the rules by which their disputes should be determined; nor why any such tribunal of either character should not be bound by such agreement among the parties. Actually, the functions, scope, and jurisdiction of

---

proved both ineffective and unpractical." Richards, *The Jurisdiction of the Permanent Court of International Justice*, 2 BRIT. Y.B. INT'L L. 1, 3 (1921) .

[19] Convention of 1907 for the Establishment of a Central American Court of Justice art. XXI. For the text of this Convention, see Report [by Mr. William I. Buchanan] of the Central American Peace Conference Held in Washington, D.C., 1907, [1907] 2 FOREIGN REL. U.S. 665, at 697 (1910) .

[20] M. HUDSON, P.C.I.J. at 82.

some of these courts, as conceived in the early twentieth century, were at least as vague as the concepts governing the bases of their decisions. Thus, in 1909, the United States proposed—repeating a suggestion made at the London Conference during the preceding year—that the International Prize Court should be invested with the jurisdiction and functions of the proposed Court of Arbitral Justice.[21] And while neither of these Courts was ever established, the framework of both, and the juridical concepts out of which their structures were designed, formed the foundations upon which the later, stronger permanent international judicial organs were erected and have endured.

There seems to be no record by which it can be ascertained how the Statute of the Permanent Court of International Justice failed to confer upon that tribunal an express direction to apply principles of international law to questions laid before it for adjudication. It must be borne in mind, in the attempt to solve this puzzle, that throughout the entire history of modern efforts to establish a permanent international tribunal as an instrument for the peaceful settlement of disputes among nations, the conviction had been expressed that this ideal could be achieved only through application of judicial principles, evolved in centuries of human striving toward the supremacy of right over might. Article 15 of the 1899 Hague Convention for the Pacific Settlement of International Disputes declares the object of international arbitration to be the settlement of disputes "on the basis of respect for laws"; and, as stated by the same instrument, tribunals of the Permanent Court of Arbitration were permitted to determine their competence in the application of "the principles of international law." [22] The provisions of the Covenant of the League of Nations, as stated, dedicate that body to the achievement of international peace and security through the establishment "of international law as the actual rule of conduct among Governments." [23] Among the classes of disputes as to which declarations of adherence to the

[21] Indentic Circular Note of the Secretary of State of the United States Proposing Alternative Procedures for the International Prize Court and the Investment of the International Prize Court with the Functions of a Court of Arbitral Justice, Nov. 3, 1909, [1910] FOREIGN REL. U.S. 597 (1915) .

[22] *See* text at note 5 *supra*.   [23] *See* note 1 *supra*.

Permanent Court of International Justice might be made under the Statute of that Court itself were disputes relating to "any question of international law." [24]

There is, however, a paucity of reference in the minutes of the 1920 Committee of Jurists to international law as a guide or yardstick to be applied by the Permanent Court of International Justice in the adjudication of controversies among nations. At one point, the 1920 Committee of Jurists referred to Article 7 of the International Price Court Convention of 1907, which provided, as a possible alternative basis for decision of disputes in the absence of governing treaty provisions or applicable generally recognized principles of international law, "the general principles of justice and equity"; but they concluded that "[t]here can be no question of giving such an unrestricted field to the decisions of the Court." [25] The only possible explanation, or perhaps rationalization, for the failure of the draftsmen of the Statute of the Permanent Court of International Justice to stipulate that international law should be a basis of decision by that Court is that they simply took it for granted that an international court would, as a matter of course, seek to resolve international disputes by the application of international law. Thus, in the course of the drafting process in 1920, M. Loder, a judge of the Supreme Court of the Netherlands and later to become the first President of the Permanent Court of International Justice, declared that "the Covenant [of the League of Nations] intended to establish" that Court "to apply international law." [26]

This view is borne out by expressions in the opinions of the Court itself over the years to the effect that its conclusions were to be based on principles of international law, just as though a direction to do so had been spelled out *in haec verba* in the Court's Statute. In the *Oscar Chinn* case, Judge Schücking declared, in his dissenting opinion, that the Court had "been set up by the Covenant as the custodian of international law." [27] In the *Case Concerning Certain German Interests in Polish Upper Silesia*

---

[24] *See* note 4 *supra*.
[25] Report of M. de Lapradelle, 1920 PROCEEDINGS at 693, 729.
[26] 1920 PROCEEDINGS at 294. *See* chapter 1 *supra*, text at note 64.
[27] [1934] P.C.I.J., ser. A/B, No. 63, at 149.

(*The Merits*), the Court referred to itself as the "organ" of international law,[28] and in the *Brazilian Loans* case, as "a tribunal of international law."[29] In the *Serbian Loans* case, the Court declared its "true function" to be to adjudicate disputes among nations "on the basis of international law," in light of the clear implication to that effect in Article 38 of its Statute. Moreover, it said, "it is international law which governs relations between those who may be subject to the Court's jurisdiction."[30]

Under Article 38 of its Statute, the first group of rules of decision which the Permanent Court of International Justice was directed to apply to cases before it were those found in "[i]nternational conventions, whether general or particular, establishing rules expressly recognized by the contesting States." As a matter of course, most of the cases brought before the Court involved interpretation of treaty provisions; and this function itself, as held by the Court in the *Advisory Opinion on the Exchange of Greek and Turkish Populations,* "involves a question of international law."[31]

Whatever may have been the intention of the framers of Article 38 of the Statute of the Permanent Court of International Justice as to the use of the general principles of international law as a basis of decision, the doctrine of such application became well fixed as a rule of the Court itself. In 1935, Judge Anzilotti, who had played an important part in the formative phases of the Court as an Under-Secretary-General of the League of Nations and had been President of the Court from 1928 to 1930, declared that "[i]t neither is nor can be disputed, . . . that the Court has been created to administer international law."[32]

[28] [1926] P.C.I.J., ser. A, No. 7, at 19.

[29] Case Concerning the Payment in Gold of the Brazilian Federal Loans Issued in France, [1929] P.C.I.J., ser. A, No. 21, at 124.

[30] Case Concerning the Payment of Various Serbian Loans Issued in France, [1929] P.C.I.J., ser. A, No. 20, at 19–20. The Court held that Article 38 of its Statute does not preclude the Court's dealing with disputes which do *not* require the application of international law.

[31] [1925] P.C.I.J., ser. B, No. 10, at 17.

[32] Advisory Opinion on the Consistency of Certain Danzig Legislative Decrees With the Constitution of the Free City, [1935] P.C.I.J., ser. A/B, No. 65, at 61. Judge Anzilotti, however, also maintained, in his dissenting opinion, that Article 38 of the Statute of the Permanent Court of International Justice should be in-

In the *Serbian Loans* case, the Court found that it was required to adjudicate some "disputes which do not require the application of international law," a possibility not excluded by Article 38 of the Statute and for which, in fact, Article 36 "expressly provides." It admitted, however, that "cases in which the Court must apply international law will, no doubt, be the more frequent. . . ."[33] In the case of *The S.S. "Lotus,"* the Court had occasion to give its own characterization of the nature and universal applicability of the international law which served as the basis of its decisions. In that case, the parties had stipulated, in Article 15 of the Lausanne Convention of 1923, that "the principles of international law" were to apply to the determination of disputes regarding delineation of jurisdiction.[34] The Court interpreted this concept to refer to those "principles which are in force between all independent nations"—that international law which "governs relations between independent States" and which "is applied between all nations belonging to the community of States."[35]

As stated, then, the Permanent Court of International Justice held repeatedly that, under Article 38 of its Statute, it was bound to adjudicate controversies before it on principles of international law. This concept of the bases of decision was explained by Manley O. Hudson, who had been one of the leading authorities of the world on international law and later, for some years a Judge of the Permanent Court of International Justice, in saying that Article 38 "serves chiefly to enumerate sources to be drawn upon in the Court's application of international law."[36]

In 1945, when the Statute of the International Court of Justice was framed and adopted, Article 38 was left in the identical form in which it had been in force for over twenty years, with one exception. Instead of providing merely that the Court was to apply the enumerated principles in the adjudication of controversies before it, the introductory clause of Article 38 of the new Statute was phrased to read: "The Court, whose function is to decide in accordance with international law such disputes as are submitted

---

terpreted as precluding the Court from rendering an opinion in a case involving "[t]he interpretation of a municipal law as such and apart from any question or dispute of an international character. . . ." *Id.* at 61–62.

[33] *See* note 30 *supra.*   [34] [1927] P.C.I.J., ser. A, No. 10, at 16.

[35] *Id.* at 16–18.   [36] M. HUDSON, TRIBUNALS at 102.

to it, shall apply" the stated principles. In other words, the oft-repeated holding of the Permanent Court of International Justice that it was to be guided in its decisions by the recognized principles of international law was translated into legislation by an express—if parenthetical—directive of the Statute of the International Court of Justice.

Because this statutory change provided merely an express recognition of the basis of decision theretofore applied by the Permanent Court of International Justice to its cases, this directive to the International Court of Justice "to decide in accordance with international law" did not lead the Court into any new jurisprudential paths. The Court simply has applied, just as did its predecessor tribunal, what it considered to be the general principles of international law relevant to the determination of disputes among nations laid before it.

In the proposed Statute of the International Court of Justice, this subject receives further consideration, and the phrase in question is reframed to avoid its parenthetical expression and to give direct emphasis to the status of the Court as an international tribunal, affirmatively charged with the determination of international disputes according to international law. The Court's basis of decision is accordingly now delineated to direct the tribunal to "adjudicate disputes before it in accordance with generally accepted, applicable principles of international law, giving due consideration, in its deliberations to" somewhat the same legal principles theretofore enumerated, with some revisions to broaden the jurisprudential powers of the Court.[37] (The deletion of the right to render decisions *ex aequo et bono* will be discussed in a subsequent chapter.) Here again, however, it is not anticipated that this rephasing of the Statute of the Court, designed to emphasize its legislative direction and to guide the course of its adjudicative processes by the gyroscopic compass of "generally accepted, applicable principles of international law," will steer it into any new, uncharted seas or channels; it will, rather, give it the assurance of a reliable check on the magnetic needle by which it has heretofore charted the same course toward the Rule of Law.

---

[37] I.C.J. STAT. (P) art. VIII, para. 5. *See* chapter 1 *supra*, text at notes 64–65.

It is a familiar principle in municipal or local law that a contract represents the law between the parties thereto. That principle applies with equal force in international law to treaties, international agreements, engagements, or conventions. By whatever name they are called, whenever they serve to regulate any phase of relationship of the signatory nations to each other, they then represent the law among the parties thereto and are referred to as "instruments of public international law." To point out the difference between such instruments and those involving only a matter of private international law (for instance, treaties respecting the rights of aliens within the territories of the contracting parties), the latter frequently require implementation by national legislation, to be applied in national courts, and the treaties themselves may no longer be the primary law between the parties thereto. However, when an international agreement is one fixing any phase of the relationship of the signatory States themselves to each other, it is an instrument of public international law, and constitutes, in the strictest sense, the law between the parties.

In bipartite treaties, as a rule, only specific commercial or other matters are regulated and as to such matters, so regulated, the regulations themselves form the law between the parties. But such treaties often include additional provisions as to the principles of law by which their interpretation is to be governed, and so express also the adjective law which the parties have agreed is to be applied to the construction of their engagement. Now, in recent times, the multipartite international convention has come more and more into use, although it was originally looked upon with considerable skepticism. For example, in 1868, when the United States was invited to accede to the Geneva Red Cross Convention of 1864, Secretary of State Seward replied that "[i]t has always been deemed at least a questionable policy, if not unwise, for the United States to become a party to any instrument to which there are many other parties." [38] Gradually, however, the national

---

[38] Letter from the Secretary of State to the French Ambassador, Mar. 31, 1868, in H.R. Exec. Doc. No. 1, 40th Cong., 3d Sess., pt. I, at 456 (1969). *See generally* J. Wright, *Humanity and Diplomacy*, 2 Essays in History 28 (1955) (published by the Corcoran Department of History, University of Virginia).

skepticism toward multipartite international engagements melted away, and they have now become an almost universally favored means of effecting resolution of international problems.

Ordinarily, such agreements originate in international conferences convened to give collective consideration to specific problems of international scope such as carriage of goods by sea in international trade, liability of owners of aircraft in the course of international transport, and, more recently and more significantly, universal disarmament and the law of treaties. The Covenant of the League of Nations itself was such a multipartite international convention of broad scope, through the functioning of which it had been hoped to create a forum for discussion and machinery for the making of other international engagements in many fields, looking toward elimination of sources of international disputes or their resolution if they should arise, as steps in the direction of universal peace. Then came failure of the League, for reasons unnecessary to discuss, followed in this evolutionary process by the Charter of the United Nations, which, for all practical intents and purposes, is a kind of universal-partite treaty to which almost all nations of the world—now over 130—are parties. To both the Covenant of the League of Nations and the Charter of the United Nations were appended so-called Statutes, in each case literally part and parcel of the Covenant and Charter, creating the Permanent Court of International Justice and the International Court of Justice, respectively.[39]

Following formation of the League of Nations, and throughout its existence and that of the United Nations, the holding of international conferences and the initiation of multipartite conventions were greatly facilitated, and their number progressively increased. All of these multipartite international engagements, dealing with specific subjects, as well as the Covenant of the League, the Charter of the United Nations, the appurtenant Statutes of the Courts, and especially the Vienna Convention of 1969 on the Law of Treaties, have created a diverse code of substantive, interpretive, and procedural law amongst the parties to them, sometimes almost all of the nations of the world. This process,

[39] LEAGUE OF NATIONS COVENANT art. 14; U.N. CHARTER art. 92.

which has now been going on actively for more than half a century, is unquestionably a legislative one–the evolution, by multipartite treaties, of an effective code of international law. This evolutionary progression has, in turn, undoubtedly done more toward the collating and clarifying of rules of public international law and the embracing of widening areas within its bounds than has been, or possibly could have been, accomplished by the early efforts of the Institute of International Law and the International Law Association, or the 1930 League of Nations Conference for the Progressive Codification of International Law; and it is, of course, facilitating the work of the International Law Commission, in its present task of compiling a Code of International Law under direction of the General Assembly of the United Nations. All of this development has resulted in the creation of a *corpus juris,* a body of international legislation enacted by treaty, without the establishment of an international parliament; and in the interpretation of this expanding treaty law, the international tribunals heretofore have begun to build, and will unquestionably continue to construct, a jurisprudence to which the late Dag Hammerskjöld referred as "a 'common law' of the United Nations," by which it is hoped that the nations of the world will ultimately be able to live in peace with each other.[40]

There may be some questions with regard to the change effected by paragraph 5 (a) of Article VIII of the proposed Statute of the International Court of Justice in the corresponding provision found in paragraph 1 of Article 38 of the Statutes of the Permanent Court of International Justice and the International Court of Justice. As this provision originally was drafted[41] and then brought over into the Statute of the International Court of Justice, it directed the Court to apply to the determinaion of issues before it, among other guilding principles, "international conventions, whether general or particular, establishing rules expressly recognized by the contesting States."[42] But the corresponding provision of the proposed Statute states that, in its deliberations, the Court is to give "due consideration," *inter alia,*

---

[40] Sec'y-Gen., Report, 10 U.N. GAOR, Supp. 1, at xiii, U.N. Doc. A/2911 (1955).
[41] P.C.I.J. STAT. art. 38, para. 1.   [42] I.C.J. STAT. art. 38, para. 1 (a).

to "the provisions of international conventions establishing rules generally recognized among nations." [43] It may be assumed that the added words, "the provisions of," are merely formal and that the present direction to the Court to apply "the provisions of international conventions" is not essentially different from the prior direction to apply the "international conventions" themselves. However, the proposed Statute no longer states that the international conventions whose provisions are to be applied by the Court may be either "general or particular." Moreover, it does not require that the rules established by such international conventions, in order to be applied by the Court, be "expressly recognized by the contesting States" but requires merely that such rules be "generally recognized among nations."

Accordingly, it is necessary to explain what practical changes, in the bases of decision to be applied by the International Court of Justice, have been effected by these revisions. May, for instance, a rule established by a particular treaty be applied by the International Court of Justice in resolving a dispute between contesting States which are not parties to the treaty?

In the first place, the term "international conventions," as used in this provision, must unquestionably be construed in its broadest sense, as including all forms of international engagements. In the *Advisory Opinion on the Customs Régime Between Germany and Austria,* the Permanent Court of International Justice held that binding international engagements "may be taken in the form of treaties, conventions, declarations, agreements, protocols, or exchanges of notes." [44] In its decision on the *Legal Status of Eastern Greenland,* the same Court even went so far as to recognize an oral statement as a binding international undertaking. [45]

An international convention may be a general one, either as viewed by the breadth of its subject matter or even because there are a large number of parties to it; or it may be particular, either as judged by the restricted nature of its subject matter or because of the limited number of parties thereto. In this connection, it is of interest to take note of a passage in the majority opinion of the

[43] I.C.J. STAT. (P) art. VIII, para. 5 (a).
[44] [1931] P.C.I.J., ser. A/B, No. 41, at 47.
[45] [1933] P.C.I.J., ser. A/B, No. 53, at 73.

International Court of Justice in the *Advisory Opinion on the Prevention and Punishment of the Crime of Genocide*. The opinion makes an exhaustive analysis of the interpretation of international treaties within "notions of contract" and then distinguishes, in decreasing order of importance, a "generally recognized principle," a "notion," and a "concept." [46] The rules established by so general an international convention as the Charter of the United Nations, to which practically all the countries of the world are now parties and which covers so broad a field of international relationships, obviously are to be applied by the International Court of Justice in the adjudication of controversies between any contesting States.

On the other hand, rules established in a treaty between two nations whose territories border on the same body of water, governing the specific fishing rights of nationals of each of the two countries in those waters and nothing more, obviously are not ordinarily to be applied by the International Court of Justice in the adjudication of different controversies between contesting States not parties to this particular international convention. But if this hypothetical fishing treaty establishes the further rule that any dispute which may arise between the parties thereto is to be adjudicated in accordance with "principles of international law, and the practices and jurisprudence established by analogous modern tribunals of highest authority and prestige," [47] then this rule may also be adopted in various circumstances by the International Court of Justice as a basis of decision in the adjudication of any controversy between any contesting States, even though they were not parties to this particular international convention.

The same principle would have applied to the Permanent Court of International Justice under paragraph 1 of Article 38 of its Statute and does apply to the International Court of Justice under the same paragraph and Article of its Statute except insofar as that paragraph required express recognition, by the contesting States,

[46] [1951] I.C.J. 15, at 21.

[47] *See, e.g.*, Convention for Arbitration Between Great Britain and Chile, Jan. 4, 1883, art. VI, 64 Martens (9 N.R.G. 2d) 445, at 446 (1883); Convention for Arbitration Between Great Britain and Chile, Sept. 26, 1893, art. 5, 77 Martens (22 N.R.G. 2d) 520, at 521 (1893).

of any rule established by such an international convention. But, in the first place, it makes no difference under those Statutes whether the international convention establishing the rule in question is general or particular. As stated by Judge Hudson in discussing this provision of Article 38 of the Statute of the Permanent Court of International Justice, "[t]he phrase *general* or *particular* seems to add little to the meaning in this connection." [48] In the second place, most such rules established by international conventions as the basis for decision by international tribunals are generally recognized by most nations. Again, as stated by Judge Hudson: "It has frequently occurred that States have admitted formulations made by other States to be proper statements of the law and as such binding for themselves." [49]

The repeated expression of a principle of international law in many international conventions and over a period of many years would seem to justify the taking of judicial notice by an international tribunal that a rule so firmly established as a basis of decision has been recognized as a binding one throughout the family of nations. Application of such a rule would certainly seem to have been permissible under the Statute of the Permanent Court of International Justice, as it is under the Statute of the International Court of Justice, as one "recognized by the contesting States," without reference to its status as "international custom" or "general principles of law recognized by civilized nations." To the extent, however, that such a rule established by an international convention must have been recognized "expressly" by contesting States, as required under the former Statutes, there undoubtedly was a limitation on the use of the rule as a basis of decision by the Court, unless, of course, such use was admissible under some other category—for instance, as an international custom.

Incidentally, in the proposed Statute of the International Court of Justice, the provision of its present Statute as to "general principles of law recognized by civilized nations" is changed, in light of modern world conditions, to read, "general principles of law, equity and justice recognized among nations." [50] In this con-

[48] M. Hudson, P.C.I.J. at 608.   [49] *Id.*
[50] I.C.J. Stat. (P) art. VIII, para. 5 (d).

nection, the international situation has changed in another very significant respect. In the last quarter of a century, many new nations have emerged on the world scene. These new nations could hardly be deemed to have recognized—much less "expressly recognized"—rules established by international conventions of a bygone era. It is accordingly considered proper, in the revision of the Statute of the International Court of Justice, to direct the Court to give consideration in its deliberations to the provisions of international conventions establishing rules "generally recognized among nations," [51] instead of "expressly recognized by the contesting States." [52]

On another point, statistics show that no less than two-thirds of the persons who have served as judges of the Permanent Court of International Justice and the International Court of Justice have been, at one time or another, professors of law. In paragraph 5 (e) of Article VIII—the article around which this discussion has centered—"legal writings of jurisconsults who are recognized authorities in international law" are to be given due consideration by the Court in its deliberations. Now, if two-thirds of the judges who have served as members of these international Courts have been professors of law, one may take the liberty of assuming that at least two-thirds, and probably more, of the "jurisconsults" to whose writings the International Court of Justice is to give due consideration in reaching its decisions have been professors of law. This seems to mean that, under the Statute of the International Court of Justice, the judges of that Court are required, in deciding cases, to give due consideration to legal writings of professors of international law recognized as authorities in that field.

There is, however (as frequently occurs in such matters), a misleading factor in the statistics. By far the greater number of these professorships have been honorary, part time, or, in the giving of occasional lectures or courses, connected with the services they have rendered in other fields. For instance, of the thirty-three judges of the International Court of Justice who have held university professorships, five have been foreign ministers of their

---

[51] *See* text at note 43 *supra*.   [52] *See* text at notes 41 and 42 *supra*.

countries; some fourteen have been legal advisers to their foreign ministries; at least nine have been judges of other international tribunals; six have been judges of their highest national courts; and fifteen have held high diplomatic posts, or other high political office.

On the other hand, there can be no question that the legal writings of jurisconsults of recognized authority in international law are frequently the work of fulltime professors of law in universities throughout the world. The direction of the Statute of the International Court of Justice to the judges of that Court to give due consideration to such writings is a well-merited tribute to the scholars who have produced these extensive and authoritative works.

Paragraph 4 of Article 38 of the Stautes of both the Permanent Court of International Justice and the International Court of Justice direct the Court, "subject to the provisions of Article 59," [53] to apply "judicial decisions and the teachings of the most highly qualified publicists of the various nations, as subsidiary means for the determination of rules of law." First of all, the term "subsidiary means" is, to say the least, obscure. It was thought by Judge Hudson perhaps to denote a direction that the Court is to draw on these sources for determination of a rule of law only when it cannot be found in international conventions, customs, or general principles of law.[54] On the other hand, the French term *auxiliaire* seems to indicate that confirmation of rules drawn from other sources may be found in judicial precedents and in the words of text writers.[55] The application of judicial decisions to the consideration of cases before the Court, and the limitations placed thereon by the provisions of Article 59, will be discussed in some detail and at some length in the next chapter. At this point, it is enough to say that, while the connection between this provision and Article 59 is not obvious, it might have been intended to preclude the use of a rule recognized in teachings, and applied by the court in an earlier case, as express precedent.

---

[53] "The decision of the Court has no binding force except between the parties and in respect of that particular case."

[54] M. HUDSON, P.C.I.J. at 612.   [55] *Id.* a 612–13; *See* 1920 PROCEEDINGS at 331–37.

The minutes of the Tenth Session of the Council of the League of Nations show that the introductory phrase "subject to the provisions of Article 59" was prefixed to paragraph 4 when Article 38 was adopted by that body.[56] The stage at which this proviso was added to the text indicates that it may have been a careless eleventh-hour afterthought; but that would not explain its retention in its incongruous context, when the 1929 amendments to the Statute of the Permanent Court of International Justice were drafted. Even less would that explain how the phrase managed to remain in the same incomprehensible context years later, in 1945, when the Statute of the International Court of Justice was drawn and adopted—despite the fact that the Statute was, as stated in Article 92 of the Charter of the United Nations, "based upon the Statute of the Permanent Court of International Justice."

At any rate, the proposed Statute of the International Court of Justice contains no such proviso, and the Court is directed by paragraph 5 (e) of Article VIII of the Statute to give "due consideration, in its deliberations," to the "legal writings of jurisconsults who are recognized authorities in international law." Of course, as in the case of judicial predecents, legal writings are not in and of themselves rules to be applied to the adjudication of causes. Rather, they are sources to which recourse is to be had for the finding or deduction of such rules so to be applied.

There has never been any standard for, or any means of determining who are, "the most highly qualified publicists of the various nations," whose teachings are to be applied in the determination of international disputes; and one may be entirely confident that there will be no undue difficulty, when and as occasion may arise under the proposed Statute, in the acceptance by the International Court of Justice of the "legal writings" of professors as "jurisconsults who are recognized authorities in international law." In the *Brazilian Loans* case, which came before the Permanent Court of International Justice, Judge de Bustamante, in a dissenting opinion, emphasized the importance of the period and environment in which an author writes and commented that "[w]riters of legal treatises just as much as anyone else, without

[56] Minutes of the Tenth Session of the Council, at 21, L.N. Doc. 20/29/16 (1920); *Id*. Annex 118, at 161.

wanting to and without knowing it, come under the irresistible influence of their surroundings, and the requirements of the national situation are reflected in their thoughts and have a great influence on their teachings." [57]

Occasionally, individual judges have referred, in concurring and dissenting opinions, to works and publications of writers in the field of international law. At times they have cited living authors, and sometimes even the collateral publications of members of the Court itself. In the case of *The S.S. "Lotus,"* the Permanent Court of International Justice held that a certain rule of international law had not been proven conclusively and commented that it had been unable to find any useful guide to the rule in any "precedents, teachings and facts. . . ." [58] But, in the final analysis, no treatise of any publicist or writer on international law has even been cited by either the Permanent Court of International Justice or the International Court of Justice as authority for any of their holdings or for any rule of international law on which any of their decisions have been based.

In any event, there can be no doubt that the professors in our universities are major contributors to the world's literature on international law. The nations of the world have evidenced their high esteem for the members of this distinguished profession in directing the judges of the International Court of Justice to give due consideration in their deliberations to "legal writings of jurisconsults who are recognized authorities in international law" as a basis of decision in the adjudication of international disputes under the International Rule of Law.

[57] [1929] P.C.I.J., ser. A, No. 21, at 133.
[58] [1927] P.C.I.J., ser. A, No. 10, at 16.

CHAPTER IX

Bases of Decision II

Paragraph 5 (b) of Article VIII of the proposed Statute of the International Court of Justice provides for application by the Court, to the decision of controversies before it, of "international custom, as evidence of a general practice accepted as law." These are precisely the terms in which the identical provision is couched in Article 38 of both the original Statute of that Court and the Statute of the Permanent Court of International Justice.

Just as with other sources, international custom is not itself a rule of law. It is a derivative pattern from which a rule may be drawn. But before a court can determine that such a rule exists, it must first find the existence of the custom. And to evidence the existence of such a custom, there must have been concurring and recurring action among a substantial number of countries in their relations to each other in such a way as to give rise to the concept among them that their own conduct is a facet of the law governing their mutual relationships, coupled with consistent absence of denial of that concept by any of them or by other countries.

This concept was illustrated interestingly in the celebrated case of *The S.S. "Lotus."* [1] That case involved a collision in 1926 on the high seas between the French mail steamer *Lotus* and the Turkish collier *Boz-Kourt*. The latter vessel was sunk, with loss of eight Turkish nationals. Following the collision, a criminal prosecution was instituted in Turkey against the first officer of the *Lotus*. The controversy was brought before the Permanent Court of International Justice under a special agreement, on a contention of the French Government that the Turkish court had no jurisdiction to prosecute the French officer under the Lausanne Convention of 1923, Article 15 of which provided that questions of jurisdiction were to be governed by "the principles of inter-

---

[1] [1927] P.C.I.J., ser. A, No. 10.

national law." [2] The principle of international law on which the French contention was based was stated to be drawn from a recognized international custom, negative in character: that because criminal prosecution of an officer charged with fault in a collision at sea in a national court other than that of the flag of the vessel involved is very rare, the maritime nations of the world must be deemed to have consented that such prosecutions should be instituted only in the courts of the country of the accused vessel's flag.

There being a French judge (M. Charles André Weiss), but no Turkish judge, on the Permanent Court of International Justice at the time, a Turkish judge *ad hoc* (M. Feïzi Daïm Bey) was appointed to sit with the Court in the case. In 1927, when the case came before the Permanent Court of International Justice, that tribunal was composed of eleven judges, so that after the Turkish judge *ad hoc* was appointed, the bench consisted of twelve judges. At the conclusion of the hearing, the bench was divided, six on each side (the French judge voting in favor of the French position, and the Turkish judge *ad hoc* standing for the Turkish side), and so the ultimate outcome of the case has no undue significance. Opinions of the various judges, however, contain language of great interest in connection with the use of "international custom, as evidence of a general practice accepted as law," as a basis of decision by the Court. Pursuant to the rule fixed for such cases by Article 55 of the Statute of the Permanent Court of International Justice, the President of the Court was required to file a casting vote to break the tie; and this was done with the casting vote favoring the Turkish thesis. The opinion on that side accordingly became the majority opinion of the Court.

In that opinion, the Court stated that it had conducted its own independent research into the problems presented in the case and had "included in its researches all precedents, teachings, and facts to which it had access and which might possibly have revealed the existence" of applicable principles of international law.[3] The Court went on to say that its research had been directed toward finding "a custom having the force of law,"[4] in the nature of "usages generally accepted as expressing principles of law,"[5]

[2] *Id.* at 16.   [3] *Id.* at 31.   [4] *Id.* at 21.   [5] *Id.* at 18.

evidencing an acknowledgment that "States recognize themselves to be under an obligation" with regard thereto.[6] The Court held that it could not recognize the existence of an international custom in the absence of a showing that the maritime nations of the world had refrained from instituting criminal proceedings in such cases because of "their being conscious of having a duty to abstain. . . ." [7]

The opinion of the Court upholding the Turkish position emphasized the absence of any national protests against such legislation as that of Turkey, authorizing criminal prosecution in the national courts of the country of the persons lost or injured as a result of a maritime collision, against an officer of the vessel charged with fault. The Court accordingly ruled against the French Government, on the ground that there was insufficient evidence to support the existence of a custom to confine the criminal prosecution of a negligent officer of a vessel involved in a collision, in whatever waters, to the national court of the country of the vessel's flag.

In his dissenting opinion, Judge Didrik G. G. Nyhold of Denmark said:

The ascertainment of a rule of international law implies consequently an investigation of the way in which customs acquire consistency and thus come to be considered as constituting rules governing international relations. . . . There must have been acts of State accomplished in the domain of international relations, whilst mere municipal laws are insufficient; moreover, the foundation of a custom must be the united *will* of several and even of many States constituting a *union of wills,* of a general *consensus of opinion* among the countries which have adopted the European system of civilization, or a manifestation of *international legal ethics* which takes place through the continued recurrence of events with an *innate consciousness of their being necessary.*[8]

Judge R. Altamira of Spain also wrote a dissenting opinion, and in it submitted that, in the evolution of a customary rule of international law, there are frequently "moments in time in which the rule, implicitly discernible, has not as yet taken shape in the eyes of the world, but is so forcibly suggested by precedents that it

[6] *Id.* at 23.   [7] *Id.* at 28.   [8] *Id.* at 59–60.

would be rendering good service to the cause of justice and law to assist its appearance in a form in which it will have all the force rightly belonging to rules of positive law appertaining to that category." [9]

In strikingly similar language of identical import, Deputy Judge O. Negulesco commented, in his dissent from the majority of the Permanent Court in the *Advisory Opinion Regarding the Jurisdiction of the European Commission of the Danube between Galaty and Braila*, on "the necessity of immemorial usage consisting both of an uninterrupted recurrence of accomplished facts in the sphere of international relations and of ideas of justice common to the participating States and based upon the mutual conviction that the recurrence of these facts is the result of a compulsory rule." [10] Judge Hudson felt that the expression "international custom, as evidence of a general practice accepted as law," in Article 38 of the Statute of the Permanent Court of International Justice, "might have been cast more clearly as a provision for the Court's applying customary international law." [11] In any event, the expression was transplanted verbatim into the original and proposed Statutes of the International Court of Justice; it does seem logical, and it is cast quite clearly in light of the construction uniformly given to it in the holdings quoted. One must agree fully with Judge Hudson that the expression, so phrased, "seems to emphasize the general law, as opposed to the special law embodied in conventions accepted by the parties." [12]

Another basis of decision laid down in the proposed Statute of the International Court of Justice is that specified in paragraph 5 (c) of Article VIII, directing the Court to give due consideration in the determination of causes pending before it to "judicial precedents recognizing legal principles"—subject, always, to the provision of paragraph 6 of Article XVI that judgments are binding as *res adjudicata* only in the case in which rendered and only as to the parties to that case. A substantially similar provision was contained in paragraph 4 of Article 38 of the Statute of the

[9] *Id.* at 106–07. [10] [1927] P.C.I.J., ser. B, No. 14, at 105.
[11] M. HUDSON, P.C.I.J. at 609.
[12] *Id.* For a draft of this provision which emphasizes custom accepted by the States party to the dispute, see 1920 PROCEEDINGS at 351.

Permanent Court of International Justice and is contained in paragraph 1 (d) of the same Article of the present Statute of the International Court of Justice. As stated, these earlier statutory provisions authorized the Courts to apply "judicial decisions" to problems before them, but they coupled "the teachings of the most highly qualified publicists of the various nations" to "judicial decisions" and directed that they were both to be treated only "as subsidiary means for the determination of rules of law;" and then they made both subject to the provisions of Article 59 of each Statute, giving binding force to a judgment of the Court only between the parties to, and in, the case decided. The incongruity of a modification of judicial consideration of dicta of text writers by a restrictive tabu dealing with the binding effect of prior decisions of the Court has already been mentioned, as have also the possible meaning and effect of the former statutory provisions for application of judicial decisions and the teachings of publicists only "as subsidiary means for the determination of rules of law." [13]

So far as is known, there is not a single reference in any opinion of either the Permanent Court of International Justice or of the International Court of Justice—as distinguished from separate and dissenting opinions of individual judges—to the work of any named writer on international law. In the case of *The S.S. "Lotus,"* it was contended, in support of the French position, that according to the "teachings of publicists," the courts of the country of the ship's flag had exclusive jurisdiction of offenses committed thereon. The Permanent Court of International Justice held that the text writers did not uniformly expand this teaching to support the French position, "apart from the question as to what [its] value may be from the point of view of establishing the existence of a rule of customary law. . . ." [14] In the *Case Concerning Certain German Interests in Polish Upper Silesia (The Merits)*, the Permanent Court referred to a "much disputed question in the teachings of legal authorities and in the jurisprudence of the principal countries." [15] In the joint opinion of

[13] *See* Chapter 8 *supra*, text at notes 53–55.

[14] [1927] P.C.I.J., ser. A, No. 10, at 26.

[15] [1925] P.C.I.J., ser. A, No. 6, at 20. The question involved was whether the doctrine of *litispendance*, the object of which is to prevent the possibility of conflicting judgments in municipal law, could be invoked in international relations in

the dissenting judges in the *Advisory Opinion Regarding Reservations to the Convention on the Prevention and Punishment of the Crime of Genocide,* it is stated that those judges had been able to find "no trace of any authority [in support of the rule stated by the majority] in any decision of this Court or of the Permanent Court of International Justice or any other international tribunal, or in any text-book." [16]

Many judges of the Courts were renowned writers on international law before their accessions to the bench; but it presumably is considered to be in poor taste to cite one's own collateral writings in support of one side or another in cases pending for adjudication before the author and his colleagues. Judges may, in all fairness and without undue inconsistency, change an abstract view of a principle when it is being applied to a concrete problem in a case presented to them. Lord Westbury is stated to have remarked, as to one of his own prior expressions cited to him as authority: "I can only say that I am amazed that a man of my intelligence should have been guilty of giving such an opinion." [17]

Of course, writers rarely present a unanimity of views on any phase of international law, and the selection by any court of the view of one group over that of another as representing an authoritative expression tends to be a judicial endorsement of that group's view rather than consideration thereof as an aid in formulating the court's own conclusion. On the other hand, the recognized standing and authority of a writer on international law would surely entitle his work to consideration in the adjudicative process and to citation by international tribunals in support of principle.

The proposed Statute of the International Court of Justice contains no provisions whatever for "subsidiary" treatment of any of the principles to be considered by the Court in reaching its conclusions, and it does not subject use of the writings of authorities

---

the sense that, in the absence of a treaty, judges of one State should refuse to entertain any suit already pending before the courts of another State. The Court made no decision on the issue because the elements which constitute *litispendance* were found to be lacking.

[16] [1951] I.C.J. 15, 42–3.

[17] *See* McGrath v. Kristensen, 340 U.S. 162, 178 (Jackson, J., concurring).

in international law to any restrictive effort of prior decisions of the Court. Further, as noted in the course of the discussion hereunder, the restriction as to the binding effect of prior judgments of the Court is narrowed to conform largely to the realistic conception given to its previous counterpart in a number of opinions by the Permanent Court of International Justice and in an even greater number by the International Court of Justice.

In 1944, Judge Hudson wrote that Article 59 of the Statute of the Permanent Court of International Justice, providing that a decision by that Court "has no binding force except between the parties and in respect of that particular case," is "a recognition of the important principle of *res judicata* or *chose jugée,* but it does not preclude the Court's reliance on precedents found in its own jurisprudence." [18] A little earlier, however, Judge Hudson had been somewhat vague and indecisive on this point. He had said then that, while Article 59 (taken with Article 38, directing the Court, in adjudicating questions before it, to apply judicial decisions, "[s]ubject to the provision of Article 59") does not "exclude the Court's adoption of the principle of *stare decisis* with respect to its own jurisprudence," it does "not encourage that course." [19] "On the other hand," Judge Hudson continued, ". . . [a]ny tribunal which seeks to administer justice in an impersonal manner will be disposed to rely upon precedents where they exist. The Court has complete freedom in this respect, and nothing prevents it from following a general rule that it will be guided by the principles applied in its earlier adjudications unless cogent reasons should appear for departing from them." [20]

When all is said and done, a decision of a court performs more than the precedential function of guiding the court itself in future adjudications. A judicial determination by an international tribunal as to the construction of a treaty provision, for instance, charts the course to be followed in the drafting of future compacts among nations. The Court has unquestionably used its own prior opinions—or rather principles of international law enunciated or recognized therein—as guiding, or at least persuasive, precedents to fortify or justify the holdings of its current decisions.

---

[18] M. HUDSON, TRIBUNALS at 124.   [19] M. HUDSON, P.C.I.J. at 627.   [20] *Id.*

The result of this general recognition of the guiding force of precedent, has been the evolution of a fairly comprehensive body of international law, serving, in itself, as a guide to the attitude and approach which the Court may be expected to take toward analogous problems. Because most of the work of the Court has been concerned with the interpretation of treaties, these precedents, laid down and followed by the Court, represent a good key to the construction which it is likely to put on provisions in, and provide an excellent guide for the draftsmen of, such international compacts. Of course, in spite of every effort to impersonalize judicial tribunals, they are, and must necessarily remain, human institutions, and as such will inevitably sometimes be inconsistent. The International Court of Justice, despite its status, is not immune to this judicial infection, and has at times hesitated in applying established precedent, and has occasionally deviated from uniform courses which it and the Permanent Court of International Justice have themselves charted. In entire fairness, it must be conceded that a too rigid adherence to precedent may entail disadvantages. Changed times and circumstances may well and properly demand changed approaches to international, as well as to sociological, problems.

There frequently are diverse precedents to be considered, just as there are frequent dissents, and the Court must choose its path among them. There also are occasions when precedents must be abandoned to give way to new and changed concepts. Courts in the United States and, in fact, in most other countries make use of legislative history—that is, the documentation of background data leading to the enactment of legislation—in arriving at what is called "legislative intent," the cornerstone of judicial construction of statutory provisions. In international jurisprudence concerning the interpretation of treaties, such legislative history as proceedings of treaty negotiations, conferences and commissions, as well as accompanying correspondence and reports, are called *travaux préparatoires,* or preparatory work. In most cases involving the interpretation of treaties, the question is raised as to the relevance and authority of *travaux préparatoires* as an element of interpretation.

It is a cardinal rule of this branch of international law that a court will not have recourse to the preparatory work preceding the signing of a treaty in order to ascertain the intention of the parties when the text of the treaty itself is clear. This rule, of course, is but one manifestation of a more fundamental legal idea embodied, for instance, in the "parol evidence rule" of contract law. As a matter of practice, the Permanent Court of International Justice frequently cited this rule; nevertheless, it invariably examined and ultimately discussed the preparatory work which led to the provision of the treaty being construed, either on the assumption that the text thereof was not clear, or perhaps to buttress the conclusion which it had reached on the basis of the clear text.

In the case of *The S.S. "Lotus,"* it will be recalled, a major part of the controversy between France and Turkey turned on Article 15 of the Lausanne Convention of 1923, under which questions of jurisdiction in disputes between the parties were to be decided according to "principles of international law." [21] The Court called attention, at the outset, to "what it has said in some of its preceding judgments and opinions, namely, that there is no occasion to have regard to preparatory work if the text of a convention is sufficiently clear in itself." Then it held that these "principles of international law," as used in the clear text of the Lausanne Convention, "can only mean international law as it is applied between all nationals belonging to the community of States." [22] But the Court then went on to uphold the French contention that the meaning of the disputed term must nevertheless be sought in the evolutionary background of the Convention. France submitted, as falling within that background, the fact that a Turkish draft of the treaty, under which Turkey had claimed jurisdiction over offenses committed outside her own territory, had been rejected. But the Court found that another draft, expressly limiting the jurisdiction of both parties to offenses committed within their own territories, had also been rejected. And the Court held, despite its own findings as to the meaning of the term in question according to the clear text of the treaty (by reason of which there was "no occasion to have regard to preparatory work"), that a minute and thorough examination of the preparatory work dis-

[21] *See* note 2 *supra*.   [22] *Id*.

closed no basis on which the Turkish jurisdiction could be found to be contrary to the "principles of international law" to which reference was made in the Convention.

In almost all cases involving interpretation of treaties, the Permanent Court of International Justice reached or confirmed its conclusions, as in the dissenting opinion of Judges Hurst, Rostworowski, and Negulesco in the *Advisory Opinion on Minority Schools in Albania,* on the basis of "events leading up to the preparation of the text," while insisting that the "natural sense of the words" alone gave the text a clear meaning.[23] Interestingly enough, in the latter case, the Court split eight to three as to the "clear meaning" of the treaty provision in question. There is rarely unanimity as to whether such a text is clear—in itself something of a judicial phenomenon—and, of course, the parties, urging different interpretations, never agree on the clarity of a treaty provision.

In any event, the frequent pronouncement by the Permanent Court of International Justice that the Court will not have recourse to *travaux préparatoires* when the provision of a treaty under consideration is clear was apparently directly contrary to the actual practice of the Court. On the other hand, the International Court of Justice, finding itself faced, and apparently somewhat awed, by the tremendous mass of preparatory work out of which the Charter of the United Nations had evolved, at first disregarded the practice established in the precedents set by the Permanent Court of International Justice, and literally followed the formula, which it incorrectly stated to be "the consistent practice" of the Permanent Court, and refused to examine preparatory work when it found a text before it to be "clear." Thus, in the *Advisory Opinion Regarding Conditions of Admission of a State to Membership in the United Nations (Article 4 of the Charter)*, the International Court of Justice stated its position to be that it should not "deviate from the consistent practice of the Permanent Court of International Justice, according to which there is no occasion to resort to preparatory work if the text of a convention is sufficiently clear in itself." [24] But then, although six of the fifteen judges, dissenting, insisted that the text under

[23] [1935] P.C.I.J., ser. A/B, No. 64, at 32.   [24] [1947–1948] I.C.J. 57, 63.

consideration required clarification, the majority of nine judges considered the "natural meaning of the words" to be "sufficiently clear" to render it improper for the Court to consider the *travaux préparatoires*.[25] And in a number of other cases decided during the earlier era of the International Court of Justice, that Court, while invoking the rigid principle, refused to adopt the flexible practice of the Permanent Court of International Justice in the matter of resort to preparatory work in treaty construction.

From about 1950 on, however, the International Court of Justice has again followed the precedents set by the Permanent Court of International Justice in adopting the general practice of referring to the *travaux préparatoires* in construing treaty provisions—sometimes without even mentioning its rule that such recourse is dependent on lack of clarity in the text itself and sometimes, as in the *Ambatielos Case* (*Jurisdiction*) after discussing and relying on preparatory work, adding incredibly: "In any case where, as here, the text to be interpreted is clear, there is no occasion to resort to preparatory work." [26]

In the international sphere, in which legislation to revise a previous holding is not available except by multipartite convention, a tribunal must be at liberty to distinguish, to modify, and even to disregard precedent while, at the same time of course, building something in the nature of *stare decisis* in rules of international law to serve as guides in the diplomatic forum. This concept undoubtedly underlies the provision of the Courts' Statutes to the effect that their decisions may be used as precedents, subject only to the overriding principle of *res adjudicata,* confining the binding force of each judgment to the parties and the cause in which rendered—leaving the Court free, as to other parties in other causes, to reconsider the substance of principles of law enunciated in prior decisions.

The opinions of the Courts demonstrate that they have departed from precedent only rarely, and never without what the Court, at least, considered good reason. But the Courts have, on occasion, changed their precedential courses, and the Court will no doubt do so again. Ordinarily, the change of course is accomplished by a process of "distinguishing" the precedent from which departure is indicated; but sometimes, in the matter of *travaux prépara-*

[25] *Id.*   [26] [1952] I.C.J. 28, 45.

toires, the Court has frankly modified its attitude in response to a realization that a prior position it has taken is no longer a tenable one.

The provision of Article 59 of the Statute of the Permanent Court of International Justice, and of the same article of the Statute of the International Court of Justice, to the effect that decisions of the Court are to have no binding force except between the parties and in the particular cases in which rendered, did not have a place in the draft statute prepared by the 1920 Committee of Jurists.[27] The provision first appeared in the draft statute adopted by the Council of the League of Nations at its Tenth Session in Brussels,[28] and probably originated in Article 84 of the Hague Convention of 1907 for the Pacific Settlement of International Disputes.[29] An Argentine proposal was rather to the effect that the Court should respect its own prior decisions,[30] somewhat as Lord Robert Cecil had suggested, as early as 1919, that the decisions of the Court should serve as its own "binding precedents." [31]

The final text of Article 59 was introduced by M. Leon Bourgeois of France. It was suggested that this complemented the negative pregnant of Article 63 of the Court's Statute, providing that nations which do not intervene in a proceeding which involves construction of a convention to which they are parties are not bound by the Court's interpretation of the document.[32] On the other hand, Lord Balfour thought it should be left to each country to protest, "not against any particular decision," but rather "against any ulterior conclusions to which that decision may seem to point"; and he predicted that the Court's opinion would "have the effect of gradually moulding and modifying international law." [33]

---

[27] *See* M. HUDSON, P.C.I.J. at 207.

[28] Minutes of the Tenth Session of the Council, at 21, L.N. Doc. 20/29/16 (1920); *Id.* Annex 118, at 161.

[29] M. HUDSON, P.C.I.J. at 207. *See* HAGUE CONVENTIONS at 75.

[30] Proposal of the Argentine Delegation, COMM. III at 514, 519.

[31] 1 D. MILLER, THE DRAFTING OF THE COVENANT 62 (1928).

[32] Report of M. Bourgeois to the Council of the League of Nations, COMM. III at 469, 478.

[33] Note by Mr. Balfour on the Permanent Court of International Justice, COMM. III at 511–12.

Senator Vittorio Scialoja, who had been Minister of Justice and Minister of Foreign Affairs of Italy, chief of the Italian Delegation to the League of Nations, and representative of that country on the Council of the League, had participated with Premier Orlando as a member of the Commission on the League of Nations, in the drafting of the League Covenant.[34] An Italian draft covenant, submitted in 1919 by Messrs. Orlando and Scialoja, expressly contemplated a permanent international court.[35] Years later, M. Scialoja, who had been an eminent professor of law at the Universities of Siena and Rome, became a member of the 1929 Committee of Jurists. During the course of the discussions in that Committee, Professor Scialoja made the unequivocal statement that the persons who created the Permanent Court of International Justice did not intend "that it should act as a factory of international law, or that its judgments should build up a system of international law." [36]

Now this would seem to be a remarkable statement for so eminent a statesman and professor of law. It will be recalled that Lord Balfour of Great Britain had said, at the Council of the League of Nations in Brussels at which the text of Article 59 of the Statute of the Permanent Court of International Justice was born, that the opinions of the Court would ultimately "have the effect of gradually moulding and modifying international law." [37] Moreover, in the report of the subcommittee of the Third Committee of the First Assembly of the League of Nations, which prepared one of the first formal drafts of the Court's Statute, it was submitted that one of the important functions of the Court would be "to contribute, through its jurisprudence, to the development of international law." [38]

Finally, as will be demonstrated in the completion of the development of this thesis, the apparent limitation in Articles 38 and 59 of the Statutes of the Permanent Court of International

---

[34] M. HUDSON, P.C.I.J. at 96 n.19.

[35] *See* Draft Scheme for the Constitution of the Society of Nations (Submitted by the Italian Delegation) , *reprinted in* 2 D. MILLER, *supra* note 31, at 246–55.

[36] 1929 PROCEEDINGS at 33.   [37] *See* note 33 *supra.*

[38] COMM. III at 526, 534 (Comment on Article 38) . *See also* H. LAUTERPACHT, DEVELOPMENT at 5.

Justice and the International Court of Justice on the binding effect of decisions of the Court did not deter either of those Courts from referring to their own precedents as establishing what they treated as accepted rules of international law.

In his report to the UN General Assembly in 1955, Secretary-General Dag Hammerskjöld, while recognizing "that the reluctance of Governments to submit their controversies to judicial settlement stems in part from the fragmentary and uncertain character of much of international law as it now exists," nevertheless postulated that, in the opinions of the Permanent and International Courts, "the beginnings of a 'common law' of the United Nations, based on the Charter, are now apparent." [39] As stated in 1957 by Shabtai Rosenne, a brilliant scholar in the field of international law, erstwhile legal adviser to the Ministry of Foreign Affairs of Israel, and latterly a member of the International Law Commission of the United Nations, the use of judicial precedents by the International Court of Justice "has become much more common, partly, no doubt, because the constant accumulation of judicial precedents is creating what has now become a relatively substantial body of international case-law." [40] In 1958, Judge Sir Hersch Lauterpacht, one of the truly great law professors of modern times, a leading authority on international law, and a judge of the International Court of Justice from 1955 until his death in 1960, wrote that the practice of the Court, in using its own decisions as guiding precedents, "has resulted, over a prolonged period of years, in the formulation—or clarification—of an imposing body of rules of international law." [41]

From time to time, both the Permanent Court of International Justice and the International Court of Justice have treated

---

[39] Sec'y-Gen., Report, 10 U.N. GAOR, Supp. 1, at xiii, U.N. Doc. 2911 (1955).

[40] S. ROSENNE, I.C.J. at 425. Rosenne later stated:

[J]udicial decisions, least of all those of the International Court, cannot be relegated to any subsidiary position; . . . the expansion of a body of international case law, which can be examined together with the full text of the relevant pleadings, is leading to a judicial codification or at least restatement of the law through application to concrete circumstances which in some respects may outstrip efforts to obtain a more complete codification by other means.

2 S. ROSENNE, LAW AND PRACTICE at 612.

[41] H. LAUTERPACHT, DEVELOPMENT at 18

decisions and dicta in the opinions of arbitral and other international tribunals as sources of persuasive precedent. The decisions of such temporary tribunals, of course, are not ordinarily guided by general rules of international law. *Ad hoc* commissions are created to decide specific situations, frequently by quasi-diplomatic processes; to find a common meeting ground to terminate a dispute, rather than to adjudicate its merits strictly by juridical standards. Nevertheless, the judgments of such temporary tribunals have been grounded, on occasion, on principles of international law, for which the permanent international courts have had occasion to cite them as authority. Despite the *ad hoc* nature of international arbitration, that process, over the centuries, also has evolved some of the significant principles and important rules of international law.

And yet, quite unaccountably, the permanent international courts have been reluctant to cite, and to rely on, decisions of arbitral tribunals as authorities recognizing such principles and rules, except in the most general terms. With three exceptions which are cited hereunder, there are no opinions of either the Permanent Court of International Justice or of the International Court of Justice in which either of these Courts referred expressly to any specific decision of an international arbitral tribunal. For instance, in the *Case Concerning the Factory at Chorzów* (*Claim for Indemnity*) (*Merits*), the Permanent Court of International Justice, in a number of passages in its opinion, referred to "a principle generally accepted in the jurisprudence of international arbitration"; to "this principle, which is accepted in the jurisprudence of arbitral tribunals"; to "a principle which seems to be established by international practice, and in particular by the decisions of arbitral tribunals"; and finally, the Court justified its refusal to make a particular award on the ground that it would be based on "contingent and indeterminate damage which, in accordance with the jurisprudence of arbitral tribunals, cannot be taken into account." [42] In somewhat similar general fashion, the International Court of Justice has also had occasion to refer to arbitral decisions. Thus, in the *Fisheries* case, the Court held that

---

[42] [1928] P.C.I.J., ser. A, No. 17, *passim*.

the ten-mile rule for bays had not acquired sufficient stature as a rule of international law because many nations had adopted a different limit, even though others had accepted it "and although certain arbitral decisions have applied it. . . ." [43] In the *Nottebohm Case (Preliminary Objection)*, the International Court of Justice relied on "earlier precedents" of arbitral tribunals for its unanimous holding that, absent any agreement to the contrary, "an international tribunal has the right to decide as to its own jurisdiction, and has the power to interpret for this purpose, the instruments which govern that jurisdiction." [44]

As stated by Judge Sir Hersch Lauterpacht: "International arbitral law has produced a body of precedent which is full of instruction and authority. Numerous arbitral awards have made a distinct contribution to international law by reason of their scope, their elaboration and the conscientiousness with which they have examined the issues before them." [45] There would seem to be no reason why the International Court of Justice should not rely more frequently on cited decisions of arbitral bodies. Despite the *ad hoc* nature of their functions, their opinions have an important place, as a basis for decision, in the international jurisprudence which is evolving in the case law of the Court.

It may, on the other hand, be said generally that neither the Permanent Court of International Justice nor the International Court of Justice has been guided to any appreciable degree by precedents in the decisions and opinions of national courts. Both in the past have considered, and the International Court of Justice will apparently continue in the future to consider, such precedents in the course of their deliberations. National courts do, of course, have occasion to pass on questions of international law. Their decisions, however, are based on, and constitute evidence only of, their own views of the rule of international law involved. When, however, such decisions of the courts of any particular State have taken on a consistent course of uniformity and are accorded recognition by other States, they may fairly be regarded as having acquired authoritative status in the sphere of international jurisprudence. Further, when a rule of international

---

[43] [1951] I.C.J. 116, 131.   [44] [1953] I.C.J. 111, 119.
[45] H. LAUTERPACHT, DEVELOPMENT at 17–18.

law has been laid down in a concordant series of authoritative opinions of the national courts of various States, the rule may fairly be regarded as having achieved the status of "recognized international custom as evidence of a general practice accepted as law," and the decisions may be treated as constituting "judicial precedents recognizing legal principles," under the express provisions of paragraph 5 of Article VIII of the proposed Statute of the International Court of Justice. Such decisions, and the rules of international law therein expressed, would be subject, on both bases, to consideration by the Court in the adjudication of disputes before it, "in accordance with generally accepted, applicable principles of international law."

There is, as stated, in the case law of the permanent international tribunals, a paucity of instances of reference to opinions of national courts as sources for rules of international law. In the Case of *The S.S. "Lotus,"* as will be recalled, a significant question at issue was as to the existence of a recognized international custom, under which prosecution of an officer of a vessel for negligence in a collision was limited to the courts of his vessel's flag. Decisions of national courts were cited by both litigants as precedents, both to prove and to disprove the existence of such "an international custom as evidence of a general practice accepted as law." The Permanent Court of International Justice reviewed these national cases, "[w]ithout pausing to consider the value to be attributed to the judgments of municipal courts in connection with the establishment of the existence of a rule of international law," but reached the conclusion that the national jurisprudence was, in any event, so divided as not to give adequate evidence of the existence of such an international rule.[46] In the *Advisory Opinion Regarding the International Status of South-West Africa,* the International Court of Justice was required to reach conclusions as to the status of a League of Nations Mandate under international law. It held that the term "had only the name in common with the several notions of mandate in national law" and that, since the Mandate under consideration was "an international institution with an international object," it is "not possible to draw any conclusion by analogy from the notions of

[46] [1927] P.C.I.J., ser. A, No. 10, at 28–29.

mandate in national law. . . ." [47] In a separate opinion, Judge Sir Arnold McNair gave it as his opinion that "the true view of the duty of international tribunals in this matter is to regard any features or terminology which are reminiscent of the rules and institutions of private law as an indication of policy and principles rather than as directly importing these rules and institutions." [48] In a lecture delivered at the Law Center of New York University in December 1953, the same distinguished jurist commended the practice of the International Court of Justice in citing precedents and submitted that, in the deliberations of that Court, the opinions of other international tribunals, as well as those of national courts, "may reasonably be supposed to have some persuasive authority. . . ." [49]

Whatever may be the limitations on use by the International Court of Justice of the decisions of other tribunals as precedents, there would seem to be no restrictions, except such as are imposed by the Court itself, on reliance by the Court on its own prior opinions and on those of the Permanent Court of International Justice. It may fairly be assumed that the Statute of the Court does not contemplate its establishment of the rigid principle of *stare decisis* through its own precedents; but it is quite certain that nothing in the Statute prohibits the Court from achieving stability in its jurisprudence by adopting a rule that it will be guided by the principles recognized and laid down in its earlier adjudications, in the absence of good reasons for departing therefrom. Both Courts have, in many instances, evidenced their intention to follow such a rule. In various opinions, the Permanent Court of International Justice has stated that it "has already had occasion to point out" a doctrine being applied; [50] or that "it is unnecessary to repeat" a principle previously enunciated; [51] or

---

[47] [1950] I.C.J. 128, 132.   [48] *Id.* at 148.

[49] A. McNair, The Development of International Justice 12 (1954).

[50] Advisory Opinion Regarding the Exchange of Greek and Turkish Populations (Lausanne Convention VI, January 30th, 1923, Article 2), [1925] P.C.I.J., ser. B, No. 10, at 21.

[51] Advisory Opinion with Regard to the Competence of the International Labour Organisation to Examine Proposals for the Organisation and Development of the Methods of Agricultural Production and Other Questions of a Like Character, [1922] P.C.I.J., ser. B, No. 3, at 57.

that it "adheres to the rule applied in its previous decision"; [52] and in one case, expressly, that it was "following the precedent" of an earlier case.[53] The International Court of Justice not only has adhered to the rule with regard to its own prior decisions, but also has extended its application to precedents of the Permanent Court of International Justice. In the *Advisory Opinion Regarding Conditions of Admission of a State to Membership in the United Nations (Article 4 of the Charter)*, the International Court of Justice stated that it did "not feel that it should deviate from the consistent practice of the Permanent Court of Internaional Justice" in giving consideration to discussions preceding the making of a treaty, when construing its terms.[54] In deciding the *Ambatielos Case (Merits: Obligation to Arbitrate)*, the Court pointed out that it was "not departing from the principle, which is well-established in international law and accepted by its own jurisprudence as well as that of the Permanent Court of International Justice, to the effect that a State may not be compelled to submit its disputes to arbitration without its consent. . . ." [55]

As stated by Judge Read of Canada, in his dissent from the *Advisory Opinion on the Interpretation of Peace Treaties With Bulgaria, Hungary and Romania (Second Phase)* :

There can be no doubt that the United Nations intended continuity in jurisprudence, as well as in less important matters. While this does not make the decisions of the Permanent Court binding, in the sense in which decisions may be binding in common-law countries, it does make it necessary to treat them with the utmost respect, and to follow them unless there are compelling reasons for rejecting their authority.[56]

In the final analysis, an international tribunal is not itself a source of international law. The Court expresses its determination as to what it has found a principle of international law to be, and this expression then simply becomes evidence of the existence of the principle. These precedents are not binding on the Court.

---

[52] Advisory Opinion Regarding the European Commission of the Danube between Galatz and Braila, [1927] P.C.I.J., ser. B, No. 14, at 28.

[53] Advisory Opinion Regarding the Interpretation of the Greco-Turkish Agreement of December 1st, 1926 (Final Protocol, Article IV), [1928] P.C.I.J., ser. B, No. 16, at 15.

[54] *See* note 24 *supra*.   [55] [1953] I.C.J. 10, 19.   [56] [1950] I.C.J. 221, 233.

It may, and occasionally does, distinguish them, and it may presumably even overrule and discard them. But as long as the principles which they embody are expressed by a permanent international tribunal, they represent, collectively, a body of international law for the guidance of nations as well as the Court itself. The International Court of Justice, while clearly not bound by precedents, will, in the ordinary course, like any other tribunal, follow its own prior decisions because they represent an expression of authoritative legal experience—they are, in effect, good law—and respect for such precedents builds stability in jurisprudence, an indispensable element in the orderly administration of justice. The International Law Commission, as an agency of the General Assembly of the United Nations, is making some progress toward a quasi-legislative codification of international law; but relatively little more has been accomplished by that body, in what must be regarded as essentially an academic rather than a scientific effort, than was achieved in similar attempts under the aegis of the League of Nations.[57] In point of fact, the Permanent Court of International Justice and the International Court of Justice have built, and the latter Court is continuing to build, a consistent and respectable body of case law through established precedents in the field of international jurisprudence. It is submitted that the expansion of this body of jurisprudence will inevitably lead to a judicial codification of international law of far greater significance and of far more practical value than a theoretically more comprehensive codification of international legislation, by which to govern the world through an International Rule of Law.

[57] The Vienna Convention of 1969 on the Law of Treaties was based on a draft originally prepared by the International Law Commission and has been one of its few concrete achievements. *See* chapter 11 *infra.* For a complete treatment of this topic, see R. DHOKALIA, THE CODIFICATION OF PUBLIC INTERNATIONAL LAW (1970).

CHAPTER X

Bases of Decision III

A large measure of the success which the International Court of Justice can achieve as a significant factor in the maintenance of world peace must come from an understanding, throughout the world, of the bases on which the Court adjudicates international disputes. There undoubtedly has been a strong popular misconception of this point. The question frequently has been asked: How it is possible, without fixed constitutional and legislative guides or an established jurisprudence based on an accepted legal philosophy, for any tribunal so to dispense international justice as to inspire the necessary confidence and respect on the part of more than a hundred nations of many differing governmental philosophies?

The question really begs the answer. Thousands of treaties— international compacts which have regulated the conduct of nations toward each other over the centuries, and more recently on a multipartite basis—form the fundamental constitutional and legislative guides of an international tribunal. Then too, long- and well-recognized international legal principles which have guided civilized nations, and judicial precedents of arbitral and other international tribunals—latterly those of the Permanent Court of International Justice and the International Court of Justice—have contributed to the formulation of an international jurisprudence in which dissents have rarely, if ever, reflected perspectives based on differing governmental philosophies. Finally, within the framework of international conventions and custom, as construed by judicial precedents, there are those broad principles of equity and justice generally recognized among nations, which also have been woven into an established international jurisprudence and which form the subject of this chapter.

Equity has a well-defined and universally accepted place in the international judicial function; but determination of controversies *ex aequo et bono* ("in equity and good conscience") is actually not a judicial function at all. In the first place, the term "equity" merely embodies a set of judicial principles by which, when construing existing reciprocal rights and liabilities of litigants, the harshness of a strict application of legal rules may be tempered in the search for justice. On the other hand, the term *ex aequo et bono,* as used in international jurisprudence, refers to a doctrine by which a controversy may be settled by *judicial legislation* — not by construing the existing rights and liabilities of the parties, but by revising them, or abrogating them, or creating new ones. As stated by Judge Sir Hersch Lauterpacht [1]:

> Adjudication *ex aequo et bono* is a species of legislative activity. It differs clearly from the application of rules of equity in their wider sense. For inasmuch as these are identical with principles of good faith, they form part of international law as, indeed, of any system of law. . . . On the other hand, adjudication *ex aequo et bono* amounts to an avowed creation of new legal relations between the parties.

Both sets of principles have their roots in Roman law, specifically in the *jus gentium* developed and applied by the praetors. The trend in modern law toward a merger of "law" and "equity" is more in the nature of a reunion: to the Romans, the concepts were one and the same.[2] Covenants, for example, were to be carried out, not only according to their letter, but in good faith. In appropriate cases, judicial tribunals were directed to apply principles of equity to the determination of controversies before them.[3] Nearly thirteen centuries later, these principles were again

---

[1] H. Lauterpacht, Development at 213.

[2] *"Iuri operam daturum prius nosse oportet, unde nomen iuris descendat. est autem a iustita appellatum: nam, ut eleganter Celsus definit, ius est ars boni et aequi."*

[When a ~~man~~ means to give his attention to law *(jus)*, he ought first to know whence the term *jus* is derived. Now *jus* is so called from *justitia;* in fact, according to the nice definition of Celsus, *jus* is the art of what is good and fair.] Digest (of Justinian) . . . .

[3] *"Actionum autem quaedam bonae fidei sunt, quaedam stricti juris. . . .*

"In bonae fidei judiciis, libera potestas permitti videtur judici ex bono et aequo aestimandi, quantum actori restitui debeat. In quo et illud continetur, ut, si quid invicem praestare actorem oporteat, eo compensato, in reliquum is, cum quo actum est, debeat condemnari. . . . Sed nostra constitutio easdem compensationes, quae

reiterated in the Napoleonic and other Continental codes.[4]

Long before the adoption of the Continental codes, it was quite common for international arbitration treaties to provide that the tribunal to which the dispute was to be referred, should be governed, in reaching its decision, by principles of equity, the term "equity" normally being coupled with the terms "law" or "justice." As early as 1661, such a direction was contained in a Portugal-Holland treaty.[5] A century and a half later, in 1815, a *reglement* adopted at the Congress of Vienna required an arbitral commission to render its decisions "en toute justice, et avec la plus grand équité." [6]

The Prize Court Convention of 1907 provided in Article 7 that the Court should be governed, when no recognized rule exists, by the general principles of justice and equity. The multipartite Spitzbergen Treaty of 1920 instructed arbitral tribunals contemplated thereunder to consider, among other factors, applicable rules of international law and "the general principles of justice and equity." [7] Finally, the Reparations Commission established under Article 233 of the Treaty of Versailles was to be guided by "justice, equity and good faith" rather than by any

---

jure aperto nituntur, latius introduxit, ut actiones ipso jure minuant, sive in rem, sive in personam, sive alias quascunque; excepta sola depositi actione. . . ."

[The fourth division [of actions] is into actions of good faith, and actions of strict right. . . .

In all actions of good faith a full power is given to the judge of calculating, according to the rules of justice and equity, how much ought to be restored to the plaintiff; and of course, when the plaintiff is found to be indebted to the defendant in a less sum, it is in the power of the judge to allow a compensation, and to condemn the defendant in the payment of the difference. . . . But we have extended compensations much farther by our constitution, when the debt of the defendant is evident, so that actions of strict right, real, personal, or of whatever kind may be diminished by compensation, except only an action of deposit. . . .]
INSTITUTES (of Justinian) 4.6.28.30.

[4] *See, e.g.,* CODE NAPOLEON art. 1134 ("Elles doivent être executées de bonne foi.") .

[5] Treaty of Peace and Alliance Between Portugal and the Netherlands, Aug. 6, 1661, art. XXV, *reprinted in* 6 Consol. T.S. 375, at 390 (in Latin) .

[6] Regulations for the Free Navigation of Rivers: Articles Concerning Navigation of the Rhine, art. XXVIII (3) , *appended to* Act of the Congress of Vienna, June 9, 1815, 10 Martens (2 N.R.) 379, at 444 (in French) .

[7] Treaty with Other Powers relating to Spitsbergen, Feb. 9, 1920, annex, § 2 (9) , 43 Stat. 1892 (1925) , T.S. No. 686 (effective June 10, 1924) , 2 L.N.T.S. 7.

particular rules of law or procedure.[8] Bipartite conventions, too, contained such provisions. For instance, the five-man Board of Commissioners established under the Jay Treaty of 1794 to ascertain British commercial claims against American citizens was to determine such claims "according to the merits of the several cases, . . . and as equity and justice shall appear to them to require." [9] And in a number of nineteenth-century claims conventions, the same countries required the commissioners to swear that their decisions would be rendered "to the best of their judgment, and according to justice and equity." [10] Under the 1910 arbitration agreement with Great Britain, the members of arbitral tribunals were to declare in writing that they would carefully examine and impartially decide all claims "in accordance with treaty rights and with the principles of international law and of equity." [11]

Like the immemorial application of equitable principles, in the absence of positive law, to the decision of private litigation in national courts, the determination of international controversies according to equity and justice has had near-universal modern acceptance. When the 1920 Committee of Jurists was drafting the Statute of the Permanent Court of International Justice, M. de Lapradelle of France suggested that the Statute should provide that "the Court shall judge in accordance with law, justice and equity." [12] M. Ricci-Busatti of Italy recommended inclusion of "principles of equity" in what was to become Article 38 of the Statute.[13] M. Hagerup of Norway, on the other hand, objected that "equity was a very vague conception and was not always in

[8] Treaty of Peace with Germany, June 28, 1919, pt. VIII, annex II, para. 11, S. DOC. 49, 66th Cong., 1st Sess. (1919), *reprinted in* 2 C. BEVANS, TREATIES AND OTHER INTERNATIONAL AGREEMENTS OF THE UNITED STATES OF AMERICA 1776–1949, at 43 (1969).

[9] Treaty of Amity, Commerce and Navigation with His Britannic Majesty, Nov. 19, 1794, art. 6, 8 Stat. 116 (1848), T.S. No. 105 (effective Feb. 29, 1796).

[10] M. HUDSON, P.C.I.J. at 616.

[11] Special Agreement with Great Britain for the Submission of Outstanding Pecuniary Claims to Arbitration, Aug. 18, 1910, art. 7, 37 Stat. 1625 (1913), T.S. No. 573 (effective Aug. 12, 1912). In fact, similar provisions have been a fixture of bilateral arbitration treaties between the United States and Great Britain, as well as between these two countries and other nations. *See* M. HUDSON, P.C.I.J. at 616.

[12] 1920 PROCEEDINGS at 295.　　　[13] *Id.* at 333–35.

harmony with justice. . . ." He proposed, therefore, that the Court have recourse to equity only if authorized to do so by the parties.[14] Mr. Elihu Root of the United States expressed the thought that, while "the world was prepared to accept the compulsory jurisdiction of a Court which applied the universally recognized rules of International Law," he was inclined to agree that it would not accept such jurisdiction of a Court "which would apply principles, differently understood in different countries." [15] Baron Descamps of Belgium suggested the "legal conscience of civilized nations" as a standard.[16] Ultimately, a directive to the Court that it was to be guided by "[t]he general principles of law recognized by civilized nations" was included in its Statute.[17]

When the Statute of the International Court of Justice was approved, there was very little discussion of this important provision. Except for the insertion in Article 38 of a provision requiring the Court to reach its decisions "in accordance with the international law," [18] no change whatever was made in the provisions of that article outlining the Court's bases of decision; and no express provision whatever was made for decisions in accordance with equitable principles.[19] But it will be recalled that both Statutes referred, in that connection, to "general principles of law recognized by civilized nations," giving to this concept the

---

[14] *Id.* at 296.

[15] *Id.* at 308. In support of this position, Mr. Root mentioned the fact that the International Prize Court, which was to apply such equitable principles, had failed to come into being mainly because of disagreement as to their scope. *Id.* at 309.

[16] *See* Proposal by Baron Descamps, *id.* at 306. Concerning Mr. Root's statement that the principles of justice varied from country to country, *see* text at note 15 *supra,* Baron Descamps answered: "[T]hat might be partly true as to certain rules of secondary importance. But it is no longer true when it concerns the fundamental law of justice and injustice deeply engraved on the heart of every human being and which is given its highest and most authoritative expression in the legal conscience of civilized nations." *Id.* at 310–11.

[17] P.C.I.J. STAT art. 38.   [18] *See generally* chapter 8 *supra,* text at notes 1–37.

[19] In fact, the only mention of equity in the entire redrafting process was a statement by Mr. Fitzmaurice of Great Britain that "there might be considerations of equity which the Court might wish to use in reaching a decision and there was no reason why the Court should not apply such considerations." U.N. Comm. of Jurists, Summary of Tenth Meeting, Doc. Jurist 58, G/46, 14 U.N.C.I.O. Docs. 204, at 205 (1945).

same status, among the bases for decision, as treaties and custom.[20] Shabtai Rosenne calls this a "positivist recognition of the Grotian concept of the co-existence, implying no subordination, of positive law and the so-called natural law of nations." [21] By thus placing the "natural law of nations" among the positivist legal principles found in conventions and custom, without subordination, the Courts have, in effect, created a doctrine of international equity within the concept of "general principles of law," inherent within the framework of international law itself, as a basis of decision of international controversies by a permanent international tribunal.

A number of arbitral courts have actually used equity as a primary basis of decision, although they have not shed much light on its scope. In 1923, an American-Norwegian tribunal said: "The majority of international lawyers seem to agree that [law and equity] . . . are to be understood to mean general principles of justice as distinguished from any particular system of jurisprudence or the municipal law of any State." [22] The following year, an American-British arbitral court held that "no ground of equity" compelled the United States to make reparation on a claim.[23] Three years later, the same court held that another claim against the United States was "just," on the basis of "general and universally recognized principles of justice." [24] Similarly, in 1933, the American-Panamanian Commission could find "no reason to

[20] President J. Gustavo Guerro and Judge Manley O. Hudson represented the Permanent Court at meetings of Committee IV/1 of the U.N. Conference on International Organization, held in San Francisco in May 1945. When asked directly if the order in which the bases of decision were enumerated in Article 38 of the Court's Statute also constituted the order in which they were to be applied, both agreed that it did not. Comm. IV/1, Summary Report of Fifth Meeting, Doc. 240, IV/1/15, 13 *id.* 163, at 164.

[21] 2 S. ROSENNE, LAW AND PRACTICE at 610 (1965).

[22] Norwegian Claims case (Norway v. United States), Hague Court Reports 2d (Scott) 39, at 65 (Perm. Ct. Arb. 1922).

[23] Eastern Extension, Australasia and China Telegraph Company, Limited, American and British Claims Arbitration 73, at 79 (1926). Fred K. Nielson, the American agent who argued the case, submitted a lengthy discussion of the meaning of "equity." *Id.* at 51–67. The British agent, Sir Cecil Hurst, who was elected to the Permanent Court but six years later, also presented his view of the term's meaning. *Id.* at 68–72.

[24] Cayuga Indians, *id.* at 307, 321. The court also considered the equitable defense of laches, sustaining it with regard to Great Britain but not to the Indians. *Id.* at 329–30.

scrutinize" international law, justice and equity, to determine whether they "embody an indivisible rule or mean that international law, justice and equity have to be considered in the order in which they are mentioned, because either of these constructions leads to the conclusion that the Commission shall be guided rather by broad conceptions than by narrow interpretations." [25]

The only instance in which the Permanent Court of International Justice appears to have applied a principle of equity is the case of *The Diversion of Water from the Meuse*, decided in 1937. In that case the Court drew an analogy between a Belgian canal lock about which Holland complained and a lock previously built by the latter country, saying that "[i]n these circumstances, the Court finds it difficult to admit that the Netherlands are now warranted in complaining of the construction and operation of a lock of which they themselves set an example in the past." [26] This may undoubtedly be considered an application of the equitable principles that "equality is equity," and that "he who seeks equity must do equity," pursuant to the holding of Judge Hudson in his separate opinion in that case, "that under Article 38 of the Statute [of the Permanent Court], if not independently of that Article, the Court has some freedom to consider principles of equity as part of the international law which it must apply." [27]

In the *Corfu Channel Case (Merits)*, the International Court of Justice based Albania's obligation to warn shipping of minefields in its territory, in part, on elementary considerations of humanity, which it found among "general and well-recognized principles." [28] The same Court took an approach to the delimitation of the disputed zone in the *Fisheries* case between Great Britain and Norway somewhat similar to that of the Permanent Court of International Justice in the *Meuse* case, by taking into consideration certain unique geographic and economic factors not directly germane to the strict legal issues involved, and relevant only as constituent elements of the concrete dispute before the Court. [29]

These equitable conceptions, so introduced by the Courts into

[25] Perry Claim, American and Panamanian Central Claims Arbitration 75 (1933).
[26] [1937] P.C.I.J., ser. A/B, No. 70, at 25.   [27] *Id.* at 77.
[28] [1949] I.C.J. 4, at 22.   [29] [1951] I.C.J. 116.

the law, are not definite or clear-cut; but, after all, law itself is not an exact science. The very use of equitable principles over the years by international tribunals certainly justifies the conclusion that equity is an element of international law, not opposed to legal principles but supplementing and tempering them in their application to international controversies.

A decision *ex aequo et bono,* on the other hand, is a horse of an entirely different color from a decision based on equitable principles. It is, in fact—as well as in law—not even a horse at all. As has been stated, an equitable decision is one in which the existing legal rights of the parties are determined, even though, in the process of such determination, the applicable legal principles may be supplemented, ameliorated, or even modified by principles of equity. A decision *ex aequo et bono* is one by which a controversy is determined by judicial legislation—not by determination of existing legal rights, but by creation of new legal relations between the parties.

No dispute has ever been submitted to either the Permanent Court of International Justice or the International Court of Justice permitting those tribunals, by agreement of both parties under Article 38 of the Statutes of both Courts, to decide a case *"ex aequo et bono,* if the parties agree thereto."[30] However, the nature of a decision *ex aequo et bono* is illustrated quite clearly in the *Free Zones* case, which came before the Permanent Court of International Justice. In the Treaty of Versailles, it was agreed

that the stipulations of the treaties of 1815 and of the other supplementary acts concerning the free zones . . . are no longer consistent with present conditions, and that it is for France and Switzerland to come to an agreement together with a view to settling between themselves the status of these territories under such conditions as shall be considered suitable by both countries.[31]

A dispute having arisen between the parties as to the effect of this provision, they submitted it to the Permanent Court of Inter-

[30] Absent such an agreement, "[i]t is the duty of the Court to interpret . . . [t]reaties, not to revise them." Advisory Opinion on the Interpretation of Peace Treaties with Bulgaria, Hungary and Romania (Second Phase) , [1950] I.C.J. 221, at 229.

[31] [1929] P.C.I.J. ser. A, No. 22, at 9; *id.* at 16.

national Justice, to determine, *first,* whether the treaty had abrogated the régime of the free zones; and, *second,* if the free zones were to remain in existence, and the parties could not themselves reach agreement as to the new régime to be established therein, to "settle for a period to be fixed by" the Court, "and having regard to present conditions, all of the questions involved in the execution" of the treaty provision.[32] The Court decided, in due course, that the Treaty of Versailles had not abrogated the free zones, and gave the parties a fixed time within which to settle the new régime in the territories.[33]

The countries having been unable to reach agreement within the given time, the second part of the submission to the Court came before it for determination. France insisted that the Court should be empowered, without limitation, to lay down the future customs régime for the territory; Switzerland, on the other hand, maintained that the submission had not been made sufficiently broad for a decision *ex aequo et bono.* The Court was divided sharply on the issue. Six of the judges felt that the submission conferred on the Court the same authority as the parties themselves would have had in negotiations and that there was no reason why it should not fix the status of the territory on the basis which it felt would be "most in conformity with the present requirements." [34] The other six judges, who became the majority of the Court through their agreement to the operative part of the judgment, held that the Court could proceed only on the basis of the existing legal rights which it had itself previously determined. Although the parties themselves might dispose of those rights by agreement, the Court was bound by existing legal rights in the absence of a "clear and explicit" submission by the parties for a determination *ex aequo et bono.*[35] In the course of his "observations" in that case, Judge Kellogg of the United States went even further in stating, quite erroneously, that "the authority given to the Court to decide a case *ex aequo et bono,* merely empowers it to apply the principles of equity and justice in the broader signification of this latter word." [36] Judge *ad hoc* Dreyfus of France observed correctly that such authority empowered the Court "to play the part of an arbitrator in order to reach the

32 *Id.*   33 *Id.* at 21.   34 *Id.* at 28.   35 *Id.* at 10.   36 *Id.* at 40.

solution which, in the light of present conditions, appeared to be the best, even if that solution required the abolition of the zones." [37]

That a decision *ex aequo et bono* is legislative, in the sense of fixing, rather than declaring, the rights of parties, as in arbitration, is demonstrated historically in innumerable references to arbitrators for such determination. As early as 1858, Chile entered into a special arbitration agreement with the United States for a decision *ex aequo et bono,* and a number of other such submissions to arbitration were made during the nineteenth century.[38] Such agreements to submit controversies to arbitral tribunals for such decision actually multiplied after adoption of the Statute of the Permanent Court of International Justice, despite its permissive provision "to decide a case *ex aequo et bono* if the parties agree thereto." For example, a Belgian-Swedish treaty of 1926 provided for submission of disputes, other than such as involved adjudication of the rights of the parties, to arbitral tribunals for decision *ex aequo et bono.* This same provision was used in many other treaties.[39] The 1928 Geneva General Act on Pacific Settlement of Disputes is particularly significant in this connection. It provided that "all disputes with regard to which the parties are in conflict as to their respective rights" were to be referred to the Permanent Court of International Justice for adjudication. All other disputes among the parties were to be referred to arbitral tribunals, for decision *ex aequo et bono,* insofar as none of the substantive rules under Article 38 of the Statute of the Court should be deemed applicable to the controversy. This provision, too, was copied into many treaties.[40]

It is reiterated that the rendition of a decision *ex aequo et bono* is not a judicial function at all; and this seems to have been demonstrated quite clearly by two decisions of the International Court of Justice.

The first is the so-called *Belize* controversy, involving a special declaration by Great Britain of acceptance of the compulsory jurisdiction of the Court "in all legal disputes concerning the interpretation, application or validity of any treaty relating to

---

[37] [1932] P.C.I.J., ser. A/B, No. 46, at 212.   [38] M. HUDSON, P.C.I.J. at 618.
[39] *Id.* at 619.   [40] *Id.*

the boundaries of British Honduras." [41] The government of Guatemala had accepted the compulsory jurisdiction of the Court, subject to the express reservation that its declaration of adherence "does not cover the dispute between England and Guatemala concerning the restoration of the territory of Belize, which the government of Guatemala would, as it has proposed, agree to submit to the Court, if the case were decided *ex aequo et bono*." [42] The provisions of the Statutes of the Courts permitting them to render decisions *ex aequo et bono* do not belong to Article 38 among the bases of decision to be applied by the Courts. The provision is really nothing more than a grant to the Courts of jurisdiction over such disputes; and Great Britain never having agreed to such submission of the Belize controversy to the Permanent Court, the jurisdiction of that tribunal never attached to the case.

In the *Asylum* and *Haya de la Torre* cases, the real controversy between the parties, as to how to terminate the confinement of Señor de la Torre in the Colombian embassy at Lima, could not be decided for the same reasons. [43] As stated by Judge Azevedo in his dissenting opinion, he felt that both the main claim of Colombia and the counterclaim of Peru should be dismissed, despite the fact that both parties had "urgently appealed to the Court to resolve the dispute." They had not "furnished it with the means to arrive at an independent solution as would have been possible" *ex aequo et bono,* but had, on the contrary, "limited the action of the Court by indicating only the legal data applicable to the case." [44] In the face of this situation, the government of Colombia declared in the *Haya de la Torre* case that it would accept a decision *ex aequo et bono* if the government of Peru would agree; but no such agreement was forthcoming. [45] So the Court could not decide that case on its merits either, not being vested with jurisdiction of the real controversy. It may well be that even if the parties had agreed, the Court would not have undertaken to render a decision *ex aequo et bono,* for, as the

---

[41] [1946–1947] I.C.J.Y.B. 217. This declaration was renewed for a further period of five years. [1950–1951] *id.* at 205.

[42] [1950–1951] I.C.J.Y.B. at 219.   [43] [1950] I.C.J. 265.   [44] *Id.* at 357.

[45] Haya de la Torre case, I.C.J. Pleadings 10 (1951).

Court held, it was unable to determine that controversy "since, by doing so, it would depart from its judicial function." [46]

It would simply not be a proper judicial function of the International Court of Justice, as a permanent tribunal with compulsory jurisdiction over disputes among nations, to act as an arbitral commission to effect compromises of such controversies for the countries involved, even with their consent. The question may perhaps be more easily understood by bringing it somewhat closer to home. Consider, for a moment, the case of an ordinary contract between an employer and a labor union, fixing terms of employment. Assume that the contract is for a term of years and provides that there are to be no strikes or lockouts during its term, but that, on the demand of either party made at the end of any year of the contract term, the agreement may be reopened for a revision of wage rates only. Assume that such a situation has arisen, that the parties have concededly bargained in good faith for new wage rates, but have simply been unable to reach agreement. Assume further, that the complaining party has filed suit in a court of otherwise competent jurisdiction, seeking relief by prayer that the court fix the wage rates on which the parties have been unable to agree and that the other party to the dispute joins squarely in the prayer of such relief.

No ordinary civil court would entertain such a proceeding, but would, on the contrary, decline jurisdiction *ex proprio motu* on the ground that the relief sought was not of a judicial nature, the controversy submitted to the court—even with the unequivocal consent of both parties—not being susceptible of juridical adjudication. A consensual controversy of that character should be submitted to arbitrators, presumably versed in the technical aspects of the problems involved and not bound by the wholesome limitations inherent in the judicial process—without regard, for the moment, to the frequently posed question as to the wisdom of making a contract by arbitration at all.

Similarly, nations which have problems requiring an alteration or fixing of their relationship, rather than an adjudication of their rights under their existing relationship, should submit such problems to arbitrators or amicable compounders, or leave them to the

[46] [1951] I.C.J. 83.

diplomatic forum in effect to adjust and compromise their differences. The majority in the *Free Zones* case at least indicated doubt as to the jurisdiction of the Court over such a case, even with the consent of the parties; and the Court expressed itself as unable to adjudicate the ultimate controversy in the *Haya de la Torre* case, "since, by doing so, it would depart from its judicial function." [47]

The question might well be asked whether the International Court of Justice, if unable for such a reason to adjudicate the ultimate issue in a case, could not go so far as to determine ,the existing reciprocal legal rights and then, with the consent of the parties, to recommend a course to be followed by them to settle their underlying controversy. In some cases, the Courts have felt themselves free, even without the express consent of the parties, to formulate such suggestions in their opinions. In the case of *The S.S. "Lotus,"* for instance, the principal issue was whether the forum of the nation of a vessel's flag had exclusive jurisdiction over an offense committed by her master in international waters, one causing collision with a vessel of a different flag. In that case, while holding that the jurisdiction of the flag forum was not exclusive, the Court suggested that the best solution of the problem in cases of collision between vessels of different flags was to recognize the concurrent jurisdiction of both the country of the offending officer's vessel and of the other country involved.[48]

In the case of *The Rights of Nationals of the United States in Morocco,* the International Court of Justice found that the relevant provision of the Act of Algeciras of April 7, 1906, did not "afford decisive evidence in support of either of the interpretations contended for by the parties" in arriving at valuations for customs purposes.[49] Since that provision "lays down no strict rule on the point in dispute," and "requires an interpretation which is more flexible" than either of those submitted by the parties, the Court suggested other factors to be taken into consideration.[50]

Interestingly, the Court has itself stated that it would be inconsistent with its position as a judicial body to express views or to announce conclusions which the parties were at liberty to dis-

[47] *Id.*   [48] [1927] P.C.I.J., ser. A, No. 10.   [49] [1952] I.C.J. 176, at 209.
[50] *Id.* at 211.

regard. In the *Free Zones* case, the Permanent Court of International Justice had occasion to say that "it would be incompatible with the Statute, and with its position as a Court of Justice, to give a judgment which would be dependent for its validity on the subsequent approval of the parties." [51] But having set up this limitation on itself, the Court went on to make the following observation in the same case: "The Court does not hesitate to express its opinion that if, by the maintenance in force of the old treaties, Switzerland obtains the economic advantages derived from the free zones, she ought in return to grant compensatory economic advantages to the people of the zones." [52]

While the Permanent Court of International Justice held, in the case of the *Serbian Loans,* that the economic changes forged by the First World War did not relieve the debtor nation of the necessity of meeting its outstanding obligations, it apparently had no feeling that it was departing from its judicial functions in adding that the circumstances "may present equities which doubtless will receive appropriate consideration in the negotiations." [53]

In the case of the *Société Commerciale de Belgique,* the Belgian government sought to enforce, and the Greek Government sought modification of, the terms of, an arbitral award in favor of a Belgian corporation against Greece. The Permanent Court of International Justice felt constrained to call attention to its judicial inability "to oblige the Belgian government . . . to enter into negotiations" looking to an amicable settlement with Greece, based on *force majeure* which had impaired the financial condition of the Greek Government, much less to "indicate the bases of such an arrangement." [54] Nevertheless, the Court held that the situation, as brought to its attention, "enabled the Court to declare that the two Governments are, in principle, agreed in contemplating the possibility of negotiations with a view to a friendly settlement, in which regard would be had, among other things, to Greece's capacity to pay." And the Court even added candidly: "Such a settlement is highly desirable." [55]

Despite these dicta of the Courts, *dehors* the judicial function

---

[51] [1932] P.C.I.J., ser. A/B, No. 46, at 161.   [52] *Id.* at 169.
[53] [1929] P.C.I.J., ser. A, No. 20, at 40.
[54] [1939] P.C.I.J., ser. A/B, No. 78 at 160, 177.   [55] *Id.* at 178.

in each case, the better view was unquestionably expressed, more recently, by the International Court of Justice, in its *Advisory Opinion on the Status of South-West Africa.* In that case the Court, confessing its inability to find, in "general considerations" in and between the lines of the record, "any legal obligation for mandatory States to conclude or negotiate" trusteeship agreements, held directly that "it is not for the Court to pronounce on the political or moral duties which these considerations may involve." [56]

On the other hand, so eminent an authority as the late Judge Sir Hersch Lauterpacht proposed that the Court should be at liberty to make recommendations – in addition to, and not in substitution for, its decisions on the law – for a nonbinding modification of the rights established in its judgments. He suggested that such authority might be effected by inserting, in the Statute of the Court, a provision reading:

If the Court finds that its decision, based on the application of the rules of law as (elsewhere herein) enumerated . . . results in a situation calling for a modification of the law either in general or in the relations of the parties to the dispute, it shall have the power to make appropriate recommendations. While such recommendations shall not be binding upon the parties, they shall give to them all due consideration.[57]

Shabtai Rosenne, in his recent book on the International Court of Justice, states that "if a broad view is taken of the functions of the Court, there is little cause for dismay that the States which have established and which maintain the Court consent that, if the parties to a dispute are in agreement, the Court may perform such a function, even though the mere existence of such a provision may offend legal purists." [58]

All in all, courts should no more presume to suggest to the diplomatic forum in international controversies than to the legislative forum in ordinary cases how the problems of the parties may be solved beyond the bounds of the judicial sphere. Diplomats are better equipped than are judges to tie up the loose ends

---

[56] [1950] I.C.J. 128, at 140.   [57] H. LAUTERPACHT, DEVELOPMENT at 219.
[58] 1 S. ROSENNE, LAW AND PRACTICE at 324 (1965).

of their disputes on the basis of rights adjudicated among nations in the juridical process, according to law, equity, and justice. If the diplomats reach an impasse, their governments can always submit their differences to arbitration—if they wish to do so—for adjustment and settlement.

For these reasons, the provision permitting the International Court of Justice to decide a cause *ex aequo et bono,* even with the consent of the parties, is omitted from the proposed Statute of that Court. Moreover, the revision of the Statute contains a direction to the Court to use general principles of law, equity, and justice as a basis of its decisions. The proper judicial perspective of a permanent international tribunal can best be preserved by holding to the straight path of its correct judicial function: to construe, and—avoiding the temptation to wander among the devious bypaths of diplomatic negotiations—to refuse to make, design, or recommend, agreements among nations. By thus confining itself to its proper role as "the principal judicial organ of the United Nations," the International Court of Justice should better be able, by its own judicial light, to reflect the image of international peace and security more clearly through the broad spectrum of the International Rule of Law.

CHAPTER XI

Vienna Convention on the Law of Treaties

Since one of the principal functions of the International Court of Justice is, and unquestionably will continue to be, the construction of treaties, there is given hereunder an outline of the recently confected Vienna Convention on the Law of Treaties. It is without question one of the most important documents of its kind ever to be drafted. As of May 1, 1973, forty-seven nations had signed the Convention and only seventeen had ratified it. The United States signed it on May 23, 1970, but the Senate, as this is written, has not yet given its advice and consent to ratification.

Actually, as will be shown hereunder, the document has no retroactive effect; that is, it is not to govern treaties made prior to its effective date. Nevertheless, as a guide to the construction of treaties among nations, it will unquestionably be used by the International Court of Justice to construe such documents, on the principle that it is largely declaratory of existing treaty law and as such undoubtedly governs the construction of their provisions.

At its opening session in 1949, the International Law Commission of the United Nations agreed that one of its first studies should concern itself with an effort to codify the law of treaties. In eighteen sessions over a period of seventeen years, the Commission held some three hundred meetings at which this subject was the principal topic of discussion. Finally, in 1966, the Commission adopted seventy-five draft articles on the law of treaties and recommended that the General Assembly of the United Nations convene an international conference of plenipotentiaries to study the draft articles and to endeavor to conclude a convention on the subject.[1] The General Assembly, by its Resolution 2166 (XXI), decided that such a conference should be convened,

[1] Int'l L. Comm'n, Report, 18 U.N. GAOR, Supp. 9, at 10, U.N. Doc. A/5509 (1963).

and in the following year (1967), decided that the first session should meet in Vienna in March 1968.

At the first session of the conference in the spring of 1968, delegations from 103 countries attended. The second and final session met again in Vienna in April and May of 1969, with representatives of 110 nations participating. The Convention, as ultimately worked out, was finally adopted on May 23, 1969, by seventy votes for, one (France) against, and nineteen abstentions, which included all of the Communist countries except Yugoslavia. It would require needless space and inordinate detail to attempt to describe all of the Convention's provisions. This chapter will accordingly mention only some of its more salient features.

The Vienna Convention on the Law of Treaties is an agreement among nations on the law governing the formation and operation of international agreements, how they should be interpreted, construed, amended, and terminated, and fixing the rules governing their invalidity. It is of particular significance that this codification should have occurred when it did, since nation-States which had only recently come into being frequently complained that they should not be bound by laws in the formation of which they had had no part. In this instance they were well represented, and all played an active role in the conferences. The result is important, not because the large number of developing countries succeeded in altering the fundamental principles of international law governing treaty arrangements among nations, but because they did not. The basic rule, *pacta sunt servanda,* that treaties are binding on the parties and cannot be broken, was affirmed. Efforts to broaden the grounds for establishing invalidity did not succeed. Satisfactory disposition was made of the problem of dispute settlement which threatened to disrupt the conference. That the contemporary international community could reach agreement on the issues involved is of paramount significance.

Part I of the Convention defines "treaty" and other terms. Part II deals with the capacity of nation-States to conclude treaties, the powers of representatives, and methods by which a nation's consent to be bound by treaties can be determined. A nation which has signed, ratified, or consented to be bound by a treaty is obligated to refrain from acts which would defeat its objects and purposes. Part III deals with reservations, entry into force, and provisional application; Part IV, with the law governing the observance and interpretation of treaties, their effect upon other nation-States, and rules governing their amendment and modification. Part V relates to invalidity, termination, and suspension, and to procedures for the settlement of disputes. The remaining parts cover succession of States, depositaries, registration, publication, signature, ratification, and other procedural matters. The Convention is to enter into force, as to the original ratifying or acceding nations, on the thirtieth day after deposit with the Secretary-General of the United Nations of the thirty-fifth instrument of ratification or accession, and thereafter, as to each subsequently ratifying or acceding nation, on the thirtieth day after such deposit of its appropriate instrument of adherence thereto.[2]

The first article states simply that the "present convention applies to treaties between States," and the second gives definitions of terms used throughout the Convention. The third provides that the fact that the Convention does not apply to certain other international agreements is not to prevent the application to such agreement of the provisions of the Convention to which they would, in any event, be subject.

The first important declaration of the Convention is that it is not retroactive. By the terms of Article 4, its provisions are to apply, *ex proprio vigore,* only to treaties concluded after the Convention shall have entered into force. A counterpart to this provision is found in Article 28 of the Convention, which declares that treaties generally are not applicable to situations which arose, or ceased to exist, before they have become effective.

Articles 6 to 17 of the Convention provide for the entry of treaties into effect by signature, ratification, approval, or accession. And Article 18 states that when a treaty has been signed subject to ratification, neither party may take any action which would defeat its objects and purposes, provided that such ratification is not "unduly delayed."

2 Vienna Convention arts. 82–84.

Under Article 19 of the Convention, reservations are admissible in connection with the ratification of, or accession to, a treaty only if not prohibited, or to the extent expressly permitted, by the treaty, and only if not incompatible with its objects and purposes.

Articles 20 through 23 regulate the manner and effect of reservations to treaties, the effect of objections thereto, the withdrawal of reservations, and the procedures regarding them. Failing any provision in a treaty to the contrary, it enters into force, under Article 24, when consent to be bound by it has been established. It is provided in Article 25 that a treaty or part of a treaty may enter into force provisionally if the parties have so agreed; but such provisional entry into force may be terminated by any party thereto by giving notice to the others that it does not intend to become a party.

Article 26 enunciates the basic doctrine, *pacta sunt servanda,* of all treaties, that they are "binding upon the parties and must be performed by them in good faith."

Under Article 29, absent a different provision, a treaty has effect in the entirety of the territory of the contracting parties; and the effect of possible conflicts between prior and later treaties when the parties thereto are the same or when they are different is regulated under Article 30.

Under Article 31 of the Convention, treaties are to be construed in accordance with the ordinary meaning of their terms, "in their context," and in the light of the treaty's objects and purposes. For the purpose of interpretation, the context of a treaty is to comprise, in addition to the text, preamble, and annexes, any agreement relating to the treaty which was made between all of the parties in connection with the conclusion of the treaty and any instrument made by one or more parties in connection with the conclusion of the treaty and accepted by the other parties as an instrument related to it. In addition, the following is to be taken into account together with the context: any subsequent agreement between the parties regarding interpretation or application, subsequent practice in the application of the treaty which establishes agreement regarding interpretation, and relevant rules of international law applicable to the relations between the parties. At the conference, the United States tried to include *travaux préparatoires,* the preparatory work of the treaty and the circumstances of its conclusion (what we would call "legislative history") among the primary guides to interpretation. In this effort, the United States was unsuccessful. Article 32 provides that recourse to supplementary means of interpretation, including such preparatory work and circumstances, may be had (and by inference may only be had) in order to confirm the meaning resulting from the application of Article 31, or to determine the meaning when the interpretation according to Article 31 leaves the meaning ambiguous or leads to a result which is manifestly absurd or unreasonable.

The Convention contains two important articles which may give rise to questions when the document is before the Senate for advice and consent to ratification. The first of these is Article 27, which states simply that "a party may not invoke the provisions of its internal law as justification for its failure to perform a treaty." This would appear to be an inevitable corollary of the basic provision in Article 26, that treaties are "binding upon the parties and must be performed by them in good faith," and seems unnecessary in view of that provision. Indeed, it was not included in the draft articles prepared by the International Law Commission during its long study of this subject. Nevertheless, its impact on our constitutional system must be recognized. For example, it would prevent justifying nonperformance by the United States on the ground that the Supreme Court had held a provision of a treaty to be invalid as in conflict with a constitutional limitation. Despite such a ruling, the invalid-treaty provision would be binding on the United States in international law, and its performance would be required. Suppose, for example, that a treaty should be made between the United States and Mexico, in which the parties agreed not to permit inflamatory, subversive broadcasts across their common border. If the treaty should be held by the Supreme Court of the United States to be violative of the free-speech guaranty of the first amendment, it would still be binding on the United States *vis-à-vis* Mexico under international law as expressed in Article 27 of the Vienna Convention.

Another significant provision is that contained in Article 46 of the Convention. This provides that "a State may not invoke the fact that its consent to be bound by a treaty has been expressed in violation of a provision of its internal law regarding competence to conclude treaties as invalidating its consent, unless that violation was manifest and concerned a rule of its internal law of fundamental importance." One may readily postulate a conceivable situation arising out of the International Anti-Dumping Code, concluded by the United States with seventeen other nations in Geneva on June 30, 1967. All of those seventeen nations treated the document as a formal treaty requiring parliamentary approval, which they gave it. The United States alone dealt with the document as an executive agreement. It was reported that, because certain of its provisions were in direct conflict with corresponding provisions of Congressional tariff acts, the Code was not submitted to the Senate for its advice and consent for fear of adverse action by that body.[3]

If such a situation should arise following the entry into force of the Vienna Convention on the Law of Treaties as to the United States, the Code would be held binding on this country even if the Supreme Court of the United States should hold that it was invalidly adopted as an executive agreement without the advice and consent of the Senate. From the text of the Constitution and the long practice of the United States in relation to executive agreements, it would appear difficult to establish that such a constitutional transgression was "manifest."

The background of Article 46 has been reviewed thoroughly in an article by Ambassador Richard D. Kearney,[4] who led the United States delegation at the Vienna conference. Prior to and at the conference, many nations supported the view that an agreement made on behalf of a government, by a person officially designated as authorized to make it, is fully binding on that government. This was the view taken by our State Department in 1950. Other states, notably developing countries, taking a

---

[3] *See* Act of Oct. 24, 1968, P.L. No. 90–634, § 201, 82 Stat. 1347 (codified at 19 U.S.C. § 160 (1970)), which suspended certain provisions of the Anti-Dumping Code. *See also* Long, *United States Law and the Anti-Dumping Code*, 3 INT'L LAW. 464 (1969).

[4] Kearney, *Internal Limitations on External Commitments—Article 46 of the Treaties Convention*, 4 INT'L LAW. 1 (1969).

"monist" point of view, saw a serious danger in drawing a distinction between the international validity of a treaty and its internal validity. There was little support for the latter position at the conference, however, with the main differences being between those countries contending that internal limitations on the capacity of nation-State representatives to conclude treaties should not invalidate their State's consent to be bound, and those insisting on adding the qualification: "unless the violation of its internal law was manifest." After the former had been defeated by a vote of fifty-six to twenty-five with seven abstentions, the final article was adopted by a vote of ninety-three in favor, none against, and three abstentions.

Ambassador Kearney says in conclusion in his above article (the Article 43 of which he speaks having become Article 46 in the final text) :

The history of Article 43 demonstrates that the text finally chosen was the culmination of an extended review of all possible courses of action. Is the solution that has been finally worked out the best available solution? It is certainly not the rule that would have the greatest appeal to either the fervid nationalist or the perfervid internationalist. But the all-or-nothing approach of true believers rarely supplies a workable formula for a workaday world. When the desirable aim of upholding the stability of the international treaty structure collides with the laudable end of placing some domestic checks and balances upon the making of international commitments, the reasonable solution should be a compromise that protects both sets of interests to the maximum extent.

The essential decision in reaching such a compromise is allocation of the burden of proceeding. Should the weight of making the argument fall upon the State that relies on its internal law to defeat a commitment or upon the latter's appearance of authority to undertake the commitment?

The decision underlying Article 43 is to accord *prima facie* validity to the appearance of authority subject to the limitation of an objectively evident violation of a fundamentally important internal law. The review of the problem has demonstrated above all, that this solution is amply supported, not only by legal theory, but by consideration of practical consequences.

Article 43 is designed for a world in which the *coup d'état* and the suspension of constitutions are endemic, but also where international business cannot be suspended until constitutional rule is restored. It is designed for a world in which assaults upon international commitments are a standard weapon in the armory of aspiring politicians. Given the facts of contemporary international existence, Article 43 represents the most reasonable rule for a world in which reason is not yet supreme.[5]

Those who contend that the internationally binding character of treaties must always be subject to domestic constitutional disabilities may well ponder the difficulties of such a position in connection with our rights against other countries. If claims under treaties were subject to being met with contentions that the treaty is not binding on the country against which the claim is made because of some internal-law limitation, the stability of an international legal order would be jeopardized. Indeed, it is difficult to see how there would be any stability at all if such a self-denying principle were universally operative. According to Ambassador Kearney's report, there fortunately appears to have been no support at the conference for such an extreme position. It is accordingly suggested that it is very much to the advantage of the United States to ratify the Vienna Convention without reservations, since if the United States ratified with reservations, under the principle of reciprocity, every other ratifying nation, large or small, would have the same right to avoid its treaty obligations by "invoking the provisions of its internal law as justification for its failure," and the only penalty which could be imposed on the United States for its own failure to comply with the terms of a treaty held invalid by the Supreme Court would be the payment of damages, with the continuing right to denounce and to withdraw from such an agreement should it permit withdrawal.

Article 33 provides that the texts of treaties in two or more languages are equally authentic, with the terms of the treaty having the same meaning in each text. Articles 34 to 38 fix the rights and obligations of third States, the methods of their revocation and modification, and state that nothing therein precludes a rule in a treaty from becoming binding on a third State as a customary rule of law.

[5] *Id.* at 21.

Under certain conditions, by Articles 39 to 41, multilateral treaties may be amended or modified, and failing an expression of a different intent, a state is to be considered a party to the treaty as amended; and under certain other conditions a multilateral treaty may be amended as to only two or more parties thereto.

Articles 42 through 45 outline the conditions under which a treaty may be held invalid, denounced, terminated, or suspended —generally only as provided in the treaty or by express terms of the Convention. And Articles 47 through 51 refer to revocation of a treaty by proof of error under certain circumstances of fraud, corruption, or coercion of a State representative.

Another important provision of the Vienna Convention is that of Article 52, which states that "a treaty is void if its conclusion has been procured by the threat or use of force in violation of the principles of international law embodied in the Charter of the United Nations." This principle would surely raise interesting legal questions as to the intergovernmental agreements between the Soviet Union and Czechoslovakia made during the 1968 invasion of the latter country by forces of the former. Termination of a treaty, or withdrawal of a party therefrom, may take place under the terms of Article 54 in accordance with the provisions of a treaty or by consent of all parties thereto; but reduction of the number of parties below the number originally necessary for the treaty to enter into force does not terminate a multilateral treaty unless the treaty provides otherwise.

Also of special interest and importance is Article 56, to the effect that a treaty containing no provision for denunciation or withdrawal is not subject thereto, unless it can be shown that the contrary was intended, directly or by implication, and then on not less than twelve months' notice.

Articles 57 to 59 and Article 61 provide for the temporary suspension of a treaty as to all or some of the parties thereto, in accordance with the provisions of the treaty or by consent of all parties, or for its termination or suspension by the conclusion of a later treaty on the same subject matter or by impossibility of performance as by disappearance or destruction of the object thereof.

Under Article 60, a material breach of a treaty by a party

thereto generally entitles the other party or parties to terminate or suspend its operation in whole or in part; but this is not to apply to provisions "in treaties of a humanitarian character," especially such as those which prohibit "any form of reprisals against persons protected by such treaties."

Another provision of great consequence to the stability of treaties, particularly those relating to the developing world, in which conditions frequently change rapidly, is Article 62, dealing with change of circumstances. Such a change, not foreseen by the parties, may not be invoked as a ground for terminating, or withdrawing from, a treaty unless the existence of those circumstances constituted an essential basis of the consent of the parties to be bound by the treaty, and the effect of the change is radically to transform the extent of obligations still to be performed. A fundamental change of circumstances may not, however, be invoked as a ground for termination or withdrawal if the treaty establishes a boundary or if the fundamental change is the result of an international breach by the party invoking it. Of particular interest in this context is the provision of Article 63, to the effect that severance of diplomatic or consular relations is not to change the legal effect of a treaty between the parties, except insofar as the existence of such relations "is indispensable for the application of the treaty."

To the same effect is the text of Article 74, which declares "that the severance or absence of diplomatic or consular relations . . . does not prevent the conclusion of treaties between" States; and that "the conclusion of a treaty does not in itself affect the situation in regard to diplomatic or consular relations."

Articles 53 and 64 of the Vienna Convention deal with the international-law concept of *jus cogens*—described as "a peremptory norm of general international law . . . accepted and recognized by the international community . . . as a norm from which no derogation is permitted and which can be modified only by a subsequent norm . . . having the same character." Article 53 states that "a treaty is void if, at the time of its conclusion, it conflicts with a permanent norm of general international law"; and article 64 provides that "if a new peremptory norm . . . emerges, any existing treaty which is in conflict with that norm

becomes void and terminates. . . ." In this connection, it is
stipulated under Article 71 of the Convention that if a treaty is
declared void as of its inception under article 53 as contrary
to a peremptory norm of international law, the parties must re-
establish the *status-quo-ante*. If, on the other hand, the treaty
becomes void because of a conflict with an emerging new peremptory norm under Article 64, the parties are relieved of further
obligations thereunder; but their prior rights and obligations
inter se remain effective — only, however, so long as these are not
themselves in conflict with the new peremptory norm.

Under Article 65, a party invoking asserted grounds of invalidity, or for termination or suspension of, or withdrawal from,
a treaty must give formal notice to the other parties of the position which it is taking. If objection is entered to such a position,
the parties must endeavor to resolve their dispute in accordance
with any agreements they may have among themselves governing
settlement of disputes, or in the absence of any such agreements,
under the terms of Article 33 of the Charter of the United Nations on "Pacific Settlement of Disputes." Failing settlement
within twelve months under the foregoing provisions, either party
may, under Article 66, submit a dispute arising under Articles 53
or 64 (*jus cogens*) to the International Court of Justice, unless
the parties agree to submit the dispute to arbitration instead; or
either party may submit a dispute as to any other matter for
conciliation under the procedure established in the Annex to the
Convention.

That Annex provides that each party to the Convention and
each other Member of the United Nations may nominate two
"qualified jurists" as conciliators for five-year terms; and the
aggregate roster of the persons so nominated is to constitute what
is called "the list." Whenever a dispute subject to conciliation
arises under Article 66, each side to the dispute appoints one
conciliator of the nationality of one of the states on that side who
need not be on "the list," and one other conciliator, not a national
of any of those states, but who must be chosen from "the list." The
four conciliators so chosen are to appoint a fifth from "the list,"
and he is to act as chairman. Any appointment not made as so
required is to be made by the Secretary-General of the United

Nations, either from "the list" or from the International Law Commission. The five persons so appointed constitute the "Conciliation Commission." It is to determine its own procedure and may hear the parties and make findings and recommendations by majority vote, and it is to make every effort to conciliate the dispute. The Conciliation Commission must make its report within twelve months of its constitution, and this report, including any conclusions stated therein regarding the facts or questions of law, shall not be binding on the parties, and it shall have no other character than that of recommendations, submitted for the consideration of the parties in order to facilitate an amicable settlement of the dispute.

By Articles 67 through 70 and Article 72 the rules of procedure and the effect of invalidity, termination, and suspension of a treaty are established. It should finally be noted that, under Article 73 of the Convention, its provisions are to be without prejudice to "any question that may arise in regard to a treaty from a succession of States, or from the international responsibility of a State, or from the outbreak of hostilities between States."

Article 75 provides that the terms of the Convention do not apply to a treaty imposed on an aggressor nation by the United Nations. Articles 76 to 80 set forth the places at which treaties may be deposited, the functions of depositaries, correction of errors in treaties, and their negotiations and publication. Signatures, ratification, accession, and entry into force are regulated under Articles 81 to 84, and Article 85 provides that the Chinese, English, French, Russian, and Spanish texts of the Convention are to be equally authentic and are to be deposited with the Secretary-General of the United Nations.

The foregoing brief outline of the more important phases of the Vienna Convention on the Law of Treaties, and of a few of the interesting problems to which it may well give rise, should suffice to indicate its overall vast scope and significance. Ambassador Kearney has referred to it as "the most far-reaching codification effort in the field of international law that has thus far been attempted." [6] It is frequently difficult, and at times even impossible, to negotiate a bipartite treaty which is eminently satis-

[6] *Id.* at 1.

factory to both sides; and it is clearly far more difficult to negotiate a multipartite convention which does not embody some provisions unacceptable, in greater or lesser degree, to most, if not all, of the several parties involved. The Vienna Convention has, as stated, only prospective effect. Since it has not yet come into effect, its provisions do not govern existing treaties. It expresses, however, many principles of existing law and sooner or later will undoubtedly govern the construction of all treaties.

CHAPTER XII

Chambers of the International Court of Justice

The system of chambers of the Permanent Court of International Justice and that of the International Court of Justice could as well have been entirely supererogatory; but chambers of general jurisdiction for which provision is made under the proposed Statute can be made to be utilitarian agencies in the development of that tribunal into a significant instrumentality for the achievement of world peace. This conclusion may best be demonstrated by an examination of the history, background, and evolution of the present statutory and regulatory provisions on the constitution and functioning of such chambers.

These chambers were originally contemplated to be smaller groups of judges or, in a sense, divisions of the Court, to provide summary procedure for the relatively rapid disposition of less complex proceedings. They were also designed to hear and determine specialized types of cases, presumably requiring technical knowledge or special consideration by the judges assigned to them, such as labor, transit, and communications cases. In the fifty years of existence of the two Courts, only one case has ever been heard by the Chamber for Summary Procedure,[1] and not a single case has ever come before any specialized chamber. Furthermore, although the Statute of the Permanent Court of International Justice provided for assessors to sit with the special chambers or with the Court when sitting in such special cases,[2] and the Statute of the International Court of Justice provides for assessors to sit with the Court or any of its chambers,[3] no assessors have ever sat with the Court or any chamber thereof.

The Hague Convention of 1899 contained no provisions for summary procedure in the settlement of international disputes. In 1907, however, the French delegation at the Hague suggested

[1] Interpretation of the Treaty of Neuilly, [1924] P.C.I.J., ser. A, Nos. 3–4.
[2] P.C.I.J. STAT. arts. 26–27.   [3] I.C.J. STAT. art. 30.

adoption of a provision for a compulsory summary arbitration procedure in cases in which disputes arose out of multipartite conventions, and such a provision was embodied, formally, in Articles 86 to 90 of the Hague Convention of 1907.

Proposals for inclusion of provisions for summary procedure in the contemplated Statute of the Permanent Court of International Justice were made in various recommendations to the 1920 Committee of Jurists.[4] Mr. Hagerup of Norway, who had been the delegate of his country to the 1907 Hague Conference, asserted "that the archives of the various Foreign Offices contain many questions left unsolved, because there had been hesitation to set going the cumbersome machinery of arbitration." He suggested that a summary system be devised "to make possible a rapid and inexpensive procedure" for such cases.[5] M. de Lapradelle of France felt that power to deal summarily with such cases might properly and effectively be reposed in a single judge, as in the *procédure des référés* of France.[6] M. Ricci-Busatti, who in 1907 had been Secretary to the Italian delegation at the Hague, suggested that, in such a case, the parties should be permitted to select any three of the judges for summary hearing and determination of their dispute.[7]

In the final analysis, there was such general agreement in principle among the members of the 1920 Committee of Jurists as to the desirability of establishing a procedure for summary disposition of cases through a division of the contemplated court that there was no undue difficulty in arriving at an agreed draft, after it was first determined that the full Court should normally sit *en banc.*[8] The draft as ultimately adopted provided simply: "With a view to the speedy dispatch of business, the Court shall form annually a chamber composed of three judges who, at the request of the contesting parties, may hear and determine cases by summary procedure."[9]

It was contemplated that proceedings in the Chamber for Summary Procedure were to be as simple as possible, and that only cases involving disputes of such a nature as to lend themselves readily to summary disposition were to be referred to

[4] *See* 1920 Proceedings at 89.   [5] *Id.* at 517.   [6] *Id.* at 524–26.   [7] *Id.*
[8] M. Hudson, P.C.I.J. at 179.   [9] P.C.I.J. Stat. art. 29.

that Chamber.[10] As stated by Judge Fromageot in 1936: "When governments addressed themselves to the Chamber for Summary Procedure, it was because they considered the case as one of minor importance, not necessarily as regards its consequences, but in the sense that the problems and difficulties to which it gave rise lent themselves to a simple solution." [11]

This Chamber was constituted regularly each year, but the only occasion on which it ever was put to use was, as stated, in the case of the *Interpretation of the Treaty of Neuilly*. Judgment was rendered in that case in September 1924; [12] on application for an interpretation of that judgment, a second judgment was rendered in March 1925.[13] In both phases of the proceeding, the Chamber was composed of the same judges, there were no oral hearings, and both judgments were rendered by the "Court sitting as a Chamber of Summary Procedure."

Otherwise:

a) A reference to the Chamber for Summary Procedure was suggested in the 1928 *Serbian Loans* case, but the Serbian government took the position that, in view of the importance of the issues involved, it was not in a position to accede to summary disposition thereof.[14]

b) In 1934, the Secretary-General of the League of Nations transmitted to the Permanent Court of International Justice the texts of certain agreements, one of which involved the contract for construction of the League buildings. The Secretary-General requested that the Court, sitting as a Chamber for Summary Procedure, undertake formation, as occasion might require, of an arbitral tribunal or tribunals for settlement of disputes under these agreements.[15] In reply to this request, the Registrar advised the Secretary-General of the League that the Court would "in all probability" be disposed to undertake the function; but when, later, a dispute did arise and the Chamber actually agreed to comply with the application for formation of an arbitral tribunal, the request was withdrawn.[16]

---

[10] M. HUDSON, P.C.I.J. at 346.   [11] [1936] P.C.I.J., ser. D, No. 2, at 666.
[12] [1924] P.C.I.J., ser. A, No. 3.   [13] [1924] P.C.I.J., ser. A, No. 4.
[14] [1929] P.C.I.J., ser. C, No. 16–III, at 792–93.
[15] 11 P.C.I.J. ANN. R. (ser. E) 152 (1935).   [16] *Id.*

c) In 1935, the Chamber for Summary Procedure was convened to act on a request that it appoint members of an arbitral tribunal, but the request was again withdrawn, and the Chamber took no action. So, while one case had been referred to and decided by the Chamber for Summary Procedure prior to the 1924 revision of the Statute of the Permanent Court for the specific purpose of encouraging summary disposition of cases, no case ever was submitted to the Chamber after that time, although some subsequent treaties did expressly contemplate that disputes arising thereunder were to be adjudicated by this Chamber.[17]

In the meantime, early during the deliberations of the 1920 Committee of Jurists, the Director of the International Labor Office (later the International Labor Organization – ILO) called the attention of the Committee to the articles of the Treaty of Versailles, under which the proposed Court was to have jurisdiction over certain types of labor disputes.[18] Despite this direction and the notice thereof brought to their attention, the Committee made no special provision for the adjudication of labor cases by the Court, on the apparent assumption that such cases would be submitted, considered, and determined just like all others.

M. Albert Thomas of France, the Director of the International Labor Office, then submitted amendments to the Committee's draft under which a certain number of the judges would have been required to be expert in labor economics and social legislation, and the membership of the Court would have had to include representatives of both management and labor for the hearing and determination of labor cases.[19] These proposals were placed before the First Assembly of the League of Nations and had the support of the French delegation when they were under consideration by a subcommittee of the Third Committee of the Assembly.[20] A plan submitted by the British representative envisaged a special chamber of five judges to adjudicate labor cases, with the assistance of four assessors sitting in a consultative capacity. This British suggestion was stated to be based on the need for a special chamber to reduce the size of the Court so that it

---

[17] *See* [1932] P.C.I.J., ser. D, No. 6, at 629.   [18] 1920 PROCEEDINGS at 248, 257.

[19] COMM. III at 537–65; LEAGUE DOCUMENTS at 74–80.

[20] COMM. III at 360, 394; LEAGUE DOCUMENTS at 129, 151.

would not be too unwieldy when the assessors were added—thus constituting a tribunal of practical size, encompassing an expertise in labor matters.[21] Strong sentiment was expressed in the subcommittee in favor of trial of labor cases before the full Court, in order to maintain the overall, worldwide, international character of the tribunal.[22] However, it was finally decided that labor cases should be heard before a small chamber, in an effort to develop, and place emphasis on, judges who would be specialists in that field.[23] But in order to satisfy, "so far as possible," those who wanted labor cases, like all others, to be heard before a representative worldwide tribunal, it was stipulated that selection of the Labor Chamber's five judges should be accomplished "with due regard for the provisions of Article 9," under which "the whole body" of judges of the entire Court "should represent the main forms of civilization and the principal legal systems of the world." [24] The Director of the International Labor Office represented to the Subcommittee that conflicts between capital and labor "were far from involving mere points of law"; and, in its report to the Third Committee, the subcommittee itself submitted that many phases of labor disputes were "not of an exclusively legal character." [25]

M. Thomas, appearing before the Third Committee, expressed irreconcilable dissatisfaction with the draft article reported to it by its Subcommittee, and demanded that "a special *locus standi* before the Court might be given the International Labor Office and that assessors be accorded an equality of status with judges." [26] In response to this submission by M. Thomas, the Third Committee added a paragraph to the Subcommittee's draft article providing that "in Labour cases, the International [Labour] Office shall be at liberty to furnish the Court with all relevant information, and for this purpose, the Director of that Office shall receive copies of all the written proceedings." [27]

[21] COMM. III at 388, 592; LEAGUE DOCUMENTS at 70, 146.
[22] COMM. III at 390 passim; LEAGUE DOCUMENTS at 149 passim.
[23] COMM. III at 396–97; LEAGUE DOCUMENTS at 153.
[24] P.C.I.J. STAT. arts. 9, 26.
[25] COMM. III at 310; LEAGUE DOCUMENTS at 106, 209.
[26] COMM. III at 309; LEAGUE DOCUMENTS at 105.   [27] P.C.I.J. STAT. art. 16.

In its final draft, as originally adopted and as revised in 1936, this article, providing for a special chamber of the Court to hear and determine labor cases, was a somewhat confusing conglomerate. It provided that in the absence of a demand by the parties that such cases be heard by this chamber, they were to be considered by the full Court or the chamber of the Court, as the case may be, to be "assisted by four technical assessors sitting with them"; but the article provided also that "recourse may always be had to the summary procedure" in which, however, there was no provision for assessors.[28] The provision for a resort to summary procedure in labor cases was recommended, along with other, lesser revisions in this article, by the 1929 Committee of Jurists, without objection by the Director of the International Labor Office; and these recommendations were adopted, without change, by the 1929 Conference of Signatories.[29]

While provision was being made for a special chamber for labor cases, similar considerations prompted formation of a special chamber of the proposed Permanent Court of International Justice for the determination of cases dealing with matters of transit and communications.[30] In other discussions taking place at this time, the technical nature of questions arising in transit and communications cases was emphasized, in light of consideration being given simultaneously by the Second Committee of the First Assembly to plans for a Transit and Communications Organization of the League of Nations.[31] This organization was to function as an agency with jurisdiction to conciliate disputes falling within the ambit of its special field; and there was considerable question as to whether this competence would not come into conflict with the Court or a chamber exercising jurisdiction over such cases.[32]

The original text of Article 27, creating a special chamber of the Court for Transit and Communications Cases, was based on a proposal made by the British delegation to the First Assembly of the League of Nations, and this was then adapted by the Subcommittee of the Third Committee to conform, generally, to the

[28] *Id.* art. 29.
[29] 1929 PROCEEDINGS at 53, 69; 1929 PROCEEDINGS (SIGNATORIES) at 38, 40.
[30] COMM. III at 592.   [31] M. HUDSON, INTERNATIONAL LEGISLATION 617 (1931).
[32] COMM. III at 310.

article providing for a special chamber to hear and determine labor cases.[33] The possible jurisdictional conflict between this new Chamber and the contemplated Transit and Communications Organization was thought to be resolved by the provision of the proposed article that such cases were to be heard and determined by the Chamber only "if the parties so demand." [34] As originally drafted, the article stipulated that the Chamber or the Court, as the case might be, was to be assisted by assessors "on all occasions." [35] The First Assembly, however, revised this stipulation to provide for such assistance by assessors only "when desired by the parties or decided by the Court," and the provision was retained in this form.[36]

When revision of this article was being considered by the 1929 Committee of Jurists, it consulted the League of Nations Advisory and Technical Committee on Communications and Transit with reference to the changes being proposed.[37] The latter body pointed out that no case had ever been referred to the special Chamber for Transit and Communications Cases; that it was extremely unlikely that assessors would be in a position "to afford the Court any real assistance" in the technical phases of such cases; and that, in the final analysis, in its view, international disputes dealing with transit and communications matters, like all other controversies among nations, should be heard and determined by the full Court.[38]

The League of Nations Advisory Committee on Communications and Transit suggested, however, as an alternative to elimination of this article from the Statute of the Permanent Court, or that it be amended to provide for summary disposition of disputes as to matters of transit and communications.[39] The 1929 Committee of Jurists nevertheless permitted the article to stand as originally drafted, with only minor modifications. That Committee did, however, add a paragraph, as in the article on the Chamber for Labor cases, to permit recourse to summary procedure under Article 29.[40] When this recommendation of the Jurists came before the 1929 Conference of Signatories, the Danish representa-

---

[33] *Id.* at 592.   [34] *Id.* at 310, 397–400.   [35] *Id.* at 498–99.   [36] *Id.*
[37] 1929 PROCEEDINGS at 69.   [38] *Id.*   [39] *Id.*   [40] *Id.* at 69, 74, 122.

tive proposed to suppress the article and to substitute in its place one to create a special chamber of the Court for consideration of international commercial disputes. The Conference of Signatories nonetheless approved the recommendation of the Committee of Jurists.[41]

No quorum of any kind has ever been fixed for a chamber of either Court. The Rules of the Courts in the past have always made provision for adjournment of a session of the full Court when a quorum is lacking, but they have contained no similar provision as to a chamber. Accordingly, it always has been assumed that the quorum of a chamber is the same as the full membership thereof, all of whom would be required to be present to constitute a valid session of the chamber.[42] Under the proposed Statute of the International Court of Justice, judges *ad hoc* are to be appointed by the Court itself when necessary to complete a quorum.[43] When forming a chamber and fixing the number of judges to compose it, presumably the Court would specify the number constituting a quorum of the chamber. The Rules of the Court, however, never have made any provision in this regard. While a Chamber of Transit and Communications cases was formed by the Permanent Court of International Justice every three years, as required under Article 29 of its Statute, that Chamber never was convened, and no case ever was brought before it.

In the early period of formulation of the Statute of the International Court of Justice, negotiations and discussions clearly were influenced by strong senses of regionalism, nations being fearful of foreign domination and correlatively anxious themselves to play influential roles in regional areas. When the Statute of the International Court of Justice was being drafted in 1945 to constitute that tribunal as the judicial organ of the United Nations, the Informal Inter-Allied Committee on the Future of the Permanent Court of International Justice, which had begun to meet in London in 1943, suggested a new approach to the problem of compulsory jurisdiction through the creation of four

---

[41] 1929 PROCEEDINGS (SIGNATORIES) at 40.
[42] [1936] P.C.I.J., ser. D, No. 2, at 15.   [43] I.C.J. STAT. (P) art. XII, para. 1.

regional chambers: one each for Europe, the Middle East and Africa, the Far East, and the Western Hemisphere.[44] The Inter-Allied Committee suggested, quite understandably in light of the history of the Permanent Court of International Justice, that non-European nations might be unwilling to submit their disputes to an international tribunal sitting in Europe, "likely to be predominantly European in composition."[45] A motivating factor behind this suggestion was unquestionably the hope that the United States, which had theretofore been unwilling to accept compulsory jurisdiction of a universal tribunal, might agree to submit to such jurisdiction of a court whose functions were circumscribed by Pan-American boundaries.[46] But because it was felt that such a system of regional chambers would inevitably undermine the salutary concept of a single permanent international tribunal with universal worldwide jurisdiction, the proposals of the Inter-Allied Committee were rejected.[47]

Two proposals in this regard had been discussed. The first of these proposals contemplated a permanent type of regional chambers which should, to all practical intents and purposes, be effectively autonomous. The second proposal, somewhat akin to a suggestion which had been made by the Department of State, envisaged regional chambers to be constituted only at the request of the parties to a particular case.[48] These proposals by the Inter-Allied Committee were submitted in response to specific Inter-American complaints that a single universal court sitting in Europe "might not altogether satisfy the needs of the world." In support of the proposals for the regional chambers, it was also urged that "only through some such regional system can it be hoped to prevent the development in the future of competing international jurisdictions for non-European parts of the world."[49]

Somewhat similar proposals were later made by Cuba and other Latin American countries to the Washington Committee of Jurists in 1945, on the submission that a single court sitting in Europe, "likely to be predominantly European in composition," was not to be expected to meet the needs of non-European na-

---

[44] R. RUSSELL, CHARTER at 381–82.
[45] *See* 1 S. ROSENNE, LAW AND PRACTICE at 201.   [46] R. RUSSELL, CHARTER at 382.
[47] *Id.* at 383–84.   [48] *Id.* at 384.   [49] *Id.*

tions.[50] There apparently was very little discussion of any of these proposals in the Washington Committee,[51] prevailing objections being based primarily on the fact that both proposals would sacrifice the highly desirable unity, cohesion, and universality of a single international tribunal with worldwide jurisdiction.[52]

The seat of the Permanent Court of International Justice had been fixed immutably, by Article 22 of the Statute of that Court, at the Hague, where its sessions and those of the Chamber for Summary Procedure were required to be held. But under the provisions of Article 28 of that Statute, as originally adopted, the special chambers might, "with consent of the parties to the dispute, sit elsewhere than at the Hague."[53] Possibly—or probably—to satisfy the demands of regionalism, when the original Statute of the International Court of Justice was adopted, it provided that the establishment of the seat of the Court at the Hague should "not prevent the Court from sitting and exercising its functions elsewhere whenever the Court considers it desirable,"[54] and that any of the chambers might also sit and function elsewhere "with the consent of the parties."[55]

It was nevertheless felt that special chambers might, on occasion, serve useful purposes, even though, to all practical intents and purposes, no use had ever been made of the chambers of the Permanent Court of International Justice.[56] In drafting a new article on chambers for the new International Court of Justice, therefore, the Court was authorized to form chambers of three or more judges from time to time, as required, to deal with particular categories of cases (disputes relating to labor and to transit and communications being kept as examples).[57] The Court was also authorized to form, at any time, a chamber composed of such number of judges as might be specified by the Court with the approval of the parties, to deal with any particular case; and it was provided expressly that cases might be tried before chambers appointed to hear particular cases, or particular categories of cases, "if the parties so request."[58] Finally, in the drafting of the Statute

---

[50] 1 S. ROSENNE, LAW AND PRACTICE at 201.   [51] 14 U.N.C.I.O. Docs. 109 (1945).
[52] R. RUSSELL, CHARTER at 384.   [53] 1 S. ROSENNE, LAW AND PRACTICE at 201.
[54] I.C.J. STAT. art. 22.   [55] *Id.* art. 28.
[56] 1 S. ROSENNE, LAW AND PRACTICE at 201.   [57] *Id.*   [58] I.C.J. STAT. art. 26.

of the International Court of Justice, the provision of Article 29 of the Statute of the Permanent Court of International Justice, requiring the Court annually to form a chamber "composed of five judges which, at the request of the parties, may hear and determine cases by summary procedure," was retained without change.[59]

Originally, since the special chambers were contemplated to deal with cases of a technical nature, it was thought that the judges composing those chambers, as well as the assessors who were to sit with them, should be persons having some knowledge of the technical subjects for consideration of which the chambers were formed.

The system of assessors had its roots in ancient Rome, where they were really trained lawyers who sat beside a provincial governor or other magistral official to guide him as to the law, in carrying out the judicial functions of his administrative office.[60] This system of assessors, as legal aides to municipal officials, is apparently still in effect in Scotland, a Roman-law jurisdiction; [61] but in England, assessors are really technical advisers to professional judges, as in the case of the Elder Brethren of Trinity House, who are frequently called, because of their "nautical skill and experience," to assist the judges of the common-law courts.[62] In the ecclesiastical courts, assessors with judicial experience are sometimes called to help officers of the Church determine disputed questions of fact; and, interestingly enough, arrangements may—in theory, at least—be made for the attendance of bishops and archbishops as assessors in trials of ecclesiastical cases by the Judicial Committee of the Privy Council of the House of Lords in England.[63] In France and in most other European countries in which the civil law prevails, an assessor is a sort of lay or assistant judge, several of whom, sitting with a trained judicial officer, constitute a court.[64]

In the courts of the United States, none of these systems of

[59] 14 U.N.C.I.O. Docs. 834–35.   [60] W. HUNTER, ROMAN LAW 803–4 (1876).
[61] 1 BOUVIER'S LAW DICTIONARY 259 (Rawle's 3d rev., 8th ed. 1914).
[62] BLACK'S LAW DICTIONARY 151 (4th ed. 1957).
[63] Church Discipline Act of 1840, 3 & 4 Vict. c. 86, § 11; Appellate Jurisdiction Act of 1876, 39 & 40 Vict. c. 59, § 14.
[64] *See* P. HERZOG AND M. WESER, CIVIL PROCEDURE IN FRANCE 149 (1967).

assessors has ever existed. In a sense, appraisers in maritime and probate proceedings, who advise the court as to valuations of vessels and property of estates, exercise functions similar to those of European assessors; and these are really expert witnesses.[65] But an assessor in this country is essentially an administrative official who fixes the value of property for purposes of *ad valorem* taxation and has no direct connection whatever with the judicial process.[66]

In light of this background and evolution of the assessorial system, it is difficult to appraise or assess the real function intended to be exercised by assessors contemplated to sit with the chambers of the Permanent Court of International Justice or of the International Court of Justice, or with those Courts themselves. But in the clear context in which provision for assessors was originally made in the Statute of the Permanent Court of International Justice, one must assume that the assessors were to be technical advisors to the judges, much like experts, who would not testify before the Court but would be available to the Court for technical consultation.[67] Provision has always been made in the Statutes of the Courts for experts, who would seem to differ from assessors in that they are witnesses—ordinarily, but not always—produced by the parties.[68] When experts are examined at the insistence of the Court, they differ from assessors only in that the assessors are an arm of the Court itself, participating in its deliberations even though not voting, whereas the experts, if present at all, by permission of the Court, during deliberations, would serve only in a consultative capacity.[69]

In the Statute of the Permanent Court of International Justice, the use of assessors was contemplated only with the Labor and Transit and Communications Chambers or with the Court in the trial of such cases.[70] In the Statute of the International Court of Justice, provisions for assessors were deleted altogether from the articles dealing with chambers of the Court, and it was enacted simply, in a separate article, that the "rules of the Court may

---

[65] The Empire, 19 Fed. 558 (E.D. Mich. 1884) .
[66] Kuhlman v. Smeltz, 171 Pa. 440 (1895) .   [67] P.C.I.J. STAT. arts. 26–27, 50.
[68] *Id*. art. 50.   [69] 1 S. ROSENNE, LAW AND PRACTICE at 212; 2 *id*. at 595.
[70] P.C.I.J. STAT. arts. 26–27.

provide for assessors to sit with the Court or with any of its Chambers, without the right to vote." [71]

While the Court has had some occasion to provide for commissions of enquiry and experts, use was made of the latter, on the initiative of the Court, only in the early *Corfu Channel* case before the International Court of Justice; [72] and neither Court has ever had occasion, in the more than fifty years of their aggregate existence, to make use of assessors at all. No real need of assessors is accordingly envisaged, and the proposed Statute of the International Court of Justice makes no provision for their appointment. The matter, however, is left to the Court for regulation by its rules, as under the preceding Statute, should need or occasion for assessors ever arise. [73]

The Rules of the Permanent Court of International Justice provided that when the members of the Chambers were elected by the full Court, consideration should be given "to any preference expressed by the judges," to give them the opportunity of serving in the special fields in which they had expert experience and knowledge. [74] But this expression of preference by the judges for places on the Chambers was discontinued in 1936, it being assumed that it was the function of the judges to bring their broad general backgrounds in international law to bear on the problems before them, in preference to any expert technical knowledge they might have as to the subjects of disputes being adjudicated. [75]

Actually, the qualities which make for competence in the judge of a permanent international tribunal are unquestionably learning in international law coupled with broad practical experience in international affairs; and if the primary requirement for settlement of an international dispute is a technical knowledge of the particular matter in controversy, the case should undoubtedly be submitted to arbitration before experts in the field rather than to a permanent judicial tribunal guided primarily by principles of international law.

In considering the future need for chambers of the Interna-

[71] I.C.J. STAT. art. 30.
[72] 5 Corfu Channel Case, I.C.J. Pleadings 170, 208 (1948).
[73] I.C.J. STAT. (P) art. XIX, para. 2.
[74] P.C.I.J.R. 14; *See* M. HUDSON, P.C.I.J. at 710.
[75] P.C.I.J.R. 24, in 13 P.C.I.J. ANN R. (ser. E) 133 (1937).

tional Court of Justice, it must be borne in mind that, with the exception of the *Neuilly* case in 1924–25,[76] decided by the Chamber for Summary Procedure of the Permanent Court of International Justice, no case had ever been submitted for trial to any chamber of either Court in the fifty years of their existence. It must also be borne in mind that special categories of cases should either be submitted to arbitrators for technical, rather than strictly legal, adjudication or to the full Court for determination according to broad principles of international law; and that there is apparently no disposition on the part of the nations of the world to submit their disputes with each other to a chamber for summary procedure.

When the original Statute of the Permanent Court of International Justice was adopted in 1922, the number of judges to constitute the special chambers for labor and for transit and communications cases was fixed at five, plus two additional judges "selected for the purpose of replacing a judge who finds it impossible to sit." [77] In addition, provision was made, as to each such special chamber, that it should be assisted by four technical assessors, sitting with the chamber but without the right to vote; [78] and as to the special chamber for labor cases, the assessors were to be "chosen with a view to ensuring a just representation of the competing interests." [79] Further, each of the articles of that Statute dealing with the formation of these special chambers specified that if there should be "a national of one only of the parties sitting as a judge" in such a chamber, the President of the Court was to "invite one of the other judges to retire in favour of a judge chosen by the other party," so that there would be either no judge of the nationality of either party or one judge of the nationality of each party sitting as a member of a special chamber in every case.[80]

When the Statute of the Permanent Court of International Justice was revised in 1929, the articles providing for special chambers for Labor and Transit and Communications cases were left substantially intact except in one important particular. It should be recalled at this point that the original Statute of the

---

[76] *See* note 1 *supra.*   [77] P.C.I.J. STAT. arts. 26–27.   [78] *Id.*
[79] *Id.* art. 26.   [80] *Id.* arts. 26–27.

Permanent Court of International Justice provided that if the Court itself should include, among its judges, a national of one of the parties, the other party might select a judge of its nationality to sit as a member of the Court for trial of the pending case; and that if the bench included no national of either party, each might select, for that case, a judge of its own nationality. Such "national" judges came to be known as judges *ad hoc*.[81] This system of providing for national judges of the parties to each case had been evolved with considerable difficulty out of conflicting views among the members of the 1920 Committee of Jurists, which then reported that "States attach much importance to having one of their subjects on the bench when they appear at the Court of Justice"; [82] and Judge Hudson later wrote that this plan represented one of the "principal achievements" of that Committee, "for the scheme for electing the judges would probably never have been adopted without it." [83]

In the 1929 Committee of Jurists, it was felt that the failure to make use of the Chamber for Summary Procedure, was probably attributable to the fact that no provision had been made for inclusion of judges of the nationalities of the parties on the bench of the chamber.[84] Now, as to that Chamber, Article 29 of the original Statute of the Permanent Court of International Justice provided simply that it was to be composed "of three judges," with no provision for national judges to assure a national balance on such a bench and none for assessors or substitutes, although the Court itself provided by rule that "two judges shall also be chosen to replace any member of the Chamber for Summary Procedure who may be unable to sit." [85] When, then, the article of the original Statute of the Permanent Court of International Justice providing for a Chamber for Summary Procedure was being studied by the 1929 Committee of Jurists, that Committee felt that the absence from the article of any provision for the selection of national judges for that chamber may have been responsible for the fact that, with the exception of the *Interpretation of the Treaty of Neuilly* case in 1924 and 1925, no resort had

---

[81] *Id*. art. 31.   [82] 1920 PROCEEDINGS at 722.   [83] M. HUDSON, P.C.I.J. at 181.
[84] 1929 PROCEEDINGS at 49–50.   [85] P.C.I.J.R. 14; *see* note 74 *supra*.

ever been had to the Chamber for Summary Procedure.[86] Actually, no cases whatever had been heard before either of the special chambers, despite the fact that some provision had been made for equality of national representation on those chambers when one of the judges was a national of either of the parties before the Court, although the Statute concededly contained no provision for national judges on the special chambers when no national of either party was a member of the chamber in the first instance. In order, then, to encourage resort to the chambers, and particularly because it was felt that provision for national judges, on a parity as to all parties, would bring about regular use of the Chamber for Summary Procedure, the number of judges on that chamber was increased from three to five in the 1929 revised Statute, with a further provision for two substitute judges for that chamber; and the article for the selection of national judges in all cases, whether or not a national of either of the parties was sitting as a judge of the Court, was made applicable to all of the chambers.[87]

But still no use was ever made of any of the chambers, and when the Statute of the International Court of Justice was drafted, the attitude of its framers toward the functions and constitution of the chambers underwent a nearly complete metamorphosis. In the first place, no use having ever been made of the special chambers for Labor and Transit and Communications, these were abandoned as such, and provision was simply made for "one or more chambers" to be formed by the Court, "from time to time," to deal "with particular categories of cases: for example, labour cases and cases relating to transit and communications." [88]

Now, although in 1929 the number of judges on the Chamber for Summary Procedure had been increased from three to five to allow for substitution of national judges for either or both of the parties, in 1945 the number of judges to constitute a chamber "for dealing with particular categories of cases" was reduced to "three or more judges as the Court may determine," while still providing, elsewhere in the Statute, for the selection of national judges *ad hoc* in all cases, as before.[89] And then, further provision was made

[86] 1929 PROCEEDINGS at 49–50.   [87] *Id.*   [88] I.C.J. STAT. art. 26.
[89] *Id.; see also* R. RUSSELL, CHARTER at 382.

under the Statute of the International Court of Justice to permit the Court, at any time, to "form a chamber to deal with a particular case," the "number of judges to constitute such a chamber" to "be determined by the Court with the approval of the parties." [90] Such a chamber might, of course, consist of only one judge; although if each of the parties wanted a judge of its own nationality to sit on the chamber, it would have to consist of two or more—and the right of the parties themselves to select such national judges was, as stated, preserved under the Statute.

And then, interestingly enough, the prior composition of the Chamber for Summary Procedure was carried over into the new Statute, with provision for five judges and two substitutes, as it had been fixed in 1929 to conform to the composition of the special chambers and to permit substitution of national judges— although, as shown, this same new Statute now provided for only two or three judges, without provision for substitutes, in the special chambers.

No reason whatever is to be found in these paradoxical provisions; and in any event, they have certainly not accomplished any salutory result in putting Chambers of the International Court to use, for, it merits reiteration, not a single case has ever been placed before any Chamber of that Court during its entire existence. Because the jurisdiction of the International Court of Justice must sooner or later be made compulsory in a realistic sense, the Court will unquestionably have a much larger docket, and may therefore really need chambers, or divisions, to enable it to dispose of its case load. So the proposed Statute is simply framed to permit the Court, "from time to time or at any time," to "form one or more chambers, to consist of three or more judges, to hear and determine, for the Court, any case or cases, by such summary or other procedure as the chamber shall direct." [91] Since the entire new philosophical concept of the Court, under its proposed Statute, involves its reconstitution as a wholly nonnational tribunal, judges no longer have nationality and there could be no occasion to justify, and no provision is made to permit selection by the parties of, national judges.

[90] I.C.J. STAT. art. 26, para. 2.   [91] I.C.J. STAT. (P) art XIII, para. 3.

Under the Rules adopted by the Permanent Court of International Justice, an application for transfer of a case from the Court to a chamber thereof for trial was required to be made at the commencement of the proceeding; and if the request was not so made, the case had to remain before the full Court for hearing.[92] The Rules governing procedure of the International Court of Justice under the Statute of that Court provide that a request "that a case should be dealt with by one of the Chambers which has been formed" for a particular category of cases, or by the Chamber for Summary Procedure, "should either be made in the document instituting the proceedings, or accompany it." [93] The same Rules provide also that a "request for the formation of a Chamber to deal with a particular case . . . can be filed at any moment until the closure of the written proceedings." [94]

Under the Statute itself, cases are to be "heard and determined by the chambers if the parties so request." [95] No provision was made in any of the Statutes, or in the Rules of either Court, for a transfer of a case from a chamber back to the Court if such a retransfer should be deemed advisable. It is considered that, under the proposed Statute of the International Court of Justice, the Court should have unrestricted power to transfer a case between a chamber and the Court at any time before judgment, and the proposed Statute accordingly provides for such transfers.[96]

Neither the Permanent Court of International Justice nor the International Court of Justice was ever given conventional general appellate jurisdiction, in the sense of adjudicating cases brought to it from inferior tribunals. Neither Court has, in other words, ever been at the summit of a hierarchy of inferior courts leading up to it. Unquestionably, the jurisdiction contemplated under the Statutes of these Courts was exclusively an original—and final—one.[97] On the other hand, by treaties, nations have frequently agreed to have recourse to the International Court to determine whether another tribunal—such as an arbitration commission—was competent to hear a case brought before it.[98]

[92] *See, e.g.,* P.C.I.J.R. 71, in 13 P.C.I.J. ANN. R. (ser. E) 140 (1937) .
[93] I.C.J.R. 76 (1) .   [94] *Id.* at 76 (3) .   [95] I.C.J. STAT. art. 26, para. 3.
[96] I.C.J. STAT. (P) art. XIII, para. 6.   [97] M. HUDSON, P.C.I.J. at 430.
[98] *See* [1932] P.C.I.J., ser. D, No. 6, at 624; 9 P.C.I.J. ANN. R. (ser. E) 333 (1933) .

The 1929 Committee of Jurists considered a proposal intended to call "attention to the possibility of widening the competence of the Permanent Court as a court of appeal." [99] This proposal was laid before the Council of the League of Nations, and the Council directed that a study be made of the matter. [100] In 1928, the Finnish delegation to the Ninth Assembly of the League recommended that nations should agree, in arbitration treaties, that recourse may be had to the Permanent Court for settlement of questions which might arise in the course of arbitration proceedings. [101] Both the proposal of the Committee of Jurists and that of the Finnish delegation were considered by the Tenth Assembly of the League, which referred to its Council for study the question as to "what would be the most appropriate procedure to be followed by States desiring to enable the Permanent Court of International Justice to assume in a general manner, as between them, the functions of a tribunal of appeal from international arbitral tribunals in all cases in which it is contended that the arbitral tribunal was without jurisdiction or exceeded its jurisdiction." [102]

The study was made by a special committee of the Council of the League, and a report was submitted suggesting various procedures by which the Permanent Court might be given a sort of appellate jurisdiction over arbitral tribunals, by recourse to the Court under agreements in conventions, by a protocol conferring such jurisdiction, or under a proposed resolution of the Assembly authorizing such recourse. [103] There was considerable hesitancy on the part of the Assembly to sanction any of these procedures. In 1931, a protocol was prepared for discussion of disputes as to the validity of arbitral awards, but the Twelfth Assembly of the League of Nations felt that the entire question "presents many aspects on which sufficient light has not yet been thrown." [104] No

[99] 1929 PROCEEDINGS at 75, 105.   [100] 10 LEAGUE OF NATIONS OFF. J. 997 (1929).
[101] LEAGUE OF NATIONS, RECORDS OF THE NINTH ASSEMBLY 76 (Spec. Supp. No. 63, 1929).
[102] LEAGUE OF NATIONS, RECORDS OF THE TENTH ASSEMBLY 174 (Spec. Supp. No. 74, 1930).
[103] 11 LEAGUE OF NATIONS OFF. J. 1359–65 (1930).
[104] LEAGUE OF NATIONS, RECORDS OF THE TWELFTH ASSEMBLY 157 (Spec. Supp. No. 92, 1932).

formal action was ever taken by the Assembly of the League or by
the General Assembly of the United Nations in this regard. In
any event, this extended discussion stimulated insertion in arbitration agreements of provisions for recourse to the International
Court for determination of questions of law arising in the course
of the arbitration proceedings.[105]

In the 1952 *Ambatielos* case, the International Court of Justice
held, in response to a submission as to whether Great Britain was
obligated to arbitrate a treaty dispute with Greece, that "the task
of the Court will have been completed when it has decided
whether the difference between Greece and the United Kingdom"
is of such a nature that "there is an obligation binding the United
Kingdom to accept arbitration." [106] Such adjudication is not,
strictly speaking, the exercise of conventional appellate jurisdiction, as evidenced, to some extent, by use of the word *recours*
rather than *appel* in the French texts, although a direct right of
appeal given in an arbitration agreement from the final decision
of a case on its merits by an arbitral tribunal to the International
Court of Justice would undoubtedly involve exercise of direct
appellate jurisdiction, even though the appeal should be heard
by trial *de novo,* as it undoubtedly would have to be.[107] In any
event, to provide for such recourse or appeal, the Rules of the
Court have since 1936 outlined procedures to be followed in such
cases, including a stipulation that when "an appeal is made to
the Court against a decision given by some other tribunal, the
proceedings before the Court shall be governed by the provisions
of the Statute and of these Rules"—not those, apparently, of the
tribunal from which the appeal was taken.[108]

It has seemingly always been taken for granted, as stated by
Judge Hudson, that since "a judgment of a Chamber is a judgment of the Court itself . . . no appeal lies from a Chamber to
the full Court." [109] This was certainly a matter of no consequence
during the fifty years in which cases were never heard before the
chambers anyway. But, in the proposed Statute of the International Court of Justice, to give it actual compulsory jurisdiction

[105] *See, e.g.,* 121 L.N.T.S. 80.   [106] [1953] I.C.J. 16.

[107] M. HUDSON, P.C.I.J. at 294.   [108] P.C.I.J.R. 67.

[109] M. HUDSON, P.C.I.J. at 345.

of all international disputes, it is assumed that many cases will be tried, in the first instance at least, before a chamber of the Court. This engendered the possibility—even the probability—of differing decisions as to the same points in different cases by different chambers of the Court, and the consequent necessity of a right of appeal from a chamber to the full Court. Provision for such an appeal is accordingly made in the proposed Statute of the International Court of Justice, while retaining the principle that, in the absence of such an appeal within sixty days, a "judgment given by a chamber shall be considered as rendered by the Court." [110]

[110] I.C.J. STAT. (P) art. XVI, para. 4.

CHAPTER XIII

Jurisdiction over
International Organizations

Paragraph 1 of Article 34 of the Statute of the International Court of Justice provides that "only States may be parties in cases before the Court." Paragraph 2 of the same article states that "in conformity with its Rules," the Court may request relevant information "of public international organizations" in any case before it and "shall receive such information presented by such organizations on their own initiative." The third paragraph of Article 34 reads: "Whenever the construction of the constituent instrument of a public international organization or of an international convention adopted thereunder is in question in a case before the Court, the Registrar shall so notify the public international organization concerned and shall communicate to it copies of all the written proceedings."

Under paragraph 3 of Article 57 of its Rules, the Court may, at any stage of the proceedings, of its own motion or at the demand of any party, "request a public international organization, pursuant to Article 34 of the Statute, to furnish information relevant to a case before it. The Court shall decide whether such information shall be presented to it orally or in writing." Paragraph 4 of the same article of the Rules of Court provides that "when a public international organization sees fit to furnish" of its own motion, information concerning a case before the Court, "it shall do so in the form of a Memorial. . . . The Court shall retain the right to require such information to be supplemented, either orally or in writing, in the form of answers to any questions which it may see fit to formulate, and also to authorize the parties to comment in writing on the information thus furnished." The fifth paragraph of Article 57 of the Rules provides that under the circumstances assigned by paragraph 3 of Article 34 of the Statute, the Registrar shall proceed "as prescribed in this paragraph." The Court may then fix a time limit "within which the public international organization concerned may submit to the Court its observations in writing. These observations shall be communicated to the parties and may be discussed by them and by the representative of the said organization during the oral proceedings."

Two international law scholars, Professors C. Wilfred Jenks and Laurent Jully, have expressed themselves strongly as favoring the right of public international organizations to be parties in their own right before the Court. The present author feels the same way. If, for instance, a State may be a party, why should not an organization of States have the same right? Actually, the practice of the Court under the provisions of the Statute and of Rule 57 of the Rules of the Court, indicates a trend in that direction, as a matter of grace if not of right; and the proposed Statute of the Court is drawn (Article IX) to give such organizations the status of parties as a matter of right before the International Court of Justice. Paragraph 1 of Article XI of the proposed Statute of the Court provides, in its relevant text, that "whenever the construction of a constituent instrument of a public international organization . . . is in question in a cause before the Court, the Registrar shall notify the public international organization concerned . . . (which) may intervene of right, by declaration, in the cause." The second paragraph of Article XI of the proposed statute provides: "Whenever there are parties to a convention whose construction is at issue in a cause between other parties, the Registrar shall notify the parties to the convention which are not parties to the cause, of the pendency of the action. Each party so notified may intervene of right, by declaration, in the cause." The parties permitted to intervene under this provision of the Statute "are parties to a convention whose construction is at issue." It has been suggested that a collective entity of separate States should be accorded a formal status before the Court, at least equivalent to that which each of its members would have separately, under the provision of the proposed revised Statute of the Court.

In support of this convention, a number of dicta are cited indicating that such a collective status might, if the question should have arisen under the present or a former Statute, be accorded to a public international body to enable it to stand in judgment before the Court. A proposal was made to the 1929 Committee of Jurists that Article 34 of the original Statute of the Permanent Court of International Justice should be amended to provide that the League of Nations might be a party before that Court. The President of the Court, at that time, was Dionisio Anzilotti, who had been a distinguished professor of international law, legal adviser to the Italian Ministry of Foreign Affairs, and, as Under-Secretary-General of the League of Nations, had played a leading part in the very creation of the Court itself. It was President Anzilotti's view that the text of Article 34 of the Statute as it stood in 1929, did not "prejudge the question whether an association of states could, in certain circumstances, appear before the Court," and that, "if the League possessed a collective personality in international law, Article 34 would not exclude it from appearing before the Court." [1]

Early in 1946 Professor Jenks, then Legal Adviser to the International Labor Office, in a brilliant paper read to the Grotius Society on *The Status of International Organizations in Relation to the International Court of Justice* said:

International organizations are increasingly becoming parties to agreements with their Members which are in the nature of treaties and are increasingly being regarded, even in cases in which they are not parties to the instrument the interpretation of which is at issue, as the natural representatives of the generality of their Members in disagreements with a particular Member.[2]

Some years later, the point never having actually arisen, it was posed somewhat rhetorically, by Laurent Jully:

It may be asked whether supposing a public international organization to be willing to take the risk of instituting proceedings against a State before the Court, the Court would consider itself strictly bound by the letter of Article 34, paragraph 1, and declare such proceedings to be inadmissible and void, or whether it would not attempt to apply the principle laid down in the *Injuries Case,* in order to give a broad interpretation of Article 34 and to find, for instance, that

---

[1] 1929 PROCEEDINGS at 59–60.   [2] 32 TRANS. GROT. SOC'Y 1, 26 (1947).

what a State can do, a group of States, even if organized as an independent legal person, can also and *a fortiori* do. . . .[3]

It is now suggested, for the first time, that public international organizations be granted, under the provisions of the revised Statute of the Court (Article IX), the right to be parties before the Court, which is to "be open [to them] at all times"; the only proviso being that any such "organizations which are not constituent agencies of the United Nations," are to enjoy the privilege subject to such conditions as shall be specified by the Security Council.[4] It would seem that a public international body, created by regional arrangement under Articles 52–54 of the Charter of the United Nations, even though not a party to that instrument, would nevertheless be a "constituent agency of the United Nations" within the meaning of that term as used in Article IX of the proposed Statute of the International Court of Justice. However, under the provisions of Article XI of the proposed Statute of the Court, the right of intervention by public international organizations is spelled out carefully. Such an organization would be entitled, as a matter of right, under paragraph 1 of that Article to intervene "in a cause before the Court," when "the construction of [its] constituent instrument" is at issue in a cause. Further, such an organization might, under paragraph 3 of that Article, apply to the Court for leave to intervene in a pending cause, whenever "it has a legal interest which may be affected by the decision of" the cause; "and the granting of such application shall be discretionary with the Court." But under paragraph 2 of Article XI of the proposed Statute, the only entities entitled to intervene in a proceeding pending before the Court are such as are parties to a convention whose construction is at issue in the cause between other parties.

When the "convention whose construction is at issue" before the Court is the Charter of the United Nations, an organization which is not itself a party to that convention does not, nor does one all of whose members are parties to the Charter, have the status of a party thereto. While, therefore, such an organization

[3] Jully, *Arbitration and Judicial Settlement—Recent Trends*, 48 Am. J. Int'l L. 380, 388 (1904); *see also* [1949] I.C.J. 174.
[4] I.C.J. Stat. (P) art. IX, para. 3.

may be considered, in a broad practical sense, to be simply a collective composite of its members, who are also component members of the United Nations, it may not intervene of right, by declaration, under Article 34 of the Statute or Article 57 of the Court's rules, in a proceeding in which the construction of that organic convention is at issue before this Court. In order to understand that principle, it is really necessary to review the background of the provisions at issue. That background is to be found in the *travaux préparatoires,* immediately underlying the Statute and Rules, and in tracing their history back through analogies of prior provisions *in pari materiae,* and even in significant past omissions of such provisions from earlier Statutes. However, a recital of the broad outlines of that history will serve better as a guide to the juridical scope of the statutory provisions in question than an endeavor to follow the devious and detailed thread of its evolution through the maze of the preliminary work underlying it; for in the achievement of sound jurisprudence, a few lines of history are worth far more than a weighty volume of logic.

A convenient starting point might well be found in the text of Article 34 of the original Statute of the Permanent Court of International Justice, which provided that "only States or Members of the League of Nations can be parties in cases before the Court." There was some discussion of this text at the time of its formulation, but that dealt primarily with the question as to whether, under any circumstances, an individual might be a party before the Court; and it seems to have been conceded that States might "present themselves as joint parties before the Court," and it was apparently agreed also that the Council of the League of Nations could not be a party.[5] The only mention of a public international organization in the original Statute of the Permanent Court, in relation to the adjudicative processes of that tribunal, came in Article 26, dealing with a somewhat conglomerate *modus procedendi* in labor cases, providing that, in such cases, "the International [Labor] Office shall be at liberty to furnish the Court with all relevant information," for which

[5] COMM. III at 378, 532, 562.

purposes, its Director "shall receive copies of all the written proceedings." There was, however, another mention of international organizations in the Statute of the Permanent Court of International Justice, as amended in 1929, in connection with the advisory jurisdiction of the Court. Article 66 of that Statute, as so amended, provided, *inter alia,* that when a request for an advisory opinion shall have been filed, the Registrar was to notify any "international organization considered by the Court . . . as likely to be able to furnish information on the question, that the Court will be prepared to receive . . . written statements, or to hear, at a public sitting to be held for the purpose, oral statements relating to the question." Actually, although Article 14 of the Covenant of the League of Nations had provided expressly that the Court was to "give an advisory opinion upon any dispute or question referred to it by the Council or Assembly," the original Statute of the Court, through a peculiar quirk of circumstances, failed even to mention the Court's advisory jurisdiction.

It is difficult to determine, from the discussions in the 1920 Committee of Jurists, just what the consensus originally was as to the advisory jurisdiction of the Court. In the report of the Committee, reference to that jurisdiction is made as being "apart from its judicial competence." [6] An opinion of the Court in such a case, said the Jurists, would amount to nothing more than an opinion "in the abstract," which would be "simply advisory," so that "the Court must not be bound by this opinion should the question come before it as a concrete case." [7] The Committee of Jurists nevertheless proposed a somewhat vague Article 36 of its draft plan, reciting the provision of the Covenant as to advisory opinions; stating that such an opinion is to be rendered, when no actual dispute is involved, by a commission of three to five members; and that when such an opinion has been requested in connection with an actual dispute, the opinion is to be rendered by the Court "under the same conditions as if the case had been actually submitted to it for decision." [8]

In a subcommittee of the Third Committee of the First Assembly of the League of Nations, M. Fromageot of France went so

[6] 1920 PROCEEDINGS at 730–31.   [7] *Id.*   [8] *Id.*

far as to state that "it was to be regretted that the Covenant gave to the Court advisory capacities." [9] At first, the Subcommittee determined to delete only the last paragraph of the proposed draft of the Committee of Jurists, but when a redraft of Article 36 was begun, the drafting committee recommended unanimously that the entire Article should be deleted, as serving no purpose not already served by Article 14 of the Covenant in directing the Court to render advisory opinions.[10] This recommendation of the drafting committee was approved unanimously by the Subcommittee, which suggested that advisory opinions "should, in every case, be given with the same quorum as that required for the decision of disputes." [11]

It must be assumed, in light of this outline, that the framers of the original Statute of the Permanent Court of International Justice did not really understand the judicial philosophy underlying the advisory function of the Court, as apparently contemplated under the Covenant of the League, and as ultimately evolved by the Court itself. This somewhat confused attitude was emphasized in the suggestion of the Subcommittee of the Third Committee that the proposed draft of Article 26 by the Committee of Jurists "entered into details which concerned rather the rules of procedure" than the competence of the Court.[12] As a result of these suggestions, the only regulation of the advisory function of the Permanent Court of International Justice was contained in rules formulated by that Court itself; and this situation continued until 1936.

Among the Rules adopted by that Court in 1922, one (Article 73) required the Registrar to give notice of any request made to the Court for an advisory opinion, "to any international organizations which are likely to be able to furnish information on the question"; and, as later revised, these Rules provided that the Court would additionally "be prepared to receive . . . written statements, or to hear . . . oral statements" from such organizations, which would be permitted also "to comment on the statements made by other" parties. However, when a study of the

[9] LEAGUE DOCUMENTS at 146; COMM. III at 386–87.
[10] LEAGUE DOCUMENTS at 156; COMM. III at 401.   [11] COMM. III at 534.
[12] *Id.*

Statute of the Permanent Court was being made in 1929, in contemplation of its revision, the prior statutory treatment of the court's advisory jurisdiction was deemed to have been attributable to the desire of the First Assembly of the League to leave the Court unhampered to evolve its own destiny in that regard. In the 1929 Committee of Jurists, Jonkheer William J. M. van Eysinga of the Netherlands, later President of the Conference of Signatories of that year and ultimately a judge of the Permanent Court, expressed the feeling, based on the early experience of the Court, that it had now become "possible to form an accurate idea of the working of the procedure in respect of advisory opinions," and that it was no longer necessary for the Court to have complete freedom in this regard.[13] Jonkheer van Eysinga accordingly suggested that the Rules of the Court be reviewed to explore the feasibility of incorporating some of their provisions into the Statute; and Judge Hans M. Huber of Switzerland, then Vice-President of the Court, concurred in this suggestion, on the ground that it should bring about a "codification" of the Court's experience.[14]

The 1926 Conference of Signatories, seeking accession of the United States to the Protocol of Signature of the Statute of the Permanent Court of International Justice, had agreed that the substantive provisions of the Rules of the Court on advisory opinions should be given the same force which they would have had if they had been contained in the text of the Statute in the first instance.[15] The 1929 Committee of Jurists pointed out that this was "particularly desirable today in view of . . . the possible accession of the United States" to the protocol of signature; and that Committee accordingly proposed that the substantive provisions of the Court's Rules on advisory opinions be "transferred" to the Statute "in order to give them a permanent character."[16] However, in "transferring" the provisions of the Rules of the Court on its advisory jurisdiction into the draft amended Statute of the Permanent Court of International Justice, the 1929 Committee of Jurists omitted the provisions of Article 73

[13] 1929 PROCEEDINGS at 66–68.   [14] *Id.*
[15] 1926 PROCEEDINGS (SIGNATORIES) at 46, 53, 77, 83.
[16] 1929 PROCEEDINGS at 125.

of the 1926 Rules, dealing with the role of international organizations in the exercise of the Court's advisory jurisdiction, from its draft of Article 66 of the Revised Statute.[17] M. Albert Thomas, Director of the International Labor Office, protested vigorously against this omission; and, after extensive debate, the 1929 Conference of Signatories, under the presidency of Jonkheer van Eysinga, agreed to retain in Article 66 of the Revised Statute the references to international organizations theretofore found in Article 73 of the Court's Rules.[18]

Article 96 of the Charter of the United Nations provides that either "the General Assembly or the Security Council may request the International Court of Justice to give an advisory opinion on any legal question," and that "other organs of the United Nations and specialized agencies, which may at any time be so authorized by the General Assembly, may also request advisory opinions of the Court on legal questions arising within the scope of their activities." While this provision expands somewhat the advisory jurisdiction of the International Court of Justice over the corresponding provisions of Article 14 of the Covenant of the League of Nations for the Permanent Court of International Justice, the provisions of Article 66 of the original Statute of the International Court of Justice remained substantially the same as those of the same Article of the revised Statute of the Permanent Court of International Justice.

In connection with its advisory functions, the Court has not confined participation in proceedings before it to public international organizations, strictly speaking, but, on the contrary, has even permitted unofficial international organizations to be heard. In its first case, in 1922, the Permanent Court of International Justice agreed to hear argument by the representative of any international organization which requested that privilege.[19] The Registrar gave notice of the pendency of that advisory proceeding to three trade-union organizations, two of which actually participated in the oral proceedings. Similarly, the Registrar of the Permanent Court of International Justice gave notice of the pendency of the Court's second advisory proceeding (*Agricultural Labor*

[17] 1929 PROCEEDINGS (SIGNATORIES) at 43–46, 49, 74–75.   [18] *Id.*
[19] Nomination of Netherlands Delegate, [1922] P.C.I.J., ser. C, No. 1, at 5, 449.

case) to unofficial international organizations dealing both with labor and with agriculture. Oral presentations were made, in that proceeding, on behalf of the International Labor Office, the International Agricultural Commission, and the International Federation of Trade Unions.[20]

The original (1945) Statute of the International Court of Justice left "unchanged the arrangements evolved by the Permanent Court of International Justice, which afford international nongovernmental organizations an opportunity to express their views in the case of advisory proceedings"; and the International Court of Justice evinced its willingness, for example, in the *South-West Africa* case, to receive a written statement from the International League for the Rights of Man.[21] But up to the point under discussion at the moment, the right of an international organization was merely one to appear in advisory proceedings, "to furnish information helpful in the determination of" the question at issue—to assist the Court, not to assert or protect an interest on its own behalf.[22]

Such a right—to assert one's own interest—was reserved to a State. Thus, under Article 63 of the Statute of the Permanent Court of International Justice, the Registrar was to notify all States not parties to a pending controversy, in which the construction of a convention to which they were parties was at issue, and "every State so notified has the right to intervene in the proceedings." This Article was proposed, in substantially the form adopted by the 1920 Committee of Jurists, which had in turn based it on Articles 56 and 84 respectively of the Hague Conventions of 1899 and 1907 on Pacific Settlement.[23]

The preceding Article (62) of the same Statute (of the Permanent Court) provides that when a State considered that it had "an interest of a legal nature which may be affected by the decision in the case, it [might] submit a request to the Court to be permitted to intervene as a third party." This text too was drafted and submitted by the 1920 Committee of Jurists, but it was not

[20] *Id.* at 481.

[21] International Status of South-West Africa, I.C.J. Pleadings, 327, 346 (1950). *See also* Jenks, *supra* note 2, at 38.

[22] *Id.*   [23] 1920 PROCEEDINGS at 594, 746.

discussed extensively in the First Assembly of the League of Nations. Significantly, however, for present purposes, the Subcommittee of the Third Committee refused to revise the draft to permit such intervention by the International Labor Office, or any other international organization.[24] When the original Statute of the International Court of Justice was drafted and adopted in 1945, the provisions of its Articles 62 and 63 were carried over, in almost exactly the same form, from the same Articles of the Statute of the Permanent Court of International Justice; and the later Statute excluded intervention by international organizations, as parties appearing in the assertion or protection of their own interests in controversies before the Court, as effectively as the earlier Statute had done.

Proposals had been made before 1945 for inclusion, in the proposed new Statute, of provisions to give public international organizations a *locus standi in judicio* before the Court. Notable among these was one submitted in April 1944 by the International Labor Office.[25] That Office suggested that

in view of the tendency to create a number of public international organizations with specialized functional responsibilities, enjoying varying degrees of independence, and likely to enter into agreements with each other analogous to treaties between States, it would seem desirable that the Permanent Court or any new court which may be established, should be empowered to assume jurisdiction of any dispute between two or more such organizations, which the parties thereto may refer to it or in respect of which it may be granted jurisdiction by treaties or conventions binding upon the organizations concerned.[26]

At the San Francisco Conference, the Venezuelan delegation called attention to the asserted necessity of making provision for settling jurisdictional conflicts among international organizations, but they conceded readily that this problem could not be settled adequately by giving such organizations the right to request advisory opinions.[27]

---

[24] LEAGUE DOCUMENTS at 30, 155, 213; COMM. III at 400, 499–500, 537.
[25] 26 OFF. BULL. I.L.O., Dec. 1, 1944, at 896.   [26] *Id.*
[27] 14 U.N.C.I.O. Docs. 839 (1945).

It has been suggested that "this proposal may perhaps have tended to place the matter in a false perspective by concentrating attention on jurisdictional conflicts between international organizations, which form only a part of the problem and can best be settled by other procedures." [28] And the same author goes on to state that "the discussions which took place at the Preliminary Conference of Jurists held in Washington in 1945, and at the United Nations Conference on International Organizations at San Francisco, showed, however, that any suggestion to give international organizations a *locus standi in judicio* before the Court, was premature in the political climate of the spring and early summer of 1945." [29] To almost the identical effect, Laurent Jully wrote eight years later:

Doubtless the learned lawyers who in 1945 undertook the revision of the Statute, could not anticipate the importance and ultimate development of international organizations. Doubtless they were anxious to avoid any controversy as to the international personality of these organizations. Furthermore, the most farsighted and progressive among these lawyers were probably afraid to 'overload the boat,' in the political climate then obtaining.[30]

Long before this time, when the original Statute of the Permanent Court of International Justice was being drafted in 1920, the Director of the International Labor Office, M. Thomas, appeared before the Third Committee of the First Assembly of the League of Nations, to criticize the draft statute which had been prepared by the Subcommittee of that Committee.[31] M. Thomas insisted that conflicts between capital and labor "were far from involving mere points of law"; and he urged that "a special *locus standi* before the Court might be given the International Labor Office"; and, as a result of his insistence, the Third Committee added a last paragraph to Article 26 of the draft Statute, dealing generally with labor cases, providing that in such controversies, "the International Labor Office shall be at liberty to furnish the Court with all relevant information." [32] The term "international organization" was really defined in this connection; but interest-

---

[28] Jenks, *supra* note 2, at 15.   [29] *Id.*   [30] Jully, *supra* note 3, at 387.
[31] COMM. III at 309–10.   [32] *Id.*

ingly, in 1924, Judge Anzilotti characterized it as an "unhappy expression which had been adopted to avoid the necessity of reference to the International Labor Office." [33] At first he sought to work out a definition of the term, but by 1926 he felt that it might be better to leave it to the Court to do so over the years by a process of inclusion and exclusion.

As indicated, a number of proposals were made when the new Statute of the International Court of Justice was being formulated in 1945, to give public international organizations the right to stand in judgment as parties before the Court. While the majority were opposed to changing the former principle of States as the only parties, most nevertheless felt that some alternative should be sought. [34] In the Washington Committee of Jurists, the United States proposed that the new Statute provide that all such international organizations be invited to furnish information to the Court, as had theretofore been the rule of Article 26 for the International Labor Office alone; and this proposal was approved. [35] The suggestion was accomplished by adding to Article 34, whose first paragraph recited that "only States may be parties in cases before the Court," a second paragraph providing that the Court might request of public international organizations information relevant to cases before it "and shall receive such information presented by such organizations on their own initiative." [36] At San Francisco, a third paragraph was added to Article 34 of the new Statute. This provided: "Whenever the construction of the constituent instrument of a public international organization . . . is in question in a case before the Court, the Registrar shall so notify the public international organization concerned. . . ." This provision was stated to have been "intended to provide necessary procedure" to implement Article 34 (2). [37] As stated, the principles embodied in these provisions were not new. They were simply an extension, to all public international organizations, of the status theretofore accorded, under Article 26, to the International Labor Office alone: "But the generalization of this principle to cover all public international organizations, and the new

[33] [1926] P.C.I.J., ser. D, No. 2 addendum, at 290.
[34] 13 U.N.C.I.O. Docs. 496 (1945).   [35] 14 *id.* at 133.   [36] *Id.* at 139.
[37] 13 *id.* at 217.

importance given to it by its inclusion in Article 34 of the Statute, combine to place the status of international organizations before the Court in a new perspective." [38]

There do not seem to be any precedential uses of these provisions of the original Statute of the Court. In the *Corfu Channel (Preliminary Objection)* [39] and *Anglo-Iranian Oil Co.*[40] cases, construction of important phrases of the Charter of the United Nations was involved; but while the Secretary-General received routine notice of the proceedings, apparently no such notice as was envisaged under Article 34 (3) of the Statute was given. In the case of the *United States Nationals in Morocco*,[41] in which construction of the Breton Woods Agreement (International Monetary Fund) was under consideration, no notice thereof was sent to that Agency, nor was it invited by the Court to furnish any information.

In commenting on the fact that "in contentious cases the International Court is not open to public international organizations," Laurent Jully held it to be "most regrettable that the framers of the Statute felt bound in 1945, in their desire to adopt as few modifications of the old Statute as possible, to adhere to so strictly limited and traditional a concept of international legal personality." [42] Jenks had expressed much the same thought a few years earlier: "One is almost tempted to suggest that the authors of the 1945 Statute, or some of them, may have felt a certain twinge of conscience in adhering to the rule that States alone may be parties in cases before the Court"; [43] but he did concede that, "of the changes made" in the 1945 Statute, "perhaps the most significant are those relating to the status before the Court of public international organizations, that is to say, of organizations governed by public international law the membership of which consists of States or governments." [44]

The very real need for a tribunal in which contentious proceedings might be instituted by or against public international organizations was demonstrated by the devices which such organizations evolved, following enactment of the 1945 Statute, to

---

[38] Jenks, *supra* note 2, at 3.   [39] [1947–1948] I.C.J. 15.   [40] [1950] I.C.J. 93.
[41] [1952] I.C.J. 176.   [42] Jully, *supra* note 3, at 386–87.
[43] Jenks, *supra* note 2, at 2.   [44] *Id.* at 1.

meet that need. The first was that of inserting in a treaty, as, for instance, the constitution of an international organization or a multilateral convention, a provision that any dispute as to its construction or application was to be submitted to the International Court of Justice for an advisory opinion, such opinion to be binding as decisive among the parties. By way of example, the second paragraph of Article 37 of the (amended) Constitution of the International Labor Organization, adopted on October 9, 1946, provides for the appointment of a special tribunal for the "expeditious determination of any dispute or question relating to the interpretation of [the constitution or] any subsequent convention"; and that "any applicable judgment or advisory opinion of the International Court of Justice shall be binding upon any tribunal established in virtue of this paragraph." Similarly, section 30 of the Convention on Privileges and Immunities of the United Nations provides that "if a difference arises between the United Nations on the one hand and a Member on the other hand, a request shall be made for an advisory opinion on any legal question involved, in accordance with Article 96 of the Charter and Article 65 of the Statute of the Court. The opinion given by the Court shall be accepted as decisive by the parties." [45] This ingenious, but highly artificial, device had been contrived to meet the demonstrated need for an adjudicative process in controversies involving public international organizations. Evolution of the device had already begun with the Permanent Court of International Justice, in its tendency to assimilate its advisory and contentious procedure. But the solution was never considered to have provided a satisfactory juridical methodology. In his treatise on *The Status of International Organizations in Relation to the International Court of Justice,* which has already been mentioned, Mr. Jenks stated that "the possibility of recourse to the advisory jurisdiction of the Court cannot be regarded as a completely satisfactory solution of the problem, either in principle or in practice." [46] "It is at best an artificial expedient," he

[45] 1 U.N.T.S. 30. Substantially the same provision is contained in section 32 of the Convention on the Privileges and Immunities of the Specialized Agencies, approved November 21, 1947.

[46] Jenks, *supra* note 2, at 35.

went on, "and although there was so strong a tendency to assimilate the advisory opinions of the Permanent Court of International Justice to judgments, that they became indistinguishable from judgments in practical effect, and the same tendency will presumably continue to prevail in the International Court of Justice, it is nevertheless true that an opinion is not a judgment and, technically, has no binding force." [47]

The second and only other device, or perhaps means, by which public international organizations could arrange for adjudication of disputes to which they were themselves parties was by arbitration through *ad hoc* tribunals. It has generally been conceded that areas in which arbitration affords an appropriate remedy are ordinarily circumscribed by the circumstances of particular cases in which adjudication cannot accomplish, by strictly judicial decision, the determination of a dispute. Such a situation arises, for instance, when the problem is one for achieving what, in the last analysis, is really a negotiated settlement, which involves bringing the parties into agreement rather than to construe the terms of an agreement which the parties have already reached—as in the determination of a controversy *ex aequo et bono* under the laws of ancient Rome. In the past, however, a number of public international organizations have had to agree to submit, or have simply submitted *ex necessitate,* to *ad hoc* tribunals for adjudication, disputes to which they were parties, even though it would concededly have been preferable, as to all parties concerned, for their controversies to be laid before, and determined by, the Court as the "principal judicial organ of the United Nations." As stated by Laurent Jully:

It is somewhat paradoxical that the numerous specialized agencies, which stand in close relationship to the United Nations, should be obliged to set up separate and *ad hoc* bodies for the settlement of future disputes, while the Charter has established, or rather confirmed, in existence, a first-class judicial organ, benefiting from a long experience as well as a high reputation, and which could certainly deal with more work than is at present being entrusted to it.[48]

Adverting again to the treatise by Professor Jenks on the status of international organizations before the Court, we find that only

[47] *Id.*   [48] Jully, *supra* note 3, at 391.

a few months after adoption of the original Statute of the International Court of Justice at San Francisco, he called attention to the fact that "the number of cases in which it is desirable to make provision for the possibility of a judicial determination of a question arising between a public international organization and one of its members had increased greatly in recent years and is likely to increase much further." [49] Writing nearly a decade later, Laurent Jully found the situation in that regard unchanged: "It would be difficult," he said, "to overemphasize the ever-increasing importance of international organizations in present-day international relations." [50] "These organizations," he continued, "whether belonging to the promotional or operational type, are called upon to enter into many international agreements, either with States or among themselves. It is thus necessary to take into account the possibility of disputes on the interpretation, application or execution of the abovementioned agreements, and the need for a settlement of such disputes by appropriate means." [51] "International organizations," said Jenks in 1946, "are increasingly becoming parties to agreements with their Members which are in the nature of treaties, and are increasingly being regarded, even in cases in which they are not parties to the instrument the interpretation of which is at issue, as the natural representatives of the generality of their Members in disagreements with a particular Member." [52] And even at that early period, just after the inception of the International Court of Justice under its present Statute, Mr. Jenks submitted that "the possibility of amending Article 34 of the Statute so as to permit public international organizations to be parties in cases before the Court would therefore appear to be worthy of serious consideration." [53] The Institut de Droit International has itself joined in the suggestion that public international organizations should be given a *locus standi in judicio* before the Court. At its 1954 Session at Aix-en-Provence, it adopted a resolution expressing its view to be that "it is a matter of urgency to widen the terms of Article 34 of the Statute so as to grant access to the Court to international organizations of States

---

[49] Jenks, *supra* note 2, at 76.   [50] Jully, *supra* note 3, at 386.   [51] *Id.*

[52] Jenks, *supra* note 2, at 26.   [53] *Id.* at 35.

of which at least a majority are members of the United Nations or parties to the Statute of the Court." [54]

In addressing the Grotius Society in February 1946, only a few months after adoption of the present Statute of the Court at San Francisco, Jenks said:

> While progress has already been made, and further progress which it is reasonable to anticipate on the basis of the present Statute, must not be underestimated, the time has surely come when international lawyers should be concerning themselves with the question whether public international organizations should not be accorded a *locus standi in judicio* before the Court equivalent to that of States. . . . The problem remains and must some day receive an appropriate solution.[55]

"The time will come," Jenks continued, "when it will be desirable to take stock of the present Statute, which is in the main a consolidation of past gains, rather than a fresh advance in international judicial organization, with a view to considering how far it is practical politics to improve it. In the course of such a stocktaking, consideration might be given to such questions as . . . the possibility of giving public international organizations a *locus standi in judicio* before the Court." [56] Jenks even concluded, in connection with his plea that "at some appropriate time Article 34 of the Statute of the Court should be amended to permit public international organizations to be parties in cases before the Court," that the Court should itself take the initiative toward that specific end.[57] "Failing a stocktaking of more comprehensive scope," he proposed that "the Court might perhaps take the initiative at an appropriate time, in suggesting an appropriate amendment to the Statute which would permit public international organizations to be parties in cases before it. A unanimous recommendation on the subject by the Court," he submitted, "would carry great weight, and would probably suffice to ensure the adoption of such an amendment. . . ." [58]

In his recent and authoritative work on *Law and Practice of the International Court*, Shabtai Rosenne, erstwhile Legal Ad-

---

[54] *Id.* at 24–25.   [55] *Id.*   [56] *Id.* at 36.   [57] *Id.* at 40.
[58] Jenks, *supra* note 2, at 37.

viser to the Ministry for Foreign Affairs of Israel and later a
member of the International Law Commission, stated that "Jully,
in a well-informed article, has returned to this question, expressing the hope that the revision of Article 34 will be one of the
first tasks to be undertaken," to give public international organizations the same status as States before the Court.[59] In 1954, the
ninth year "following the coming into force of the" Charter of
the United Nations, Laurent Jully wrote that it was "to be hoped
that if the United Nations decide, in 1955, to undertake the revision of the Charter and the Statute, the revision of Article 34
will be one of the first tasks to be undertaken as being capable of
bringing about an important improvement in this special province of international law." [60]

It is in this background that the provisions of the proposed
revised Statute of the Court, giving to public international organizations the right to appear, to intervene, and to stand in judgment before the Court, were drafted. Article IX of the proposed
Statute contains the provisions governing parties generally. Paragraph 1 of that Article stipulates that "only public international
organizations or States may be parties before the Court"; and
paragraph 2 provides that the Court is "to be open at all times
to all public international organizations which are constituent
agencies, or are created under the terms, of the Charter of the
United Nations, and to all States which are members of the
United Nations." Paragraph 3 of Article IX states expressly that
"the Court shall be open to public international organizations
which are not constituent agencies, or are not created under the
terms of the Charter of the United Nations, and to States other
than those which are members of the United Nations," under
such conditions as may be specified by the Security Council; provided that "in no case shall such conditions place the parties in
positions of inequality before the Court."

Next, under paragraphs 3 and 4 of Article XVIII of the proposed Statute of the Court, the Registrar is to "give notice of
any request for an advisory opinion, to all public international

[59] 1 S. ROSENNE, LAW AND PRACTICE at 289.
[60] Jully, *supra* note 3, at 391.

organizations or States which, on the face of the request, have in his opinion, an apparent interest in the question," and also, "through the Secretary-General, to all other public international organizations which are constituent agencies of the United Nations, and to all States which are members of the United Nations." Then, such notices having been given, paragraph 5 of Article XVIII expressly permits "any public international organization or State which feels that it has an interest in the determination of a question which has been submitted to the Court for an advisory opinion, or which feels that it may be in a position to furnish information helpful in the determination of such question, may, under such rules as the Court may prescribe, file memorials and counter-memorials with the Court, and, with leave of Court, make an oral presentation on the question before the Court."

On the specific question of intervention, paragraph 1 of Article XI of the proposed revised Statute of the Court, as hereinabove already indicated, requires the Registrar to notify the public international organization concerned, "whenever the construction of" its "constituent instrument, or of an international convention adopted thereunder, is in question in a cause before the Court," and permits "such public international organization" to "intervene of right, by declaration, in the cause." Finally, as also already stated above, paragraph 3 of Article XI provides that "a public international organization" which "considers that it has a legal interest which may be affected by the decision of a cause . . . may apply to the Court for permission to intervene in the cause, and the granting of such application shall be discretionary with the Court."

In speaking of the original Statute of the Court, Jully suggested that if such a case arose, the Court should give Article 34 "a broad interpretation," and should find "that what a State can do, a group of States, even if organized as an independent legal person, can also and *a fortiori* do." [61] In light of the foregoing history, and of the comments of Messrs. Jenks and Jully, it is submitted that the provisions of the proposed Revised Statute of

[61] *Id.* at 388.

the International Court of Justice, fixing the status of public international organizations as parties, as special pleaders in advisory proceedings, and as intervenors before the Court, are fully warranted and justified, and should be adopted.

CHAPTER XIV

Domestic Jurisdiction I

Perhaps the most controversial subject of discussion, throughout the history of the Permanent Court of International Justice and the International Court of Justice, has been that of domestic versus international jurisdiction. In order to get a proper view of the entire matter, one must study the *travaux préparatoires* of the relevant provisions of the Covenant of the League of Nations, the Statute of the Permanent Court of International Justice, the Charter of the United Nations, and the Statute of the International Court of Justice, as well as the analogous opinions of both Courts, of relevant discussions on the floor of the Security Council and the General Assembly, and the voluminous writings on the subject by eminent commentators on international law; and finally, the proposed Statute of the International Court of Justice. An extensive volume could unquestionably be written on the history of the struggle of national interests to preserve, throughout the background of international organization, the sanctity of matters of domestic concern against international encroachment. Interestingly enough, one will find in the discussions arguments on both sides of the question by the same representatives of nations, depending largely on whether they are the subject of proposed action or are urging action against some other, politically inimical, nation.

It has become increasingly customary among nations to enter into compacts, especially of a multilateral character, governing matters which in earlier times were never thought to form appropriate subjects of international scope. A treaty regulating tariffs or immigration quotas among nations should not be subject to construction by an international tribunal, on allegation of breach, as against objection that tariffs and immigration are matters of solely domestic concern. The same principle would unquestionably be applied in the matter of a treaty guaranteeing human rights and fundamental freedoms.

While there have, on occasion, as stated, been sharp differences of opinion, engendered largely by political currents, as to whether in particular circumstances a dispute over a matter of internal concern has become so serious a threat to international peace as to lose its domestic character, there has been no disagreement as to the general applicability of the principle in an appropriate situation. Under the Covenant of the League of Nations, any dispute claimed by a party thereto, and found by the Council "to arise out of a matter which by international law is solely within the domestic jurisdiction" of the complaining party, might not be the subject of a recommendation of settlement by the Council.[1]

In substantial conformity to this provision of the Covenant of the League, Article 39 of the 1928 Geneva General Act for the Pacific Settlement of International Disputes permitted a reservation excluding from its procedure disputes arising out of questions which, by international law, were solely within the domestic jurisdiction of the States concerned. Judge Hudson says that this, in turn, seems to have led to the provision in the British declaration of adherence of September 1929 to the jurisdiction of the Permanent Court, except as to "disputes with regard to questions which by international law fall exclusively within the jurisdiction of the United Kingdom," [2] a precedent followed by most of the British dominions and nine other countries.[3]

Following adoption of the Moscow Declaration of October 31, 1943, agreeing that an international organization was to be established after the war, officials of the United States Department of State prepared a memorandum for use in negotiations in that regard.[4] Secretary of State Hull was keenly aware of the American opposition to the right of the League of Nations, and of the Permanent Court of International Justice, to decide whether a controversy arose out of questions within the international or domestic jurisdiction—either political or juridical—as a result of

[1] LEAGUE OF NATIONS COVENANT art. 15, para. 8.

[2] M. HUDSON, P.C.I.J. at 470–71.

[3] *Id.* at 471. These countries are Albania, Argentina, Brazil, Egypt, Iran, Iraq, Poland, Romania, and Yugoslavia.

[4] R. RUSSELL, CHARTER at 290.

which the Senate of the United States had refused to ratify the League Covenant.[5] With this thought uppermost in the minds of the drafters, the memorandum provided expressly that "assumption on its own initiative or on reference to it of jurisdiction over a dispute" by the Council should require the concurrence of all of its permanent members; so that the Council would be the agency to decide whether a dispute involved a matter of international concern or fell within the domestic jurisdiction of a State, and the United States would be in a position to block any such decision of which it did not approve.[6] The memorandum stated that this provision "would permit the great powers to interpose a veto against the consideration by the Council of a dispute which they deem to involve a matter of domestic jurisdiction." It was suggested particularly that this "power would seem to be necessary in the event that the Council, as is now provided, has the authority to take jurisdiction over a dispute, determine the terms of settlement, and assure compliance therewith." [7] In addition, because of the historic United States objection to the possibility of intervention by an international organization in its domestic affairs, a general overall reservation on domestic jurisdiction was considered necessary over and above the veto power in the Council, as to which it was further to be provided that "no State should be required to abstain from voting on any question which by international law is solely within [its own] domestic jurisdiction." [8]

Shortly after its creation, the Permanent Court of International Justice was asked by the Council of the League to render an advisory opinion as to whether a dispute between France and Great Britain with reference to the validity of certain decrees of Tunis (a French protectorate) and of French Morocco, to the effect that natives of those principalities born of British subjects, were, despite certain applicable treaties, nationals of the principalities and thus subject to compulsory service in the French Foreign Legion, was "by international law, solely a matter of domestic jurisdiction" under Article 15 (8) of the Covenant of the League.[9] In the British brief in that case, it was submitted by

---

[5] *Id.* at 298.　　[6] *Id.* at 298–99.　　[7] *Id.* at 405.　　[8] *Id.* at 407.
[9] Nationality Decrees in Tunis and Morocco, [1923] P.C.I.J, ser. B, No. 4.

"His Majesty's Government . . . that the interpretation of a treaty between two Powers concerning reciprocal rights and imposing reciprocal obligations, cannot by international law, be a matter solely within the domestic jurisdiction of one of them." [10] In the brief of the British Government also, counsel "submitted that the relevant words" as to domestic jurisdiction in Article 15 (8) of the Covenant of the League of Nations, should be read "to include only matters of ordinary domestic and internal activity, such, for example, as immigration and tariff laws and regulations, in contradistinction to matters which, in any degree, involve external operation or application." [11] In its "Countercase," or reply brief, the British agreed that the domestic jurisdiction provision of the Covenant "owes its origin to the desire of the American people or Government to reserve certain questions in regard to which the control of the League appeared to them unacceptable"; they stated that "His Majesty's Government share the view of the French Government that tariff and immigration questions were aimed at; but they are unable to agree, as suggested in the French case, that questions of naturalization were included." [12]

The Court held that, in the abstract (aside from the facts of that particular case which required a different conclusion), "in the present state of international law, questions of nationality are . . . in principle within this reserved domain"; and that "the question whether a certain matter is or is not solely within the jurisdiction of a State is an essentially relative question; it depends upon the development of international relations." [13] The court went on to hold

that it may well happen that, in a matter which, like that of nationality, is not, in principle, regulated by international law, the right of a State to use its discretion is nevertheless restricted by obligations which it may have undertaken toward other States. . . . Article 15, paragraph 8 then ceases to apply . . . and the dispute as to the question whether a State has or has not the right to take certain measures, becomes in these circumstances a dispute of an international charac-

---

[10] [1923] P.C.I.J., ser. C., No. 2, at 62.   [11] *Id.* at 64.   [12] *Id.* at 467.
[13] [1923] P.C.I.J., ser. B, No. 4, at 24.

ter, and falls outside the scope of the exception contained in this paragraph.[14]

The Court accordingly answered the question in the negative, and held that the dispute there under consideration was not "by international law, solely a matter of domestic jurisdiction" of Tunis and Morocco.[15] It is extremely significant to note, however, that this was not a holding that the case fell within the jurisdiction of the Court despite any provisions of Article 15 (8) of the Covenant in that regard. That Article provided merely that the Council of the League was to "make no recommendation" as to settlement of a dispute arising out of a matter "which by international law is solely within the domestic jurisdiction" of a party thereto.[16] It follows, the Court continued, that

the League's interest in being able to make such recommendations as are deemed just and proper in the circumstances with a view to the maintenance of peace must, at a given point, give way to the equally essential interest of the individual State to maintain intact its independence in matters which international law recognizes to be solely within its jurisdiction.[17]

However, said the Court, when, as to

a matter which, by international law, is, in principle, solely within the domestic jurisdiction of one Party . . . the other Party invokes international engagements which, in the opinion of that Party, are of a nature to preclude in the particular case such exclusive jurisdiction, [the matter ceases] to be one solely within the domestic jurisdiction of the State [and] enters the domain governed by international law.[18]

Accordingly, the Permanent Court of International Justice expressed no opinion, in the case of the *Nationality Decrees in Tunis and Morocco,* as to its own jurisdiction *quoad* Article 15 (8) —or otherwise. It merely held, by advisory opinion, that, as a matter of international law (which it was of course competent to construe), the dispute in question in that case did not arise out of a matter "solely within the domestic jurisdiction" of the countries involved, so that the Council of the League might properly make recommendations as to settlement of the controversy.

[14] *Id.*   [15] *Id.* at 32.   [16] *Id.* at 26.   [17] *Id.* at 25.   [18] *Id.* at 25–26.

The history and background of the provisions of the Charter of the United Nations on human rights and fundamental freedoms is a long and devious one, but for purposes of the present treatise may be stated relatively simply. These provisions had their origin in a United States proposal at Dumbarton Oaks, it being explained by the American delegate that there was great interest throughout the United States in the establishment of some sort of an international bill of rights; but this and other similar proposals were received with marked skepticism by the British and Soviet representatives.[19] At one point in the discussions, the United States delegation, especially sensitive to the problems of domestic jurisdiction, submitted the following paragraph for inclusion in the draft Charter:

The International Organization should refrain from intervention in the internal affairs of any state, it being the responsibility of each state to see that conditions prevailing within its jurisdiction do not endanger international peace and security and, to this end, to respect the human rights and fundamental freedoms of all its people, and to govern in accordance with principles of humanity and justice.[20]

The British representative immediately pointed out that the second portion of the proposed provision was clearly contradictory to the first, on nonintervention, and constituted what would unquestionably be treated as a grant of plenary authority to the international organization to intervene in the internal administration of Member States.[21] The United States insisted that the second part of the paragraph was nothing more than a declaration of principle; and the Soviet delegate said that he could not understand what relationship the whole subject had to the functions of an international security organization, but the Soviet Union indicated that it would go along with a proposal of that sort if it referred specifically to "Fascist states and states of a Fascist type."[22] The United States delegation was unwilling to accept such a vague substitute and persisted in pressing for a human rights provision in either the statement of purposes at the beginning of the Charter, or among the functions of the General Assembly, or with the outline of the scope of duties of the Economic

---

[19] R. Russell, Charter at 423.   [20] *Id.*   [21] *Id.*   [22] *Id.* at 424.

and Social Council. Neither the British nor the Soviet representative seemed to relish the concept as applied to either area, but both were anxious to avoid basic disagreement with the United States over inclusion in the Charter of a general declaration on respect for human rights and fundamental freedoms.[23]

There is little legislative, and a paucity of judicial, history to serve as a guide between the decision of the Permanent Court in the *Tunis and Morocco* case and the commencement of negotiations looking to formulation of the Charter of the United Nations; but the issue of domestic versus international jurisdiction loomed large on the horizon throughout the framing of Article 2 (7) of the Charter. There was general agreement from the outset that the contemplated new organization was to be excluded from intervention in the domestic affairs of member countries. The representatives of the United States were apparently particularly zealous in that regard, being consciously sensitive to congressional jealousy of American domestic prerogatives.[24] The position of the Soviet Union was in entire accord with that of the United States, but was motivated by Soviet insistence that there should be no international interference in its own imposed settlements of controversies which it might have with its neighbors —actually international disputes.[25] The American proposals, at least on their surface, were aimed at widening the domestic jurisdiction reservation to be inserted in the Charter, to assure prohibition of interference in matters "essentially" within the internal domain of nations, and by omission of any reference to international law as a determinative criterion to govern the limits of that domain.

During the course of the drafting negotiations at San Francisco, while a clause of the proposed Charter allowing unlimited freedom of discussion and recommendation in the Assembly was being considered, Ambassador Gromyko of the Soviet Union sought to restrict the right of such discussion to matters "within the sphere of international relations" only if they would affect "the maintenance of international peace and security," because otherwise any member might bring up in the Assembly any action

[23] *Id.*   [24] *Id.* at 407, 606.   [25] *Id.* at 770–71.

of a State which it did not like, such as tariffs and immigration, clearly matters within domestic jurisdiction.[26] Australian Foreign Minister Evatt objected to this proposal, on the ground that the contemplated general reservation on domestic jurisdiction would clearly apply throughout the entire Charter; and while Mr. Gromyko replied that this "would not be sufficient," he abandoned his suggestion, and did not bring it up again.[27] This was, in effect, the submission of the British Government, in the case of the *Nationality Decrees in Tunis and Morocco,* in which they urged the words "solely within the domestic jurisdiction," as used in paragraph 8 of Article 15 of the Covenant, "will be found to bear a narrow and restricted meaning, and to include only matters of ordinary domestic and internal activity, such, for example, as immigration and tariff laws and regulations, in contradistinction to matters which, in any degree, involve external operation and application." [28]

At another point in the debates at San Francisco, the British delegate indicated that, without a proposed Australian amendment intended to strengthen the domestic jurisdiction text being considered, "such matters as immigration policy would have become subject to the jurisdiction of the Security Council" under some circumstances.[29] In his report to the President after the San Francisco Conference, Secretary of State Stettinius explained, somewhat ambiguously, that "it is quite conceivable that there might be an international dispute with reference to such matters as tariffs, immigration and the like, but where such a dispute related to matters which are essentially domestic in character, settlement through international processes should not be required." [30]

At Dumbarton Oaks in the Spring of 1945, the matter of domestic jurisdiction was the subject of extensive discussion. At one point, the American representatives suggested insertion, in the "Proposals," of a statement of general principle prohibiting the proposed new international organization "from intervention in the internal affairs of any State." [31] Section VIII-A of the "Proposals," dealing with pacific settlement, contained no protection,

26 *Id.* at 771.   27 *Id.*   28 [1923] P.C.I.J., ser. C, No. 2, at 64.
29 R. RUSSELL, CHARTER at 904.   30 *Id.* at 903.   31 *Id.* at 463.

by way of veto, for the permanent members of the Council, who were not to participate in measures taken under paragraphs 1 to 6 of that Section, looking toward peaceful settlement of disputes to which they were themselves parties. Great Britain accordingly proposed, with the concurrence of the United States, and ultimately the approval of the Soviet Union, that a seventh paragraph be added to this section, declaring, in terminology borrowed from paragraph 8 of Article 15 of the Covenant of the League, that the provisions of the first six paragraphs thereof "should not apply to situations or disputes arising out of matters which by international law are solely within the domestic jurisdiction of the State concerned." [32] Section VII-B, on the other hand, dealing with measures to enforce peace, contained protection for the Great Powers, through the veto, since they were not required to abstain from voting on such measures even when they were parties to a dispute; and they could thus forestall any action which they felt infringed on their domestic domain. [33]

At about that time, China raised a question which was to plague the framers of the Charter throughout its formulation, and has actually never really been settled since. "Where," they asked, is the power of decision to lie, "in determining whether a question was within domestic jurisdiction?" It was agreed tentatively that the determining organ would probably be the Council, which could always ask the Court for an advisory opinion. But this raised another issue since, if one of the Great Powers should be a party to a dispute, it could not veto a Council decision on jurisdiction; and retention by a State of plenary and exclusive authority over matters within its domestic jurisdiction was considered to be an issue of transcendental importance. [34]

In the course of preparations for the San Francisco Conference officials of the United States Department of State suggested that the wording of the reservation be revised to provide that the terms of the relevant paragraphs of Section A "should not apply to situations or disputes which the International Court of Justice finds, upon reference by any party or the Security Council, to arise solely out of matters which by international law are within the domestic jurisdiction of the State concerned." [35] However,

[32] *Id.*   [33] *Id.* at 464.   [34] *Id.*   [35] *Id.* at 605.

senatorial feeling that no international agency should be permitted to decide whether any matter was or was not one of domestic American concern was so strong that the United States delegation to the San Francisco Conference was constrained to reject both proposals—for determination of such issues either by the Council or by the Court. The delegation thereupon eliminated the words "solely," "by international law," and reference to the Court from the original proposal for paragraph 7, to provide that the preceding paragraphs of Section A "should not apply to situations or disputes arising out of matters which are within the domestic jurisdiction of the State concerned," [36] thus granting a veto to every State involved in a dispute, by permitting it to decide the jurisdictional issue for itself.

As stated above, at Dumbarton Oaks the reservation on domestic jurisdiction was inserted in the section on pacific settlement, which had raised difficulties by the absence of the right of veto by the Great Powers. At San Francisco, there developed a strong, ultimately successful movement to make this domestic jurisdiction reservation one of general principle effective throughout the entirety of the instrument being drafted. [37]

Three other material questions as to the sanctity of the domestic jurisdiction reservation became the subject of extensive and intensive discussion throughout the negotiations at San Francisco. The first was as to the organ which should decide whether a question was one of international or domestic jurisdiction; the second, as to whether international law should furnish the criteria for such determination; and the third question was whether the principle of nonintervention should apply only to matters "solely" within domestic jurisdiction, or should be widened to cover all matters "essentially" within such jurisdiction.[38]

There are significant passages in three days' proceedings at San Francisco. On June 12, 1945, the Norwegian delegation filed a statement, in essence recommending that all of the participating nations agree that the new Organization be allowed a wider latitude of authority, because it would "be a very grave limitation on the efficiency of" the Organization, "to deny it the right to suggest to one or both parties that they make concessions in mat-

[36] *Id.* at 606.   [37] *Id.* at 900.   [38] *Id.* at 900–901.

ters which, under international law and treaties, are within their domestic jurisdiction." [39]

To prohibit the Security Council, said the Norwegian statement, from touching "upon any matter belonging essentially in the domestic jurisdiction of any party," would be placing "very severe limitations" on the proposed system of international conciliation; and therefore the "Norwegian Delegation sincerely hopes that it will be realized that the cause of peace by conciliation cannot be realized without a certain willingness on the part of member states to recede from rigid concepts of national sovereignty." [40] In the course of this discussion, the Mexican delegate pointed out that while "non-intervention was one of the essential principles of the inter-American system" which had recently been "formally endorsed" at the Conference of Chapultepec, "that was not to say that at some future date the international Organization might not have so much authority and prestige that it could be permitted to intervene, even in matters which were normally within the domestic jurisdiction of the State." [41]

A number of countries—notably the Latin American States— felt that decisions as to whether a question was or was not one of domestic jurisdiction should ultimately be made by the Court. This concept was thought to be consonant with the widely supported sponsorship of compulsory jurisdiction for the Court. Other countries—notably Great Britain—favored determination of such a question "by the body to which it is sought to submit the dispute or situation." [42] The United States insisted, throughout the negotiations, that the standard of international law was too vague and indefinite as a measuring rod for domestic jurisdiction, despite considerable insistence to the contrary based largely on the provision of Article 38 of the Statute, then also being drafted for the Court, declaring that its (the Court's) "function is to decide in accordance with international law." [43]

---

[39] 6 U.N.C.I.O. Docs. 430 (1945).

[40] *Id.* at 431–32. "Sovereignty, with such an interpretation as this, is not compatible with a legal order, or even with a system of political security such as the United Nations was planned to be." Eagleton, *The United Nations: Its Aims and Structure*, 55 YALE L.J. 974, 980 (1946).

[41] 6 U.N.C.I.O. Docs. 495 (1945).   [42] R. RUSSELL, CHARTER at 901.

[43] *Id.* at 902.

In the Big Four, China consistently urged retention of the international law standard, and was supported by Great Britain, while the Soviet Union agreed with the American position.[44] The United States and the Soviet Union ultimately prevailed in their demand for a strengthened reservation for matters within the domestic jurisdiction of a State; the reservation was to be included among the general principles governing all organs of the United Nations; the word "essentially" was substituted for "solely"; the reference to international law was omitted; and the clause contained no provision as to who should decide whether a dispute arose out of domestic or international issues.[45]

This latter express omission was then widely construed as vesting in the country concerned the right to judge for itself whether a matter involved in a controversy to which it was being made a party fell within its domestic jurisdiction.[46]

[44] *Id.*   [45] *Id.*   [46] 6 U.N.C.I.O. Docs. 111 (1945).

CHAPTER XV

Domestic Jurisdiction II

Ever since the movement in 1919 for a League of Nations, the Senate of the United States had been almost violently hostile to the concept of an international organization which might have or exercise authority to encroach on American domestic preserves. The representatives of the State Department of the United States at San Francisco were keenly aware of this hostility and of the need for Senate ratification of the instruments to be negotiated there in 1945.[1]

It may be noted that at the Big Four discussions at San Francisco, Great Britain submitted that, should a dispute arising out of a matter within the domestic jurisdiction of a country "constitute a threat to international peace or security, or should a breach of the peace occur in consequence of such a situation or dispute, it should be open to the Security Council, acting in accordance with Section VIII-B, to take such action as it may deem appropriate"; and this suggestion met with the approval of the three other powers.[2] A further British proposal, to allay fears as to the scope of the Charter provision that members of the United Nations were to be required to "settle their disputes by peaceful means," involved insertion of "international" before the word "disputes," and inclusion of a provision in the domestic reservation clause, that Member States should, under no circumstances, be required to submit matters of domestic concern to settlement under the Charter.[3] The amended domestic jurisdiction reservation as finally accepted by the four "Sponsoring Powers," to be included among the general principles governing the entirety of the Charter, then took the following form: "Nothing contained in this Charter shall authorize the Organization to intervene in matters which are essentially within the domestic

---

[1] R. Russell, Charter at 464, 606, 960.   [2] *Id.* at 901.   [3] *Id.*

jurisdiction of the State concerned, or shall require Members to submit such matters to settlement under this Charter; but this principle shall not prejudice the application of Chapter VIII, Section B." [4]

This amendment, as proposed by the sponsoring governments, was referred to Committee I/1 (on Preamble, Purposes and Principles), and was referred by it in turn to a drafting sub-committee, which conferred with a subcommittee of Committee III/2 (on Peaceful Settlement).[5] The latter committee agreed that because the reservation was to be moved to Chapter II on Principles, and was accordingly to involve "a change in the *portée* of the text," it should continue to be considered by Committee I/1. Considerable opposition arose from the smaller countries to the sponsors' amendment; and the Subcommittee was unwilling to take a formal position on the matter, beyond recommending, "in principle," that the full committee consider the sponsoring governments' text (with a minor change of verbiage).[6]

At one point during the Committee consideration of the provision, Foreign Minister Evatt of Australia charged "that the sponsoring governments would not themselves have included in the Charter this principle of general intervention, had it not been for" the "significant fact" that there was reserved "to each of them an individual veto on action by the Council under Chapter VIII, Section B"; so that they could "assure their legislatures that these drastic powers of intervention in domestic matters can never be put into operation against themselves." [7] The primary problem which arose at this juncture concerned the final clause in the sponsoring governments' amendment, providing that the principle of nonintervention by the United Nations in the domestic affairs of States "shall not prejudice the application of Chapter VIII, Section B." This section, as it then stood, contained two general provisions—one permitting the Security Council to make recommendations for settlement of a dispute whenever there is a "threat to the peace," and the other to take direct enforcement measures to maintain or restore peace when occasion arose.[8] The smaller States feared that because of this authority the Great

[4] *Id.* at 902.   [5] 6 U.N.C.I.O. Docs. at 722–23 (1945).   [6] *Id.* at 723.
[7] R. Russell, Charter at 906.   [8] *Id.* at 463–64.

Powers, as permanent members of the Security Council, might "in certain circumstances and eventualities in deciding the terms of settlement of a dispute or adjustment of a situation, require a member to abide by the will of the great powers in a matter of domestic concern" whenever they saw fit, for their own purposes, to consider that such a matter seemed to involve a "threat to the peace." [9] Australia's concern was over immigration, her policies in that regard having given rise, for many years, to loudly voiced objections throughout Asia. A number of other countries which did not have the power to veto, each of which had "its own internal problems, its own vital spheres of domestic policy, in which it cannot without forfeiting its very existence as a state permit external intervention," also joined in the Australian position.[10] It was felt that "such a provision is almost an invitation to use or threaten force, in any dispute arising out of a matter of domestic jurisdiction, in the hope of inducing the Security Council to extort concessions from the State that is threatened"; but because "enforcement action to prevent aggression is not an exception at all to the general rule of non-intervention in matters of domestic jurisdiction," it was submitted that, while intervention by the United Nations in the domestic affairs of a State should be permitted in the taking of enforcement measures to heal a breach of the peace or to prevent aggression, it should be prohibited as to making recommendations in the event of a mere threat to the peace.[11]

The Norwegian delegate, Dr. Arnold Raestad, assured the other delegates that his country

is not more disposed than any other of those represented here to admit foreign interference in its domestic affairs . . . but the Norwegian people are at the same time profoundly attached to the cause of international peace, and international peace cannot be maintained in the long run without a system of international investigation, conciliation and arbitration. . . . [I]t will be a very grave limitation on the efficiency of the organ charged with this work to deny it the right to

[9] *Id.* at 905.
[10] COMMONWEALTH OF AUSTRALIA, UNITED NATIONS CONFERENCE ON INTERNATIONAL ORGANIZATION, 25 APRIL–26 JUNE 1945, at 28–30 (1945).
[11] 6 U.N.C.I.O. Docs. 438 (1945).

suggest to one or both parties that they make concessions in matters which, under international law and treaties, are within their domestic jurisdiction. . . . One is reminded of the caustic remark of Mr. Elihu Root: "The people of the State of New York are in favor of prohibition, but opposed to its enforcement." [12]

The Norwegian delegation submitted "that the cause of peace by conciliation cannot be realized without a certain willingness on the part of member states to recede from rigid concepts of national sovereignty"; and that insistence "upon what may be called the domestic jurisdiction veto . . . would represent a retrogression from the state of development which the world had attained in this field under the Covenant of the League of Nations." [13]

When Commission I met, on June 19, 1945, to consider paragraph 8 of Chapter II, as thus reported to it by its Committee I, only two voices were raised in opposition to the Committee's recommendation. The first was that of Uruguay, whose delegate, Mr. Paysse, assured the Commission that his country was "in accord with the incorporation in the text of the rule of respect for what we call domestic jurisdiction, still necessary in this stage of evolution that international order has achieved. . . . But for the delegation of Uruguay, in the proposed text, there are two serious technical mistakes of great importance. . . ." [14]

In the first place . . . how is the matter of domestic jurisdiction to be defined? In the second place, who shall define the matter of domestic jurisdiction? . . . The delegation of Uruguay has supported and voted for two concrete proposals presented by the delegates of Greece and Belgium, and which refer to the rules of international law. The Dumbarton Oaks Proposals also respected this criterion with reference to international law which had been already adopted by the League of Nations in paragraph 8 of Article 15 of the Covenant of the League. In the presence of this thesis, it is now desired to affirm that the criterion of whether any question is of a domestic character, is to be decided and determined by the interested State. It has been stated by the illustrious representative of the United States, Mr. John Foster Dulles, that the criteria of international law in this matter are [too] vague and indefinite . . . [but] the Delegation of Uruguay defends the principle enunciated in the Dumbarton Oaks Proposals.[15]

[12] *Id.* at 430.   [13] *Id.* at 432.   [14] *Id.* at 109.   [15] *Id.* at 109–10.

With reference to the question as to "which authoritative organ will decide on the internal, domestic or reserved character of the question," the Uruguayan delegate stated pointedly: "Since Versailles, and with the acceptance of the proposal of President Wilson regarding respect for domestic jurisdiction inspired by ex-President Taft and the policy of the Republican Party, the jurisdictional definition was to be by the Council with the necessary advisory opinion of the International Court. . . ."[16] Mr. Paysse warned his colleagues that

with the rule now proposed, a great jump backwards will be taken: the definition of the question according to domestic law made by the interested member itself, made according to a political criterion, and not according to a juridical criterion. . . . In this debate on article 8, there is implied an unfortunate regression which will indicate to the world, a state of mistrust regarding the rule of international law and the organs of international justice.[17]

The negotiators of the United States at the San Francisco Conference in 1945 were content to give the impression that failure to designate a body to decide the basic issue of the domestic jurisdiction reservation left it to the country concerned to decide for itself. At the same time, they approved paragraph 6 of Article 36 of the Statute of the International Court of Justice, in which it was provided expressly that "in the event of a dispute as to whether the Court has jurisdiction, the matter shall be settled by the decision of the Court."[18] Senator Morse had offered a resolution for a limited declaration of adherence by the United States, recognizing the jurisdiction of the Court under Article 36 of its original Statute, but excepting "disputes with regard to questions which by international law fall exclusively within the jurisdiction of the United States"—substantially the language employed in the Covenant of the League of Nations and in the Dumbarton Oaks Proposals.[19]

As stated by Dr. Evatt, the Australian delegate at San Francisco, "[t]he proper method of dealing with matters of this kind was to take them out of the ambit of domestic jurisdiction by

[16] *Id.* at 110.   [17] *Id.* at 110–11.   [18] R. RUSSELL, CHARTER at 901, 908–9.
[19] *Id.* at 946.

concluding an international convention for the protection of basic human rights and fundamental freedoms. . . . [T]he Dumbarton Oaks text was being amended to give full opportunity for the conclusion of a convention along these lines." [20] In a memorandum filed by the Australian delegation, it was stated that "if the members of the Organization really desire to give the Organization the power to" deal with matters of domestic concern to a State, "their proper course is either to declare that they recognize" such matters to be "of legitimate 'international' and not merely of 'domestic' concern, or to make a formal international convention" with regard thereto. "The Charter, as already amended, gives full opportunity for such an agreement. If such a declaration were made, or such a convention were drawn up, it would be plain that nothing in the paragraph proposed . . . would limit the right of the Organization to intervene." [21]

As stated by the Belgian delegate, M. Dehousse, in his address before Commission I at San Francisco on June 19, 1945,

> most cases in which the Court will be called upon to decide will very probably be cases in which the application of treaties will have to be considered. And it is the most elementary truth that the existence of such treaties, even if they bear on matters within the jurisdiction of the national country, such as questions of nationality or tariff barriers, draws those questions out of the exclusive jurisdiction of the parties and makes the Court competent to deal with them. The clause [in question] therefore does not seem of such a nature as to impede the functioning of the International Court. . . .[22]

Australia ultimately offered an amendment to insert the words "enforcement measures under" in the final clause of the sponsors' amendment, so that it would prohibit intervention by organs of the United Nations in the domestic affairs of States, on condition that this should "not prejudice the application of enforcement measures under Chapter VIII, Section B." [23] The session of Committee I/1 for June 13, 1945, was devoted to a debate on the relative merits and demerits of this amendment.

This debate on the Australian amendment took place under the chairmanship of M. Manuilsky of the Ukrainian SSR. Ac-

[20] *Id.* at 906.   [21] 6 U.N.C.I.O. Docs. 439 (1945).   [22] *Id.* at 112.
[23] *Id.* at 494 *passim.*

cording to the official report of that meeting, "some delegates wished to go further in safeguarding the domestic jurisdiction of the several states, by suppression altogether of the final clause defining the exception in favor of action by the Organization," so that the Council would be prohibited from intervening in domestic affairs of a State under any circumstances whatever.[24] The delegate of Peru, for instance, stated that "in the opinion of many jurists," the proposed paragraph "represented a retrograde step in comparison with the position under the Covenant of the League of Nations." He added that "the nature of the exception stated was a matter of serious importance to the smaller states, since it implied that the Security Council might take all manner of measures overriding domestic jurisdiction." It was, he said, the conviction of his delegation "that, even in the case of enforcement measures, it should be specifically stated that these would be operative, 'with due regard to domestic jurisdiction and the sovereignty of the State,' and action should be limited to the minimum necessary." [25]

In a memorandum filed by Dr. Evatt of Australia in support of his country's proposed amendment to the text on the domestic jurisdiction reservation, he conceded that "the line between matters of domestic jurisdiction and matters of international concern is not fixed and immutable. It is being altered all the time, as States agree—formally or informally—to handle more and more of their affairs in concert." [26] In another connection, Dr. Evatt said that "he agreed with Mr. Dulles that matters *solely* within domestic jurisdiction were constantly contracting. For example, international agreement to promote full employment would have been unheard of a few years ago." [27]

The French delegate expressed himself as in agreement with the objective of the Australian amendment, but not entirely satisfied with its phraseology. He agreed that the prohibition against international intervention in the domestic affairs of a State should always be "subject to the general obligation incumbent on the Security Council, to insure the maintenance of international peace and security"; but he felt that this general obligation should not accrue unless, in the words of a prior

[24] *Id.*   [25] *Id.* at 495.   [26] *Id.* at 439.   [27] *Id.* at 511–12.

amendment proposed by France, "the clear violation of essential liberties and of human rights constitutes in itself a threat capable of compromising peace." [28]

The delegate of Greece expressed the view "that the emphatic wording of the first part of the paragraph was sufficient to fulfill the purpose desired," but that the concluding clause "was inconsistent with the main section of the paragraph," and should be deleted. The Greek delegation felt also that the sanctity of the domestic jurisdiction of a State could be safeguarded adequately only by a provision (which they proposed as a further amendment to the paragraph) under which the Court would "decide whether or not such situation or dispute arises out of matters which, under international law, fall within the domestic jurisdiction of the State concerned." [29]

There was some dissension, notably that of China, whose delegate took the view that "any limitation to the case of enforcement measures might well be irreconcilable with the primary object of the organization, which was the maintenance of peace and security." [30] And Norway was frankly opposed to both the sponsors' proposal and the Australian amendment, and filed a written memorandum in support of its position.[31] Even the delegate of Uruguay, who strongly favored the Australian amendment, conceded, in the course of his remarks, that he "was in full sympathy . . . with the statements made by the Delegates of Mexico, Peru and Greece," and that, "ideally, a community of nations organized according to democratic methods, should, through its organization, keep a watchful eye on all matters, whether or not within the domestic sphere of the State." [32] The Chinese delegate "took the view that the Australian amendment was restrictive, and any limitation to the case of enforcement measures might well be irreconcilable with the primary object of the Organization, which was the maintenance of peace and security." [33]

During the discussion in Committee I/1 on the proposed Australian amendment to permit intervention in domestic affairs in "the application of enforcement measures," Viscount Cranborne, delegate of the United Kingdom, said that he realized fully

[28] *Id.* at 498.   [29] *Id.* at 495.   [30] *Id.* at 497.   [31] *Id.* at 498.
[32] *Id.* at 496.   [33] *Id.* at 497.

"that certain States were jealous of their rights of national jurisdiction," and he conceded that "the principle should not be infringed until and unless a question or dispute had become the cause of such serious differences that there was the threat of war." [34] Viscount Cranborne explained that "the sponsoring governments' text had sought to obtain a proper balance between the rule and the exception"; that his delegation "saw considerable force" in the Australian amendment, "and the United Kingdom was quite prepared to modify the original text by the inclusion of the words proposed." [35] Nevertheless, of the ten delegates who took part in the discussion in the Committee, all of the others agreed that the paragraph proposed by the sponsoring governments, with the amendment submitted by Australia, warranted the two essential principles: (1) of nonintervention by the United Nations in the domestic affairs of States; and (2) of assurance that the hands of the Security Council should not be tied in the imposition of enforcement measures to maintain peace.[36] France and Greece then withdrew their proposed amendments, and Mr. John Foster Dulles of the United States delegation, which had apparently refrained from participating in the discussion of the Australian amendment, "mentioned that he would wish to intervene later as a spokesman of the sponsoring governments to explain their motives in proposing" the paragraph in question.[37] The paragraph so adopted then simply provided that "nothing contained in the present Charter shall authorize the United Nations to intervene in matters which are essentially within the domestic jurisdiction of any State, or shall require the Members to submit such matters to settlement under the present Charter; but this principle shall not prejudice the application of enforcement measures under Chapter VII." [38]

During the course of discussions in Committee II/2 at San Francisco with regard to the role to be assigned to the General Assembly in matters of Peace and Security, Mr. Andrei Gromyko, the Soviet delegate, objected to "the committee phraseology in the new paragraph" on the ground that it "conflicted with the prohibition against intervention in domestic affairs"; and he stated that unless this language were revised or limited, "members

[34] *Id.* at 498.   [35] *Id.*   [36] *Id.* at 494.   [37] *Id.* at 499.   [38] *Id.* at 512.

could raise any kind of question—for example, immigration issues
. . . the discussion of which would infringe on state sovereignty." [39] While the debate in the Committee as hereinabove
outlined, was confined primarily to the merits of the Australian
amendment, it showed also, very clearly, that there was still
widespread support for reinsertion in the sponsors' amendment,
of the criterion of international law for determination of what
constituted domestic jurisdiction; for substitution of "solely" for
"essentially" to narrow the bounds of that jurisdiction; and for
the designation of a specific organ—preferably the International
Court of Justice—to adjudicate domestic status by those standards. [40]

The Australian amendment was adopted by the Committee in
face of these objections—not really controverted—that "it implied
that the Security Council might take all manner of measures
overriding domestic jurisdiction"; [41] and on the next day—June
14, 1945—the Committee took up for consideration and final
action the text of the paragraph under discussion, as revised
by the Australian amendment. [42] Prior to the next session of
the Committee therefore, at which Mr. Dulles was to address the
group on behalf of the sponsoring governments' amendment, the
United States delegation reconsidered the issues mentioned, giving considerable weight to the strong feelings which had been
expressed by the Latin American nations, as evidenced in the
statement quoted above, by the delegate of Peru. [43] But Senators
Vandenburg and Connally urged opposition to any provisions
whatever which might possibly impinge "on the right of the
United States to determine for herself, what matters were within
her domestic jurisdiction"; and they warned that any other
course would definitely be inviting an affirmative Senate reservation to that effect when ratifying the Charter. [44]

When the Committee met on June 14, 1945, to consider the
paragraph proposed by the sponsoring governments, as amended
by the Australian provision, the chairman suggested that further
amendments proposed by Greece and Belgium might be better

[39] R. Russell, Charter at 770.   [40] *Id.* at 906.
[41] 6 U.N.C.I.O. Docs. 495 (1945).   [42] *Id.* at 507.
[43] R. Russell, Charter at 495.   [44] *Id.* at 907.

understood if the article were first explained in its entirety by Mr. Dulles.[45] According to the official report of the meeting, Mr. Dulles stated "that the four-power amendment dealt with domestic jurisdiction as a basic principle, and not, as had been the case in the original Dumbarton Oaks proposals and in Article 15 of the Covenant of the League of Nations, as a technical and legalistic formula. . . ." "This change in concept," Mr. Dulles continued, had been brought about "by the change in the character of the Organization as planned in the discussions at San Francisco . . . now broadened to include functions," such as those of the Economic and Social Council, "which would enable the Organization to eradicate the underlying causes of war, as well as to deal with crises leading to war." [46] Mr. Dulles asserted that he was opposed to determination of domestic jurisdiction by rules of international law, because "international law was subject to constant change and therefore escaped definition. It would, in any case," he said, "be difficult to define whether or not a given situation came within the domestic jurisdiction of a State. In this era," he pointed out, "the whole national life of a country was affected by foreign conditions"; and he felt that it would be impractical "to provide that the World Court determine the limitations of domestic jurisdiction or that it should be called upon to give advisory opinions. . . ." [47] "The principle," he said, that the "Organization in one of its branches or organs should intervene in what was essentially the domestic life of the member States . . . was subject to evolution. The United States had had long experience in dealing with a parallel problem, *i.e.,* the relationship between the forty-eight states and the Federal Government. Today, the Federal Government of the United States exercises an authority undreamed of when the Constitution was formed." He foresaw "that if the Charter contained simple and broad principles, future generations would be thankful to the men at San Francisco who had drafted it." [48]

It is perhaps not entirely without latent significance that Mr. Dulles, with his internationally minded perspective, was designated to make this presentation in place of Dean Virginia Gildersleeve of Barnard College, the chief United States delegate on

[45] 6 U.N.C.I.O. Docs. 507 (1945).   [46] *Id.*   [47] *Id.* at 508.   [48] *Id.*

this Committee,[49] or that, at the conclusion of his presentation, the Chairman of the Committee, M. Manuilsky of the Ukrainian Soviet Socialist Republic, "moved a vote of thanks to Mr. Dulles for his masterly exposition of the problem of domestic jurisdiction." [50] His explanation is particularly enlightening and indicates clearly how far open he was leaving the door to ultimate intervention by the United Nations in the internal affairs of its members, despite his assurances to the contrary for the benefit of the United States Senate, when read in context with the previous day's pertinent discussion in the same Committee.

In any event, the Greek delegate thereupon "said that his Government felt that the basic issue was one of determining what was domestic jurisdiction"; and that "his delegation felt that the International Court was the body which should determine this matter" to "safeguard the application of the Australian amendment which had been voted the preceding day," and thus to "proclaim the supremacy of justice as a rule governing the organization." To that end, he proposed an amendment providing that "it should be left to the International Court of Justice, at the request of a party, to decide whether or not such situation or dispute arises out of matters that under international law, fall within the domestic jurisdiction of the State concerned." [51] The delegate of Peru spoke in favor of the Greek amendment, stating that "many of the Latin-American countries felt that the principle of respect for domestic jurisdiction was of the greatest importance," and that "there had been a long evolutionary development of rules of international law in treaties and other bodies of jurisprudence which could be called upon to interpret questions of domestic jurisdiction." [52] Mr. Dulles opposed the Greek amendment vigorously on various grounds which he laid before the Committee, closing with the suggestion that "the fact remained that the Security Council, the Assembly and the Economic and Social Council could always ask for Advisory Opinions from the International Court"; [53] although less than an hour earlier he had stated categorically to the Committee that "he did not consider that it would be practicable to provide that the World Court

---

[49] R. Russell, Charter at 907.   [50] 6 U.N.C.I.O. Docs. 508 (1945).
[51] *Id.* at 509.   [52] *Id.*   [53] *Id.*

determine the limitations of domestic jurisdiction, or that it should be called upon to give advisory opinions" in this field.[54] It was accordingly not at all surprising that when the chairman called for a vote, seventeen were in favor of the Greek amendment, and only fourteen against, although the amendment failed of adoption because it had not received the required two-thirds majority.[55]

The delegate of Belgium thereupon submitted that because, "as a result of the Conference, the scope and functions of the Economic and Social Council had been greatly expanded . . . there should be some provision by which excessive activity on the part of any organs set up under the Charter should be controlled." He conceded "that even within domestic jurisdiction very little was still *solely* within its scope, due to the changing world . . . but he did not feel that these matters, still regarded as solely within domestic jurisdiction, should be disregarded now." [56] Belgium was convinced, he said, that "there was a source for international law in Article 38 of the Statute of the Permanent Court of International Justice, which had been continued in the draft for the new Court; and also in treaties and other sources which had contributed to the establishment of principles and rules of international law"; by all of which, questions as to whether a matter fell within or without the domestic jurisdiction of a country could most fairly be determined.[57] The Belgian delegate accordingly proposed that the article sponsored by the four powers be amended to prohibit intervention by the United Nations in matters which, "in the judgment of the Organization," are "solely" or "exclusively" within the domestic jurisdiction of a State, "according to international law." [58] The delegate of Peru said "that he preferred that the International Court should be the body to decide questions of interpretation regarding domestic and international jurisdiction." [59]

Dr. Evatt of Australia agreed with the delegate of Peru that "the Court could provide the best judgment on these matters, and that whenever delay was permissible, advisory opinions could be secured." The first Belgian amendment, he said, "made the

[54] *Id.* at 508.   [55] *Id.* at 510.   [56] *Id.* at 510–11.   [57] *Id.* at 511.
[58] *Id.* at 510.   [59] *Id.* at 512.

Organization the judge of its own activities," which "should not be the case." He "agreed with Mr. Dulles that matters solely within domestic jurisdiction were constantly contracting"; and he felt that

the wording of the amendment of the sponsoring governments contained a more modern concept in keeping with international relations today. . . . He paid a tribute to the contribution of Latin American jurists to this problem, and asked the delegates from the Latin American countries to consider whether the word "essentially" was not more appropriate, and provided a broader interpretation of the Organization's power than the word "solely." [60]

Twenty-seven members of the Committee voted against, and only seven in favor of, determination of domestic jurisdiction "in the judgment of the Organization"; and six for, and twenty-eight against, substitution of "solely" or "exclusively" for "essentially." However, only eighteen were in favor of, with fourteen opposed to, fixing the criterion of international law for determination of domestic jurisdiction *vel non,* so that proposal lost also for lack of the necessary two-thirds majority.[61] Finally, then, by thirty-three votes for and four against, the article, in the following form, was adopted by the Committee: "Nothing contained in this Charter shall authorize the Organization to intervene in matters which are essentially within the domestic jurisdiction of any State or shall require the Members to submit such matters to settlement under this Charter; but this principle shall not prejudice the application of enforcement measures under Chapter VIII, Section B." [62]

Committee 1, which had drafted the foregoing article, functioned under Commission I on "General Provisions." In his report on the article to the Commission, the Committee's rapporteur (Syria) stated that "the Organization we are developing is assuming, under the present Charter, functions wider in their scope than those previously assumed by the League of Nations or other international bodies, or even wider than those which were first contemplated at Dumbarton Oaks, especially in the economic, social and cultural fields." [63] He continued:

[60] *Id.* at 511–12.   [61] *Id.* at 512.   [62] *Id.* at 512–13.   [63] *Id.* at 486.

The tendency . . . to provide the United Nations with a broad jurisdiction is, therefore, relevant and founded. The necessity, on the other hand, to make sure that the United Nations under prevalent world conditions should not go beyond acceptable limits or exceed due limitations, called for [an expression of principle] to determine the scope of the attributes of the Organization and to regulate its functioning in matters at issue.[64]

"Conceived under that tendency and the corresponding necessity," the rapporteur went on, the article is "clear and explicit enough to establish a rule of general application, and then to allow an exception. . . . Stated positively, the paragraph means: (1) that each State has entire liberty of action in matters which are essentially within its domestic jurisdiction; (2) that the Organization may intervene in such matters provided they fall definitely within the purview of enforcement measures provided for under Section B of Article VIII." [65]

Three particular questions had arisen, he reported:

(1) Whether international law, given what it actually is, should be explicitly established as the criterion of differentiation between international and domestic jurisdictions, or whether it is preferable to leave out such an explicit mention of international law; (2) which organ or organs should be empowered to decide whether a given matter lies in the domestic or international fields; (3) whether it is more appropriate to use the word "essentially" as it stands in the text before you, or to go back to the terminology of the original Dumbarton Oaks Proposals, and thus replace "essentially" by "solely." Other questions and suggestions were also made, but, says the report, "the Committee finally preferred to keep" the paragraph as now submitted, and accordingly "recommends the present text." [66]

"Uruguay," said its delegate, "along with Belgium, Greece and Norway, voted against this provision. Now the delegation of Uruguay," he concluded, "limits itself to stating that it will abstain from voting on this provision, with a firm conviction that no small and weak State can renounce the rules of international law and judicial jurisdiction which are its firmest guaranties." [67] The delegate of Belgium joined in the views expressed by the delegate of Uruguay. He regretted that the Committee had "done

[64] *Id.*   [65] *Id.* at 487.   [66] *Id.* at 487–88.   [67] *Id.* at 111.

away with" the "formula used in the Covenant of the League of Nations," as the criterion "for the determination of the limits of exclusive jurisdiction . . . so that there is a risk that the article may be interpreted in such a way that each country would finally be the judge of the extent of that exclusive jurisdiction. Such a conception, he insisted, "would have the most deplorable results" in that it "would be a continual obstacle to the action of the Security Council. . . . Therefore, the Belgian delegation regrets that Committee 1 of Commission I should have deleted any reference to international law . . . and should also have replaced the words 'exclusive competence' by that of 'domestic jurisdiction,' " and "for the reasons given it will abstain from taking part in the vote." [68]

[68] *Id.* at 111–12.

CHAPTER XVI

Domestic Jurisdiction III

Shortly after commencement of the San Francisco Conference in June 1945, in the course of discussion in Committee I/1 of the text of the paragraph ultimately to become Article 2 (7) of the Charter of the United Nations, M. Dehousse, the delegate of Belgium, had occasion to analyze the point here under discussion, in relation to the case of the *Nationality Decrees in Tunis and Morocco,* the opinion in which, he submitted, really "pointed out that nationality remained within the reserved domain, and that each state was the sole judge if the matter did not clearly fall under international agreement." [1] The report of Committee I/1, which finally approved the text of Article 2 (7) at San Francisco, is not entirely clear on this point. For instance, the Belgian delegate, conceding that "there should be some provision by which excessive activity on the part of any organs set up under the Charter should be controlled," in light of the fact that "as a result of the Conference, the scope and functions of the Economic and Social Council had been greatly expanded," nevertheless preferred the "solely domestic" criterion set forth in the Covenant of the League and in the Dumbarton Oaks Proposals.[2] Dr. Evatt of Australia "disagreed with the Delegate of Belgium," and "agreed with Mr. Dulles that matters *solely* within domestic jurisdiction were constantly contracting." He suggested, for example, that while "international agreement to promote full employment would have been unheard of a few years ago," it nevertheless remained " 'essentially' within domestic jurisdiction," although no longer " 'solely' within domestic jurisdiction." [3] Significantly, the Belgian amendment to substitute "exclusively" or "solely" for "essentially" in the text of Article 2 (7) of the Charter was defeated in the Committee by twenty-eight votes to six and was

[1] 6 U.N.C.I.O. Docs. 511 (1945).   [2] *Id.* at 510.   [3] *Id.* at 511–12.

not renewed thereafter.[4] No poll was actually taken in the Commission on the paragraph, the President simply announcing that "if no other member of the Commission wishes to be recognized, we shall consider the conclusions of the Committee as adopted"; and the paragraph, worded as above (at the end of the preceding chapter) became Article 2 (7) of the Charter.[5]

The substitution of "essentially" for "solely" in the text of Article 2 (7) of the Charter of the United Nations and the omission of the standard of international law from that text were perhaps not the most significant departures from the corresponding provisions of Article 15 (8) of the Covenant of the League of Nations. The prohibition of the Covenant against recommendations as to settlement of a dispute within the domestic jurisdiction of a party thereto—the only situation to which Article 15 (8) applied at all—came into play only when the claim of domestic jurisdiction was made by one of the parties and was held by the Council to be well founded. In some of the early opinions of the International Court of Justice, there are indications of some doubt as to whether the Court is bound by those provisions of the Charter, especially its statement of general purposes, which concededly restricts the freedom of action of the other organs of the United Nations. However, these doubts never crystallized into a pro-or-con holding.

During the latter part of June 1945, M. Dehousse submitted that the mere fact that Article 38 of the Statute of the Permanent Court of International Justice referred to treaties as one of the sources from which the Court was to draw principles of international law, "did not mean that any treaty automatically brought its substance into the realm of international law. For example . . . nationality was a common subject of treaties, but these treaties did not bring nationality *ipso facto* under international law. This still remained within domestic jurisdiction, and fell under international law only so far as treaties specifically so provided." [6]

The mere fact that a treaty deals with a matter of concededly domestic character does not transmute that subject into one of international import. Even if this were the effect of treaties under

[4] *Id.* at 512.   [5] *Id.* at 113.   [6] *Id.* at 511.

the Covenant of the League, as to matters theretofore "solely" of domestic concern, it could hardly be said that the mere declaration of principle against racial discrimination in the Charter of the United Nations could remove that subject from the "essentially" domestic jurisdiction of a State within the concept of Article 2 (7) of that instrument. However, in "the situation contemplated by the Charter," Joseph Nisot, an eminent Belgian authority on international law and delegate of that country to the 1945 Conference of Jurists at Washington, points out that "the existence of treaty provisions is, of itself, by no means conclusive." A matter, he said "may be *essentially* within the domestic jurisdiction, despite the fact that it is covered by a treaty. In a matter of that nature," he went on, Article 2 (7) would bar "the Organization from intervening, except with the consent of the State concerned," which "consent would endow the Organization with the extra-constitutional power to intervene"; but "unless it should express such a specific consent, a treaty, as such, would, in principle, be of no avail." [7]

Following an early suggestion at Dumbarton Oaks for a protective clause on human rights in connection with a proposal for "international cooperation in political, economic and social fields," as to which there was some opposition based on an asserted objection that this might involve an invasion into the domestic affairs of a State, a draft putting the two concepts into juxtaposition was submitted. That proposed text provided that the "[o]rganization should refrain from intervention in the internal affairs of any State, it being the responsibility of each State to see that conditions prevailing within its jurisdiction do not endanger international peace and security and, to this end, to respect the human rights and fundamental freedoms of all its people and to govern in accordance with principles of humanity and justice." [8] Some suggestion was made, by the British representative, that this really presented a contradiction between domestic and international concepts, rather than a reconciliation of the two; but ultimately, a tentatively satisfactory proposal was

[7] Nisot, *Art. 2, para. 7 of the United Nations Charter as compared with Art. 15, para. 8 of the League Covenant*, 43 AM. J. INT'L L. 776, 779 (1949).

[8] R. RUSSELL, CHARTER at 423.

worked out for Chapter IX on International Economic and Social Cooperation, in substantially the form later accepted for Article 55 at San Francisco, declaring that "the United Nations shall promote . . . universal respect for, and observance of, human rights and fundamental freedoms for all. . . ." [9] The Charter, as finally adopted at San Francisco, provided that the Economic and Social Council "may make recommendations for the purpose of promoting respect for, and observance of, human rights and fundamental freedoms," and, to that end, "may prepare draft conventions for submission to the General Assembly." [10]

But Article 55 is only one of some seven places in the Charter of the United Nations in which the promotion of human rights and fundamental freedoms is commended to the members of that organization in various contexts. Thus, elsewhere in the Charter, the "People of the United Nations" declared that they were combining their efforts to "promote social progress and better standards of life in larger freedom"; and they reaffirmed their "faith in fundamental human rights [and] in the dignity and worth of the human person," which they agreed to assure by "international machinery for the purpose of economic and social advancement of all peoples." [11] In the very first article of the Charter, one of the "Purposes of the United Nations" is stated to be to "achieve international cooperation . . . in promoting and encouraging respect for human rights and for fundamental freedoms for all"; and the General Assembly is charged with the duty of implementing the "Purposes and Principles of the United Nations," by initiating studies and making recommendations "for the purpose of . . . assisting in the realization of human rights and fundamental freedoms for all." [12] Finally, the Charter declares that among the "basic objectives of the trusteeship system, in accordance with the Purposes of the United Nations laid down in Article 1 of the present Charter, shall be . . . to encourage respect for human rights and for fundamental freedoms for all." [13]

In the end, by the time the San Francisco Conference had completed its labors, provisions "to promote universal respect

[9] *Id.* at 424; U.N. CHARTER art. 55.   [10] U.N. CHARTER art. 62.
[11] *Id.* preamble.   [12] *Id.* arts. 13–14.   [13] *Id.* art. 76.

for, and observance of, human rights and fundamental freedoms for all without distinction as to race, sex, language or religion" were inserted, in one form or another, in all three sections of the Charter, and in the chapter on the International Trusteeship System as well. For instance, in the memorandum filed on June 12, 1945, at San Francisco by Dr. Arnold Raestad on behalf of the Norwegian delegation, urging "member States to recede from rigid concepts of national sovereignty," [14] it has been conceded "that under the Charter some matters, such as the treatment of racial elements, have [already] been removed from the sphere of domestic jurisdiction and that, in consequence, the scope of the matters which are essentially within the domestic jurisdiction of member States has been to some extent diminished." [15] A reading of the record of the committees at San Francisco demonstrates, however, that ultimately most of the delegates felt that the general overall reservation on domestic jurisdiction in what was to become Article 2 (7) constituted an adequate bulwark against invasion of internal affairs by all of the organs of the United Nations. They accordingly acceded to emphatic expressions throughout the Charter on promotion of respect for human rights and fundamental freedoms; and the United States representative then asserted that his country was just as anxious as any other to achieve the Charter's lofty goals, while insisting that the revised texts did no more than to endeavor to reach those goals through international cooperation.[16] "It is an established fact," the Iranian delegate to the Security Council submitted, "that any question which has a bearing on violation of human rights, when these violations are of particular importance, and are capable of affecting the cordial relations which should exist between the Members of the United Nations, is not essentially within the domestic jurisdiction of a State." [17]

It is submitted, from a mere reading of the foregoing provisions, that they cannot logically be construed as anything more than commendable expressions of human aspirations, toward the achievement of which the new world organization was to extend the combined efforts of its members by "assisting in the realiza-

---

[14] 6 U.N.C.I.O. Docs 432 (1945).   [15] *Id.* at 431.
[16] R. RUSSELL, CHARTER at 939.   [17] 1 U.N. SCOR, 1st ser., No. 2, at 18 (1946).

tion of" these essential rights and freedoms; and in particular light of the stated contemplation of the future submission of international conventions toward the desired end, it may be assumed that even the frequently reiterated allusions to these liberties in the Charter of the United Nations did not of themselves transmute them from matters of "essentially" domestic, into matters of "essentially" international, concern.

The jurisdiction of the League of Nations to exercise authority even in a matter within the domestic jurisdiction of a State was applied, for example, in 1938, during the Spanish civil war, when the Council of the League appointed investigative commissions in connection with the interventions of Germany and Italy, although the status of the Spanish rebels was concededly within Spain's domestic jurisdiction. In April 1946, this question became the subject of discussion in the Security Council, when the representative of Poland insisted that, by the resolution of the General Assembly itself, "it was established that the question of the Franco regime is not an internal affair of interest to Spain alone but an international problem which concerns all of the United Nations"; [18] while the representative of the Netherlands, with whom the representative of France concurred, called attention to the fact that "while the Dumbarton Oaks plan spoke of 'matters solely within the domestic jurisdiction of States,' this was considered as being too narrow and too restricted and therefore was changed in the Charter to 'matters . . . essentially within the domestic jurisdiction of any State.' " [19]

While the presence of British troops in Indonesia was under discussion before the Security Council in February 1946, the representative of the Netherlands declared that the only fighting involved was for the sole purpose of subduing armed bands who tried to prevent the British troops from disarming the Japanese and obtaining their surrender.[20] On February 10, 1946, however, the representative of the Soviet Union reminded the members of the Council that "[t]here are matters . . . which though formally comprised in the domestic jurisdiction of a given State,

[18] *Id.* at 157 (1946).   [19] *Id.* at 177.
[20] 1 U.N. SCOR, 1st ser., No. 1, at 185 (1946).

border upon external political relations . . . threatening the peace and security of the peoples. Such matters cannot be left to be settled by the State itself, notwithstanding the principle of sovereignty." [21]

A little later, in connection with the second Indonesian question the representative of the Netherlands objected to a successful resolution to establish a United Nations Commission for Indonesia, saying that it represented "a drastic and deep interference in the domestic affairs of a State, such as no Member of the United Nations ever accepted when signing the United Nations Charter"; and he warned that "[i]f this resolution is adopted," Article 2 (7), "which is one of the cornerstones of the United Nations Charter, will from now on be a dead letter." [22] But the representative of India said that he was "astonished that in these times anybody could urge that the Indonesian question was a domestic issue, when it had produced the gravest repercussions throughout the world, and has forced 19 different countries in Asia and in the Pacific to meet at very short notice and to pass a unanimous resolution indicating the gravity of the situation, and the possibilities of a menace to world peace." [23]

In April 1946, a proposed Polish resolution condemning the Franco regime in Spain as a threat to international peace and security was rejected by the Security Council, on the ground that it constituted interference in the domestic affairs of Spain, in violation of Article 2 (7) of the Charter.[24] In the debate on that resolution, both sides conceded the principle, as expressed by the French representative, that events which, though taking place within the frontiers of one country, endanger world peace, cease to be domestic affairs.[25] The representative of the Soviet Union stated that "the Charter leaves no doubt whatever under which circumstances the United Nations . . . both can and should take certain measures required by the situation arising even out of the internal affairs of a State when these internal affairs constitute a menace to international peace and security"; and he branded

[21] *Id.* at 206.   [22] 4 U.N. SCOR, 406th meeting 9, 11 (1949).
[23] 4 U.N. SCOR, 403d meeting 3 (1949).
[24] *See* 1 U.N. SCOR, 1st ser., No. 2, at 167 (1946).   [25] *See id.* at 169.

the assertions of the opponents of the Polish resolution as "ill-founded and a distortion of the true facts." [26] The representative of the Netherlands summed up the position in his statement that "[s]o long as Franco does not really threaten international peace and security, whether Spain wants to keep that regime or not is a matter for Spain and for Spain alone." [27]

In December 1946, on submission of France and Mexico, the Joint First and Sixth Committees recommended to the General Assembly of the United Nations adoption of a resolution reciting that because of the discriminatory treatment of Indians in the Union of South Africa, friendly relations between the two countries have been, and were likely to be further, impaired and declaring "that the treatment of Indians in the Union should be in conformity with the international obligations under the agreements concluded between the two Governments and the relevant provisions of the Charter." [28] In the course of the debate on the resolution as to the treatment of Indians in South Africa, Sr. Castro of El Salvador stated that his delegation, having made [29]

a careful study of this matter . . . has come to the conclusion that, in order to eliminate from the legislation of all countries such existing provisions as those which accept or establish discriminatory treatment based upon differences of race, religion or others, it is necessary to implement the Charter of the United Nations in such a way as to give to the International Court of Justice . . . compulsory jurisdiction in such matters. . . . If this is not done . . . every contemplated solution of concrete cases will always find as an insurmountable barrier the provision contained in paragraph 7 of Article 2 of the Charter, which forbids our international Organization from taking action in matters which are essentially within the domestic jurisdiction of any State.

Following the statement by the delegate of El Salvador, Mme. Pandit, in behalf of India, pleaded that the General Assembly "created for the United Nations the abounding confidence of the common people in it as a defender of justice, public law and morality"; [30] but the decisive answer to the Salvadorean submission was made, on the following day, in a direct, carefully pre-

[26] *Id.* at 185–86.   [27] *Id.* at 177.   [28] 1 U.N. GAOR 1007 (1946).
[29] *Id.* at 1015.   [30] *Id.* at 1019.

pared, and devastating reply thereto by Sr. Alfaro of Panama.[31]

Sr. Ricardo J. Alfaro had been Vice-President and President of his country and its Minister for Foreign Affairs, and he had held many diplomatic posts. Following his service as delegate of Panama to the San Francisco Conference, he served as his country's representative in the General Assembly of the United Nations. He had been a founder-member and Secretary General of the American Institute of International Law. He subsequently became a member, and then chairman, of the International Law Commission, and ultimately a judge and Vice-President of the International Court of Justice. The world has known few more learned or more justly renowned juris-consults in the field of international law. To the assertion of Dr. Castro of El Salvador that Article 2 (7) of the Charter would be "an insurmountable barrier" to action by the United Nations or by the International Court of Justice as against national legislation establishing "discriminatory treatment based upon differences of race," Sr. Alfaro asked:

Now, is paragraph 7 a real barrier? Are human rights essentially within the domestic jurisdiction of the State? My answer is no, and a hundred times, no. . . .[32] I submit that by the San Francisco Charter, human rights have been taken out of the province of domestic jurisdiction, and have been placed within the realm of international law. I submit that the United Nations have undertaken collectively to proclaim, to promote and to protect human rights, and by so doing, the Members of the community of States, by the greatest of all covenants of history, the San Francisco Charter, have given birth to a new principle of the law of nations. . . .[33] Therefore . . . we are bound to conclude that although human rights must be exercised and can be violated within the frontiers of the State, the promotion and protection of human rights and freedoms is a matter essentially within the jurisdiction of international law, esentially within the sphere of action of the United Nations.[34]

"The delegation of Panama," Sr. Alfaro stated squarely, "does not agree with the proposal that this matter be referred to the International Court of Justice." That would be, he concluded, "tantamount to a manifestation by the General Assembly that it

[31] *Id.* at 1026–28.   [32] *Id.* at 1026.   [33] *Id.*   [34] *Id.* at 1027.

thinks that the provisions of the Charter relative to human rights are ineffective, because they are nullified by the provisions on domestic jurisdiction." [35]

Field Marshal Ian Smuts, for the Union of South Africa, insisted "that the proper constitutional legal procedure should be followed to provide an answer to the question whether South Africa has broken any international treaty obligations or violated fundamental rights or freedoms enjoined upon her by the Charter"; and that, to that end, the proposed resolution be amended to provide that the "International Court of Justice is requested to give an advisory opinion on the question whether the matters referred to in the Indian application are, under Article 2, paragraph 7 of the Charter, essentially within the domestic jurisdiction of the Union." [36] Sir Hartley Shawcross of the United Kingdom agreed with Field Marshal Smuts. He asked:

What does this clause about domestic jurisdiction really mean? How does it relate to the provisions of our Charter, repeated over and over again, about fundamental human rights. . . . Until the measure of the domestic-jurisdiction clause in Article 2, paragraph 7 of our Charter has been authoritatively defined, this doubt . . . as to what we are entitled to deal with, and what is excluded from our jurisdiction, must always bedevil the relations between our member States and endanger our Organization. . . . If it is justice that is sought . . . what better way is there to secure justice than by the Court which we have established as our own organ to administer justice between the nations of the world? [37]

The representative of the Soviet Union, Mr. Andrei Y. Vyshinsky, replied:

Unfortunately, I cannot agree with Sir Hartley Shawcross in his interpretation of paragraph 7 of Article 2, and I cannot agree with his recommendation to refer the whole matter to the International Court of Justice. . . . The Indian Government's complaint against the South African Government, in this matter of a discriminatory régime, is justified in the fullest sense, from the juridical standpoint, precisely by the fact that it deals with the violation of an intergovernmental, bilateral agreement . . . between the Governments of India and of

[35] *Id.*   [36] *Id.* at 1009–10.   [37] *Id.* at 1035–36.

the Union of South Africa. . . . In these circumstances, how can it be said that this is a domestic matter of the Union of South Africa, that it comes under domestic jurisdiction and cannot have any significance of an international character, and that it is not one of those questions which must be included in the international category? That is why reference to paragraph 7 of Article 2 is unjustified. . . . The Soviet delegation considers that justice must indeed be secured, and that it should be secured by an international court; but this international court is here, it is yourselves, it is all of us, it is our Organization which should deliver its verdict.[38]

The proposed South African amendment to refer the matter to the Court was defeated; and the Franco-Mexican resolution was thereupon adopted by thirty-two votes to fifteen, with several abstentions.[39] The resolution demanding "that the treatment of Indians in the Union of South Africa should be in conformity with the international obligations under the agreements concluded between the two Governments and the relevant provisions of the Charter," was accordingly adopted by the General Assembly by an overwhelming majority.[40]

No disputes as to tariffs or immigration have come before either Court, but in May 1948 a question of immigration, as one of domestic jurisdiction, was the subject of discussion in the Security Council in connection with the then recent military operations between Egypt and Israel. The representative of the United Kingdom had introduced a draft resolution, calling on "both parties to undertake that they will not introduce fighting personnel or men of military age into Palestine during the cease-fire." [41] The representative of the Jewish Agency for Palestine submitted that, under article 2 (7) of the Charter, the Council would be exceeding its powers if it intervened in the immigration policies of Israel. This view was supported by the representative of the Ukrainian Soviet Socialist Republic, who insisted that any question as to immigration into Israel was an internal affair of that country, as to which the Security Council had "neither the right nor the power to encroach upon the sovereign rights of a

---

[38] *Id.* at 1042–45 *passim.*   [39] *Id.* at 1061.   [40] *Id.,* at 1007.
[41] 3 U.N. SCOR, 306th meeting 29 (1948).

State." [42] The members of the Security Council, in apparent recognition of the exclusively domestic character of a question of immigration raised under such circumstances, amended the proposed draft resolution to call on all "concerned to undertake that they will not introduce fighting personnel" into Palestine or the Arab countries "during the cease-fire," and that any men of military age entering those countries would not be mobilized or given military training during that period.[43]

The strong undertow of political currents in the determination as to whether a matter of concededly domestic concern has evolved into a threat to international peace and security under given circumstances is well illustrated—insofar as it has not already been demonstrated above—by a series of discussions in the Security Council during the period of five years from 1946 through 1950, involving demands for intervention by the United Nations in Greece, Czechoslovakia, and Korea. These demands were made, in each case, on the ground that the situations in the countries concerned constituted threats to international peace and security and were opposed, in each case, on the assertion that the disputes arose out of "matters which are essentially within the domestic jurisdiction" of the States involved, within the intendment of Article 2 (7) of the Charter. The basis of the contention that the Security Council should consider the situation in Algeria in June 1956 was, as stated by the representative of Iran, that France's refusal to allow the Algerian people the right of self-determination was a violation of paragraph 2 of Article 1 of the Charter, which provides that development of "respect for the principle of . . . self-determination of peoples" is one of the "Purposes of the United Nations." He, too, dealt at length with the provisions of Article 2 (7) .[44]

As early as 1946, the delegates of the Communist-bloc nations urged, in the Security Council, intervention in Greece on the contention that asserted mistreatment of political prisoners by dominant British forces in that country had become a matter of essentially international, rather than of essentially domestic, con-

[42] 3 U.N. SCOR, 307th meeting 15 (1948) .
[43] 3 U.N. SCOR, 309th meeting 52 (1948) .
[44] 11 U.N. SCOR, 729th meeting 13–15 (1956) .

cern; [45] but they took a diametrically opposite position two years later, with reference to the ruthless suppression of political opponents of the Communist regime in Czechoslovakia by Soviet troops supporting it.[46] Conversely, while the Australian delegate submitted to the Security Council, in October 1956, that paragraph 7 of Article 2 of the Charter could not possibly be construed as preventing the Council "from investigating the situation created in Hungary by the violent action taken by foreign [Soviet] military forces in repressing the civil rights and political freedoms of the Hungarian people," [47] the representative of the United Kingdom had insisted, earlier in the same year, that the Council was precluded from considering the Algerian question, since to do so would inevitably constitute interference in a matter lying essentially within the domestic jurisdicton of France.[48]

In the summer of 1946, the Ukranian Socialist Soviet Republic brought a complaint before the Security Council, charging that a situation in the Balkans which endangered international peace and security had resulted from the policy of the Greek government, carried out with the use of British troops, to suppress a significant Communist faction in Greece.[49] The representative of the Soviet Union declared that this complaint raised "a very important and serious question directly connected with the maintenance of international peace and security," and that it must be placed on the agenda of the Security Council for discussion, since while "[i]t may be said that the state of affairs in Greece is an internal Greek affair," just "[a]s soon as an internal state of affairs causes a serious external complication and gives rise to a threat to peace, the Charter of the United Nations obliges the Security Council to consider the situation even if it arises out of the internal position. In the present case precisely such a situation occurs." [50] The Greek Question was put on the agenda of the Council, and in the course of the general debate thereon, the representative of the Soviet Union repeated his

---

[45] E. TETLOW, THE UNITED NATIONS 84 (1970).

[46] L. GOODRICH, THE UNITED NATIONS IN A CHANGING WORLD 70 (1974).

[47] 11 U.N. SCOR, 746th meeting 23 (1956).

[48] 11 U.N. SCOR, 730th meeting 9 (1956).

[49] *See* 1 U.N. SCOR, 2d ser., No. 1, at 200–12 (1946).   [50] *Id.* at 170.

position as to the meaning of Article 2 (7) of the Charter, which, he said "is absolutely clear. It permits the United Nations to undertake appropriate measures for removing a threat to the peace, even though such a threat might have arisen from the internal situation in a particular country. This paragraph not only justifies but also obliges the Security Council to undertake measures against countries having a fascist regime, the very existence of which represents a threat to the peace." [51] Conversely, he continued, "[i]t is impossible, on the basis of this paragraph in the Charter, to justify foreign intervention [by British forces] in the internal affairs of Greece, all the more so because it is a matter of an intervention which is responsible to a considerable extent for the aggressive policy of ruling Greek circles." [52] The representatives of both Greece and the United Kingdom showed that British troops had landed in Greece at the time of the liberation of that country in 1944 and had remained in Greece since then at the request of the Greek government; and the item was removed from the agenda of the Council.[53]

On August 31, 1950, the Soviet Union again brought up the Greek Question before the Security Council through its representative Mr. Yakov Malik, then President of the Council, by including in its provisional agenda, an item on "The Unceasing Terrorism and Mass Executions in Greece." During the discussion, he offered a proposed resolution under which the Security Council would request "the Greek Government to suspend the execution of the death sentences on 45 active members of the national resistance movement . . . to prohibit any further executions of political prisoners and not to allow the transfer of tubercular political prisoners to desert islands with an unhealthy climate." [54] Sir Gladwyn Jebb, representative of the United Kingdom, insisted that it was "perfectly clear that the Security Council had no jurisdiction in the matter at all, and that it would be wholly improper for the item to be included in the definitive agenda. The matters with which the resolution deals, he continued, "obviously do not constitute a threat to the peace. They

[51] *Id.* at 304.   [52] *Id.*   [53] *Id.* at 417–22.
[54] 5 U.N. SCOR, 493d meeting 19–20 (1950).

are clearly within the sphere of Greek domestic jurisdiction, and the United Nations under Article 2, paragraph 7 of the Charter is therefore precluded from discussing them" [55] and the Soviet proposal to include the item on the agenda was defeated by nine votes to two.[56]

[55] *Id.* at 22–23. [56] *Id.* at 30.

CHAPTER XVII

Domestic Jurisdiction IV

In the spring of 1948, it was proposed to place on the agenda of the Security Council a complaint by Chile that the political independence of Czechoslovakia had been violated by a threat of the use of Soviet military forces poised on the Czech border, so that the Czechoslovak *coup d'état* had been accomplished only because of official Soviet participation therein. "I am instructed by the Government of the USSR," said its representative, Andrei Gromyko, "to object categorically to the Chilean communication being placed on the Security Council's agenda. . . . Discussion of the Chilean communication would be crass interference by the Security Council in the internal affairs of Czechoslovakia . . . flatly prohibited by . . . one of the most important clauses of the Charter, Article 2, paragraph 7. . . ." [1]

It would almost seem that those who drew up the United Nations Charter knew that there would be hotheads who would try to use the authority of the United Nations to intervene in the internal affairs of other States and would attempt to seize control of their internal and external policy. But, as we see, the Charter of the United Nations safeguards the independence of States and protects in this respect the interest of all peoples. . . . All States and all peoples must themselves settle their own domestic affairs, including the internal form of government in their State. No one is entitled to . . . impose upon a particular nation a conception of state organization held by other States or their ruling circles. Yet, it is just such a tendency in the internal affairs of Czechoslovakia that underlies the Chilean communication which we are asked to consider. [2]

The representative of France, M. Parodi, asked leave to "add a reminder. More than once already, when dealing with questions which arose earlier, we have had occasion to discuss whether certain matters should be included in the agenda or not. We had

[1] 3 U.N. SCOR, 268th meeting 90 (1948). [2] *Id.*

this discussion, for instance, on the occasion of a complaint, which was made by the Ukrainian SSR itself regarding the Greek question. . . . [I]f it is contended, as the representative of the USSR contended a moment ago, that a complaint submitted to the Council has no facts to support it, we must still be able to examine it to find out whether or not that is really the case; to do that we must first of all include it in the agenda. That is what was decided in the previous case of the complaint of the Ukrainian SSR. I really do not see any reason why we should not take the same decision today." [3]

On behalf of the Ukrainian Soviet Socialist Republic, Mr. Tarashenko, its representative, simply reiterated:

To place the Chilean letter on the Security Council's agenda would mean a direct and completely unjustified intervention by the Security Council in the internal affairs of the Czechoslovak Republic and the internal life of the Czechoslovak people, which would be incompatible with the principles of the United Nations Charter. The authors of that letter must be aware that the people of Czechoslovakia alone have the right to decide the character of their own government, regardless of whether or not it pleases certain gentlemen in certain foreign States. [4]

Sir Alexander Cadogan of the United Kingdom pointed out that there had been no suggestion that the United Nations "intervene in matters of domestic jurisdiction in Czechoslovakia. . . . What is before us is an allegation" that the Soviet Union "has intervened in the affairs of another State with the threat of the use of force. . . . It is true that the representative of the USSR has said that this charge is pure invention, unfounded assertion and gross slander; but that is no reply. . . ." [5] "If these allegations are true," Mr. Warren R. Austin summed up in behalf of the United States, "the matter would clearly not be essentially within the domestic jurisdiction of Czechoslovakia, because it would be a situation resulting from illegal action by one Member of the United Nations against another. Consequently, in order to be able to determine whether the case comes within the meaning of Article 2, paragraph 7, the Security Council must consider the Chilean complaint; and of course, it cannot consider the Chilean

[3] *Id.* at 98.   [4] *Id.* at 97.   [5] *Id.* at 94.

complaint if it is not put on the agenda." [6] And the agenda containing the Chilean complaint was adopted by nine votes to two.[7]

Thereafter, the question as to whether the Chilean complaint (as supported by the Argentine) should be investigated by the Security Council was debated at length over a period of several weeks, the members of the Council reiterating, in substance, what they had said during the discussion on whether the question should be put on the agenda in the first instance; and Mr. Gromyko charged again that the assertions which had been made that the changes in the Government of Czechoslovakia had been brought about by the intervention of the Soviet government were "ludicrous" and "absurd" slander and that the "Soviet delegation flatly rejects them." [8] The representative of the United States submitted that the charges against the governments of the Soviet Union and Czechoslovakia were based on the allegation of an illegal intervention by one State in the internal affairs of another State, leading to the impairment of its political independence. Moreover, the restoration and maintenance of democratic institutions in liberated Europe, including Czechoslovakia, was the subject of an international agreement concluded at Yalta by Marshal Stalin, Prime Minister Churchill, and President Roosevelt in February 1945. Consequently, if the charges are true, Article 2, paragraph 7, clearly could not be a bar to Security Council jurisdiction over this question.[9] The Chilean-Argentine proposal failed of adoption, with nine votes in favor and two against, one of the latter being the veto of the Soviet Union.

On August 22, 1968, a resolution was introduced by seven countries in the Security Council, which was "gravely concerned that, as announced by the Presidium of the Central Committee of the Communist Party of Czechoslovakia, troops of the Soviet Union and other members of the Warsaw Pact have entered their country without the knowledge and against the wishes of the Czechoslovakian Government," and condemned "the armed intervention of the Union of Soviet Socialist Republics and other members of the Warsaw Pact in the internal affairs of the Czechoslovak Socialist Republic"; and the proposed resolution called

[6] *Id.* at 99.   [7] *Id.* at 101.   [8] *Id.* at 91.   [9] *See id.* at 99.

"upon them to take no action of violence or reprisal that could result in further suffering or loss of life, forthwith to withdraw their forces and to cease all other forms of intervention in Czechoslovakia's internal affairs." [10] The action of the USSR was almost universally condemned, only the Soviet bloc affirming the right of the Soviet Union to intervene in Czechoslovakia. Ambassador Malik, defending the action of his country, said that "this is a purely internal affair" of Czechoslovakia "and the common business of its allies through the socialist community and the Warsaw Treaty." [11] "What possible relation does the Security Council have," he continued, "to the internal affairs of Czechoslovakia? The answer, based on the United Nations Charter, Article 2, paragraph 7, can be one only: none." [12]

Ambassador George Ball of the United States condemned the Soviet conduct unequivocally. "The world is revolted by the attempt to justify the invasion and occupation of a sovereign country on the preposterous grounds that it was undertaken in the interests of peace and security. The world is disgusted by the pious assertion that this invasion and occupation of a sovereign country are merely 'fraternal assistance. . . .' What shocks us all," he went on, "is the low appraisal that the Soviet leadership places on human intelligence. How gullible, how childishly credulous does it think humankind really is? No, the whole world can recognize naked aggression when it sees it and the frantic and frightened leaders of the Soviet Union cannot conceal it or disguise it, for the world has already found them out . . . and it despises and is disgusted by their furtive and fraudulent efforts to drape tyranny with sanctimony and anoint it with piety. . . . In the view of the Soviet representative," Ambassador Ball continued, "there is the apparent assumption that Czechoslovakia either is or should be a colony of the Soviet Union. . . . For what the Soviet representative describes as an internal matter of Czechoslovakia becomes for him a matter in which the Soviet Union is not only free but has some obligation to interfere. Thus, if it is in fact an internal matter for Czechoslovakia, then I find it very hard to understand how one reaches this extraordinary

---

[10] 23 U.N. SCOR, 1442d meeting 3–4 (1968).
[11] *Id.* 1141st meeting 20 (1968).   [12] *Id.* at 26.

conclusion without any request from the Czechoslovak Government." For "this invasion did take place," without any such request. "Unless one assumes some colonial hypothesis on the part of the Soviet representative, I find it is impossible to understand the very tortured logic which he has put forward." [13]

After lengthy debate, the chairman put the resolution to a vote, with the result of ten in favor, two against (Hungary and the USSR) and three abstentions. The resolution was accordingly defeated by the Soviet veto.[14]

At the end of July 1950, the representative of the United States had submitted a draft resolution to condemn the North Korean authorities for their persistent defiance of the United Nations. But the President of the Security Council, speaking as the representative of the Soviet Union, stated that it should be "clear to anyone . . . that a civil war is in progress in Korea. . . . The military operations between the North and South Koreans are of an internal character. . . . As is known, the United Nations Charter also directly prohibits intervention by the United Nations in the domestic affairs of any State when the conflict is an internal one. . . . Accordingly, the United Nations Charter provides for intervention by the Security Council only in events of an international rather than of an internal nature. . . ." [15] The representative of the United Kingdom pointed out that the Soviet representative had neglected to mention that the Government of the Republic of Korea had already been recognized by the United Nations as the lawful government of that country; and that, accordingly, the country was, in a sense, "existing under the mantle of [the United Nations]." "Quite apart from this," he added, ". . . [a] civil war in certain circumstances might well . . . constitute a 'threat to the peace,' or even a 'breach of the peace,' and if the Security Council so decided, there would be nothing whatever to prevent its taking any action it liked in order to put an end to the incident, even if it should involve two or more portions of the same international entity. Indeed, paragraph 7 of Article 2 of the Charter so

[13] *Id.* 1442d meeting 506, 1441st meeting 28 (1968).
[14] *Id.* 1443d meeting 28–29 (1968).
[15] 5 U.N. SCOR, 482d meeting 6, 8 (1950).

provides"; and the concluding words of that paragraph "make it quite clear that the United Nations has full authority to intervene actively in the internal affairs of any country if this is necessary for the purpose of enforcing its decisions as regards the maintenance of international peace and security." [16]

The draft resolution proposed by the United States to condemn the Government of North Korea was nevertheless not adopted since, although it received nine votes in its favor with only one abstention, it was again vetoed by the Soviet Union. [17]

In 1949, in the case of the *Interpretation of the Peace Treaties with Bulgaria, Hungary and Romania,* the International Court of Justice did have occasion to pass on the question as to whether human rights guaranteed by treaty were within the jurisdiction of the United Nations. Complaint was first made in the Assembly in April by Australia and Bolivia that Bulgaria and Hungary had committed "acts contrary to the purposes of the United Nations and to their obligations under the Peace Treaties, to ensure to all persons within their respective jurisdictions the enjoyment of human rights and fundamental freedoms." [18] A few months later, while this matter was still being considered, it was proposed by the Government of Australia that the General Assembly consider the same question as it related to Romania, and the matter as to all three countries was put on the Assembly's agenda, and was referred to the Ad Hoc Political Committee. [19] Reference was made to the provisions of the Charter, particularly Article 55, which states that "the United Nations shall promote . . . universal respect for, and observance of, human rights and fundamental freedoms for all without distinction as to race, sex, language or religion." [20] Each of the peace treaties which had been executed between the Allies and these Balkan countries provided that the latter were to "take all measures necessary to secure to all persons under [their jurisdiction], without distinction as to race, sex, language or religion, the enjoyment of human rights

---

[16] *Id.* 486th meeting 5–6 (1950).   [17] *Id.* 496th meeting 18–19 (1950).

[18] Liang, *Observance in Bulgaria, Hungary and Rumania of Human Rights and Fundamental Freedoms: Request for an Advisory Opinion on Certain Questions,* 44 AM. J. INT'L L. 100, 103 (1950).

[19] *Id.* at 111.   [20] *Id.* at 105.

and of the fundamental freedoms, including freedom of expression, of press and publication, of religious worship, of political opinion and of public meeting." [21] In the course of the debates, it was charged that the acts alleged to have been committed by these countries included the maladministration of justice and the denial of free expression of political opinion and of religious worship. The trial of Cardinal Mindzenty of Hungary, that of fifteen Protestant pastors in Bulgaria, the arrest and detention without trial of six bishops of the Uniate Church and the dissolution of the Greek Orthodox Church in Romania, and the suppression of political parties in all three countries were cited as evidence in support of the allegations. [22]

The truth of the averments was denied by each of the Balkan countries (none being Members of the United Nations) in telegrams to the Secretary-General, on the floor of the General Assembly, and in the *Ad Hoc* Political Committee by the Soviet Union, Byelorussia, Poland, Yugoslavia, and Czechoslovakia. [23] The representatives of these nations insisted that all civil, political, and religious freedoms existed in the countries concerned and that the proceedings against Cardinal Mindzenty in Hungary, the Protestant pastors in Bulgaria, and the Uniate bishops in Roumania had no connection whatever with their religious activities, but were based on crimes under local penal law, such as treason, espionage, and illicit traffic in currencies; and it was stated further that the acts charged were done in pursuance of those provisions in the peace treaties which obliged the Balkan nations not to "permit in future the existence and activities of organizations of a Fascist type which have as their aim denial to the people of their democratic rights." [24] The representatives of the Soviet bloc countries, upholding the position of the Balkan States, insisted also that the question put in issue was essentially within their domestic jurisdictions and that under Article 2 (7) of the Charter the United Nations were prohibited from intervening therein. [25]

---

[21] *Id.* at 105, 111; A large part of the debate, and of the subsequent legal proceedings, centered about the contention that asserted violations of the treaties must be dealt with by arbitration machinery for which provision was made therein, each to appoint an arbitrator, which the Balkan countries had simply refused to do, thus frustrating any such proceeding. Discussion of that phase of the controversy is pretermitted herein, as essentially irrelevant.

[22] *Id.* at 104, 111.　　　[23] *Id.* at 104, 111–12.　　　[24] *Id.* at 104.　　　[25] *Id.* at 106.

To this, the representative of Panama, Sr. Alfaro, later to become, as stated above, a member and Vice-President of the International Court of Justice, replied with the statement that, in seven different places, the Charter declared it to be the obligation of the United Nations, as such, to safeguard human rights and fundamental freedoms and to ensure their universal observance; and that these provisions would be meaningless if the United Nations were not authorized to intervene when a violation of such rights or freedoms occurred in any country.[26]

The debate ultimately centered about a joint resolution introduced by Bolivia, Canada, and the United States, proposing to submit to the International Court of Justice, for adjudication, the questions involved in the dispute, including that as to asserted violations of the Charter provisions on human rights and fundamental freedoms—notably in Article 55, to which specific reference was made.[27] It was urged by a number of delegates that the very existence of the peace treaties themselves had the direct legal effect of making the asserted Balkan denials of human rights and fundamental freedoms subjects of essentially international jurisdiction to which Article 2 (7) of the Charter did not apply.[28]

Sir Alexander Cadogan of the United Kingdom—with rather doubtful consistency *vis-à-vis* the position taken three years earlier by his colleague, Sir Hartley Shawcross, in the debates on the treatment of Indians in the Union of South Africa—submitted that the Balkan controversy was governed by the decision of the Permanent Court in the *Tunis and Morocco* case, holding that the otherwise unhampered right of a State to legislate in a matter of domestic jurisdiction, must be deemed to give precedence to rights created by obligations which it may have undertaken in treaties with other States.[29] Sr. Hernan Santa Cruz, the representative of Chile, pointed out that in the 1946 debate on the matter of the Indian nationals in South Africa, the Soviet delegate, Mr. Vyshinski, had taken the firm position that the very existence of an agreement between the two countries precluded the possibility of a juridical conclusion that the controversy there in issue was essentially within the domestic jurisdiction of the Union of South Africa, under paragraph 7 of Article 2 of the Charter.[30] When,

[26] *Id.*   [27] *Id.* at 112.   [28] *Id.* at 106.   [29] *Id.* at 107.   [30] *Id.*

however, Mr. Vyshinski took the floor on behalf of Hungary and
Romania, he simply insisted that these countries had not violated the Peace Treaties, that there was no dispute among the parties to the treaties within the meaning of their terms, and that
there was accordingly no basis on which to request the Court's
advisory opinion; [31] but when the joint resolution for submission
of the controversy to the Court for its opinion was put to a vote in
the General Assembly, it was adopted by forty-seven votes to five,
with seven abstentions.[32]

The Court held directly that the contention against the exercise "of its advisory function" under "Article 2 paragraph 7 of
the Charter" was "based on a misunderstanding"; and it held
further that, for "the purpose of the present Opinion, it suffices
to note that the General Assembly justified the adoption of its
resolution by stating that 'the United Nations, pursuant to Article
55 of the Charter, shall promote universal respect for and observance of human rights and fundamental freedoms for
all. . . .' " [33] The Court then did state that the request for its
advisory opinion was limited to "the applicability of the procedure for settlement of disputes by the Commissions provided
for in the express terms" of the treaties; and it held that "the
interpretation of the terms of a treaty for this purpose could not
be considered as a question essentially within the domestic jurisdiction of a State. It is a question of international law which, by
its very nature, lies within the competence of the Court." [34] This
holding, the Court felt, should "suffice to dispose of the objection
based on the principle of domestic jurisdiction, and directed
especially against the competency of the Court," bound, as an
organ of the United Nations, "to observe the provisions of the
Charter, including Article 2, paragraph 7." [35]

The opinion of the Court in that case might well have been
put in clearer terms. But a question as to whether there has been
a violation of human rights and fundamental freedoms under the
Charter of the United Nations—a matter involving "the interpretation of the terms of a [multilateral] treaty"—said the Court,
cannot be a question "essentially within the domestic jurisdiction

---

[31] *Id.* at 113.   [32] *Id.* at 115.   [33] [1950] I.C.J. 64, at 70.   [34] *Id.* at 70–71.
[35] *Id.* at 71.

of a State," but, on the contrary, presents "a question of international law which, by its very nature, lies within the competence of the Court." [36] It is true that Judge Krylov of the Soviet Union dissented in the *Peace Treaties* case, saying that "the question of human rights and fundamental freedoms, which, it is alleged, Bulgaria, Hungary and Roumania have failed to observe . . . belongs to the essentially domestic jurisdiction of the State and, as such, is out of the jurisdiction of this Court. . . ."[37] The wording of this text [Article 2 (7)] contemplates that this case might come within the domestic jurisdiction of the State, despite the fact that it has been dealt with in a treaty. Even in that case, the matter might still remain essentially within the domestic jurisdiction." [38] "The drafting of this article" at San Francisco, in connection with "the competence of the Economic and Social Council," said Judge Krylov, was simply aimed "at promoting respect for these rights and liberties [and] was intended to avoid the possibility of interference by the Organization in the national domain of the State," and not to remove them from that domain into the broad field of international jurisdiction.[39] Judge Krylov called attention to the circumstance that it was found at San Francisco to be "necessary to broaden the domestic jurisdiction of the State to set aside the difficulties which might arise from the competence of the Economic and Social Council," and particularly "Article 55 of the Charter on human rights and fundamental freedoms," aimed "at promoting respect for these rights and liberties . . . to avoid the possibility of interference by the Organization in the national domain of the State." [40]

It must be borne in mind, however, that failure of the Court to achieve its destined stature as an international tribunal with compulsory jurisdiction over all nations was unquestionably due to the fear of States that the Court might invade their domestic domains. "As an example" of this fear, Judge Krylov noted that many States, in subscribing to the original Statute of the Court, "retained the right to give the final definition of what comes within their domestic jurisdiction." [41] As Judge Krylov said, the wording of Article 55 of the Charter, on human rights and

[36] *Id.* at 70.　　[37] *Id.* at 111.　　[38] *Id.* at 112.　　[39] *Id.* at 112–13.
[40] *Id.*　　[41] *Id.* at 112.

fundamental freedoms, "was prepared mainly at the suggestion of the delegation of the United States of America." Of this there can really be no doubt.[42] Even Judge Zoričíc of Yugoslavia, dissenting on other grounds from the opinion of the majority, added: "I agree that the objection to the Court's jurisdiction raised by several States, and which is based on the argument that the questions put to the Court relate to a subject falling exclusively within the domestic jurisdiction of the State [Article 2, paragraph 7 of the Charter] is ill-founded and cannot be upheld." [43]

Judge Sir Hersch Lauterpacht stated that "it is not clear . . . whether in the view of the Court, the fact that the General Assembly in adopting a Resolution relies on Article 55 of the Charter in the matter of human rights and freedoms is sufficient to render inoperative the prohibition in paragraph 7 of Article 2"; but, he continued, "if any issue which is dependent upon the interpretation of a treaty ceases to be a matter of domestic jurisdiction, then this applies also to the provisions of the Charter in the matter of human rights and fundamental freedoms." [44] Under Article 2 (7) of the Charter, on the other hand, the Security Council could not have intervened in such a situation, because "the United Nations Organization," as stated by Joseph Nisot, the distinguished Belgian scholar, "is, *in principle,* incompetent to intervene in matters which are essentially within the domestic jurisdiction of a State," which "incompetence results from the mere operation of the provision [*ipso jure* incompetence]." Further, as stated by the same authority: "The prohibition against intervening in domestic matters is the general rule of the Charter. It is a rule of interpretation, binding, in principle, on any organ of the United Nations [not only on the Council], and governing all the provisions of the Charter." [45] The criterion of "solely" in the Covenant, M. Nisot wrote, "is wholly at variance" with that of "essentially," established by the Charter.

---

42 *Id.* at 113.   43 *Id.* at 98.

44 H. Lauterpacht, Development at 272–73. *See generally* 1 S. Rosenne, Law and Practice at 105.

45 Nisot, *Art. 2, para. 7 of the United Nations Charter as Compared with Art. 15, para. 8 of the League of Nations Covenant,* 43 Am. J. Int'l L. 776, 776–78 (1949).

"Thus," he continued, "a matter [nationality, for instance] may, through the conclusion by a State of a treaty relating to it, cease to be *solely* within the domestic jurisdiction of that State, although continuing *essentially* to be within its domestic jurisdiction." [46] In the case of the *Nationality Decrees in Tunis and Morocco,* therefore, M. Nisot emphasized that the Permanent Court of International Justice "could hold that the existence of international contractual provisions relating to the matter at issue was sufficient ground for the conclusion that domestic jurisdiction was no longer *solely* involved" under the provision in the Covenant of the League. [47]

"It is probable," said Judge Sir Hersch Lauterpacht, in the latest (1958) edition of his renowned treatise on *The Development of International Law by the International Court,* that the General Assembly's reference, in its Resolution at issue in the *Peace Treaties* case, to "Article 55 of the Charter on human rights and freedoms . . . is no more than a statement of fact." [48]

Shortly after adoption of the Charter, Professor Clyde Eagleton of New York University questioned whether, for example, under Article 2 (7), "the United States could prevent the General Assembly or the Economic and Social Council from making recommendations upon, or even discussion of, such matters as tariffs or immigration." [49] Professor Eagleton, erstwhile Legal Adviser to the Department of State of the United States, actually went so far as to criticize Article 2 (7) on the ground that, under it, "a State has only to assert that a matter is within its domestic jurisdiction in order to exempt it from such small jurisdiction as the United Nations might otherwise have over it." This provision, he said, for which the "United States was primarily responsible . . . was intended to give assurance to the Senate that the United Nations would not be able to intervene in what we might regard as our internal affairs." [50] Professor Eagleton expressed the view that Article 2 (7) is gravely detrimental to the progress of the organized community of nations. "Sovereignty," he wrote, "with such

[46] *Id.* at 779.   [47] *Id.*   [48] H. LAUTERPACHT, DEVELOPMENT at 273.
[49] Eagleton, *The United Nations: Aims and Structure,* 55 YALE L.J. 974, 979 (1946).
[50] *Id.*

an interpretation as this, is not compatible with a legal order, or even with a system of political security such as the United Nations was planned to be." [51] "If this clause is strictly applied," Professor Eagleton submitted, "the United Nations can be no more than machinery through which cooperation can be sought in matters upon which all members agree. It is a gain to have such machinery available," he concluded, "but a system in which each nation has its own veto falls far short of satisfying the needs of the world today." [52]

Shabtai Rosenne, on the other hand, maintains that the disability of the Court in matters of domestic jurisdiction existed independently of the provisions of Article 2 (7) of the Charter, as "fundamentally a question of the legitimate sphere of activity of international law, and *ipso facto* a limiting factor on the role of the Court"; so that "the jurisprudence of the Court . . . and the practice of various UN organs which have been faced with the problem, does not support a view that the domestic jurisdiction exception of the Charter is broader than it was under the Covenant. This approach," he submits, "appears to have been adopted by the Court in the *Nottebohm* case (second phase), where the Court did not discuss Article 2 (7) of the Charter in connection with the domestic jurisdiction of a State in the matter of nationality laws, and based itself on general international law." [53]

Nevertheless, several members of the United States delegation continued to have grave misgivings as to the reaction of the Senate to such provisions as those of Chapter IX of the Charter on International Economic and Social Cooperation, binding the United Nations to promote "higher standards of living" and "full employment," which, some delegates felt, a number of Senators might well consider to be a blanket invitation to the Organizations to intervene in the domestic field by embarking on a wide program of economic and social reforms.[54] A careful study of the proceedings in the United States Senate, on consideration of the Charter of the United Nations for ratification, confirms a continuing skepticism on the domestic jurisdiction issue, despite

[51] *Id.*   [52] *Id.*   [53] 1 S. ROSENNE, LAW AND PRACTICE at 68–69.
[54] R. RUSSELL, CHARTER at 784.

Mr. Dulles's assurances. Nevertheless, the Senate Foreign Relations Committee ultimately did report that domestic jurisdiction of the States was protected adequately as against Security Council action, which would, in any event, always be subject to the right of veto of the United States.[55] But, when it came to the declaration of adherence to the original Statute of the Court, in which, on matters of domestic jurisdiction, there was to be no veto available to the United States, the Senate not only proceeded more cautiously—it expressly refused to accept Mr. Dulles's assurances and specifically repudiated his assertions that he had safeguarded adequately the domestic jurisdiction of the United States with the tacit, and sometimes stated, acquiescence of the Senate members of the San Francisco delegation.[56] During the course of his testimony before the Senate Foreign Relations Committee, Mr. Dulles said [57]:

I recall occasions when I myself was asked to go to committee meetings to present the agreed American case. I accepted to do so on the understanding that one, at least, of two Senators [Connally and Vandenberg] would come with me. In each case, after I had finished speaking, the Senator present nodded his head to indicate support of what I had said. That senatorial nod carried far more potency than any words which I had been able to utter.

But as events were soon to demonstrate quite conclusively, Mr. Dulles was apparently having trouble with his eyes when he "saw" Senators Connally and Vandenberg nodding acquiescence in equivocal assurances of "the agreed American case" which he was presenting to the Nations of the world at San Francisco. At the instance of Senator Connally, however, this language was brought into conformity with that of Article 2 (7) of the Charter. And then Senator Connally, far from acquiescing in Mr. Dulles's assertion that he had "nodded his head to indicate support of what [Mr. Dulles] had said," expressed his dissatisfaction with the assurances of Mr. Dulles that the domestic jurisdiction of the United States was adequately protected by Article 2 (7) of the Charter of the United Nations, by insisting that his country's

[55] *Id.* at 939.   [56] *Id.* at 946.

[57] *Hearings on the Charter of the United Nations Before the Senate Comm. on Foreign Relations,* 79th Cong., 1st Sess., pt. 5, at 469 (1945).

declaration of adherence to the Court should cover disputes essentially within her own domestic jurisdiction only as determined by the United States of America. Senator Vandenberg, who had also been cited by Mr. Dulles as having nodded acquiescence in his (Mr. Dulles's) assurances at San Francisco, concurred in the Connally Reservation, which was thereupon adopted by the Senate.[58]

It may, perhaps, safely be stated that if a matter is to be removed from the domestic jurisdiction of a State, it must be put into a treaty expressly—not as a declaration of principle, but as a statement directly subject to construction by the International Court of Justice. It may fairly be said, in any event, on the basis of the discussions which have taken place, that when a matter of a concededly domestic nature within a State has international repercussions of such scope as to constitute a threat to, or a breach of, international peace or security, the organs of the United Nations, despite the provisions of Article 2, paragraph 7 of the Charter, are no longer prohibited from intervening therein to prevent the breach or to restore the peace.

There remain to be considered only the provisions of the proposed Statute of the Court, dealing expressly with the matter of domestic jurisdiction. The first of these is contained in section 3 of Article VIII, and simply provides, in substantially the same terms as Article 2 (7) of the Charter, that the Court "shall have no jurisdiction over, and nothing contained in the present statute shall be construed as requiring any member of the United Nations to submit to the Court for adjudication, any matter essentially within its domestic jurisdiction." This provision was inserted in the Statute of the Court only to avoid doubts which had been expressed as to whether Article 2 (7) of the Charter was intended to apply to the Court the same prohibition against intervention in the internal affairs of a State which it set up against "the United Nations," alone mentioned in that article. This clearly does not narrow the jurisdiction of the Court from the breadth of its competence as limited by Article 2 (7), since the two provisions are identical to all practical intents and pur-

---

[58] 92 Cong. Rec. 10695–97 (1946).

poses; just as, in the words of Rosenne, "the jurisprudence of the Court, for example in the *Peace Treaties* case itself, and the practice of various UN organs which have been faced with the problem, does not support a view that the domestic-jurisdiction exception of the Charter is broader than it was under the Covenant." [59]

Next, in section 4 of Article VIII of the proposed Statute, it is provided that while any "dispute as to the jurisdiction of the Court shall be determined by the Court," nevertheless, "when any State, party to the cause, shall contend that a matter brought before the Court for adjudication is essentially within the domestic jurisdiction of the State, the Court shall not exercise jurisdiction over the proceeding unless at least ten of its judges concur in holding the matter to be within the jurisdiction of the Court." The foregoing provisions are really the crux of the proposed revised Statute. Assuming, as one must, that States have failed to declare their unreserved adherence to the Court primarily, if not exclusively, because they fear invasion of their domestic jurisdiction and are jealous of their national sovereignties, it is felt that they will ultimately trust ten of the fifteen members of the Court to protect their national interests. And then, to make assurance doubly sure, although judges are prone to feel that there can be no doubt about their expressed opinions, the proposed Statute finally provides that any "doubts as to whether any matter is essentially within the domestic jurisdiction of a State, shall be resolved by the Court in favor of such domestic jurisdiction." [60]

[59] 1 S. ROSENNE, LAW AND PRACTICE n. 3 at 68.
[60] I.C.J. STAT. (P) art. VIII, para. 4.

CHAPTER XVIII

Enforcement of Decrees

Of what value is a decree of the International Court of Justice in favor of one sovereign nation and against another? Are there any precedents involving a nation's refusal to comply with the terms of a decree of the Court against it? Can a decree of the Court be enforced against the will of the nation cast therein? What means does international law provide to aid or compel enforcement of a decree of the Court against a sovereign nation? These and related significant questions are necessarily posed, must inevitably be considered, and should be answered forthrightly in the light of the ever-increasing need for definitive adjudication of international disputes.

The people of each nation may be presumed to prefer its form of government—at least in its essentials—to that of any other. Despite the pious protestations of a small minority of Utopians, world government must be as much anathema to others as it apparently is to a vast number of the people of the United States. But peace, especially in a world in which war must inevitably bring destruction to practically all sovereign nations, can be assured if those nations will agree in advance—as they can without undue surrender of their sovereignty—to adjudication of their international disputes by such an impartial tribunal. The International Court of Justice, reconstituted as proposed in this volume, could, it must be conceded, go far to fulfill the fundamental "Purposes and Principles" proclaimed in the first article of the Charter of the United Nations. But how can the decree of such a tribunal, ordering a sovereign nation to perform or refrain from performing an act, be enforced without impinging on the sovereignty of the nation cast in the judgment? Or is there a real or undue surrender of sovereignty in agreement in advance by a nation to abide by, and submit to, the decree of an acceptably impartial international tribunal?

The questions posed in undertaking a study of such a problem may perhaps find varying answers when examined in the light of strictly logical scrutiny. But, as has been stated before, a page of history is worth more than a volume of logic, and a safe guide for the future can unquestionably be found in an intelligent analysis of the past. In the first place, enforcement of decrees is not normally a part of the judicial process at all. It is true that under the practice of many national and local municipal courts, enforcement is carried out under direction of their judicial tribunals; but even then the enforcement process is really undertaken by the court in its administrative rather than in its judicial capacity. Further, in countries in which suits against the State or its autonomous subdivisions are permitted, judgments against public bodies may not be enforced under direction of the tribunal which rendered them, but only by separate legislative or administrative proceedings. In these cases the only function of the court—a strictly judicial one—is to determine the abstract question of liability *vel non* and to audit the amount due, if any, not the disposition to be made of any decree which may be rendered against the State. There may, therefore, be said to be a universally accepted distinction between adjudication followed by enforcement in proceedings against States, and in proceedings against private parties.

This principle applies *a fortiori* to proceedings between States in international tribunals, both arbitral and judicial. The legal element—the tribunal's findings of fact and conclusions of law governing the dispute between the national parties—necessarily enters into the process of enforcement; but the enforcement process itself can neither be undertaken nor directed by the court. By the very nature and constitution of an international tribunal, it can have no power of coercion against nations.[1] Its judgments are purely declaratory. Nor is there—certainly not in the ordinary sense—any legislative, executive, or administrative governmental body in the world, with authority over nations, that might lend

---

[1] As was stated in 1945 at the Washington Committee of Jurists, convened to draft a statute for the proposed new international tribunal: "It was not the business of the court itself to ensure the execution of its decisions." 14 U.N.C.I.O. Docs. 853, 886 (1945).

its aid to a successful party in a dispute between States before an international tribunal to compel compliance with a judgment rendered against the will of the country cast in the decree. The function of enforcement of the decree of an international court is therefore neither a legislative nor an administrative one, but is rather the bringing into play of a political responsibility in a diplomatic sphere. The exercise of this political function is not a concomitant or attendant incident of the judicial decree; it is a separate process in which a new and independent policy is formulated.

These abstract statements of principle are brought into the focus of concrete and immediate reality by noting that the provisions for enforcement of judgments of the International Court of Justice are not found in the Statute of the Court as a responsibility of that tribunal, whose function is simply defined in paragraph 1 of Article 38 of its present Statute to be "to decide in accordance with international law such disputes as are submitted to it." Enforcement of judgments has been confided by the Charter of the United Nations to the Security Council, "which may," under paragraph 2 of Article 94, "if it deems necessary, make recommendations or decide upon measures to be taken to give effect to the judgment."

Similarly, it was no part of the function of the Permanent Court of International Justice to see to, or to provide ways and means for, the execution or enforcement of its judgments, although it does not seem to have been unusual to provide arrangements in bipartite treaties for the enforcement of judicial decisions entered thereunder. For instance, in the Protocol of May 24, 1934, between Peru and Colombia, the high contracting parties convenanted in Article 7 that if they should be unable to agree on measures to put into effect any judgment which might be rendered under the Protocol by the Permanent Court of International Justice, the Court should be authorized, "in addition to its ordinary competence, to make effective the judgment in which it has declared" that one of the parties has prevailed.[2] In the first contentious case before the Permanent Court of International

---

[2] 164 L.N.T.S. 21.

Justice—that of the *S.S. "Wimbledon"* [3]—the Court expressly refused to specify means for coercion of its decree by awarding "interim interest at a higher rate in the event of the judgment not being complied with at the expiration of the time fixed for compliance." It reiterated such a refusal in the *Chorzow Factory* case.[4] Since, therefore, enforcement of decrees of an international tribunal is under international law an entirely political function, completely separate from adjudication of the dispute which resulted in the decree, the enforcement process is, in effect, a new dispute to be resolved politically.

Of course, the Security Council cannot reopen the original dispute and review, in the judicial appellate sense, the issues adjudicated by the Court. Nevertheless, the Council unquestionably may, in the course of carrying out its political enforcement function, treat the entirety of the problem as a new dispute in which the judicial decree is only one of the elements and bring it to an ultimate solution by viewing its overall reflection in a broad political mirror.

The fundamental distinguishing feature between national and international tribunals is, not that the latter do not have enforcement means or authority to carry out their decrees, but that a national court functions for and in the name of a sovereign entity, a concept entirely absent from an international tribunal which adjudicates, without the aid of sovereignty, disputes between sovereign entities themselves.[5] This absence of sovereign authority for the enforcement of judicial decrees in international practice as well as the lack of the means and agencies for enforcement normally available to a judgment creditor in a national court have both given rise to the international legal doctrine of self-help, under which a prevailing nation may take its own steps to enforce a judgment in its favor, provided that, under the modern concept, such steps do not themselves lead to a breach of international peace. Therefore, while there is a superficial analogy

[3] [1923] P.C.I.J., ser. A, No. 1, at 32.   [4] [1928] P.C.I.J., ser. A, No. 17, at 63.

[5] It is interesting to note that it was once proposed, during the formulation of the Rules of Procedure for the Permanent Court of International Justice, that judgments should be rendered "in the name of the community of civilized nations," although the court did not find this proposal to be acceptable. [1922] P.C.I.J., ser. D, No. 2, at 266, 274.

between enforcement of national and international judgments, international law has had, and must continue to lay out, its own routes toward its own objectives through difficult terrain.

Generally speaking, coercion to compel involuntary compliance with the decrees of international tribunals is an exceptional and rarely required remedy. Instances, concededly very rare, in which nations have refused to abide by decisions have involved arbitral awards establishing boundaries on a give-and-take basis rather than formal juridical adjudications of legal rights and liabilities. In practically no other types of recorded instances in modern history (until very recently) have governments refused to be bound by or to execute decisions of international tribunals. In nearly all cases in which a decree has required affirmative action, the party cast has taken the action voluntarily and without question—even in cases in which the losing country has bitterly denounced the decision against it and has persisted in its denial of its liability as found. By way of example, in 1923 the United States paid a substantial amount under an arbitral award in favor of Norway, to evidence its "devotion to the principle of arbitral settlements even in the face of a decision proclaiming certain theories of law which it cannot accept." [6] During the twenty years of the incumbency of the Permanent Court of International Justice, there was not a single recorded instance in which any nation refused to comply with the decision of that Court in any case. This universal recognition of the accepted principle of compliance with international decrees apparently accounts for the initial failure, when the Charter of the United Nations was being formulated, to give thought to codification of the principle in that document. No provision of any kind was contained in the original Dumbarton Oaks Proposal, under which the members of the United Nations were to undertake expressly to abide by, and to comply with, decisions of what was to be the principal judicial

[6] M. HUDSON, TRIBUNALS at 129. Actually, a long time before that, Mexico paid to the United States the amounts of awards made by a claims commission established under an international convention of 1868, despite the position taken by Mexico that the claims on which the awards were based were fraudulent. Interestingly enough, some twenty years later, when the United States learned that at least some of the claims had in fact been fraudulent, it refunded the amounts thereof to Mexico. *Id.*

organ of their proposed new international organization. Australia later submitted a new paragraph to be added to the draft Charter, expressing the promise of each member of the organization to comply with any decree of the Court rendered in a case to which it was a party.[7] This proposal was adopted[8] and ultimately became paragraph 1 of Article 94 of the Charter: "Each member of the United Nations undertakes to comply with the decision of the International Court of Justice in any case to which it is a party."[9]

Countries which are not members of the United Nations may, in accordance with the provisions of Article 93 (2) of the Charter, become parties to the Statute of the International Court of Justice, "on conditions to be determined in each case by the General Assembly upon the recommendation of the Security Council." These countries have always been required, as one of the conditions of becoming parties to the Statute, to be bound by the enforcement provisions of Article 94 to the same extent as are members of the United Nations;[10] and by a general resolution of the Security Council, adopted October 15, 1946, these same conditions were imposed on nonmember States seeking access to the Court in particular cases.[11]

The fact that the United States is so meticulous in complying with her treaty obligations, undoubtedly accounts, in large measure, for the refusal of the Senate to accept unreserved compulsory jurisdiction of the International Court, with unequivocal agreement given in advance to comply with any decision which that tribunal might render in any case to which the United States might be a party. Actually, it was suggested at San Francisco, in

---

[7] 13 U.N.C.I.O. Docs. 553 (1945).   [8] *Id.* at 297, 386.

[9] Similarly, Paragraph 4 of Article 13 of the Covenant of the League of Nations provided that "the Members of the League agree that they will carry out in full good faith any award or decision that may be rendered" by the Permanent Court of International Justice; and then, in a sort of left-handed recognition of the occasional mutability of national attitudes toward compliance with adverse awards, the members of the League added the negative covenant "that they will not resort to war against a member of the League which complies therewith."

[10] *See, e.g.,* G.A. Res. 91 (I) (Dec. 11, 1946), fixing conditions on which Switzerland was permitted to become a party to the Statute of the Court. [1947–48] I.C.J.Y.B. 30–31.

[11] [1947] I.C.J., ser. D, No. 1, at 98.

1945, that a refusal to comply with a decision of the International Court of Justice should be considered to be, and dealt with as, an act of aggression.[12] In the course of studies to define what constitutes "aggression," the International Law Commission has given repeated consideration to inclusion of refusal to comply with a decision of the Court within the definition. But the suggestions have not been received favorably.[13] Invasion of disputed territory in violation of a judgment of the International Court of Justice would be an affirmative infringement of sovereignty already recognized by the Court. It would unquestionably constitute aggression—not because of the violation of the court's decree, but because of the nature of the act itself, tending to a breach of international peace by infringement of the sovereignty of the nation invaded, aggravated by the precedent judicial adjudication recognizing that sovereignty. It is for that reason—because of the differences between various kinds of judgments in various classes of cases involving various types of issues, calling for various kinds of remedies—that the Charter of the United Nations gives the creditor party "recourse to the Security Council, which may, if it deems necessary, make recommendations or decide upon measures to be taken to give effect to the judgment." [14] This brief outline of this phase of the law governing enforcement of international decrees also explains clearly why the provisions governing enforcement are found in the Charter of the United Nations, rather than in the Statute of the International Court of Justice. Such provisions are not part of the adjudicative process of the Court, but relate only to the powers of the United Nations organization as a whole, to be exercised by the Security Council within its political discretion.

In the last analysis, the question as to how decisions of the International Court of Justice are to be enforced is simply one phase of the overall problem as to how compliance with any other international obligation is to be compelled. This is, after all, the fundamental problem which faces a world community made up

[12] 13 U.N.C.I.O. Docs. 579 (1945) .
[13] *See* Int'l L. Comm'n, Report, 6 U.N. GAOR, Supp. 10, at 8, U.N. Doc. A/1858 (1952) . *See also* 1 S. ROSENNE, LAW AND PRACTICE at 120.
[14] U.N. CHARTER art. 94, para. 2.

of independent States, each desiring and determined to maintain its national sovereignty. How are the members of such an international society to be required to comply with the decisions of a tribunal which they have themselves set up to adjudicate their disputes? And is not failure of a sovereign nation to comply with such a decision the equivalent of failure to comply with any other international obligation arising out of any other agreement among sovereign States to be bound by one of its terms, or out of a political determination reached pursuant to an undertaking contained in such an agreement, in accordance with the maxim *pacta sunt servanda?* If not the only, then certainly the most notable, instance of outright and unequivocal refusal to comply with the decree of an international tribunal is found in the position of Albania *vis-à-vis* the judgment of the International Court of Justice in one of its earliest decisions, the *Corfu Channel* case.[15]

It is conceivable that the Government of Bolivia may have had some premonition of such a difficulty as was to arise in the *Corfu Channel* case, when the representative of that country proposed in 1945, at San Francisco, that a refusal to comply with a decision of the International Court of Justice should be considered to be, and should be dealt with as, an act of aggression.[16] On December 15, 1949, judgment was rendered by the Court in favor of the United Kingdom and against Albania for £843,947, representing an award for loss of the destroyer *Saumarez,* for damage to the destroyer *Volage,* and for the deaths of forty-five of the ships' officers and men and injuries to forty-two others of their complements. The loss occurred when the vessels struck mines in the Corfu Channel off the coast of Albania as a result of Albania's fault in failing to warn the approaching ships of the danger from the mines, of whose existence Albania was aware.[17]

From the date of rendition of that judgment, the case became one illustrating the problems of enforcement of international decrees, although it never found or pointed to an effective route toward their solution. Nevertheless, an outline of the postjudgment proceedings in that case will provide a significant background for an understanding of various phases of the problem.

[15] [1949] I.C.J. 244.   [16] [1947–48] I.C.J. 244.   [17] *Id.*

Discussions between representatives of the two governments to endeavor to find mutually acceptable ways and means to effect settlement of the judgment led to nothing except an Albanian offer to pay £40,000 to Great Britain in full settlement. This offer was rejected in January 1951 as completely unrealistic.[18] Next, the British, in an exercise of economic self-help for enforcement, sought Albanian property which might be seized within the geographical jurisdiction of the United Kingdom to satisfy the judgment, but no such property being found, this effort was unsuccessful.[19]

During World War II, in September 1943, German military units had looted a vault in Rome and had carried away to Germany some 2,340 kilograms of monetary gold, ultimately found and captured by the Allied forces. Under the 1946 Act of Paris on Reparations, restitution of the gold was to be made by the United States, British, and French Governments, which established a tripartite commission to carry out the distribution.[20] Both Italy and Albania made claim to the gold, and the commission referred the controversy back to their governments, which by an agreement confected at Washington on April 25, 1951, arranged for appointment of an arbitrator to render an opinion as to whether either Albania or Italy (or neither) was entitled to the gold, his opinion to be binding on the governments. The arbitrator rendered his decision on February 20, 1953, holding that under the Act of Paris, Albania was entitled to the gold. The British Government then took the position that, as stated in the Washington Agreement, "if Albania establishes a claim to the gold under Part III of the Paris Act, it should be delivered to the United Kingdom in partial satisfaction of the judgment of the International Court of Justice against Albania." The governments were prepared to recognize this claim and to deliver the gold to Great Britain in partial satisfaction of the judgment. At this point, however, a new factor entered upon the scene. Italy

[18] 473 Parl. Deb. H. L. (5th ser.) (1951); 1168; 474 *id.* at 113; 477 *id.* at 958; 483 *id.* at 569; 488 *id.* at 201.

[19] 483 *id.* at 570; 488 *id.* at 981.

[20] The substance of the facts as to the postadjudicative phases of the Corfu Channel case, is to be found in the opinion of the International Court of Justice in Monetary Gold Removed from Rome in 1943, [1954] I.C.J. 19.

asserted an independent claim—not under the Act of Paris—against Albania, submitting that this claim had priority over that of Great Britain against the gold. But the governments agreed to turn the gold over to the United Kingdom, unless either Albania or Italy should apply within ninety days to the International Court of Justice for adjudication of the conflicting claims, in which event they bound themselves "to conform in the matter of the delivery of the gold with any decision of the International Court given as the result of such application by Italy or by Albania."

Albania neither instituted nor participated in any proceedings before the Court, but within the time limitation, Italy filed her application with the tribunal requesting determination (1) as to whether any part of the gold should under any circumstances be turned over to Italy rather than to Albania; and (2) whether the claim of Italy to the gold should not have priority over that of the United Kingdom, on the ground that Italy's cause of action against Albania had arisen before that of Great Britain. But now Italy, having by institution of her action in the International Court of Justice stopped delivery of the gold to the United Kingdom, took the ingenious step of filing a plea to the Court's jurisdiction over her own action. The ground was that Albania, which was not before the Court, was a necessary party to the controversy between Albania and Italy, involving the first question submitted to the Court for adjudication. Italy then requested that her plea to the jurisdiction be considered by the Court as a preliminary question, before decision of the merits of the controversy. The British representative contended that Italy's plea to the jurisdiction had the effect of a withdrawal of her action, with consequent perfection of the United Kingdom's title to the gold under the Washington Agreement. The Court held that it "is indeed unusual that a state which has submitted a claim by the filing of an application should subsequently challenge the jurisdiction of the court to which of its own accord it has applied," but that nevertheless "Italy's acceptance of jurisdiction is one thing, while her raising of a legal issue on jurisdiction is quite another. It cannot be inferred from the making of the preliminary objection, that Italy's acceptance of jurisdiction has become less complete or less

positive than was contemplated in the Washington Statement."
Italy continues, said the Court,

to hold herself out as being subject to the court's jurisdiction in these
proceedings after the raising of the preliminary objection as much
as she did before taking that step. . . . The court accordingly finds
that it has been validly seized of the application and that this application, contrary to the submissions of the United Kingdom Government, still subsists.

Next, the Court found that the first question submitted to it for
adjudication "centers around a claim by Italy against Albania
. . . for the redress of an international wrong. . . . In order,
therefore, to determine whether Italy is entitled to receive the
gold, it is necessary to determine whether Albania has committed
an international wrong against Italy." But the Court said, it
"cannot decide such a dispute without the consent of Albania"
to the Court's jurisdiction, and "it is not contended by any party
that Albania has given her consent in this case either expressly
or by implication." It was accordingly held "that, although Italy
and the three respondent States have conferred jurisdiction on the
court, it cannot exercise this jurisdiction to adjudicate on the first
claim submitted by Italy." Finally, the Court concluded that a
necessity for determination of the second Italian submission—
that "Italy's right to receive the said share of monetary gold must
have priority over the claim of the United Kingdom"—"will only
arise in the event that the court has decided on the merits of the
first question, as requested by the Italian Government." The
Court accordingly found "inasmuch as it cannot adjudicate on
the first Italian claim, it must refrain from examining the question of priority between the claim of Italy and that of the United
Kingdom."

And so enforcement of the judgment of the International
Court of Justice in favor of the United Kingdom against Albania
in the *Corfu Channel* case was—and remains to this day—
frustrated on all fronts, although no effort was ever made in that
case to seek enforcement through the Security Council under the

second paragraph of Article 94 of the Charter of the United Nations, expressly directed to that end.[21]

The enforcement provision of the Covenant of the League of Nations stipulated that, "in the event of any failure to carry out such an award or decision, the Council shall propose what steps should be taken to give effect thereto." [22] The Charter of the United Nations gives to the prevailing party "recourse to the Security Council, which may, if it deems necessary, make recommendations or decide upon measures to be taken to give effect to the judgment." [23] A fundamental difference between these two provisions arises from, and is emphasized by, the words "if it deems necessary" in Article 94 (2) of the Charter, but absent from Article 13 (4) of the Covenant. Under the express language of the Charter provision, the exercise by the Security Council of its enforcement function is discretionary, not obligatory. This conclusion is amply supported by the background as well as the words of Article 94 (2). A proposal for addition of this phrase was made in 1945 at San Francisco by the Advisory Committee of Jurists, and it was adopted formally at the twenty-second meeting of Committee IV/1 (Judicial Organization—International Court of Justice), the summary report of which contains the following:

It was observed that the use of this phrase might tend to weaken the position of the court. In answer to this argument it was pointed out that the action to be taken by the Security Council was permissive rather than obligatory, and that the addition of the aforementioned phrase merely made more clear the discretionary power of the Security Council.[24]

"Presumably," wrote Judge Green H. Hackworth only two months after adoption of the Charter and the Statute of the

[21] "Although the damages awarded to the United Kingdom against Albania in the *Corfu Channel* case (£843,947) have not been paid over—the only instance so far as is known, of complete failure to comply with a judgment of the court—the competence of the Security Council has not yet ever been invoked in order to secure compliance with a judgment." S. ROSENNE, THE WORLD COURT 43–44 (1962).

[22] LEAGUE OF NATIONS COVENANT art. 13, para. 4.

[23] U.N. CHARTER art. 94, para. 2.   [24] 14 U.N.C.I.O. 495 (1945).

Court, "the Security Council would not think it necessary to decide upon 'measures to be taken' unless it should feel that failure to respect the decision of the court constituted a threat to the peace, in which event it might proceed under the provision of Chapter VII of the charter relating to threats to the peace, breaches of the peace, and acts of aggression." [25] In light of the *travaux préparatoires* in the background of the phrase "if it deems necessary" and of the simple, explicit meaning of the words themselves, it can hardly be contended that action of the Security Council in the enforcement of judgments of the International Court of Justice is not an entirely discretionary exercise of a politico-diplomatic function.[26]

The Council has discretion to determine whether it will discuss enforcement of a judgment of the International Court of Justice at all, or whether it will simply not put the issue on its agenda; and if it should put the matter on its agenda, whether it should "make recommendations or decide upon measures to be taken"— and if so, what the measures should be—"to give effect to the judgment." Of course, the measures must always be "to give effect to the judgment." The Council may not reverse the judgment or take away adjudicated rights secured or created thereunder. The judgment remains *res judicata* between the parties, whatever the Security Council may, or may not, do to enforce it.

With exclusive power to enforce decrees of the International Court of Justice vested in the Security Council, the question arises as to the applicability of the right of veto to enforcement measures proposed by the Council. Some doubt has been expressed in this regard, but there seems little real question that decisions as to enforcement measures, as a protective reservation to the Great Powers, require unanimity of votes by the Council's permanent members. As stated by Shabtai Rosenne, a member of

---

[25] 13 DEP'T. STATE BULL. 126 (1945). Mr. Hackworth was Legal Adviser to the Department when the Charter was adopted. He later became a judge of the Court and served as such for fourteen years, during three of which he was its President.

[26] "Not only was the authority of the council thus made unquestionably discretionary, but the new phrase—'if it deems necessary'—clearly implied, after the argument just described, that the council would consider enforcement necessary only when failure to execute a court judgment appeared to create a threat to the peace." R. RUSSELL, CHARTER at 895.

the International Law Commission: "The question also arises
. . . whether the 'veto' is applicable to action by the Security
Council under Article 94. He suggests that 'no clear answer is
possible,' but that it can be presumed, without much risk of
error, that the Security Council is unlikely to set about willfully
destroying the power of the court." [27]

The final problem for consideration is what effective measure
can be devised to compel compliance with a judgment of the
International Court of Justice, against a recalcitrant nation, without resorting to the use of force and provoking a breach of international peace. What practical measure may, for instance, be
employed to compel Albania to satisfy the court's money decree
in favor of Great Britain? An eminently practical answer to this
eminently practical question may be found in the provisions of
Articles 5 and 19 of the United Nations Charter, aimed at contingencies closely analogous to those arising from delinquencies
in compliance with judgments of the Court. Article 5 of the
Charter states that "a Member of the United Nations against
which preventive or enforcement action has been taken by the
Security Council may be suspended from the exercise of the
rights and privileges of membership by the General Assembly
on recommendation of the Security Council." Under Article 19
a member of the United Nations in arrears in its financial contributions in excess of a specified amount beyond a specified
length of time "shall have no vote in the General Assembly." It
is not suggested that these articles of the Charter are directly
applicable to procedures for enforcement of decrees; but they do
supply a practical guideline by which the Security Council "may,
if it deems necessary," decide that a nation in default under a
judgment of the International Court of Justice, is to "be suspended from the exercise of the rights and privileges of membership" in the United Nations, and "shall have no vote in the
General Assembly" until it shall comply with the decree, as "a
measure to be taken to give effect to the judgment" under the
second paragraph of Article 94 of the Charter. Adoption of these
measures, it is submitted, would give strong impetus to ac-

---

[27] 1 S. ROSENNE, LAW AND PRACTICE at 153–54.

complishment of the "Purposes and Principles" stated in the Charter of the United Nations, for "prevention and removal of threats to the peace," by effecting "adjustment or settlement of international disputes" in "conformity with the principles of justice and international law." [28]

[28] U.N. CHARTER art. 1, para. 3.

CHAPTER XIX

Recent Movements

In August 1965, the House of Delegates of the American Bar Association put the Association on record as favoring world peace through a strengthened international judiciary. In its preambular paragraphs, the resolution recited that "the International Court of Justice, although now performing a useful function in resolving international differences, is not being utilized to its maximum capacity"; that "the private bar has long been committed to the principle of resolving all differences, public and private, by sound judicial processes"; and that "a re-examination of the Statute of the Court may well point to ways and means of making the Court an institutional structure having greater usefulness in meeting the requirements for world peace." [1] On these premises, the American Bar Association recommended "that the members of the United Nations be asked to consider a revision of the Statute of the International Court of Justice . . . to give the Court jurisdiction over all members of the United Nations . . . consideration [to] be given to the Court being composed of international judges having tenure for life . . . and to prohibiting the overruling of a plea to the jurisdiction on the ground that a controversy is domestic except by a vote of two-thirds of its entire membership." [2]

On August 14, 1970, several countries (supplemented by others on September 10 and 11) requested that "Review of the Role of the International Court of Justice" be placed on the agenda of the General Assembly.[3] As required by Rule 20 of the Assembly's Rules of Procedure, an explanatory memorandum was attached. It stated that a "study should be undertaken . . . of the obstacles to the satisfactory functioning of the International Court of Justice, and ways and means of removing them." [4]

[1] 1965 A.B.A. Rep. 580.   [2] Id.   [3] U.N. Doc A/8042, at 1–2 (1970).
[4] Id. at 3.

In discussing the draft resolution (U.N. Doc. A/C.6/L.800 [1970]) in the Sixth (Legal) Committee on October 30, 1970, Mr. Olivier Deleau of France stated: "The reluctance of states to accept the compulsory jurisdiction of the Court in regard to disputes, had minimized the effectiveness of the judicial body."[5] Mr. Dimitri L. Kolesnik of the Soviet Union replied that

it was clear . . . from a recent statement by the United States Secretary of State that at least one of the sponsors of the present item sought to revise the Statute of the Court . . . thus amending its role and character. Such a position . . . would be tantamount to a revision . . . of the United Nations Charter itself. . . . Under the present circumstances any revision of the United Nations Charter and that of the Court's Statute would mean a weakening of the whole system and structure of the United Nations. . . .[6]

If the Court changed the character of its decisions, then states would be willing to bring their disputes before the Court. . . . His delegation could not agree with the ways and means suggested to overcome the difficulties faced by the Court. Some of these suggestions . . . might even lead to a disintegration of the body of international law. The idea of converting the Court into a sort of world judicial body, whose jurisdiction would have a binding character for all parties, was totally and wholly unacceptable. . . .[7]

The setting up of an *ad hoc* committee to exercise the role of the Court might be dangerous. . . . Instead of asking views of Governments first, the sponsors, from the very beginning, were trying to establish a new body. . . . His delegation was resolutely opposed to the very idea of revising the role and Statute of the Court as well as to the establishment of any body to deal with the matter.[8]

The delegate of Brazil, Themistocles B. Cavalcanti, stated that the "compulsory jurisdiction of the Court was a prerequisite for its effectiveness. . . . He expressed the hope that the time might come when states would readily submit their disputes to the Court

[5] U.N. Release No. GA/L 1420 at 1 (Oct. 30, 1970).

[6] *Id.* at 2. Mr. Kolesnik apparently overlooked the fact that Article 94 of the Charter of the United Nations provides that if "any party to a cause fails to perform the obligations incumbent upon it under a judgment rendered by the Court, the other party may have recourse to the Security Council [where the right of veto remains], which may, if it deems necessary, make recommendations or decide upon measures to be taken to give effect to the judgment."

[7] *Id.* at 2–3. *See* note 33 *infra.*   [8] *Id.* at 3.

for a peaceful settlement. It was with this expectation that his delegation would vote in favor of the draft resolution." [9]

On November 19, 1970, at a meeting of the Sixth Committee, Mr. Brewer, delegate of Liberia, reminded his colleagues that "in 1945, in the preparatory work in connection with drafting the Statute of the Court, the question whether the Court's jurisdiction was to be made obligatory . . . had been the subject of debate. . . . Since the issue of the Court's jurisdiction still raised essentially the same kind of political considerations, his government had decided that only an inquiry undertaken by a committee of experts appointed by the General Assembly would insure a fully objective investigation of the problem. . . ." [10] At a subsequent meeting of the Committee, Mr. Gastli, the delegate of Tunisia, in introducing a draft resolution (U.N.Doc. A/C.6/L.806 [1970]), said that under it, States "would submit their comments to the Secretary General; the Court itself would be invited to express its views; and a working group . . . would be instructed, on the basis of the opinions and suggestions put forward by states and by the Court, to prepare a preliminary report which would bring together the various ideas expressed. . . ." [11] The delegate of Chile, Mr. Zegers, said that even "if it was true that the question of the functioning of the Court was more than simply a matter of its Rules, it was still necessary to ascertain the views of the Court itself on the subject before making any recommendations. His delegation therefore welcomed [the] draft resolution submitted by the French delegation (U.N. Doc. A/C.6/L. 801 [1970]), under which Member states . . . would be invited to submit their opinions and suggestions and the Court itself would be requested to state its views. . . ." [12] "In general," Mr. Zegers continued,

the French proposal represented a half-way house between the establishment of an *ad hoc* committee . . . as proposed in the sixteen-Power draft and the simple transmission to the International Court of Justice of the records of the discussion on the question in the Sixth Committee, as proposed in the draft of Czechoslovakia and the Ukrainian SSR [U.N.Doc. A/C.6/L.802 (1970)]. The French draft,

[9] *Id.* at 4.   [10] U.N. Doc. A/C.6/SR.1226, at 2 (1970).
[11] U.N. Doc. A/C.6/SR.1224, at 2 (1970).   [12] *Id.* at 3.

which in any case did not exclude the possibility of an *ad hoc* committee being established at the twenty-sixth session, should therefore be able to command unanimous support.[13]

Mr. Koleznik of the Soviet Union stated "that the sixteen-Power draft resolution . . . was not only unacceptable but might well be harmful to the interests of the United Nations. . . . In addition, the purpose of the contemplated revision of the Statute seemed to be to make the Court's jurisdiction compulsory. But the discussion had clearly shown that the functioning of the Court . . . depended first of all on the General Assembly and the Security Council, which elected the Court's judges. . . . The French draft resolution provided a compromise solution in keeping with United Nations tradition." [14]

The representative of Australia, Mr. Brennan, replied:

[the] representative of the Soviet Union had stated that the members of the Sixth Committee were perhaps less well placed than the judges of the Court to examine the problems facing the Court. The reply to that argument was that the issue was not the problems of the Court itself but those of Governments, and more specifically the attitudes of Governments toward the judicial settlement of disputes through the intermediary of the Court. . . . The sixteen-Power draft resolution also provided that the views submitted by Governments and the Court should be referred to an *ad hoc* committee . . . which would analyze them.[15]

The task of that Committee . . . would not, as the representative of the USSR had suggested, be to prepare a revision of the Statute of the Court, but to consider how Governments could make better use of the services of the Court within its present Statute, though it would not set its face against considering amendments to the Statute if that proved necessary. It would then rest with Governments, if they so wished to avail themselves of the procedure provided for in Chapter V of the Statute for amendments to that instrument.[16]

Mr. Gimer, representative of the United States, rather startlingly assured the group that "his delegation had no intention of amending the Statute, Article 36 included"; to which the Hungarian delegate, Mr. Prandler, replied that "he was glad to hear . . . assurances that they did not intend to undertake a

13 *Id.*   14 *Id.* at 3–4.   15 *Id.* at 5.   16 *Id.* at 6.

revision of the Statute of the Court. If that was the case, however, why was it necessary to set up an *ad hoc* committee?" [17] Mr. Fartash, the delegate of Iran, "said that it was traditional for the Sixth Committee to resolve the difficulties it encountered by preparing a compromise text. His delegation felt that the French draft resolution was the one most likely to fulfill that role. His delegation believed that nothing but good could come from carrying out a preliminary inquiry of that kind before establishing a new body, and would support the French draft resolution." [18]

The delegate of Bulgaria, Mr. Kostov, said "that the views of the Court itself should be heard before any decision of any kind was adopted. . . . His delegation . . . was prepared, for the sake of compromise, to support the French draft resolution." [19] Mr. Deleau, the French representative, asked: "Why would it not be preferable to request the Secretary-General to prepare a report on the basis of the comments made by Governments and the views of the Court?" [20] The delegates of a number of countries made statements as to whether it was necessary or advisable to get the views of governments before appointing an *ad hoc* committee, or whether such a committee should be appointed at all.[21] The Chairman, Mr. Engo of the Cameroon, "suggested that a vote on the documents before the Committee should be postponed in order to allow the sponsors time to consult together," and "it was so decided." [22]

The delegate of Kenya, Mr. Njenga, on November 13, 1970, said that since the negotiations had not yet made it possible to arrive at an agreed text, the delegations of Guyana, Kenya, Uganda, and Zambia had felt it necessary to submit amendments to U.N. Doc. A/C.6/L 808 (1970). The debates in the Committee indicated that all States wanted action with a view to enhancing the effectiveness of the Court.[23] "However," said Mr. Njenga, "the sponsors of the proposed amendments believed that an *ad hoc* committee would be premature until states had had an opportunity to express their views on the subject. That did not

[17] *Id.*   [18] *Id.* at 7.   [19] *Id.* at 7–8.   [20] *Id.* at 8.   [21] *Id.* at 2–6.
[22] *Id.* at 7.   [23] U.N. Doc. A/C.6/SR 1225, at 13 (1970).

at all exclude the possibility of establishing such a body at a later time, if Governments so wished." [24] Mr. Deleau (France) stated that his country "did not insist that the Sixth Committee take . . . its draft resolution. It fully supported the proposed amendments and requested that France be included among the sponsors of the document containing them." [25]

The Chairman, Mr. Engo of the Cameroon, "said that he understood that informal consultations had resulted in a consensus agreement" for "a recommendation to the General Assembly to adopt draft resolution A/C.6/L. 800, Rev. 1, as modified by A/C.6/L. 808, Rev. 2," and "it was so decided." [26] The resolution so adopted provided that Member States should be invited "to submit to the Secretary-General, by 1 July 1971, views and suggestions concerning the role of the Court," inviting "the Court to submit its views, should it so desire," and requesting the Secretary-General "to prepare a comprehensive report in the light of the opinions expressed by the states and the Court." [27]

In accordance with custom, the delegates of the various countries were thereupon invited to state the reasons which motivated their votes. Ceylon's delegate, Mr. Pinto, stated that the "draft resolution adopted seemed to embody the soundest of the approaches proposed. . . . However the proviso should be reiterated that any future study on the role of the Court should be wide-ranging, encompassing the opinions of both lawyers and experts in the political and social sciences. . . ." [28] The delegate of the United States, Mr. Reis, stated that the "resolution called for concrete action by States, the Court and the Secretary-General. . . . The United States regarded the effort to take a new and creative look at the Court as satisfactorily launched." [29] Mr. Zegers, representative of Chile, agreed that "the views of both States and the Court deserved the consideration of all Governments. . . ." [30]

The delegate of Morocco, Mr. Kabbaj, said that although "not all (of the Court's) decisions had commanded approval, it had generally served to safeguard the rule of law and justice. Morocco had cause to be thankful for the decision the Court had handed

24 *Id.*   25 *Id.*   26 U.N. Doc. A/C.6/SR 1229, at 2 (1970).
27 *Id.* at 28.   28 *Id.* at 4.   29 *Id.*   30 *Id.* at 4–5.

down in 1951 in the *Case Concerning Rights of Nationals of the United States of America in Morocco.* . . . A decision at the present stage to establish an *ad hoc* committee to review its functions would be premature. His delegation therefore welcomed the draft resolution which the Committee had approved and was glad that it had secured a consensus." [31] Mr. Robertson, representative of Madagascar, "welcomed the consensus decision, which allowed his and other Governments, and the Court, the necessary time to crystallize their views on a complex problem, and identify the obstacles to the proper functioning of the Court." [32]

The Soviet delegate, Mr. Kolesnik, said that "his delegation was glad to see that the consensus resolution did not provide for the creation of an *ad hoc* committee immediately, nor prejudge the need for States or the United Nations to review the Court's role. Moreover, it did not conflict with the USSR's basic position that the reason for the Court's present lack of activity was that it had handed down unjust decisions and not that its Statute was defective." [33] "His delegation," he said "re-emphasized the fact that any review of the Court's role and any attempt to undermine its Statute and the United Nations Charter were unacceptable; nor could it agree to States having the Court's compulsory jurisdiction imposed on them in violation of their sovereign rights." [34]

Mr. Brennan, the Australian delegate, stated "that his delegation welcomed the adoption of the consensus text. . . . The problem was not so much whether an *ad hoc* committee should be established; the real division of opinion was between those who wanted the item to be further discussed and those who did not. . . . The intention of the review was not to examine the way in which the Court carried on its business, but rather to ascertain the attitude of Governments to the pacific settlement of disputes, the judicial settlement of legal disputes and the settlement of legal disputes by the Court." [35] The Finnish delegate, Mr. Castren, said that the "discussions on the role of the Court had proved most useful; his delegation . . . hoped that when the General

[31] *Id.* at 5.   [32] *Id.* at 6.

[33] *Id.* The record discloses that out of twenty-seven cases, the Soviet judges concurred in the decision of twenty-two.

[34] *Id.*   [35] *Id.* at 7.

Assembly resumed its discussion of the item in 1971, on the basis of views by Governments and by the Court itself, it would be in a position to take more effective decisions in line with the intentions of the initiators of the question." [36]

Mr. Francis, representing Jamaica, said that "his delegation was particularly pleased at the consensus achieved in the draft resolution. . . . The opposing views turned out to be nothing more than a difference of opinion as to the spirit in which the item should be dealt with at the twenty-sixth session." [37] The delegate of the United Kingdom "concurred in the unanimous adoption of the draft resolution. . . . It had already expressed its reason for preferring the establishment of an *ad hoc* committee during the current year. . . . His delegation was confident that a decision to establish an *ad hoc* committee would be taken at the twenty-sixth session." [38]

The representative of the Ukrainian SSR, Mr. Makarevich, said that "his delegation and that of Czechoslovakia had not opposed the compromise text of the resolution adopted unanimously by the Committee. . . . The main purpose of opposing the inclusion of the item concerning the role of the Court had been to revise the statute of the Court and hence the Charter." [39] "However," he went on, "any modification of the character, functions and authority of one of the main organs of the United Nations would jeopardize the other main organs, particularly the Security Council. In the long-term interests of international peace and security, and adherence to the Charter, his delegation would oppose any attempt to impose the compulsory jurisdiction of the Court, a step which would undermine the foundations of the United Nations." [40]

Mr. Deleau (France) remarked that "his delegation welcomed the unanimous adoption of [the] resolution. . . . The Committee's decision would make it possible to continue consideration of the complex question of the role of the Court in an atmosphere of general agreement." [41] Mr. Chamas, Lebanon's delegate, stated that he "had not agreed with the view that the establishment of an *ad hoc* committee would imply the threat of a revision of the

[36] *Id.* at 8.   [37] *Id.*   [38] *Id.* at 8–9.   [39] *Id.* at 9.   [40] *Id.*
[41] *Id.* at 9–10.

Charter. However, the question now remained open, leaving Governments plenty of time to consider what further action was needed"; [42] and the representative of Zambia, Mr. Chaila, "expressed his delegation's satisfaction at the unanimous decision reached by the Committee." [43]

The Sixth Committee's report, submitted on December 11, 1970, reviewed the positions expressed by the Member States during the debates. It stated that certain States "hesitated to make greater use of the Court" because "they doubted the adequacy of existing international law to meet their needs. . . . It was asserted that the international law applied by the Court still reflected essentially the legal systems of European and American states," although "juridical norms were gradually emerging which corresponded to contemporary reality." [44] The report continued that some "representatives recalled that at the United Nations Conference on International Organization at San Francisco, the smaller nations had expressed opposition to the system established in article 36, for they had hoped to be able to offset their military weakness by their ability to bring even large countries into court, and that it was only to avoid jeopardizing the Court's future that they had bowed to the will of the great Powers. It was also said that the Court would not become an effective institution until judicial settlement became compulsory." [45] "Some delegations," the report went on, suggested that "one of the matters which might be studied was ways and means of encouraging the unconditional acceptance of the Court's compulsory jurisdiction"; but "it was also observed that to make the Court's jurisdiction compulsory would amount to making it a supra-national organ, with greater power than the Security Council, which was, of course, unacceptable, and would infringe the principles of national independence and sovereignty and other basic rights of states." [46] Finally, the report went on to say that some representatives "stated that they did not oppose the idea of an *ad hoc* committee, but rather felt that it should not be established too hastily at the current session," since "some delegations intended to propose the establishment of an *ad hoc* committee to study the question of a

[42] *Id.* at 10.　　[43] *Id.*　　[44] U.N. Doc. A/8238, at 14 (1971).　　[45] *Id.* at 17.
[46] *Id.* at 17–18.

review of the Charter . . . it would be desirable to delay taking a decision on the review of the role of the Court until the position with regard to the review of the Charter had become more clear." [47] The General Assembly considered the report of the Sixth Committee on December 15, 1970. Mr. Javits spoke on behalf of the United States,[48] and Mr. Kolesnik on behalf of the Soviet Union.[49] The Assembly adopted the resolution (G.A. Res. 2723 [XXV]) proposed by the Committee.[50] Mr. Kolesnik, in a brief statement, repeated that the "Court has fallen into a period of idleness not because of any flaw in the Statute of the Court but because it has compromised itself by erroneous decisions.[51] Pursuant to the terms of the Resolution, the Secretary-General prepared a questionnaire to governments, and in due course, answers were received from many countries. On September 15, 1971, the Secretary-General issued his report (U.N. Doc. A/8382 [1971]), from which the following excerpts are reproduced.

Cyprus responded simply that, in its opinion, the main difficulty lay in the fact that the "jurisdiction of the Court remained optional"; [52] and "the adoption of the compulsory jurisdiction of the Court . . . and the recourse to the Court in general are subject to political manipulation as instruments of a state's foreign policy." [53] Denmark was equally direct in stating that ". . . the crux of the matter is the unwillingness of Governments to accept the compulsory jurisdiction of the Court. . . ." [54] Japan replied that it "is also true that the climate itself may change if steps are taken to alleviate the misgivings of Member States against the Court, and if institutional reforms succeed in increasing the confidence of States in the role of the Court." [55] France stated with equal directness, if not simplicity, that it "appears that the real reason for the rejection of compulsory jurisdiction lies in the structure of international relations itself." [56]

Finland stated that "the fact that international law as a judicial system is still underdeveloped and deficient in many respects, causes many states to adopt an attitude of reserve in bringing

[47] *Id.* at 25.   [48] U.N. Doc A/FV.1931, at 7–12 (1971).   [49] *Id.* at 13–15.
[50] *Id.* at 7.   [51] *Id.* at 15. *See* note 33 *supra.*
[52] U.N. Doc. A/8382, at 15 (1971).   [53] *Id.* at 19.   [54] *Id.*
[55] *Id.* at 20.   [56] *Id.* at 21.

cases to the International Court of Justice, particularly on issues involving recognition of its jurisdiction as compulsory." [57] Laos, consistent with her prior opinion as theretofore expressed, said that "the jurisdiction of the Court should be . . . made compulsory"; [58] and again that "all states Members of the United Nations should be required to submit to the jurisdiction and decisions of the Court." [59]

"The effectiveness of the Court can be enhanced," stated the Ukrainian SSR, "not by strengthening its role, broadening its competence and making States subject to its compulsory jurisdiction, which could be prejudicial to the national sovereignty of States, but by strict observance of the provisions of the United Nations Charter and the Statute of the Court." [60] Czechoslovakia echoed the thoughts of its Communist contemporaries in stating that to "recognize an obligatory jurisdiction of the International Court of Justice would amount to transforming it into a suprastate organ, with which the Czechoslovak Socialist Republic cannot agree." [61]

"As to the optional clause in Article 36 of the Statute," Mr. Alcivar of Ecuador stated that:

his delegation did not share the view that the acceptance of the compulsory jurisdiction of the Court conflicted with the principle of state sovereignty. The scope of the Charter went far beyond that of a general multilateral treaty, and it could be regarded as a kind of constitution for the universal international community as judicially represented by the United Nations. States, as judicial persons, were therefore objects of national and international rights and obligations, and thus subjects of a national and international legal order. [62]

Mr. Osei Tutu of Ghana expressed the opinion of his Government that ". . . if the international community's faith in the Court was to be restored, the permanent members of the Security Council should accept the Court's compulsory jurisdiction in conformity with their obligations under the Charter." [63]

According to a United Nations press release of December 7, 1972, Vladimir N. Federoff of the Soviet Union stated "that the

[57] *Id.* at 24. [58] *Id.* at 66. [59] *Id.* at 28. [60] *Id.* at 32.
[61] *Id.* at 69. [62] U.N. Doc. A/C.6/SR 1284, at 3 (1972).
[63] U.N. Doc. A/C.6/SR 1281, at 16 (1972).

Soviet delegation rejected any proposals attempting artificially to enforce obligatory jurisdiction of the Court upon States." [64]

Tiny Laos stated squarely that the "Statute of the Court should be revised on the principle of compulsory adherence whereby all States Members of the United Nations would undertake *in advance* to comply with the decisions of the Court and to enforce them in the same way as decisions of their national courts." [65] Yugoslavia, at odds with the generally expressed Communist view, replied to the questionnaire of the Secretary-General as follows:

> The fact that jurisdiction of the International Court of Justice is not compulsory but facultative, constitutes one of the main obstacles to the work of the Court. The Yugoslav Government feels that in the contemporary conditions it would not be realistic to expect a larger number of countries to accept the compulsory jurisdiction of the Court. . . . The acceptance of the compulsory jurisdiction, in essence, depends upon the further democratization of the international community.[66]

Poland, quite remarkably, stated that the "practice of accepting compulsory jurisdiction of the Court with reservations makes the acceptance only apparent. The experience indicates that the efforts aimed at enhancing the effectiveness of this judicial organ should be primarily directed at overcoming distrust and encouraging States to bring disputes before the Court, and this could be done by making improvements within the present framework of the Statute." [67]

France stated that its "Government considers that more general acceptance of the compulsory jurisdiction of the Court . . . can only come about after a change in the position of States regarding the judicial settlement of disputes." [68] Finland added the thought that the "reasons why States have refrained from accepting the optional clause concerning the recognition of the International Court of Justice's jurisdiction as compulsory obviously cannot be removed easily and quickly." [69] Mr. Bejasa of the Philippines suggested that first the Court "should endeavor to encourage States

[64] U.N. Release No. GA/L/1593, at 6 (Dec. 7, 1972).

[65] U.N. Doc. A/8382, at 120 (1971).   [66] *Id.* at 70.   [67] *Id.* at 66.

[68] *Id.* at 69.   [69] *Id.* at 72.

to accept the compulsory jurisdiction of the Court, in accordance with Article 36 of the Statute, without expressing any reservations that would deprive such acceptance of any real meaning. . . ." [70]

Two countries suggested the adoption of General Assembly resolutions to solve the compulsory jurisdictional problem. Thus Austria suggested that efforts "to induce Governments to recognize the Court's jurisdiction as compulsory should be continued —if necessary by means of resolutions of the General Assembly." [71] Switzerland stated that its "Government would like the General Assembly, by means of a solemn resolution, to invite States to accept the compulsory jurisdiction of the Court, and to invite those which have already done so to abandon restrictive reservations. . . ." [72]

In a supplementary reply published by the Secretary-General on September 30, 1971, Senegal stated:

[D]espite the term "compulsory jurisdiction of the Court," States are not bound by it unless they so desire, stating voluntarily that they accept the jurisdiction of the Court. All the efforts made so far to impose the jurisdiction automatically have met with resistance from states which consider that their sovereignty would be impaired. It is probable that, if the Charter and the Statute were amended to that effect, a number of states would prefer to leave the United Nations. [73]

In addition to the problem of compulsory jurisdiction, other matters were, of course, considered. Thus, in the Sixth Committee, Mr. Bikoutha of the Congo expressed the interesting thought that "a review of the role of the Court was imperative, and in the view of his delegation, it implied amendment of some of the provisions of the Statute. . . . It should be borne in mind that some of the Court's shortcomings derived from the unfortunate fact that some of its judges had not always displayed the impartiality expected of them. . . . It would be unrealistic to attempt to enhance the Court's role without revising its Statute." [74] Mr. Mtango of Tanzania hit the nail more closely on the head. He stated that his country "also deplored the fact that judges who

[70] U.N. Doc. A/C.6/SR 1281, at 14 (1972).
[71] U.N. Doc. A/8382, at 69 (1971).   [72] *Id.* at 67.
[73] U.N. Doc. A/8382/Add. 1, at 12 (1971).
[74] U.N. Doc. A/C.6/SR 1229, at 3 (1970).

were nationals of permanent members of the Security Council were defending in the Court the views expressed by their countries in the United Nations bodies. That was the reason for the Court's unpopularity. . . . The independence of the Court should be reinforced. . . ." [75]

In the report of the Sixth Committee to the General Assembly, it was stated that "mention was made of the fact that of the forty-two judges elected to the Court since its establishment, seventeen had come from Europe, fourteen from the American continent, eight from Asia and Australia and three from Africa." On the other hand, the report stated that "some representatives . . . were very doubtful whether better use would have been made of the Court if its composition would have been different . . . and that the current composition of the Court could be properly said to be in accordance with Article 9 of the Statute." [76] The use of the term "civilized nations" (in paragraph 1 (a) of Article 38 of the present Statute of the Court) came in for its share of criticism, as was to be expected. Guatemala said that "various objections have been raised to this Article [38], particularly to the expression 'civilized nations' in paragraph 1 (c) . . . ." [77] Mexico stated that ". . . we agree with those who favor the deletion of the qualifying phrase, 'by civilized nations' in paragraph 1 (c) on the grounds that it is a verbal relic of the old colonialism." [78]

Interestingly, the United States expressed the opinion that, as had been suggested, "the Court might decide cases by a two-thirds vote rather than by simple majority, thereby assuring that the views of all legal systems be fully taken into account in the Court's deliberations. A judgment based on less than a two-thirds majority might be delivered in declaratory form, on the basis of which the parties would negotiate a settlement. This alternative might be studied further." [79]

The system of *ad hoc* judges too was criticized quite severely. Switzerland, in its reply to the Secretary-General's questionnaire, stated that "the dissenting vote of the judge *ad hoc* chosen by the State which loses the case, when it is a constant phenomenon, as

[75] U.N. Doc A/C.6/SR 1281, at 15 (1972).
[76] U.N. Doc. A/8238, at 15–16 (1971).   [77] U.N. Doc. A/8382, at 23–24 (1971).
[78] *Id.* at 24–25.   [79] *Id.* at 37.

has been the case thus far, constitutes an insurmountable obstacle to unanimity, although the latter is certainly a desirable ideal and would tend to strengthen the authority of the Court's decisions." [80] The reply of Cyprus was somewhat more subtle:

Regarding judges *ad hoc* . . . there exists a divergence of views, some supporting them as satisfying diplomatic susceptibilities and others being against them as contrary to the idea of justice. If they were allowed to die a natural death, it would be more consistent with the standing and the decorum of a Court administering justice in accordance with law.[81]

Denmark was of the opinion that ". . . it could be considered to allow international organizations to be parties to cases before the Court"; [82] a concept in which Guatemala,[83] Argentina,[84] Switzerland,[85] Sweden,[86] and Canada [87] joined. The "United States believes that . . . international organizations should be permitted to appear before the Court as plaintiffs or defendants." [88] Madagascar,[89] Iraq,[90] and Austria [91] expressed themselves to the same effect. France, on the other hand, felt that it "would seem that allowing international organizations to be parties to contentious cases before the Court would raise serious problems of principle and procedure." [92]

In her replies to the Secretary-General's questionnaire, Switzerland had said:

[I]f it was felt that a further step should be taken to ensure continuity within the Court, this could be achieved by taking up the proposal adopted in 1954 by the Institute of International Law at its session in Aix-en-Provence:

With a view to reinforcing the independence of the judges, it is suggested that members of the Court should be elected for 15 years and should not be re-eligible. . . .[93]

With a view to strengthening the independence of the judges and depoliticizing the elections, it would be desirable either to elect judges for life . . . or to appoint them for a long fixed period without the possibility of re-election.[94]

---

[80] *Id.* at 63.   [81] *Id.* at 62.   [82] *Id.* at 71.   [83] *Id.*   [84] *Id.* at 72.
[85] *Id.* at 73–75.   [86] *Id.* at 76.   [87] *Id.*   [88] *Id.* at 71.   [89] *Id.* at 76.
[90] *Id.* at 77.   [91] *Id.*   [92] *Id.* at 76.   [93] *Id.* at 42.   [94] *Id.* at 43.

"It is the opinion of the United States," the reply of that government stated, "that the present nine-year term is the minimum length needed to encourage independence of the judges." [95] Yugoslavia, on the other hand, stated that "the possibility for shortening the terms should be explored. This would enable the Court to renew itself more often, and at the same time provide a possibility for re-election." [96]

Mr. Mtango, for Tanzania, stated to the Sixth Committee that "consideration might also be given to fixing a maximum age limit for candidates for judgeships and a mandatory retirement age"; [97] for Ghana, Mr. Tutu expressed the same thought at the same place: "With regard to the term of office of the judges of the Court . . . it might be desirable to consider the possibility of fixing a mandatory retirement age for judges." [98]

In response to the invitation to the Court to express its views, the President of the Court addressed the Secretary-General as follows: "While the Court is fully mindful of the responsibilities entrusted to it by the Charter and its Statute, it does not consider that it could at this stage usefully state its views on the question involved." [99]

On December 7, 1972, an eighteen-Power Resolution was introduced in the Sixth Committee by the Netherlands. [100] Under it, the Assembly would establish an *ad hoc* committee to study the role of the International Court of Justice. "The Committee would hold a three-week session 'at an appropriate time' in 1973 and a further two-week session in 1974. It would report to the General Assembly at its twenty-ninth session in 1974." [101] On the same date, the Committee, by a record vote of sixty-three in favor to thirty-three against with twenty abstentions, adopted a resolution, [102] recommending that the General Assembly postpone until 1974 further discussion of the item, "Need to consider suggestions

95 *Id.* at 41.   96 *Id.* at 45.   97 U.N. Doc. A/C.6/SR 1281, at 15 (1972).
98 *Id.* at 16.   99 *Id.* at 120.

100 U.N. Doc. A/C.6/L. 887 (1973). Further resolutions were introduced on December 8, 1972, by Mauritania and others (U.N. Doc. A/C.6/L. 892 [1973]), by the Soviet Union (U.N. Doc. A/C.6/L. 893 [1973]) and by France [U.N. Doc. A/C.6/L. 894 (1973)].

101 UN Press Release, GA/L 1594, 8 December 1972.
102 U.N. Doc. A/C.6/L. 886 (1972).

regarding review of the Charter of the United Nations." [103] Accordingly, on the following day, at the request of some representatives, the Committee decided to postpone its vote on the item (on review of the role of the International Court of Justice) in order to allow delegations more time to consider an eighteen-Power draft resolution before the Committee." [104]

It may perhaps be said that little or no progress has been made toward meeting the recommendations of the American Bar Association in its 1965 resolution, mentioned at the outset of this chapter. The truculence of the Soviet Union throughout the discussions demonstrates certain veto of such amendments of the Statute of the Court as would be required to carry out the beneficent purposes of the Association's resolution. On the other hand, it may be that the very fact that there have been such discussion and correspondence as are outlined above does indicate some progress after all.

[103] *Id.* GA/L. 1592.   [104] U.N. Release No. GA/L 1594 (Dec. 8, 1972).

CHAPTER XX

The Future of the Court

After the First World War the League of Nations was instituted to provide a worldwide body in which international disputes could be aired, and even sanctions imposed, to minimize the possibility of renewed warfare. Coupled with the League of Nations, the Permanent Court of International Justice was established as a tribunal in which, under restricted circumstances, international disputes of a justiciable nature might be determined if need for submission thereof to the Court arose, or if such submission was agreed.

Primarily because the United States was not a party to the League of Nations, and largely too because the Covenant of the League was so loose as not to permit of strong economic or other measures of enforcement, it ultimately failed completely under the weight of Mussolini, Hitler, and other impacts. Without going into detail, the Permanent Court of International Justice, while surviving in theory for some years, suffered, in a practical sense, much the same fate as its parent, the League, for want of a virile constitution. As early as July 1941, Under-Secretary of State Sumner Welles had expressed the view that the failure of the League of Nations was attributable to the fact that it had never been able to function, as originally intended, to bring about "peaceful and equitable adjustments between nations." Mr. Welles accordingly concluded that "some adequate instrumentality must unquestionably be found to achieve such adjustments when the nations of the earth again undertake the task of restoring law and order to a disastrously shaken world." [1]

When President Roosevelt and Prime Minister Churchill met to draft the Atlantic Charter, the Prime Minister suggested a paragraph in which it was to be declared that the ultimate peace should, "by effective international organization," afford security

[1] 5 DEP'T STATE BULL. 75–76 (1941).

to all States and peoples of the world.[2] The President objected to this language because of the widespread feeling throughout the United States, which he shared, "against creation of a new Assembly of the League of Nations." [3] In the final draft of the Atlantic Charter, signed on August 14, 1941, the President of the United States of America and the Prime Minister "representing His Majesty's Government of the United Kingdom," declared their belief "that all of the nations of the world . . . must come to the abandonment of the use of force," and that, "pending the establishment of a wider and permanent system of general security," the disarmament of aggressor nations is essential.[4] In a "Declaration by United Nations" issued at Washington on January 1, 1942, some twenty-six nations then at war with the Axis powers subscribed to the principles embodied in the Atlantic Charter.[5] Nearly two years later, on October 31, 1943, the governments of the United States, the United Kingdom, the Soviet Union, and China issued the Declaration of Four Nations on General Security, better known as the Moscow Declaration, in which they recognized expressly "the necessity of establishing at the earliest practicable date a general international organization . . . for the maintenance of international peace and security." [6] Out of that, despite the frustration of the League of Nations, came Dumbarton Oaks and ultimately, at San Francisco, the Charter of the United Nations and the Statute of the International Court of Justice.

The Court has been endeavoring to function within its hobbles for over twenty-five years. It is still hampered by bonds of the distant past. It is unable to progress because nations will not subscribe to its unreserved compulsory jurisdiction. They remain distrustful of judges who echo the views of their governments. They are jealous of their own national sovereignties and fear encroachments on their domestic domains. The within plan was devised to avoid that fear by safeguarding the sovereign rights

[2] W. CHURCHILL, THE GRAND ALLIANCE 434 (1950).

[3] S. WELLES, WHERE ARE WE HEADING? 15 (1946).

[4] U.S. DEP'T STATE, PUB. NO. 1732, COOPERATIVE WAR EFFORT 4, E.A.S. No. 236 (1942).

[5] *Id.* at 1.

[6] U.S. DEP'T STATE, PUB. NO. 2298, TOWARD THE PEACE DOCUMENT 6 (1945).

of all nations—principally through the internationalization of the Court's judges, their appointment for life, and the requirement of the affirmative vote of ten judges to overrule a motion to jurisdiction of the Court over a controversy asserted to be within the domestic jurisdiction of a party to the action. It certainly does seem likely that when every nation of the world is amenable to the jurisdiction of the Court—when all international legal disputes are subject to adjudication by an impartial tribunal established for that purpose—tensions will inevitably be eased, and the use of war as an instrument for the settlement of such disputes will certainly be lessened materially, if not eliminated entirely.

As long ago as 1944, Judge Hudson of the Permanent Court of International Justice made a wise observation. He said: "The most vital question as to the future of the Court relates to the extent of its compulsory jurisdiction over legal disputes. If such jurisdiction could be made universal, a great advance would be registered toward the supremacy of law in international relations." [7] One must bear in mind, however, that mere adjudication of disputes cannot avoid the use of force by a nation dissatisfied with a judgment against it. In 1961, the General Assembly of the United Nations called on the Soviet Union to refrain from detonating an immense atomic explosion, as it had announced it would do; but the detonation took place. A blot on the escutcheon of the United Nations was unquestionably the invasion of Czechoslovakia by the Soviet Army and forces of her allies in 1968, to coerce the will of that country to Communist principles.

It is undoubtedly true, on the other hand, that the Members of the United Nations are legally bound by the decrees of the International Court of Justice. In the Charter of the United Nations itself, each member of that body "undertakes to comply with the decisions of the" Court "in any case in which it is a party." [8] But there is reserved to every nation something in the nature of a suspensive appeal with reference to enforcement of decrees of the Court, as heretofore stated, to the diplomatic forum of the Security Council, which is charged by the Charter with deciding upon, or recommending, "if it deems necessary,"

[7] M. HUDSON, TRIBUNALS at 153.   [8] U.N. CHARTER art. 94, para. 1.

any "measures to be taken to give effect to the judgment." [9]

So far as the present writer is aware, the only case in which a decree of the International Court of Justice has been ignored completely, is the *Corfu Channel* case, in favor of Great Britain and against Albania—a simple money judgment, the first decree of the present Court.[10] Albania has simply refused to pay the judgment, and despite extensive efforts and complex litigation, the decree has never been satisfied, and the matter has never been brought before the Security Council.[11]

Each of the permanent members of the Security Council has, under the proposed Statute, an express right of veto over any measure proposed by the Security Council to enforce a judgment; so that a permanent member of the Council may effectively block enforcement of a judgment against it, or against a political ally. But even if a defaulting party is not a permanent member, or a political ally of such a member, of the Security Council, effective means must still be found to enforce international judicial decrees against nations; and economic sanctions have not, historically, proved effective. Unless the nations of the world can be persuaded to disarm realistically, there will always remain the danger of recourse to force, even in disregard of a decision of the International Court of Justice; but there can be no question that such a danger will be lessened immeasurably by the existence of an impartial Court with compulsory jurisdiction over international disputes.

Under the proposed Statute of the Court, each of its judges is "internationalized" and becomes, for his natural life, a citizen of the United Nations, with diplomatic immunity in every country of the world; [12] and the same is true as to the judge's wife except that, within a limited time after the death of the judge, she must give up her United Nations citizenship; but she may then become a national of any country of her choice.[13] Judges of the International Court of Justice unquestionably will be willing to give up their right to vote in their own national and local elections. They may, of course, reacquire that right on retirement if

9 *Id.* art. 94, para. 2.   10 [1949] I.C.J. 244.
11 Monetary Gold case, [1954] I.C.J. 19.   12 I.C.J. STAT. (P) art. IV, para. 1.
13 *Id.* art. IV, para. 2.

they wish. Obviously, this internationalization of the judges and their wives was intended to remove from the judges any trace or vestige of national prejudice or influence to which they might conceivably otherwise remain subject. To the foregoing must be added appointment of the judges for life, subject to permissible retirement at seventy and compulsory retirement at seventy-five; and decisions as to domestic jurisdiction by a majority of ten votes, whatever the composition of the Court may be. These provisions constitute, in a sense, the keystone in the arch of the revised Statute of the International Court of Justice. Their purpose was to assure the Members of the United Nations that they might safely agree to submit themselves in advance to the compulsory jurisdiction of the Court, without fear that any one, or group, of its judges might be swayed by national or regional influences in reaching determinations in the course of adjudication of international disputes.

It is, perhaps, true that not a single opinion of the Court— majority, concurring, or dissenting—reflects any deliberate or studied national prejudice on the part of any of the judges involved. It must be recognized, however, that the mind of every human being—and judges are all human beings—is, to a large extent, the product of the influences and prejudices of the environment in which it has been molded and to which it remains subject; and that is sometimes as it should be, for out of discussions and conflicts among minds so influenced, fair conclusions are normally likely to evolve. But it must also be conceded that there have heretofore been presented to the Court for determination few issues framed in a strong, sharply defined, supercharged nationalistic atmosphere in which national prejudices— if they existed in the minds of any of the judges—might have played a significant part.

Moreover, under the Statute of the International Court of Justice, if none of the judges of the Court is a national of a country which is a party to a case before the Court, that country has the right to demand that a judge of its nationality sit with the Court if a judge of the nationality of the other party to the case is a member of the Court.[14] Such designations of judges *ad hoc* have

[14] I.C.J. STAT. art. 31, para. 2.

quite frequently been made. Of the thirty-seven "contentious" cases brought before the present Court between 1945 and 1970, judges *ad hoc* were appointed in no less than seventeen. Now, it cannot be gainsaid that, in every such instance, without exception, when orders were entered and judgments were rendered, the judges *ad hoc* were on the side of the nation which had appointed them, even when they stood alone or almost alone. For instance, in the famous *Corfu Channel* case, the first international controversy to come before the International Court of Justice, Great Britain sought indemnity from Albania for damage to warships and loss of life resulting when the vessels struck mines in Albanian territorial waters. Albania sought dismissal of the case. The Court contained a British judge, and Albania accordingly requested appointment of M. Igor Daxner (of Czechoslovakia) as judge *ad hoc*. Dividing the other judges into groups, they included nationals of (1) the United States, France, Belgium, Canada, and (Nationalist) China; (2) Brazil, Chile, El Salvador, and Mexico; (3) Norway and Egypt; and (4) Yugoslavia, Poland, and the Soviet Union.

On the preliminary question, Albania's request for dismissal was rejected in March 1948, by fifteen votes to one, Judge *ad hoc* Daxner for Albania alone dissenting.[15] Later, in December 1949, on the merits of the same case, M. Bohuslav Eyer (also of Czechoslovakia) sat with the same Court as Albania's judge *ad hoc,* and he and Soviet Judge Krylov were the only dissenters from the Court's judgment in favor of Great Britain.[16]

Similarly, in a case decided in November 1950 in favor of Peru and against Colombia, the only dissenting vote was cast by Colombia's judge *ad hoc,* Sr. Calcedo Castilla;[17] and as late as November 1960, the Court held, by a vote of fourteen to one, that an arbitral award made by the King of Spain in 1906, in a boundary dispute between Nicaragua and Honduras, was binding on Nicaragua—the only dissenting vote being that of Nicaragua's judge *ad hoc,* Sr. Urrutia Holguin.[18] Each of these judges *ad hoc,* and each of the others who has served with the Court, was a distinguished lawyer, a renowned scholar, an authority in in-

[15] [1947–48] I.C.J. 33.   [16] [1949] I.C.J. 68, 115, 251, 252.
[17] [1950] I.C.J. 404.   [18] [1960] I.C.J. 221.

ternational law, a diplomat of note, and a brilliant jurist of unimpeachable personal and judicial integrity; but he was unquestionably selected because of, and his honest judgment was undoubtedly induced at least in part by, the predilections inherent in his nationality.

As heretofore stated, in 1933 Professor (later Sir Hersch) Lauterpacht, himself to become, in time, a judge of the International Court of Justice, published an analysis of some of the cases which had been decided up to that time by the Permanent Court of International Justice. He found that in three of fifteen of these cases lending themselves to such analysis, in which national judges had been appointed by the parties, they had voted with the majority in favor of their own States; and that, in the remaining twelve, the national judges had dissented, frequently as a minority of one, in favor of their own States; so that, in the last analysis, no judge *ad hoc* ever voted against his own country.[19]

There have unquestionably also been suggestions that when cases involving significant national issues have arisen before the Court, even permanent judges of the nationalities concerned have leaned to the side of their own countries or blocs. As stated by Professor Lauterpacht, it is possible that even some of the permanent judges, when the interests of their own or even of an allied country are involved, have not "succeeded in overcoming the powerful influence of national allegiance." [20] It has been pointed out on a number of occasions—and there has been considerable comment on the fact—that in practically no cases has a national judge voted against his own State when it prevailed, or failed to dissent from an opinion unfavorable to his own State or to members of its political alliances.[21] For example, the Yugoslav, Polish, and Soviet judges alone dissented from the advisory opinion of the remaining members of the International Court of Justice on the main question (Number II) in the case of the *Interpretation of the Peace Treaties with Bulgaria, Hungary and Romania*.[22] Similarly, in another advisory opinion of that Court in the case relating to *Certain Expenses of the United Nations in the Congo*, rendered in 1962, the dissents of the French and Soviet judges

---

[19] H. LAUTERPACHT, FUNCTION at 230 (1966 reprint).   [20] *Id*. at 238.
[21] *Id*. at 237.   [22] [1950] I.C.J. 89, 98, 105.

(in which the Argentinian, Peruvian, and Polish judges joined) followed the policies which had been expressed by the representatives of those countries in the General Assembly, as did for that matter, by and large, those of the judges who joined in the majority opinion, and whose governments (including those of the United States and Great Britain) had taken that position in the Assembly's diplomatic forum.[23]

It simply cannot be doubted that human judges with limited terms and subject to reelection may be inclined, in doubtful cases, to lean toward the cause of that party to a proceeding before them which has ties to the electorate. History and psychology demonstrate that human beings are ordinarily prone to react humanly. However, it must be conceded that statistics alone can be, and sometimes are, misleading. As stated by Judge Hudson, a conclusion as to the tendency of national judges on an international tribunal, to partisanship in favor of their own nations, "should not be based upon a mere tabulation of the votes which led to the adoption of the Court's judgments and opinions."[24] But then, on the other hand, a decade earlier, Professor Lauterpacht had expressed his conviction that, without impugning the motives of the national judges, the result of the analysis he had made of their votes in the fifteen cases which he cited could not "be regarded as a mere coincidence."[25] In fact, Professor Lauterpacht went even further and stated quite candidly that, while he could not say that there had been no legal basis whatever for the positions of these national (*ad hoc*) judges, he found the fact that in not a single case had any one of them ever voted against his own country to be "profoundly disturbing."[26]

Not very long ago, the point was illustrated in sharp perspective in the southern states of the United States. Federal judges, holding their posts under life tenure and free of local influences, rendered politically unpopular decisions in strict accord with constitutional law as confirmed by precedents laid down by the Supreme Court of the United States. At about the same period, movements to improve the caliber of local judges throughout the same area by providing for their life tenure were uniformly un-

---

[23] [1962] I.C.J. 227, 235, 253, 239, 288. [24] M. Hudson, P.C.I.J. at 355.
[25] H. Lauterpacht, Function at 230. [26] *Id.* at 231.

successful under pressures for shortening terms of local judges to as little as two years, by popular election, to assure their responsiveness to local political influences. And so, although no such situation has ever demonstrably arisen on the docket of the International Court of Justice, the internationalization of judges of the Court and their spouses and the election of its judges for life, under the revised Statute of the Court, will tend to purge the Court's adjudicative process of any possible national, regional, or "bloc" bias with which it might otherwise conceivably have been tainted.

Prior to his being knighted and elevated to the International Court of Justice, Professor Lauterpacht unquestionably felt that much of the difficulty with the Court lay in the reluctance of nations to submit their disputes for adjudication to a tribunal, as to the impartiality of whose judges they were at least doubtful —an impartiality which he felt, as he put it, required that they consider themselves to be "citizens of the world." [27] Professor Lauterpacht was elected to the Court in the fall of 1954 and took his place on the bench in the following February. Three or four years later he published his renowned work on the *Development of International Law in the International Court*. In that book, published (as stated) after he had been a judge of the International Court for three or four years, he said that a government by law rather than by men was of even greater importance in international than in local tribunals, because of the inherent suspicion with which sovereign nations looked upon foreign judges.[28] He said also, in this, his last textual work on the subject, that he could not really overstress the importance of an assurance of impartiality of judges of an international tribunal; and he referred as support for this statement, with direct approval thereof, to the chapter on the impartiality of international tribunals which he had written a quarter of a century earlier in his *Function of Law in the International Community*.[29]

Appointment of judges for life, as provided under the proposed Statute, must also strengthen the Court.[30] The maximum and

[27] *Id.* at 202, 239.   [28] H. Lauterpacht, Development at 40.   [29] *Id.*
[30] I.C.J. Stat. (P) art. III, para. 1.

minimum ages of the judges, when appointed to the Court under the present Statute, have been forty-nine and seventy-eight, with an average of sixty-two, and many judges have died in office. Judges have been reelected in significant numbers, for terms of nine years under the present Statute, when they have already passed the age of seventy-five, and even more frequently when their new terms will run substantially beyond their seventy-fifth birthdays. Under the proposed Statute of the Court, there will be permissible retirement of judges at more frequent intervals. So that, under the proposed Statute, there will not only be ample opportunity for new appointments of judges but there will be continuity of the Court and the advantage of security of tenure of individual judges with complete independence from national influences.

There can be no question that failure of the nations of the world to declare their adherence to the International Court of Justice, except to some extent subject to emasculating reservations, has been caused by their fear of being overruled on pleas to the jurisdiction of the Court on the ground that a matter before it is one of domestic, rather than of international, concern. Questions of immigration, nationalization, human rights (including race relations), discrimination on account of sex, and other similar matters falling in the shadow or border zone may fairly be cited as examples. Suppose, for instance, that Nation *A* contends that Nation *B*'s immigration quota policies are discriminatory on the ground that they tend to exclude members of certain racial groups. Such a question undoubtedly raises interesting points of law. Under its present Statute and Rules, the International Court of Justice might, quite conceivably, sit with nine judges and the cited issue might be decided by a vote of five to four. But under the proposed Statute of the Court, a majority of ten judges would be necessary to overrule a plea to its jurisdiction on such a ground, with a full Court of fifteen judges sitting on the demand of either party. This is probably the most, certainly one of the most, significant features of the proposed Statute of the Court. It should give ample assurance to nations, now skeptical as to the impartiality of the members of the present Court and jealous of their sovereignties when faced with such problems, that they will get a fair hearing and decision in matters of asserted domestic jurisdiction.

Declarations of adherence to the new International Court of Justice would be without reservations, and jurisdiction of the Court would be compulsory over international disputes as to all members of the United Nations and, as a practical matter, over all nations of the world.

With adoption and ratification of the proposed Statute, "effective collective measures" will indeed have been taken, in the words of the first article of the Charter of the United Nations, to achieve "international peace and security" through "prevention and removal of threats to the peace," by bringing about "adjustment or settlement of international disputes" in "conformity with the principles of justice and international law." It is submitted that the Court, reconstituted as herein suggested, will assure the Nations of the World of impartial verdicts in the solutions of their disputes, and will give to the world itself, and to humanity, new hope for Justice and an International Rule of Law.

Appendixes
Index

Charter of the United Nations

WE, THE PEOPLE OF THE UNITED NATIONS,

DETERMINED

to save succeeding generations from the scourge of war, which twice in our life-time has brought untold sorrow to mankind, and

to reaffirm faith in fundamental human rights, in the dignity and worth of the human person, in the equal rights of men and women and of nations large and small, and

to establish conditions under which justice and respect for the obligations arising from treaties and other sources of international law can be maintained, and

to promote social progress and better standards of life in larger freedom,

AND FOR THESE ENDS

to practice tolerance and live together in peace with one another as good neighbors, and to unite our strength to maintain international peace and security, and

to ensure, by the acceptance of principles and the institution of methods, that armed force shall not be used, save in the common interest, and

to employ international machinery for the promotion of the economic and social advancement of all peoples,

HAVE RESOLVED TO COMBINE OUR EFFORTS
TO ACCOMPLISH THESE AIMS.

Accordingly, our respective Governments, through representatives assembled in the city of San Francisco, who have exhibited their full powers found to be in good and due form, have agreed to the present Charter of the United Nations and do hereby establish an international organization to be known as the United Nations.

CHAPTER I

PURPOSES AND PRINCIPLES

Article 1

The purposes of the United Nations are:

1. To maintain international peace and security, and to that end: to take effective collective measures for the prevention and removal of threats to the peace, and for the suppression of acts of aggression or other breaches of the peace, and to bring about by peaceful means,

and in conformity with the principles of justice and international law, adjustment or settlement of international disputes or situations which might lead to a breach of the peace;

2. To develop friendly relations among nations based on respect for the principle of equal rights and self-determination of peoples, and to take other appropriate measures to strengthen universal peace;

3. To achieve international cooperation in solving international problems of an economic, social, cultural, or humanitarian character, and in promoting and encouraging respect for human rights and for fundamental freedoms for all without distinction as to race, sex, language, or religion; and

4. To be a center for harmonizing the actions of nations in the attainment of these common ends.

Article 2

The Organization and its Members, in pursuit of the purposes stated in Article 1, shall act in accordance with the following principles.

1. The Organization is based on the principle of the sovereign equality of all its Members.

2. All Members, in order to ensure to all of them the rights and benefits resulting from membership, shall fulfil in good faith the obligations assumed by them in accordance with the present Charter.

3. All Members shall settle their international disputes by peaceful means in such a manner that international peace and security, and justice, are not endangered.

4. All Members shall refrain in their international relations from the threat or use of force against the territorial integrity or political independence of any State, or in any other manner inconsistent with the purposes of the United Nations.

5. All Members shall give the United Nations every assistance in any action it takes in accordance with the present Charter, and shall refrain from giving assistance to any State against which the United Nations is taking preventive or enforcement action.

6. The Organization shall ensure that States which are not Members of the United Nations with these Principles so far as may be necessary for the maintenance of international peace and security.

7. Nothing contained in the present Charter shall authorize the United Nations to intervene in matters which are essentially within

the domestic jurisdiction of any State or shall require the Members
to submit such matters to settlement under the present Charter; but
this principle shall not prejudice the application of enforcement
measures under Chapter VII.

CHAPTER II

MEMBERSHIP

Article 3

The original Members of the United Nations shall be the States
which, having participated in the United Nations Conference on
International Organization at San Francisco, or having previously
signed the Declaration by United Nations of January 1st, 1942, sign
the present Charter and ratify it in accordince with Article 110.

Article 4

1. Membership in the United Nations is open to all other peace-
loving States which accept the obligations contained in the present
Charter and, in the judgment of the Organization, are able and willing to carry out these obligations.

2. The admission of any such State to membership in the United
Nations will be effected by a decision of the General Assembly upon
the recommendation of the Security Council.

Article 5

A Member of the United Nations against which preventive or enforcement action has been taken by the Security Council may be
suspended from the exercise of the rights and privileges of membership by the General Assembly upon the recommendation of the Security Council. The exercise of these rights and privileges may be
restored by the Security Council.

Article 6

A Member of the United Nations which has persistently violated the principles contained in the present Charter may be expelled from the Organization by the General Assembly upon the recommendation of the Security Council.

CHAPTER III

ORGANS

Article 7

1. There are established as the principal organs of the United Nations: a General Assembly, a Security Council, an Economic and Social Council, a Trusteeship Council, an International Court of Justice, and a Secretariat.

2. Such subsidiary organs as may be found necessary may be established in accordance with the present Charter.

Article 8

The United Nations shall place no restrictions on the eligibility of men and women to participate in any capacity and under conditions of equality in its principal and subsidiary organs.

CHAPTER IV

THE GENERAL ASSEMBLY

Composition

Article 9

1. The General Assembly shall consist of all the Members of the United Nations.

2. Each Member shall have not more than five representatives in the General Assembly.

Functions and Powers

Article 10

The General Assembly may discuss any questions or any matters within the scope of the present Charter or relating to the powers and functions of any organs provided for in the present Charter, and, except as provided in Article 12, may make recommondations to the Members of the United Nations or to the Security Council or to both on any such questions or matters.

Article 11

1. The General Assembly may consider the general principles of cooperation in the maintenance of international peace and security, including the principles governing disarmament and the regulation of armaments, and may make recommendations with regard to such principles to the Members or to the Security Council or to both.

2. The General Assembly may discuss any questions relating to the maintenance of international peace and security brought before it by any Member of the United Nations, or by the Security Council, or by a State which is not a Member of the United Nations in accordance with Article 35, paragraph 2, and, except as provided in Article 12, may make recommendations with regard to any such questions to the State or States concerned or to the Security Council or to both. Any such question on which action is necessary shall be referred to the Security Council by the General Assembly either before or after discussion.

3. The General Assembly may call the attention of the Security Council to situations which are likely to endanger international peace and security.

4. The powers of the General Assembly set forth in this Article shall not limit the general scope of Article 10.

Article 12

1. While the Security Council is exercising in respect of any dispute or situation the functions assigned to it in the present Charter, the General Assembly shall not make any recommendation with regard to that dispute or situation unless the Security Council so requests.

2. The Secretary-General, with the consent of the Security Council, shall notify the General Assembly at each session of any matters relative to the maintenance of international peace and security which are being dealt with by the Security Council and shall similarly notify the General Assembly, or the Members of the United Nations if the General Assembly is not in session, immediately the Security Council ceases to deal with such matters.

Article 13

1. The General Assembly shall initiate studies and make recommendations for the purpose of:

(a) promoting the international cooperation in the political field and encouraging the progressive development of international law and its codification;

(b) promoting international cooperation in the economic, social, cultural, educational and health fields, and assisting in the realization of human rights and fundamental freedoms for all without distinction as to race, sex, language, or religion.

2. The further responsibilities, functions and powers of the General Assembly with respect to matters mentioned in paragraph 1 (b) above set forth in Chapters IX and X.

Article 14

Subject to the provisions of Article 12, the General Assembly may recommend measures for the peaceful adjustment of any situation, regardless of origin, which it deems likely to impair the general welfare or friendly relations among nations, including situations resulting from a violation of the provisions of the present Charter setting forth the purposes and principles of the United Nations

Article 15

1. The General Assembly shall receive and consider annual and special reports from the Security Council; these reports shall include an account of the measures that the Security Council has decided upon or taken to maintain international peace and security.

2. The General Assembly shall receive and consider reports from the other organs of the United Nations.

Article 16

The General Assembly shall perform such functions with respect to the international trusteeship system as are assigned to it under Chapters XII and XIII, including the approval of the trusteeship agreements for areas not designated as strategic.

Article 17

1. The General Assembly shall consider and approve the budget of the Organization.

2. The expenses of the Organization shall be borne by the Members as apportioned by the General Assembly.

3. The General Assembly shall consider and approve any financial and budgetary arrangements with specialized agencies referred to in Article 57 and shall examine the administrative budgets of such specialized agencies with a view to making recommendations to the agencies concerned.

Voting

Article 18

1. Each member of the General Assembly shall have one vote.

2. Decisions of the General Assembly on important questions shall be made by a two-thirds majority of the members present and voting. These questions shall include: recommendations with respect to the maintenance of international peace and security, the election of the non-permanent members of the Security Council, the election of

the members of the Economic and Social Council, the election of members of the Trusteeship Council in accordance with paragraph 1 (*c*) of Article 86, the admission of new Members to the United Nations, the suspension of the rights and privileges of membership, the expulsion of Members, questions relating to the operation of the trusteeship system, and budgetary questions.

3. Decisions on other questions, including the determination of additional categories of questions to be decided by a two-thirds majority, shall be made by a majority of the members present and voting.

Article 19

A Member of the United Nations which is in arrears in the payment of its financial contributions to the Organization shall have no vote in the General Assembly if the amount of its arrears equals or exceeds the amount of the contributions due from it for the preceding two full years. The General Assembly may, nevertheless, permit such a Member to vote if it is satisfied that the failure to pay is due to conditions beyond the control of the Member.

Procedure

Article 20

The General Assembly shall meet in regular annual sessions and in such special sessions as occasion may require. Special sessions shall be convoked by the Secretary-General at the request of the Security Council or of a majority of the Members of the United Nations.

Article 21

The General Assembly shall adopt its own rules of procedure. It shall elect its President for each session.

Article 22

The General Assembly may establish such subsidiary organs as it deems necessary for the performance of its functions.

CHAPTER V

THE SECURITY COUNCIL

Composition

Article 23

1. The Security Council shall consist of fifteen Members of the United Nations. The Republic of China, France, the Union of Soviet Socialist Republics, the United Kingdom of Great Britain and Northern Ireland, and the United States of America shall be permanent members of the Security Council. The General Assembly shall elect ten other Members of the United Nations to be non-permanent members of the Security Council, due regard being specially paid, in the first instance to the contribution of Members of the United Nations to the maintenance of international peace and security and to the other purposes of the Organization, and also to equitable geographical distribution.

2. The non-permanent members of the Security Council shall be elected for a term of two years. In the first election of the non-permanent members after the increase of the membership of the Security Council from eleven to fifteen, two of the four additional members shall be chosen for a term of one year. A retiring member shall not be eligible for immediate re-election.

3. Each member of the Security Council shall have one representative.

> As amended 17 Dec. 1963,
> effective 31 Aug. 1965.

Functions and Powers

Article 24

1. In order to ensure prompt and effective action by the United Nations, its Members confer on the Security Council primary responsibility for the maintenance of international peace and security, and agree that in carrying out its duties under this responsibility the Security Council acts on their behalf.

2. In discharging these duties the Security Council shall act in accordance with the purposes and principles of the United Nations. The specific powers granted to the Security Council for the discharge of these duties are laid down in Chapters VI, VII, VIII, and XII.

3. The Security Council shall submit annual and, when necessary, special reports to the General Assembly for its consideration.

Article 25

The Members of the United Nations agree to accept and carry out the decisions of the Security Council in accordance with the present Charter.

Article 26

In order to promote the establishment and maintenance of international peace and security with the least diversion for armaments of the world's human and economic resources, the Security Council shall be responsible for formulating, with the assistance of the Military Staff Committee referred to in Article 47, plans to be submitted to the Members of the United Nations for the establishment of a system for the regulation of armaments.

Voting

Article 27

1. Each member of the Security Council shall have one vote.

2. Decisions of the Security Council on procedural matters shall be made by an affirmative vote of nine members.

3. Decisions of the Security Council on all other matters shall be made by an affirmative vote of nine members including the concurring votes of the permanent members; provided that, in decisions under Chapter VI, and under paragraph 3 of Article 52, a party to a dispute shall abstain from voting.

As amended 17 Dec. 1963,
effective 31 Aug. 1965.

Procedure

Article 28

1. The Security Council shall be so organized as to be able to function continuously. Each member of the Security Council shall for this purpose be represented at all times at the seat of the Organization.

2. The Security Council shall hold periodic meetings at which each of its members may, if it so desires, be represented by a member of the government or by some other specially designated representative.

3. The Security Council may hold meetings at such places other than the seat of the Organization as in its judgment will best facilitate its work.

Article 29

The Security Council may establish such subsidiary organs as it deems necessary for the performance of its functions.

Article 30

The Security Council shall adopt its own rules of procedure, including the method of selecting its President.

Article 31

Any Member of the United Nations which is not a member of the Security Council may participate, without vote, in the discussion of any question brought before the Security Council whenever the latter considers that the interests of that Member are specially affected.

Article 32

Any Member of the United Nations which is not a member of the Security Council or any State which is not a Member of the United

Nations, if it is a party to a dispute under consideration by the Security Council, shall be invited to participate without vote, in the discussion relating to the dispute. The Security Council shall lay down such conditions as it deems just for participation of a State which is not a Member of the United Nations.

CHAPTER VI

PACIFIC SETTLEMENT OF DISPUTES

Article 33

1. The parties to any dispute, the continuance of which is likely to endanger the maintenance of international peace and security, shall, first of all, seek a solution by negotiation, enquiry, mediation, conciliation, arbitration, judicial settlement, resort to regional agencies or arrangements, or other peaceful means of their own choice.

2. The Security Council shall, when it deems necessary, call upon the parties to settle their dispute by such means.

Article 34

The Security Council may investigate any dispute, or any situation which might lead to international friction or give rise to a dispute, in order to determine whether the continuance of the dispute or situation is likely to endanger the maintenance of international peace and security.

Article 35

1. Any Member of the United Nations may bring any dispute, or any situation of the nature referred to in Article 34, to the attention of the Security Council or of the General Assembly.

2. A State which is not a Member of the United Nations may bring to the attention of the Security Council or of the General Assembly any dispute to which it is a party if it accepts in advance, for the

purposes of the dispute, the obligations of pacific settlement provided in the present Charter.

3. The proceedings of the General Assembly in respect of matters
brought to its attention under this Article will be subject to the
provisions of Articles 11 and 12.

Article 36

1. The Security Council may, at any stage of a dispute of the nature referred to in Article 33 or of a situation of like nature, recommend appropriate procedures or methods of adjustment.

2. The Security Council should take into consideration any procedures for the settlement of the dispute which have already been
adopted by the parties.

3. In making recommendations under this Article the Security
Council should also take into consideration that legal disputes should
as a general rule be referred by the parties to the International Court
of Justice, in accordance with the provisions of the Statute of the
Court.

Article 37

1. Should the parties to a dispute of the nature referred to in
Article 33 fail to settle it by the means indicated in that Article, they
shall refer it to the Security Council.

2. If the Security Council deems that the continuance of the dispute is in fact likely to endanger the maintenance of international
peace and security, it shall decide whether to take action under Article 36 or to recommend such terms of settlement as it may consider
appropriate.

Article 38

Without prejudice to the provisions of Articles 33 to 37, the Security Council may, if all the parties to any dispute so request, make
recommendations to the parties with a view to a pacific settlement of
the dispute.

CHAPTER VII

ACTION WITH RESPECT TO THREATS TO THE PEACE, BREACHES OF THE PEACE, AND ACTS OF AGGRESSION

Article 39

The Security Council shall determine the existence of any threat to the peace, breach of the peace, or act of aggression and shall make recommendations, or decide what measures shall be taken in accordance with Articles 41 and 42, to maintain or restore international peace and security.

Article 40

In order to prevent an aggravation of the situation, the Security Council may, before making the recommendations or deciding upon the measures provided for in Article 39, call upon the parties concerned to comply with such provisional measures as it deems necessary or desirable. Such provisional measures shall be without prejudice to the rights, claims, or position of the parties concerned. The Security Council shall duly take account of failure to comply with such provisional measures.

Article 41

The Security Council may decide what measures not involving the use of armed force are to be employed to give effect to its decisions, and it may call upon the Members of the United Nations to apply such measures. These may include complete or partial interruption of economic relations and of rail, sea, air, postal, telegraphic, radio and other means of communication, and the severance of diplomatic relations.

Article 42

Should the Security Council consider that measures provided for in Article 41 would be inadequate or have proved to be inadequate, it may take such action by air, sea or land forces as may be necessary to maintain or restore international peace and security. Such action may include demonstrations, blockade, and other operations by air, sea or land forces of Members of the United Nations.

Article 43

1. All Members of the United Nations, in order to contribute to the maintenance of international peace and security, undertake to make available to the Security Council, on its call and in accordance with a special agreement or agreements, armed forces, assistance and facilities, including rights of passage, necessary for the purpose of maintaining international peace and security.

2. Such agreement or agreements shall govern the numbers and types of forces, their degree of readiness and general location, and the nature of the facilities and assistance to be provided.

3. The agreement or agreements shall be negotiated as soon as possible on the initiative of the Security Council. They shall be concluded between the Security Council and Members or between the Security Council and groups of Members, and shall be subject to ratification by the signatory States in accordance with their respective constitutional processes.

Article 44

When the Security Council has decided to use force, it shall, before calling upon a Member not represented on it to provide armed forces in fulfillment of the obligations assumed under Article 43, invite that Member, if the Member so desires, to participate in the decisions of the Security Council concerning the employment of contingents of that Member's armed forces.

Article 45

In order to enable the United Nations to take urgent military measures, Members shall hold immediately available national air-force contingents for combined international enforcement action. The strength and degree of readiness of these contingents and plans for their combined action shall be determined, within the limits laid down in the special agreement or agreements referred to in Article 43, by the Security Council with the assistance of the Military Staff Committee.

Article 46

Plans for the application of armed force shall be made by the Security Council with the assistance of the Military Staff Committee.

Article 47

1. There shall be established a Military Staff Committee to advise and assist the Security Council on all questions relating to the Security Council's military requirements for the maintenance of international peace and security, the employment and command of forces placed at its disposal, the regulation of armaments, and possible disarmament.

2. The Military Staff Committee shall consist of the Chiefs of Staff of the permanent members of the Security Council or their representatives. Any Member of the United Nations not permanently represented on the Committee shall be invited by the Committee to be associated with it when the efficient discharge of the Committee's responsibilities requires the participation of that Member in its work.

3. The Military Staff Committee shall be responsible under the Security Council for the strategic direction of any armed forces placed at the disposal of the Security Council. Questions relating to the command of such forces shall be worked out subsequently.

4. The Military Staff Committee, with the authorization of the Security Council and after consultation with appropriate regional agencies, may establish regional subcommittees.

Article 48

1. The action required to carry out the decisions of the Security Council for the maintenance of international peace and security shall

be taken by all the Members of the United Nations or by some of them, as the Security Council may determine.

2. Such decisions shall be carried out by the Members of the United Nations directly and through their action in the appropriate international agencies of which they are members.

Article 49

The Members of the United Nations shall join in affording mutual assistance in carrying out the measures decided upon by the Security Council.

Article 50

If preventive or enforcement measures against any State are taken by the Security Council, any other State, whether a Member of the United Nations or not, which finds itself confronted with special economic problems arising from the carrying out of those measures, shall have the right to consult the Security Council with regard to a solution of these problems.

Article 51

Nothing in the present Charter shall impair the inherent right of individual or collective self-defence if an armed attack occurs against a Member of the United Nations, until the Security Council has taken measures necessary to maintain international peace and security. Measures taken by Members in the exercise of this right of self-defence shall be immediately reported to the Security Council and shall not in any way affect the authority and responsibility of the Security Council under the present Charter to take at any time such action as it deems necessary in order to maintain or restore international peace and security.

CHAPTER VIII

REGIONAL ARRANGEMENTS

Article 52

1. Nothing in the present Charter precludes the existence of regional arrangements or agencies for dealing with such matters relating to the maintenance of international peace and security as are appropriate for regional action, provided that such arrangements or agencies and their activities are consistent with the purposes and principles of the United Nations.

2. The Members of the United Nations entering into such arrangements or constituting such agencies shall make every effort to achieve pacific settlement of local disputes through such regional arrangements or by such regional agencies before referring them to the Security Council.

3. The Security Council shall encourage the development of pacific settlement of local disputes through such regional arrangements or by such regional agencies, either on the initiative of the States concerned or by reference from the Security Council.

4. This Article in no way impairs the application of Articles 34 and 35.

Article 53

1. The Security Council shall, where appropriate, utilize such regional arrangements or agencies for enforcement action under its authority. But no enforcement action shall be taken under regional arrangements or by regional agencies without the authorization of the Security Council, with the exception of measures against any enemy State, as defined in paragraph 2 of this Article, provided for pursuant to Article 107, or in regional arrangements directed against renewal of aggressive policy on the part of any such State, until such time as the Organization may, on request of the governments concerned, be charged with the responsibility for preventing further aggression by such a State.

2. The term "enemy State" as used in paragraph 1 of this Article applies to any State which during the second world war has been an enemy of any signatory of the present Charter.

Article 54

The Security Council shall at all times be kept fully informed of activities undertaken or in contemplation under regional arrangements or by regional agencies for the maintenance of international peace and security.

CHAPTER IX

INTERNATIONAL ECONOMIC AND SOCIAL COOPERATION

Article 55

With a view to the creation of conditions of stability and well-being which are necessary for peaceful and friendly relations among nations based on respect for the principle of equal rights and self-determination of peoples, the United Nations shall promote:

(*a*) higher standards of living, full employment, and conditions of economic and social progress and development;

(*b*) solutions of international economic, social, health and related problems; and international cultural and educational cooperation; and

(*c*) universal respect for, and observance of, human rights and fundamental freedoms for all without distinction as to race, sex, language, or religion.

Article 56

All Members pledge themselves to take joint and separate action in cooperation with the Organization for the achievement of the purposes set forth in Article 55.

Article 57

1. The various specialized agencies, established by intergovernmental agreement and having wide international responsibilities, as defined in their basic instruments, in economic, social, cultural, educational, health and related fields, shall be brought into relationship with the United Nations in accordance with the provisions of Article 63.

2. Such agencies thus brought into relationship with the United Nations are hereinafter referred to as "specialized agencies."

Article 58

The Organization shall make recommendations for the coordination of the policies and activities of the specialized agencies.

Article 59

The Organization shall, where appropriate, initiate negotiations among the States concerned for the creation of any new specialized agencies required for the accomplishment of the purposes set forth in Article 55.

Article 60

Responsibility for the discharge of the functions of the Organization set forth in this Chapter shall be vested in the General Assembly and, under the authority of the General Assembly, in the Economic and Social Council, which shall have for this purpose the powers set forth in Chapter X.

CHAPTER X

The Economic and Social Council

Composition

Article 61

1. The Economic and Social Council shall consist of twenty-seven Members of the United Nations elected by the General Assembly.

2. Subject to the provisions of paragraph 3, nine members of the Economic and Social Council shall be elected each year for a term of three years. A retiring member shall be eligible for immediate re-election.

3. At the first election after the increase in the membership of the Economic and Social Council from eighteen to twenty-seven members, in addition to the members elected in place of the six members whose term of office expires at the end of that year, nine additional members shall be elected. Of these nine additional members, the term of office of three members so elected shall expire at the end of one year, and of three other members at the end of two years, in accordance with arrangements made by the General Assembly.

4. Each member of the Economic and Social Council shall have one representative.

As amended 17 Dec. 1963,
effective 31 Aug. 1965.

Functions and Powers

Article 62

1. The Economic and Social Council may make or initiate studies and reports with respect to international economic, social, cultural, educational, health and related matters and may make recommendations with respect to any such matters to the General Assembly, to the Members of the United Nations, and to the specialized agencies concerned.

2. It may make recommendations for the purpose of promoting respect for, and observance of, human rights and fundamental freedoms for all.

3. It may prepare draft conventions for submission to the General Assembly, with respect to matters falling within its competence.

4. It may call, in accordance with the rules prescribed by the United Nations, international conferences on matters falling within its competence.

Article 63

1. The Economic and Social Council may enter into agreements with any of the agencies referred to in Article 57, defining the terms on which the agency concerned shall be brought into relationship with the United Nations. Such agreements shall be subject to approval by the General Assembly.

2. It may coordinate the activities of the specialized agencies through consultation with and recommendations to such agencies and through recommendations to the General Assembly and to the Members of the United Nations.

Article 64

1. The Economic and Social Council may take appropriate steps to obtain regular reports from the specialized agencies. It may make arrangements with the Members of the United Nations and with the specialized agencies to obtain reports on the steps taken to give effect to its own recommendations and to recommendations on matters falling within its competence made by the General Assembly.

2. It may communicate its observations on these reports to the General Assembly.

Article 65

The Economic and Social Council may furnish information to the Security Council and shall assist the Security Council upon its request.

Article 66

1. The Economic and Social Council shall perform such functions as fall within its competence in connection with the carrying out of the recommendations of the General Assembly.

2. It may, with the approval of the General Assembly, perform services at the request of Members of the United Nations and at the request of specialized agencies.

3. It shall perform such other functions as are specified elsewhere in the present Charter or as may be assigned to it by the General Assembly.

Voting

Article 67

1. Each member of the Economic and Social Council shall have one vote.

2. Decisions of the Economic and Social Council shall be made by a majority of the members present and voting.

Procedure

Article 68

The Economic and Social Council shall set up commissions in economic and social fields and for the promotion of human rights, and such other commissions as may be required for the performance of its functions.

Article 69

The Economic and Social Council shall invite any Member of the United Nations to participate, without vote, in its deliberations on any matter of particular concern to that Member.

Article 70

The Economic and Social Council may make arrangements for representatives of the specialized agencies to participate, without vote, in its deliberations and in those of the commissions established by it, and for its representatives to participate in the deliberations of the specialized agencies.

Article 71

The Economic and Social Council may make suitable arrangements for consultation with non-governmental organizations which are concerned with matters within its competence. Such arrangements may be made with international organizations and, where appropriate, with national organizations after consultation with the Member of the United Nations concerned.

Article 72

1. The Economic and Social Council shall adopt its own rules of procedure, including the method of selecting its president.
2. The Economic and Social Council shall meet as required in accordance with its rules, which shall include provision for the convening of meetings on the request of a majority of its members.

CHAPTER XI

DECLARATION REGARDING NON-SELF-GOVERNING TERRITORIES

Article 73

Members of the United Nations which have or assume responsibilities for the administration of territories whose peoples have not yet attained a full measure of self-government, recognize the principle that the interests of the inhabitants of these territories are paramount, and accept as a sacred trust the obligation to promote to the utmost, within the system of international peace and security established by the present Charter, the well-being of the inhabitants of these territories, and, to this end:

(*a*) to ensure, with due respect for the culture of the peoples concerned, their political, economic, social and educational advancement, their just treatment and their protection against abuses;

(*b*) to develop self-government, to take due account of the political aspirations of the peoples, and to assist them in the progressive development of their free political institutions, according to the particular circumstances of each territory and its peoples and their varying stages of advancement;

(*c*) to further international peace and security;

(*d*) to promote constructive measures of development, to encourage research, and to cooperate with one another and, when and where appropriate, with specialized international bodies with a view to the practical achievement of the social, economic and scientific purposes set forth in this Article; and

(*e*) to transmit regularly to the Secretary-General for information purposes, subject to such limitation as security and constitutional considerations may require, statistical and other information of a technical nature relating to economic, social and educational conditions in the territories for which they are respectively responsible other than those territories to which Chapters XII and XIII apply.

Article 74

Members of the United Nations also agree that their policy in respect of the territories to which this Chapter applies, no less than in respect of their metropolitan areas, must be based on the general principle of good-neighborliness, due account being taken of the interests and well-being of the rest of the world, in social, economic and commercial matters.

CHAPTER XII

INTERNATIONAL TRUSTEESHIP SYSTEM

Article 75

The United Nations shall establish under its authority an international trusteeship system for the administration and supervision of such territories as may be placed thereunder by subsequent individual agreements. These territories are hereinafter referred to as "trust territories."

Article 76

The basic objectives of the trusteeship system, in accordance with the purposes of the United Nations laid down in Article 1 of the present Charter, shall be:

(*a*) to further international peace and security;

(*b*) to promote the political, economic, social and educational advancement of the inhabitants of the trust territories, and their progressive development towards self-government or independence as may be appropriate to the particular circumstances of each territory and its peoples and the freely expressed wishes of the peoples concerned, and as may be provided by the terms of each trusteeship agreement;

(*c*) to encourage respect for human rights and for fundamental freedoms for all without distinction as to race, sex, language or religion, and to encourage recognition of the interdependence of the peoples of the world; and

(*d*) to ensure equal treatment in social, economic and commercial matters for all Members of the United Nations and their nationals, and also equal treatment for the latter in the administration of justice, without prejudice to the attainment of the foregoing objectives and subject to the provisions of Article 80.

Article 77

1. The trusteeship system shall apply to such territories in the following categories as may be placed thereunder by means of trusteeship agreements:

(*a*) territories now held under mandate;

(*b*) territories which may be detached from enemy States as a result of the second world war; and

(*c*) territories voluntarily placed under the system by States responsible for their administration.

2. It will be a matter for subsequent agreement as to which territories in the foregoing categories will be brought under the trusteeship system and upon what terms.

Article 78

The trusteeship system shall not apply to territories which have become Members of the United Nations, relationship among which shall be based on respect for the principle of sovereign equality.

Article 79

The terms of trusteeship for each territory to be placed under the trusteeship system, including any alteration or amendment, shall be agreed upon by the States directly concerned, including the mandatory power in the case of territories held under mandate by a Member of the United Nations, and shall be approved as provided for in Articles 83 and 85.

Article 80

1. Except as may be agreed upon in individual trusteeship agreements, made under Articles 77, 79, and 81, placing each territory under the trusteeship system, and until such agreements have been concluded, nothing in this Chapter shall be construed in or of itself to alter in any manner the rights whatsoever of any States or any

peoples or the terms of existing international instruments to which Members of the United Nations may respectively be parties.

2. Paragraph 1 of this Article shall not be interpreted as giving grounds for delay or postponement of the negotiation and conclusion of agreements for placing mandated and other territories under the trusteeship system as provided for in Article 77.

Article 81

The trusteeship agreement shall in each case include the terms under which the trust territory will be administered and designate the authority which will exercise the administration of the trust territory. Such authority, hereinafter called the "administering authority," may be one or more States or the Organization itself.

Article 82

There may be designated, in any trusteeship agreement, a strategic area or areas which may include part or all of the trust territory to which the agreement applies, without prejudice to any special agreement or agreements made under Article 43.

Article 83

1. All functions of the United Nations relating to strategic areas, including the approval of the terms of the trusteeship agreements and of their alteration or amendment, shall be exercised by the Security Council.

2. The basic objectives set forth in Article 76 shall be applicable to the people of each strategic area.

3. The Security Council shall, subject to the provisions of the trusteeship agreements and without prejudice to security considerations, avail itself of the assistance of the Trusteeship Council to perform those functions of the United Nations under the trusteeship system relating to political, economic, social and educational matters in the strategic areas.

Article 84

It shall be the duty of the administering authority to ensure that the trust territory shall play its part in the maintenance of international peace and security. To this end the administering authority may make use of volunteer forces, facilities and assistance from the trust territory in carrying out the obligations towards the Security Council undertaken in this regard by the administering authority, as well as for local defence and the maintenance of law and order within the trust territory.

Article 85

1. The functions of the United Nations with regard to trusteeship agreements for all areas not designated as strategic, including the approval of the terms of the trusteeship agreements and of their alteration or amendment, shall be exercised by the General Assembly.

2. The Trusteeship Council, operating under the authority of the General Assembly, shall assist the General Assembly in carrying out these functions.

CHAPTER XIII

THE TRUSTEESHIP COUNCIL

Composition

Article 86

1. The Trusteeship Council shall consist of the following Members of the United Nations:

(*a*) those Members administering trust territories;

(*b*) such of those Members mentioned by name in Article 23 as are not administering trust territories; and

(*c*) as many other Members elected for three-year terms by the

General Assembly as may be necessary to ensure that the total number of members of the Trusteeship Council is equally divided between those Members of the United Nations which administer trust territories and those which do not.

2. Each member of the Trusteeship Council shall designate one specially qualified person to represent it therein.

Functions and Powers

Article 87

The General Assembly and, under its authority, the Trusteeship Council, in carrying out their functions, may:

(*a*) consider reports submitted by the administering authority;

(*b*) accept petitions and examine them in consultation with the administering authority;

(*c*) provide for periodic visits to the respective trust territories at times agreed upon with the administering authority; and

(*d*) take these and other actions in conformity with the terms of the trusteeship agreements.

Article 88

The Trusteeship Council shall formulate a questionnaire on the political, economic, social and educational advancement of the inhabitants of each trust territory, and the administering authority for each trust territory within the competence of the General Assembly shall make an annual report to the General Assembly upon the basis of such questionnaire.

Voting

Article 89

1. Each member of the Trusteeship Council shall have one vote.

2. Decisions of the Trusteeship Council shall be made by a majority of the members present and voting.

Procedure

Article 90

1. The Trusteeship Council shall adopt its own rules of procedure, including the method of selecting its president.

2. The Trusteeship Council shall meet as required in accordance with its rules, which shall include provision for the convening of meetings on the request of a majority of its members.

Article 91

The Trusteeship Council shall, when appropriate, avail itself of the assistance of the Economic and Social Council and of the specialized agencies in regard to matters with which they are respectively concerned.

CHAPTER XIV

THE INTERNATIONAL COURT OF JUSTICE

Article 92

The International Court of Justice shall be the principal judicial organ of the United Nations. It shall function in accordance with the annexed Statute, which is based upon the Statute of the Permanent Court of International Justice and forms an integral part of the present Charter.

Article 93

1. All Members of the United Nations are *ipso facto* parties to the Statute of the International Court of Justice.

2. A State which is not a Member of the United Nations may become a party to the Statute of the International Court of Justice on

conditions to be determined in each case by the General Assembly upon the recommendation of the Security Council.

Article 94

1. Each Member of the United Nations undertakes to comply with the decision of the International Court of Justice in any case to which it is a party.

2. If any party to a case fails to perform the obligations incumbent upon it under a judgment rendered by the Court, the other party may have recourse to the Security Council, which may, if it deems necessary, make recommendations or decide upon measures to be taken to give effect to the judgment.

Article 95

Nothing in the present Charter shall prevent Members of the United Nations from entrusting the solution of their differences to other tribunals by virtue of agreements already in existence or which may be concluded in the future.

Article 96

1. The General Assembly or the Security Council may request the International Court of Justice to give an advisory opinion on any legal question.

2. Other organs of the United Nations and specialized agencies, which may at any time be so authorized by the General Assembly, may also request advisory opinions of the Court on legal questions arising within the scope of their activities.

CHAPTER XV

The Secretariat

Article 97

The Secretariat shall comprise a Secretary-General and such staff as the Organization may require. The Secretary-General shall be appointed by the General Assembly upon the recommendation of the Security Council. He shall be the chief administrative officer of the Organization.

Article 98

The Secretary-General shall act in that capacity in all meetings of the General Assembly, of the Security Council, of the Economic and Social Council and of the Trusteeship Council, and shall perform such other functions as are entrusted to him by these organs. The Secretary-General shall make an annual report to the General Assembly on the work of the Organization.

Article 99

The Secretary-General may bring to the attention of the Security Council any matter which in his opinion may threaten the maintenance of international peace and security.

Article 100

1. In the performance of their duties, the Secretary-General and the staff shall not seek or receive instructions from any government or from any other authority external to the Organization. They shall refrain from any action which might reflect on their position as international officials responsible only to the Organization.

2. Each Member of the United Nations undertakes to respect the

exclusively international character of the responsibilities of the Secretary-General and the staff and not to seek to influence them in the discharge of their responsibilities.

Article 101

1. The staff shall be appointed by the Secretary-General under regulations established by the General Assembly.

2. Appropriate staffs shall be permanently assigned to the Economic and Social Council, the Trusteeship Council, and, as required, to other organs of the United Nations. These staffs shall form a part of the Secretariat.

3. The paramount consideration in the employment of the staff and in the determination of the conditions of service shall be the necessity of securing the highest standards of efficiency, competence and integrity. Due regard shall be paid to the importance of recruiting the staff on as wide a geographical basis as possible.

CHAPTER XVI

Miscellaneous Provisions

Article 102

1. Every treaty and every international agreement entered into by any Member of the United Nations after the present Charter comes into force shall as soon as possible be registered with the Secretariat and published by it.

2. No party to any such treaty or international agreement which has not been registered in accordance with the provisions of paragraph 1 of this Article may invoke that treaty or agreement before any organ of the United Nations.

Article 103

In the event of a conflict between the obligations of the Members of the United Nations under the present Charter and their obligations under any other international agreement, their obligations under the present Charter shall prevail.

Article 104

The Organization shall enjoy in the territory of each of its Members such legal capacity as may be necessary for the exercise of its functions and the fulfillment of its purposes.

Article 105

1. The Organization shall enjoy in the territory of each of its Members such privileges and immunities as are necessary for the fulfillment of its purposes.

2. Representatives of the Members of the United Nations and officials of the Organization shall similarly enjoy such privileges and immunities as are necessary for the independent exercise of their functions in connection with the Organization.

3. The General Assembly may make recommendations with a view to determining the details of the application of paragraphs 1 and 2 of this Article or may propose conventions to the Members of the United Nations for this purpose.

CHAPTER XVII

TRANSITIONAL SECURITY ARRANGEMENTS

Article 106

Pending the coming into force of such special agreements referred to in Article 43 as in the opinion of the Security Council enable it to begin the exercise of its responsibilities under Article 42, the parties to the Four-Nation Declaration, signed at Moscow, October 30th, 1943, and France, shall, in accordance with the provisions of paragraph 5 of that Declaration, consult with one another and as occasion requires with other Members of the United Nations with a view to such joint action on behalf of the Organization as may be necessary for the purpose of maintaining international peace and security.

Article 107

Nothing in the present Charter shall invalidate or preclude action, in relation to any State which during the second world war has been an enemy of any signatory to the present Charter, taken or authorized as a result of that war by the governments having responsibility for such action.

CHAPTER XVIII

AMENDMENTS

Article 108

Amendments to the present Charter shall come into force for all Members of the United Nations when they have been adopted by a vote of two thirds of the members of the General Assembly and ratified in accordance with their respective constitutional processes by two thirds of the Members of the United Nations, including all the permanent members of the Security Council.

Article 109

1. A general conference of the Members of the United Nations for the purpose of reviewing the present Charter may be held at a date and place to be fixed by a two-thirds vote of the members of the General Assembly and by a vote of any nine members of the Security Council. Each Member of the United Nations shall have one vote in the conference.

2. Any alteration of the present Charter recommended by a two-thirds vote of the conference shall take effect when ratified in accordance with their respective constitutional processes by two thirds of the Members of the United Nations, including all the permanent members of the Security Council.

3. If such a conference has not been held before the tenth annual session of the General Assembly following the coming into force of the present Charter, the proposal to call such a conference shall be placed on the agenda of that session of the General Assembly, and the conference shall be held if so decided by a majority vote of the members of the General Assembly and by a vote of any seven members of the Security Council.

> As amended 20 Dec. 1965,
> effective 12 June 1968.

CHAPTER XIX

RATIFICATION AND SIGNATURE

Article 110

1. The present Charter shall be ratified by the signatory States in accordance with their respective constitutional processes.

2. The ratifications shall be deposited with the Government of the United States of America, which shall notify all the signatory States of each deposit as well as the Secretary-General of the Organization when he has been appointed.

3. The present Charter shall come into force upon the deposit of ratifications by the Republic of China, France, the Union of Soviet Socialist Republics, the United Kingdom of Great Britain and Northern Ireland and the United States of America, and by a majority of the other signatory States. A protocol of the ratifications deposited shall thereupon be drawn up by the Government of the United States of America, which shall communicate copies thereof to all the signatory States.

4. The States signatory to the present Charter which ratify it after it has come into force will become original Members of the United Nations on the date of the deposit of their respective ratifications.

Article 111

The present Charter, of which the Chinese, French, Russian, English and Spanish texts are equally authentic, shall remain deposited in the archives of the United States of America. Duly certified copies thereof shall be transmitted by that Government to the governments of the other signatory States.

IN FAITH WHEREOF the representatives of the governments of the United Nations have signed the present Charter.

DONE at the city of San Francisco the twenty-sixth day of June, one thousand nine hundred and forty-five.

Present Statute of the International Court of Justice

Article 1

THE INTERNATIONAL COURT OF JUSTICE established by the Charter of the United Nations as the principal judicial organ of the United Nations shall be constituted and shall function in accordance with the provisions of the present Statute.

CHAPTER I

ORGANIZATION OF THE COURT

Article 2

The Court shall be composed of a body of independent judges, elected regardless of their nationality from among persons of high moral character, who possess the qualifications required in their respective countries for appointment to the highest judicial offices, or are jurisconsults of recognized competence in international law.

Article 3

1. The Court shall consist of fifteen members, no two of whom may be nationals of the same State.

2. A person who for the purposes of membership in the Court could be regarded as a national of more than one State shall be deemed to be a national of the one in which he ordinarily exercises civil and political rights.

Article 4

1. The members of the Court shall be elected by the General Assembly and by the Security Council from a list of persons nominated by the national groups in the Permanent Court of Arbitration, in accordance with the following provisions.

2. In the case of Members of the United Nations not represented in the Permanent Court of Arbitration, candidates shall be nominated by national groups appointed for this purpose by their governments under the same conditions as those prescribed for members of the Permanent Court of Arbitration by Article 44 of the Convention of The Hague of 1907 for the pacific settlement of international disputes.

3. The conditions under which a State which is a party to the present Statute but is not a Member of the United Nations may participate in electing the members of the Court shall, in the absence of a special agreement, be laid down by the General Assembly upon recommendation of the Security Council.

Article 5

1. At least three months before the date of the election, the Secretary-General of the United Nations shall address a written request to the members of the Permanent Court of Arbitration belonging to the States which are parties to the present Statute, and to the members of the national groups appointed under Article 4, paragraph 2, inviting them to undertake, within a given time, by national groups, the nomination of persons in a position to accept the duties of a member of the Court.

2. No group may nominate more than four persons, not more than two of whom shall be of their own nationality. In no case may the number of candidates nominated by a group be more than double the number of seats to be filled.

Article 6

Before making these nominations, each national group is recommended to consult its highest court of justice, its legal faculties and schools of law, and its national academies and national sections of international academies devoted to the study of law.

Article 7

1. The Secretary-General shall prepare a list in alphabetical order of all the persons thus nominated. Save as provided in Article 12, paragraph 2, these shall be the only persons eligible.

2. The Secretary-General shall submit this list to the General Assembly and to the Security Council.

Article 8

The General Assembly and the Security Council shall proceed independently of one another to elect the members of the Court.

Article 9

At every election, the electors shall bear in mind not only that the persons to be elected should individually possess the qualifications required; but also that in the body as a whole the representation of the main forms of civilization and of the principal legal systems of the world should be assured.

Article 10

1. Those candidates who obtain an absolute majority of votes in the General Assembly and in the Security Council shall be considered as elected.

2. Any vote of the Security Council, whether for the election of judges or for the appointment of members of the conference envisaged in Article 12, shall be taken without any distinction between permanent and non-permanent members of the Security Council.

3. In the event of more than one national of the same State obtaining an absolute majority of the votes both of the General Assembly and of the Security Council, the eldest of these only shall be considered as elected.

Article 11

If, after the first meeting held for the purpose of the election, one or more seats remain to be filled, a second and, if necessary, a third meeting shall take place.

Article 12

1. If, after the third meeting, one or more seats still remain unfilled, a joint conference consisting of six members, three appointed by the General Assembly and three by the Security Council, may be formed at any time at the request of either the General Assembly or the Security Council, for the purpose of choosing by the vote of an absolute majority one name for each seat still vacant, to submit to the General Assembly and the Security Council for their respective acceptance.

2. If the joint conference is unanimously agreed upon any person who fulfills the required conditions, he may be included in the list, even though he was not included in the list of nominations referred to in Article 7.

3. If the joint conference is satisfied that it will not be successful in procuring an election, those members of the Court who have already been elected shall, within a period to be fixed by the Security Council, proceed to fill the vacant seats by selection from among those candidates who have obtained votes either in the General Assembly or in the Security Council.

4. In the event of an equality of votes among the judges, the eldest judge shall have a casting vote.

Article 13

1. The members of the Court shall be elected for nine years and may be re-elected; provided, however, that of the judges elected at the first election, the terms of five judges shall expire at the end of three years and the terms of five more judges shall expire at the end of six years.

2. The judges whose terms are to expire at the end of the above-

mentioned initial periods of three and six years shall be chosen by lot to be drawn by the Secretary-General immediately after the first election has been completed.

3. The members of the Court shall continue to discharge their duties until their places have been filled. Though replaced, they shall finish any cases which they may have begun.

4. In the case of the resignation of a member of the Court, the resignation shall be addressed to the President of the Court for transmission to the Secretary-General. This last notification makes the place vacant.

Article 14

Vacancies shall be filled by the same method as that laid down for the first election, subject to the following provision: the Secretary-General shall, within one month of the occurrence of the vacancy, proceed to issue the invitations provided for in Article 5, and the date of the election shall be fixed by the Security Council.

A member of the Court eletced to replace a member whose term of office has not expired shall hold office for the remainder of his predecessor's term.

Article 15

A member of the Court elected to replace a member whose term of office has not expired shall hold office for the remainder of his predecessor's term.

Article 16

1. No member of the Court may exercise any political or administrative function, or engage in any other occupation of a professional nature.

2. Any doubt on this point shall be settled by the decision of the Court.

Article 17

1. No member of the Court may act as agent, counsel, or advocate in any case.

2. No member may participate in the decision of any case in which he has previously taken part as agent, counsel, or advocate for one of the parties, or as a member of a national or international court, or of a commission of enquiry, or in any other capacity.

3. Any doubt on this point shall be settled by the decision of the Court.

Article 18

1. No member of the Court can be dismissed unless, in the unanimous opinion of the other members, he has ceased to fulfil the required conditions.

2. Formal notification thereof shall be made to the Secretary-General by the Registrar.

3. This notification makes the place vacant.

Article 19

The members of the Court, when engaged on the business of the Court, shall enjoy diplomatic privileges and immunities.

Article 20

Every member of the Court shall, before taking up his duties, make a solemn declaration in open Court that he will exercise his powers impartially and conscientiously.

Article 21

1. The Court shall elect its President and Vice-President for three years; they may be re-elected.

2. The Court shall appoint its Registrar and may provide for the appointment of such other officers as may be necessary.

Article 22

1. The seat of the Court shall be established at The Hague. This, however, shall not prevent the Court from sitting and exercising its functions elsewhere whenever the Court considers it desirable.

2. The President and the Registrar shall reside at the seat of the Court.

Article 23

1. The Court shall remain permanently in session, except during the judicial vacations, the dates and duration of which shall be fixed by the Court.

2. Members of the Court are entitled to periodic leave, the dates and duration of which shall be fixed by the Court, having in mind the distance between The Hague and the home of each judge.

3. Members of the Court shall be bound, unless they are on leave or prevented from attending by illness or other serious reasons duly explained to the President, to hold themselves permanently at the disposal of the Court.

Article 24

1. If, for some special reason, a member of the Court considers that he should not take part in the decision of a particular case, he shall so inform the President.

2. If the President considers that for some special reason one of the members of the Court should not sit in a particular case, he shall give him notice accordingly.

3. If in any such case the member of the Court and the President disagree, the matter shall be settled by the decision of the Court.

Article 25

1. The full Court shall sit except when it is expressly provided otherwise in the present Statute.

2. Subject to the condition that the number of judges available to constitute the Court is not thereby reduced below eleven, the Rules of the Court may provide for allowing one or more judges, according to circumstances and in rotation, to be dispensed from sitting.

3. A quorum of nine judges shall suffice to constitute the Court.

Article 26

1. The Court may from time to time form one or more Chambers, composed of three or more judges as the Court may determine, for dealing with particular categories of cases; for example, labor cases and cases relating to transit and communications.

2. The Court may at any time form a Chamber for dealing with a particular case. The number of judges to constitute such a chamber shall be determined by the Court with the approval of the parties.

3. Cases shall be heard and determined by the Chambers provided for in this Article if the parties so request.

Article 27

A judgment given by any of the Chambers provided for in Articles 26 and 29 shall be considered as rendered by the Court.

Article 28

The Chambers provided for in Articles 26 and 29 may, with the consent of the parties, sit and exercise their functions elsewhere than at The Hague.

Article 29

With a view to the speedy despatch of business, the Court shall form annually a Chamber composed of five judges which, at the request of the parties, may hear and determine cases by summary procedure. In addition, two judges shall be selected for the purpose of replacing judges who find it impossible to sit.

Article 30

1. The Court shall frame rules for carrying out its functions. In particular, it shall lay down rules of procedure.

2. The Rules of the Court may provide for assessors to sit with the Court or with any of its Chambers, without the right to vote.

Article 31

1. Judges of the nationality of each of the parties shall retain their right to sit in the case before the Court.

2. If the Court includes upon the Bench a judge of the nationality of one of the parties, any other party may choose a person to sit as judge. Such person shall be chosen preferably from among those persons who have been nominated as candidates as provided in Articles 4 and 5.

3. If the Court includes upon the Bench no judge of the nationality of the parties, each of these parties may proceed to choose a judge as provided in paragraph 2 of this Article.

4. The provisions of this Article shall apply to the case of Articles 26 and 29. In such cases, the President shall request one or, if necessary, two of the members of the Court forming the chamber to give place to the members of the Court of the nationality of the parties concerned, and, failing such, or if they are unable to be present, to the judges specially chosen by the parties.

5. Should there be several parties in the same interest, they shall, for the purpose of the preceding provisions, be reckoned as one party only. Any doubt upon this point shall be settled by the decision of the Court.

6. Judges chosen as laid down in paragraphs 2, 3 and 4 of this Article shall fulfil the conditions required by Articles 2, 17 (paragraph 2), 20, and 24 of the present Statute. They shall take part in the decision on terms of complete equality with their colleagues.

Article 32

1. Each member of the Court shall receive an annual salary.

2. The President shall receive a special annual allowance.

3. The Vice-President shall receive a special allowance for every day on which he acts as President.

4. The judges chosen under Article 31, other than members of the Court, shall receive compensation for each day on which they exercise their functions.

5. These salaries, allowances, and compensation shall be fixed by the General Assembly. They may not be decreased during the term of office.

6. The salary of the Registrar shall be fixed by the General Assembly on the proposal of the Court.

7. Regulations made by the General Assembly shall fix the conditions under which retirement pensions may be given to members of the Court and to the Registrar, and the conditions under which members of the Court and the Registrar shall have their traveling expenses refunded.

8. The above salaries, allowances, and compensation shall be free of all taxation.

Article 33

The expenses of the Court shall be borne by the United Nations in such a manner as shall be decided by the General Asembly.

CHAPTER II

COMPETENCE OF THE COURT

Article 34

1. Only States may be parties in cases before the Court.

2. The Court, subject to and in conformity with its Rules, may request of public international organizations information relevant to cases before it, and shall receive such information presented by such organizations on their own initiative.

3. Whenever the construction of the constituent instrument of a public international organization or of an international convention adopted thereunder is in question in a case before the Court, the

Registrar shall so notify the public international organization concerned and shall communicate to it copies of all the written
proceedings.

Article 35

1. The Court shall be open to the States parties to the present
Statute.

2. The conditions under which the Court shall be open to other
States shall, subject to the special provisions contained in treaties in
force, be laid down by the Security Council, but in no case shall such
conditions place the parties in a position of inequality before the
Court.

3. When a State which is not a Member of the United Nations is a
party to a case, the Court shall fix the amount which that party is to
contribute towards the expenses of the Court. This provision shall not
apply if such State is bearing a share of the expenses of the Court.

Article 36

1. The jurisdiction of the Court comprises all cases which the
parties refer to it and all matters specially provided for in the Charter
of the United Nations or in treaties and conventions in force.

2. The States parties to the present Statute may at any time declare that they recognize as compulsory *ipso facto* and without special
agreement, in relation to any other State accepting the same obligation, the jurisdiction of the Court in all legal disputes concerning:

a. the interpretation of a treaty;

b. any question of international law;

c. the existence of any fact which, if established, would constitute
a breach of an international obligation;

d. the nature or extent of the reparation to be made for the
breach of an international obligation.

3. The declarations referred to above may be made unconditionally
or on condition of reciprocity on the part of several or certain States,
or for a certain time.

4. Such declarations shall be deposited with the Secretary-General
of the United Nations who shall transmit copies thereof to the parties
to the Statute and to the Registrar of the Court.

5. Declarations made under Article 36 of the Statute of the Permanent Court of International Justice and which are still in force shall be deemed, as between the parties to the present Statute, to be acceptances of the compulsory jurisdiction of the International Court of Justice for the period which they still have to run and in accordance with their terms.

6. In the event of a dispute as to whether the Court has jurisdiction, the matter shall be settled by the decision of the Court.

Article 37

Whenever a treaty or convention in force provides for reference of a matter to a tribunal to have been instituted by the League of Nations, or to the Permanent Court of International Justice, the matter shall, as between the parties to the present Statute, be referred to the International Court of Justice.

Article 38

1. The Court, whose function is to decide in accordance with international law such disputes as are submitted to it, shall apply:

a. international conventions, whether general or particular, establishing rules expressly recognized by the contesting States;

b. international custom, as evidence of a general practice accepted as law;

c. the general principles of law recognized by civilized nations;

d. subject to the provisions of Article 59, judicial decisions and the teachings of the most highly qualified publicists of the various nations, as subsidiary means for the determination of rules of law.

2. This provision shall not prejudice the power of the Court to decide a case *ex aequo et bono,* if the parties agree thereto.

CHAPTER III

PROCEDURE

Article 39

1. The official languages of the Court shall be French and English. If the parties agree that the case shall be conducted in French, the judgment shall be delivered in French. If the parties agree that the case shall be conducted in English, the judgment shall be delivered in English.

2. In the absence of an agreement as to which language shall be employed, each party may, in the pleadings, use the language which it prefers; the decision of the Court shall be given in French and English. In this case the Court shall at the same time determine which of the two texts shall be considered as authoritative.

3. The Court shall, at the request of any party, authorize a language other than French or English to be used by that party.

Article 40

1. Cases are brought before the Court, as the case may be, either by the notification of the special agreement or by a written application addressed to the Registrar. In either case the subject of the dispute and the parties shall be indicated.

2. The Registrar shall forthwith communicate the application to all concerned.

3. He shall also notify the Members of the United Nations through the Secretary-General, and also any other States entitled to appear before the Court.

Article 41

1. The Court shall have the power to indicate, if it considers that circumstances so require, any provisional measures which ought to be taken to preserve the respective rights of either party.

2. Pending the final decision, notice of the measures suggested shall forthwith be given to the parties and to the Security Council.

Article 42

1. The parties shall be represented by agents.
2. They may have the assistance of counsel or advocates before the Court.
3. The agents, counsel, and advocates of parties before the Court shall enjoy the privileges and immunities necessary to the independent exercise of their duties.

Article 43

1. The procedure shall consist of two parts: written and oral.
2. The written proceedings shall consist of the communication to the Court and to the parties of Memorials, Counter-Memorials and, if necessary, Replies; also all papers and documents in support.
3. These communications shall be made through the Registrar, in the order and within the time fixed by the Court.
4. A certified copy of every document produced by one party shall be communicated to the other party.
5. The oral proceedings shall consist of the hearing by the Court of witnesses, experts, agents, counsel, and advocates.

Article 44

1. For the service of all notices upon persons other than the agents, counsel, and advocates, the Court shall apply direct to the government of the State upon whose territory the notice has to be served.
2. The same provision shall apply whenever steps are to be taken to procure evidence on the spot.

Article 45

The hearing shall be under the control of the President or, if he is unable to preside, of the Vice-President; if neither is able to preside, the senior judge present shall preside.

Article 46

The hearing in Court shall be public, unless the Court shall decide otherwise, or unless the parties demand that the public be not admitted.

Article 47

1. Minutes shall be made at each hearing and signed by the Registrar and the President.
2. These minutes alone shall be authentic.

Article 48

The Court shall make orders for the conduct of the case, shall decide the form and time in which each party must conclude its arguments, and make all arrangements connected with the taking of evidence.

Article 49

The Court may, even before the hearing begins, call upon the agents to produce any document or to supply any explanations. Formal note shall be taken of any refusal.

Article 50

The Court may, at any time, entrust any individual, body, bureau, commission, or other organization that it may select, with the task of carrying out an enquiry or giving an expert opinion.

Article 51

During the hearing any relevant questions are to be put to the witnesses and experts under the conditions laid down by the Court in the rules of procedure referred to in Article 30.

Article 52

After the Court has received the proofs and evidence within the time specified for the purpose, it may refuse to accept any further oral or written evidence that one party may desire to present unless the other side consents.

Article 53

1. Whenever one of the parties does not appear before the Court, or fails to defend its case, the other party may call upon the Court to decide in favor of its claim.

2. The Court must, before doing so, satisfy itself, not only that it has jurisdiction in accordance with Articles 36 and 37, but also that the claim is well founded in fact and law.

Article 54

1. When, subject to the control of the Court, the agents, counsel, and advocates have completed their presentation of the case, the President shall declare the hearing closed.

2. The Court shall withdraw to consider the judgment.

3. The deliberations of the Court shall take place in private and remain secret.

Article 55

1. All questions shall be decided by a majority of the judges present.

2. In the event of an equality of votes, the President or the judge who acts in his place shall have a casting vote.

Article 56

1. The judgment shall state the reasons on which it is based.

2. It shall contain the names of the judges who have taken part in the decision.

Article 57

If the judgment does not represent in whole or in part the unanimous opinion of the judges, any judge shall be entitled to deliver a separate opinion.

Article 58

The judgment shall be signed by the President and by the Registrar. It shall be read in open Court, due notice having been given to the agents.

Article 59

The decision of the Court has no binding force except between the parties and in respect of that particular case.

Article 60

The judgment is final and without appeal. In the event of dispute as to the meaning or scope of the judgment, the Court shall construe it upon the request of any party.

Article 61

1. An application for revision of a judgment may be made only when it is based upon the discovery of some fact of such a nature as to be a decisive factor, which fact was, when the judgment was given, unknown to the Court and also to the party claiming revision, always provided that such ignorance was not due to negligence.

2. The proceedings for revision shall be opened by a judgment of the Court expressly recording the existence of the new fact, recognizing that it has such a character as to lay the case open to revision, and declaring the application admissible on this ground.

3. The Court may require previous compliance with the terms of the judgment before it admits proceedings in revision.

4. The application for revision must be made at latest within six months of the discovery of the new fact.

5. No application for revision may be made after the lapse of ten years from the date of the judgment.

Article 62

1. Should a State consider that it has an interest of a legal nature which may be affected by the decision in the case, it may submit a request to the Court to be permitted to intervene.

2. It shall be for the Court to decide upon this request.

Article 63

1. Whenever the construction of a convention in which states other than those concerned in the case are parties is in question, the Registrar shall notify all such states forthwith.

2. Every state so notified has the right to intervene in the proceedings; but if it uses this right, the construction given by the judgment will be equally binding upon it.

Article 64

Unless otherwise decided by the Court, each party shall bear its own costs.

CHAPTER IV

ADVISORY OPINIONS

Article 65

1. The Court may give an advisory opinion on any legal question at the request of whatever body may be authorized by or in accordance with the Charter of the United Nations to make such a request.

2. Questions upon which the advisory opinion of the Court is asked shall be laid before the Court by means of a written request containing an exact statement of the question upon which an opinion is required, and accompanied by all documents likely to throw light upon the question.

Article 66

1. The Registrar shall forthwith give notice of the request for an advisory opinion to all States entitled to appear before the Court.

2. The Registrar shall also, by means of a special and direct communication, notify any State entitled to appear before the Court or international organization considered by the Court, or should it not be sitting, by the President, as likely to be able to furnish information on the question, that the Court will be prepared to receive, within a time limit to be fixed by the President, written statements, or to hear, at a public sitting to be held for the purpose, oral statements relating to the question.

3. Should any such State entitled to appear before the Court have failed to receive the special communication referred to in paragraph 2 of this Article, such State may express a desire to submit a written statement or to be heard; and the Court will decide.

4. States and organizations having presented written or oral statements or both shall be permitted to comment on the statements made by other States or organizations in the form, to the extent, and within the time-limits which the Court, or, should it not be sitting, the President, shall decide in each particular case. Accordingly, the Registrar shall in due time communicate any such written statements to States and organizations having submitted similar statements.

Article 67

The Court shall deliver its advisory opinions in open Court, notice having been given to the Secretary-General and to the representatives of Members of the United Nations, of other States and of international organizations immediately concerned.

Article 68

In its exercise of its advisory functions, the Court shall further be guided by the provisions of the present Statute which apply in contentious cases to the extent to which it recognizes them to be applicable.

CHAPTER V

AMENDMENT

Article 69

Amendments to the present Statute shall be effected by the same procedure as is provided by the Charter of the United Nations for amendments to that Charter, subject however to any provisions which the General Assembly upon recommendation of the Security Council may adopt concerning the participation of States which are parties to the present Statute but are not Members of the United Nations.

Article 70

The Court shall have power to propose such amendments to the present Statute as it may deem necessary, through written communications to the Secretary-General, for consideration in conformity with the provisions of Article 69.

Proposed Revised Statute of the International Court of Justice

Article I

Constitution

The International Court of Justice, established by the Charter of the United Nations as the principal judicial organ of the United Nations, shall be constituted, and shall function, in accordance with the provisions of the present Statute.

Article II

Composition of the Court

1. The Court shall be composed of a body of independent judges, nationals, at the time of their election, of Members of the United Nations, elected from among persons of high moral character, who possess the qualifications required in their respective countries for appointment to the highest judicial offices, or are jurisconsults of recognized competence in international law.

2. The Court shall consist of fifteen members, no one of whom shall, at the time of his election, be less than fifty nor more than sixty-five years of age, and no two of whom shall have been of the same national origin. A person who, for purposes of membership on the Court, could be regarded as a national of more than one State, shall be deemed to be a national of that one in which he ordinarily exercises civil and political rights.

Article III

Election of Judges

1. The members of the Court shall be elected for life, by the General Assembly and by the Security Council, from a list of persons

nominated by the Members of the United Nations, all as provided hereunder.

2. The members of the Court, serving as such upon ratification of the present Statute, shall be deemed to have been elected for life under the terms of the present Statute, with tenure for determination of their retirement pensions as of the date of their original election to membership on the Court.

3. Promptly following the occurrence of any vacancy in the membership of the Court, or in anticipation of a forthcoming vacancy to occur by resignation or retirement, the Secretary-General of the United Nations shall invite each of the members of the General Assembly to nominate, within thirty days, for each such vacancy, not more than two persons of any nationality not already represented prior to election to the Court, qualified, and in a position, to serve as members of the Court.

4. The Secretary-General shall prepare a list, in alphabetical order, of all of the persons so nominated, and shall submit this list to the General Assembly and to the Security Council, which bodies shall proceed, independently of one another, to elect a member of the Court to fill each vacancy thereon.

5. At each election to membership on the Court, every effort shall be made to reflect in the Court as a whole, a composite of the principal civilizations and legal systems of the world.

6. The nominee or nominees, equal in number to the vacancy or vacancies to be filled, obtaining the greatest number of votes, and not less than a majority of the votes cast in both the Security Council and the General Assembly, shall be elected; provided that only the eldest among nominees who are nationals of the same State, and who may have received such number of votes, shall be considered to have been so elected.

7. If, after the first meeting held for such election, one or more seats remain to be filled, a second and, if necessary, a third meeting shall take place.

8. If, after the third meeting, one or more seats still remain unfilled, a Joint Conference consisting of six members, three appointed by the General Assembly and three by the Security Council, may be formed at any time at the request of either the General Assembly or the Security Council, for the purpose of choosing, by vote of a majority of all of the members of the Joint Conference, one name for each seat still vacant, for submission to the General Assembly and the Security Council for their respective acceptances.

9. If the Joint Conference is unanimously agreed on any qualified person, he may be elected even though he was not included in the list of nominations submitted by the Secretary-General to the General Assembly and the Security Council as hereinabove provided.

10. If the Joint Conference should not be successful in procuring an election, it shall so advise the General Assembly and the Security Council, and those members of the Court who shall already have been elected shall proceed to fill the vacant seat or seats by selection from among those nominees who have obtained any votes either in the General Assembly or in the Security Council. In the event of any equality of votes among the judges, the eldest judge shall have a casting vote.

11. Any vote of the Security Council, whether for the election of judges or for the appointment of members of a Joint Conference, shall be taken without any distinction between permanent and non-permanent members of the Security Council.

Article IV

Civil Status of Judges

1. Each person elected as a member of the Court shall, as a condition precedent to his accession to office as such, renounce his or her allegiance to the State of which he or she was a national when elected, and shall be deemed to have become *ipso facto,* for his natural lifetime, a citizen of the United Nations.

2. The spouse of each member of the Court shall, as of her date of the judge's accession, be deemed to have renounced (his or her) allegiance to the State of which she was a national when the judge was elected, and shall, during the lifetime of such member of the Court, and for two years thereafter, be deemed to hold United Nations citizenship; but prior to the expiration of such term of two years, such spouse shall be obligated to take, and shall be eligible for, citizenship in any State of her choice, and she shall thereupon surrender her United Nations passport to the Secretary-General.

3. Members and former members of the Court, and their spouses who shall be deemed to hold United Nations citizenship as in the present Statute provided, shall receive passports as such from the Secretary-General, and may freely enter into, reside in, and depart from, any State which is a Member of the United Nations; and they shall enjoy diplomatic privileges and immunities in all such States.

4. Each judge of the Court, and the spouse of each judge, shall be deemed to have his or her national domicile at the seat of the Court; and each retired judge of the Court and his spouse, as long as they shall be deemed to be citizens of the United Nations as in the present Statute provided, shall be deemed to have his (or her) national domicile at his permanent residence; in each case in so far as, but no farther than, his United Nations citizenship and his diplomatic status and immunities do not fully cover or define his personal status, rights and liabilities.

5. Every member of the Court shall, before taking up his duties as such, make a solemn declaration in open court that he will exercise his functions conscientiously and impartially.

6. No member of the Court may exercise any political or other functions, or engage in any occupation whatever, other than as a member of the Court; nor may any member of the Court participate in the decision of any case with which he has had any prior connection whatever, direct or indirect, in any capacity, except that members of a chamber shall be eligible to sit on the full Court on an appeal from the chamber to the Court, under the provisions of section 4 of Article XVI of the present Statute.

Article V

Officers of the Court

1. The Court shall elect its President and Vice-President for terms of three years. These shall be eligible for re-election. The Court shall appoint its Registrar, and shall provide for the appointment of such other officials and employees as may be necessary.

2. The seat of the Court shall be established at the Hague, but the Court may sit, and exercise its functions, elsewhere as it may deem advisable. The President and Registrar shall reside at the seat of the Court.

Article VI

Resignations, Retirement and Dismissal

1. Any member of the Court may resign at any time, except while under impeachment (para. 4 hereunder), by addressing his resigna-

tion to the Secretary-General, upon receipt by whom the resignation shall be effective. Six months after a judge shall have resigned, he and his (or her) spouse shall lose their United Nations citizenship. Within said period of six months, they shall be eligible for, and shall take, citizenship in any State of their choice, and shall surrender their United Nations passports to the Secretary-General.

2. Any member of the Court who shall, during his tenure of office, have reached the age of seventy years, may retire at any time.

3. Any member of the Court who shall have reached the age of seventy-five years, shall be retired as of his seventy-fifth birthday; except that such retirement shall not, as to any member of the Court serving as such upon ratification of the present revised Statute, take effect until six months after such ratification.

4. Any member of the Court may be dismissed, for violation of any provision of the present Statute, of any provision of rules or regulations of the Court, or for conduct in any wise unbecoming a member of the Court, by vote of not less than two-thirds of the members of the Security Council (without distinction as to permanent or non-permanent members), on trial under impeachment by a majority of the members of the General Assembly.

5. A member of the Court who has been dismissed, and his (or her) spouse, shall forfeit their United Nations citizenship; they shall revert to the citizenship which they had at the time of his election to the Court; they shall forthwith surrender their United Nations passports to the Secretary-General; and the dismissed judge shall have no right to any pension or other emoluments of his office, effective from the date of his dismissal.

6. The Registrar may be dismissed at any time by the Court, and any other official or employee of the Court may be dismissed at any time by the appointing authority. Pension and other rights of such dismissed officials or employees of the Court shall be as fixed under regulations of the General Assembly.

Article VII

Salaries and Expenses

1. Each member of the Court shall receive an annual salary. The President shall receive a special annual allowance, and the Vice-

President shall receive a special allowance for every day on which he acts as President.

2. Judges *ad hoc* shall receive compensation for each day on which they exercise their functions, including days on which they travel in connection with the exercise of their functions.

3. The salaries and allowances of members of the Court, and the compensation of the judges *ad hoc,* shall be fixed by the General Assembly, and shall never be decreased during the terms of office of persons for whom fixed.

4. The salary of the Registrar shall be fixed by the General Assembly on recommendation of the Court, and the compensation of all other officials and employees of the Court shall be fixed by the Court.

5. Expenses of the members of the Court and judges *ad hoc,* for their reasonable expenses of traveling to and from, attendance at, and otherwise on business of, the Court, shall be reimbursed to them.

6. Expenses of the Registrar, and of other officials and employees of the Court, incurred in connection with the exercise of their functions, shall be reimbursed to them.

7. Members of the Court who shall have retired after not less than ten full years of service, shall receive, for life, retirement pensions equal to their annual salary at the time of their retirement; and members of the Court who shall have retired after less than ten full years of service, shall receive, for life, retirement pensions equal to that portion of their annual salary at the time of their retirement, as the number of years served by them as members of the Court bears to ten.

8. The widow of a member or retired member of the Court, who was his wife during his tenure of office as a member of the Court, shall receive a pension for life. In the case of a widow of a member of the Court, this pension shall be one-half of the pension which would have been payable, according to his years of service, to the member of the Court if he had retired as of the date of his death with not more than ten years of service. In the case of the widow of a retired judge, this pension shall be one-half of the pension to which such retired judge was entitled at the time of his death.

9. Conditions of retirement, and pensions of the Registrar and other officials, shall be as fixed by the General Assembly.

10. The salaries, allowances, compensation, pensions and reimbursements of expenses, fixed as provided in the present Statute, shall be free of any and all taxation.

Article VIII

Jurisdiction

1. All Members of the United Nations shall be subject to the compulsory jurisdiction of the Court in all justiciable disputes concerning:

a. the interpretation of a treaty;

b. any question of international law;

c. the existence of any fact which, if established, would constitute a breach of an international obligation;

d. the nature and extent of any reparation to be made for the breach of an international obligation; and

e. any matter which, by treaty or convention in force between parties to the present revised Statute, provides for reference thereof to the Court, to a tribunal to have been instituted by the League of Nations, or to the Permanent Court of International Justice.

2. The jurisdiction of the Court shall extend also to:

a. all justiciable cases which the parties may refer to it;

b. all matters specially provided for in the Charter of the United Nations; and

c. matters referred to the Court for advisory opinions, as elsewhere in the present revised Statute provided.

3. The Court shall have no jurisdiction over, and nothing contained in the present Statute shall be construed as requiring any Member of the United Nations to submit to the Court for adjudication, any matter essentially within the domestic jurisdiction of any State.

4. Any question or dispute as to the jurisdiction of the Court shall be determined by the Court; but when any State, party to the cause, shall contend that a matter brought before the Court for adjudication is essentially within the domestic jurisdiction of the State, the Court shall not exercise jurisdiction over the proceeding unless at least ten of its judges concur in holding the matter to be within the jurisdiction of the Court. Any doubt as to whether a matter is essentially within the domestic jurisdiction of a State shall be resolved by the Court in favor of such domestic jurisdiction.

5. The Court shall adjudicate disputes before it in accordance with generally accepted, applicable principles of international law, giving due consideration, in its deliberations, to:

a. the provisions of international conventions establishing rules generally recognized among nations;

b. international custom, as evidence of a general practice accepted as law;

c. judicial precedents recognizing legal principles (subject, in all cases, to the provisions of paragraph 6 of Article XVI, that a judgment of the Court shall be *res adjudicata* only as between the parties to the cause, and as to the cause, in which the judgment was rendered) ;

d. general principles of law, equity and justice recognized among nations; and

e. legal writings of jurisconsults who are recognized authorities in international law.

Article IX

Parties

1. Only public international organizations or States may be parties in cases before the Court.

2. The Court shall be open at all times to all public international organizations which are constituent agencies, or are created under the terms of the Charter, of the United Nations, and to all States which are Members of the United Nations.

3. The Security Council of the United Nations shall specify the conditions under which—subject to special provisions contained in treaties in force—the Court shall be open to public international organizations which are not constituent agencies, or are not created under the terms of the Charter, of the United Nations, and to States other than those which are Members of the United Nations; but in no case shall such conditions place the parties in positions of inequality before the Court.

Article X

Institution and Prosecution of Causes

1. Cases may be brought before the Court by notification of a special agreement, or by application, by one or more parties, addressed

in either case to the Registrar, and indicating the subject of the dispute and the parties thereto.

2. The Registrar shall forthwith communicate the notification or application to all parties immediately concerned therein on the face thereof, and also to the Members of the United Nations through the Secretary-General.

3. The parties shall file pleadings and other documents as required, and within the time fixed, or permitted, by the Court, in its Rules, or in each case.

4. The parties shall be represented by agents, and may have the assistance of advocates throughout the proceedings. The agents and advocates shall enjoy the privileges and immunities necessary to the independent exercise of their duties as such.

5. Unless otherwise ordered by the Court, or by a chamber before which the cause is to be heard, all oral evidence shall be heard, and all documentary evidence shall be introduced, before a referee appointed by the Court or chamber, by letters rogatory or by deposition *de bene esse.*

6. The Court may, at any time, request any individual, body, bureau, commission or other organization to carry out an enquiry and report to the Court, or to give the Court an expert opinion.

7. The Court may request information relevant to cases before it, from public international bodies, and shall receive any information transmitted to it by such bodies on their own initiative.

8. Copies of all documents filed by a party in a proceeding, shall be given to every other party to the cause.

9. All notices shall be served on the advocates of the parties, in person, by delivery at, or by mail addressed to, the places at which they are to be found, elsewhere as the Court may direct, or through the government of the State upon whose territory the services is to be effected.

Article XI

Intervention

1. Whenever the construction of a constituent instrument of a public international organization, or of an international convention adopted thereunder, is in question in a cause before the Court, the Registrar shall notify the public international organization concerned,

and shall transmit to it copies of all the written proceedings. Such public international organization may intervene of right, by declaration, in the cause.

2. Whenever there are parties to a convention whose construction is at issue in a cause between other parties, the Registrar shall notify the parties to the convention which are not parties to the cause, of the pendency of the action. Each such party so notified may intervene of right, by declaration, in the cause.

3. Whenever a public international organization or a State considers that it has a legal interest which may be affected by the decision of a cause, such public international organization or State may apply to the Court for permission to intervene in the cause, and the granting of such application shall be discretionary with the Court.

4. A judgment in any cause shall be binding on all intervenors, as well as on the original parties to the cause.

Article XII

Provisional Measures

1. Pending hearing and determination of a cause, the Court may, *ex proprio motu,* or on application of any party, if it considers that circumstances so require, specify any provisional measures to be taken to preserve, *pendente lite,* the respective rights of any party or parties.

2. Notice of the provisional measures so specified by the Court, shall be given forthwith by the Registrar to the parties and to the Security Council, which may, if it deems necessary, decide upon measures to be taken to give effect thereto.

Article XIII

Sessions of the Court

1. The Court shall remain in session permanently, except during judicial vacations as fixed by the Court. Members of the Court shall have periodic leave as fixed by the Court, and shall, except when prevented by compelling reasons, hold themselves permanently at the disposal of the Court.

2. The full Court shall sit in each cause, except as expressly other-

wise provided in the present Statute. By general rule, or by special ruling of the Court in any case, a member of the Court may be dispensed from sitting in special circumstances, provided that, except as stipulated in paragraph 6 of this Article, the number of judges available to constitute a full Court shall not thereby be reduced below eleven.

3. From time to time, or at any time, the Court may, from one or more chambers, to consist of three or more judges, to hear and determine, for the Court, any case or cases by summary or other procedure as the chamber may direct. Three judges shall consitute a quorum of a chamber.

4. A case shall be heard by a chamber only at the request, or by the consent, of all parties to the cause, or by direction of the Court; and a chamber may, at such request, or by such consent or direction, sit and exercise its functions elsewhere than at the Hague.

5. By direction of the Court, *ex proprio motu* or at the request of any party or parties thereto, a case may be transferred for hearing or determination, at any time after institution of the proceeding and prior to judgment, from the Court to a chamber, or from a chamber to the Court.

6. Any question as to the jurisdiction of the Court may be considered and determined only by the full Court, with not less than fifteen judges sitting, if demanded by any party to the cause.

7. If a member of the Court feels that he should not, for any reason, take part in the decision of a particular case, he shall so advise the President; or if any member of the Court feels that, for any reason, any other member of the Court should not sit in a particular case, he shall so advise the President. Any party to a cause before the Court may suggest to the Court that, for a particular reason given, a member of the Court should not take part in the decision of the case. The Court shall determine any dispute as to whether a member should be allowed or required to take part in the decision of any case, the questioned member not participating in such determination, nor in the adjudication of any case in which the Court shall have decided that he is not eligible to sit.

Article XIV

Completion of The Court

1. Whenever, for any reason, it shall not be possible to have the required number of judges for the Court, in any particular cause, or if, for any reason, no reguar judge is available for designation as an additional judge under paragraph 1 of Article XVI of this Statute, the Court may designate as a judge or judges *ad hoc*, a retired member or members of the Court who may be willing and able to participate in the determination of the case; or, if such retired member or members should not be available, the Court shall designate, as a judge or judges *ad hoc*, some other person or persons from among those theretofore nominated—although never elected by the United Nations—to serve as a judge of the Court.

2. A judge or judges *ad hoc* shall not be of the nationality of any party to the cause and shall retain his or their nationalities.

Article XV

Hearings

1. Whenever any party fails to defend its case or to appear before the Court, any other party may call upon the Court to decide the controversy against the defaulting party; provided that before entering a judgment against a party in default, the Court shall determine that it has jurisdiction of the case, and that the claim or claims of the non-defaulting party or parties are well founded.

2. Unless otherwise ordered by the Court or chamber before which the cause is to be heard, the hearing before the Court shall consist of an oral presentation by the advocates of the parties.

3. Memorials and counter-memorials may be filed before and after oral presentation, pursuant to the Rules, or to orders, of the Court.

4. The official languages of the Court shall be English and French, and, unless otherwise ordered by the Court at the request of any party, the pleadings shall be drawn, and the proceedings shall be conducted, in either English or French.

5. Hearings before the Court and chamber shall be public unless the Court or chamber shall direct otherwise.

6. The President, or if he is unable to preside, the Vice-President, and if the latter should not be able to preside, the senior judge present, shall preside over sessions of the Court. The President or Vice-President, if a member of the Chamber, or the senior judge present shall preside over sessions of a chamber.

7. Minutes of each session of the Court shall be maintained by the Registrar, and these alone shall be the authentic evidence of the proceedings.

8. The deliberations of the Court shall take place in private and shall remain secret.

Article XVI

Decisions

1. All questions (except a question raised by the contention of a State party to a cause, under paragraphs 3 and 4 of Article VIII of the present Statute, that a matter before the Court is essentially within that State's domestic jurisdiction) and all cases shall be decided by a majority of the judges sitting; and, in the event of an equality of votes, the Court shall designate an additional judge or judges to sit with the Court for rehearing and determination of the question or cause.

2. The Court or chamber shall render an opinion in support of its judgment. If the opinion is not unanimous, it shall state the names of the judges concurring therein, and both concurring and dissenting judges shall be entitled to render separate opinions.

3. Opinions and decisions of the Court shall be rendered in both English and French, the Court designating which of the texts is to be considered authoritative.

4. A judgment given by a chamber shall be considered as rendered by the Court; except that any party which may have objected to a hearing before a chamber shall have a right, within sixty days from rendition of an adverse judgment by a chamber, to appeal therefrom to the full Court, on which the members of the chamber which decided the case shall be eligible to sit. Except as otherwise ordered by the Court, the presentation of a case on appeal shall be on the record made up before the chamber.

5. The judgment of the Court, and a judgment of a chamber which is not subject to appeal, shall be signed by the President and Registrar of the Court. Subject to the provisions of paragraph 2 of Article 94 of the Charter of the United Nations, there shall be no appeal from any judgment of the Court, nor from any judgment of a chamber except as provided in the preceding paragraph of this Article.

6. Judgments shall have no binding force as *res adjudicata,* except between the parties to the cause and intervenors therein, and in respect of the cause in which rendered. In the event of a dispute as to the meaning or scope of a judgment, the Court or chamber which rendered it may construe it upon application of any party to the cause.

7. Any party may apply to the Court for revision of a judgment, on discovery of a fact of such a nature as to warrant revision, provided that such fact was unknown to the party, without negligence on its party, prior to judgment.

8. An application for revision of judgment must be made within six months of discovery of the new fact on which it is based; but such application may not be made, in any event, after the lapse of ten years from the date of judgment.

9. The granting of a hearing on such application for revision of a judgment shall be discretionary with the Court, which may require previous compliance with the terms of the judgment as a condition precedent to proceedings for revision.

10. Recommendations made, or decisions rendered, by the Security Council, under paragraph 2 of Article 94 of the Charter of the United Nations, upon measures to be taken to give effect to a judgment of the Court, shall be made or rendered by an affirmative vote of eight members including the concurring votes of the permanent members.

Article XVII

Costs

1. The expenses of the Court shall be borne by the United Nations in such a manner as shall be determined by the General Assembly.

2. Each party to a cause shall bear its own costs, unless otherwise decreed by the Court.

3. The Court shall, by its rules, fix the charges, fees and costs which parties shall pay in connection with proceedings before the Court.

4. When a public international organization which is not a constituent agency of the United Nations, or a State which is not a member of the United Nations, is a party to a cause, the Court shall fix the amount which such party is to contribute toward the expenses of the Court in addition to the charges, fees and costs payable by all parties.

Article XVIII

Advisory Opinions

1. The Court shall give an advisory opinion on any legal question laid before it by any body which may be authorized by, or in accordance with, the Charter of the United Nations to make such request.

2. Questions upon which the advisory opinion of the Court is requested shall be laid before it in a written application, accompanied by all documents which may be of assistance in reaching an answer to the questions.

3. The Registrar shall forthwith give notice of any request for an advisory opinion to all public international organizations or States which, on the face of the request, have, in his opinion, an apparent interest in the question.

4. The Registrar shall also forthwith give notice of any request for an advisory opinion, through the Secretary-General, to all other public international organizations which are constituent agencies of the United Nations, and to all States which are Members of the United Nations.

5. Any public international organization or State which feels that it has an interest in the determination of a question which has been submitted to the Court for an advisory opinion, or which feels that it may be in a position to furnish information helpful in the determination of such questions, may, under such rules as the Court may prescribe, file memorials and counter-memorials with the Court, and, with leave of Court, make an oral presentation on the question before the Court.

6. In the exercise of its advisory functions, the Court shall be guided, in addition to the provisions of the within Article, by the provisions of the present Statute, and of its own rules governing controverted cases, in so far as applicable.

Article XIX

Rules and Regulations

1. The Court shall make all rules necessary or advisable for the conduct of proceedings pending before it, including rules to cover all matters provided by the present Statute, to be governed by such rules.

2. The Rules of the Court may provide for assessors to sit with the Court or with any of its chambers, but assessors shall not have the right to vote.

Article XX

Ratification and Amendment

1. Reservations shall not be admissible in ratifications of the present Statute, which shall come into force unconditionally, as written, for all Members of the United Nations, after it shall have been adopted by a vote of two-thirds of the members of the General Assembly, upon deposit with the Secretary-General of instruments of ratification thereof, without reservations, in accordance with their respective constitutional processes, by two-thirds of the Members of the United Nations, including all of the permanent members of the Security Council. A protocol of the instruments of ratification deposited shall communicate copies thereof to all of the Members of the United Nations, and to all States not Members of the United Nations who shall then have become parties to the former Statute of the International Court of Justice.

2. Amendments to the present Statute shall be effected by the same procedure as is provided by the Charter of the United Nations for amendment to that Charter.

3. The Court may propose such amendments to the present revised Statute as it may deem necessary or advisable, by written communication to the Secretary-General, for consideration pursuant to the first paragraph of the within Article.

Index